ED BROOKE

Biography of a Senator

ED BROOKE

BIOGRAPHY OF A SENATOR

by John Henry Cutler

THE BOBBS-MERRILL COMPANY, INC.
INDIANAPOLIS · NEW YORK

THE BOBBS-MERRILL COMPANY, INC.
INDIANAPOLIS • NEW YORK
COPYRIGHT © 1972 BY JOHN HENRY CUTLER
ALL RIGHTS RESERVED
LIBRARY OF CONGRESS CATALOGUE CARD NUMBER 72-80809
DESIGNED BY JACK JAGET
MANUFACTURED IN THE UNITED STATES OF AMERICA

for

Robert
Margaret
David
Abigail
John

CONTENTS

CONTENTS

ACKNOWLEDGMENTS

Most of the primary source material in this authorized biography, which represents two years of research on Edward Brooke alone, came from personal interviews with friends, colleagues, political opponents or supporters, and members of the Brooke family, including the Senator's mother, wife and two daughters. A big help in tracing the family background was Dr. Adelaide Hill, the Senator's cousin, who is professor of sociology and director of Afro-American Studies at Boston University. Dr. Hill, who grew up with Brooke and went to school with him through the early grades, high school, and college, read and corrected early chapters after giving me family background information. As a biographer of the "What porridge had John Keats?" school I am indebted to Senator Brooke for his cooperation as well as to his close associates in whose memories the untold story of his life exists. This book was written with their cooperation.

Special mention should be made of early backers of Brooke who detected his catch-fire political potential long before he became known even in Massachusetts: John Bottomly, Roger Woodworth, Glendora and Harold Putnam, Gael Mahony, Georgia Ireland and Joseph Fitzgerald. Giving intimate glimpses of Brooke at work and at play during his early years in Roxbury, Boston's Harlem, were Clarence Elam, Alfred Brothers, Melnea Cass, Lionel Lindsay, Moe Robinson, Clyde Christmas, Herbert Jackson, James Mahone, Otto Snowden, Royal Bolling, George V. Medeiros, Herbert E. Tucker, Jr., and Judge Elwood McKenney.

ACKNOWLEDGMENTS

Behind-the-scenes data came from Brooke's Washington staff—especially from Betsy Warren, his personal secretary; Sally Saltonstall, his receptionist; Caryle Connelly, Marilyn Dexheimer, Eather Higginbotham, Linda Bunce, Ann Cunningham, Patricia Caroleo, Philip Heller, Rosemary Murphy, Hardy Nathan, James McCauley, Melinda Smith, and Hamilton Wood, Jr. In the Boston office warm thanks go to Maura O'Shaughnessy, Georgia Ireland, Claire Alfano, Barbara Masters, Carolyn Stewart and Evan Dobelle, also to Ruth Spaulding, one of the many volunteer workers who supplied anecdotal material.

I thank Mayor Kevin White of Boston and his former adviser, William I. Cowin; former Mayor John Collins, Secretary of Transportation John Volpe, Governor Francis Sargent, former State Senator William Weeks, George C. Lodge, Congressman Hastings Keith and Gerry Studds, his opponent in the 1960 campaign, and former Representative Francis W. Perry and his successor, Representative Roger Babb, and Representative Martin Linsky, all of whom gave a perspective on Brooke. Sidelights came from Frederick C. Dumaine, Jr., Lloyd Waring, Elmer Nelson, Anthony DeFalco, Mary Newman, Harcourt Wood and John Wheatley.

Former assistant attorneys general who helped with the book include J. Walter Skinner, Edward M. Swartz, John E. Sullivan, and Judges Benjamin Gargill, Edward T. Martin, and Herbert E. Travers. Among scores of other associates interviewed were Frankland W. L. Miles, William Jackson and Leo Martin—the latter two former state troopers who served as drivers and bodyguards for Brooke; Mrs. James Pye, Mrs. Gael Mahony, J. Alan MacKay, Harold Haestnes, and Margaret McKinney, Brooke's first secretary back in Roxbury days.

Thanks also to Albert Gammal, Jr., Jerome Sadow (Brooke's former press secretary), Rudolph A. Sacco, Graham Champey, Joseph McMahon, William Hayden, Donald Whitehead and Harold Appleton.

Newsmen who helped include David Wilson, Salvatore J. Micchiche, Al Benjamin, Frank Bucci, J. J. Smith, Jim Morse, Thomas Gallagher, and Cornelius R. Owens. I am especially grateful to Peter Lucas, who loaned me his unpublished material on his trip with Brooke to Southeast Asia, and to Howard S. Knowles, political editor of the *Worcester Telegram and Gazette,* the only reporter to trail Brooke on his African trip in 1968. Marilyn Dexheimer, Brooke's legislative assistant, who went on the same trip, not only proofread the chapter on Africa, but added many sidelights.

ACKNOWLEDGMENTS

Greatly appreciated was the cooperation from librarians of Boston newspapers: the *Globe, Herald Traveler* and *Record American.* I also spent happy hours lost in the files of the Boston Public Library and in Harvard University's Lamont Library, which has *The New York Times* and *The Washington Post* on microfilm. My daughter, Gail, who was then an assistant to the society editor of the *Boston Herald Traveler,* helped my research by combing the files of that newspaper for material on Brooke.

Information from Brooke's colleagues in the Senate and elsewhere in high places, and from newspaper, magazine and book sources, is acknowledged in the text or in chapter notes in the appendix.

ED BROOKE

Biography of a Senator

CHAPTER ONE

Light in the Tunnel

T HE MOST exciting step forward for American blacks since Lincoln freed the slaves was the election by popular vote of Edward William Brooke III of Massachusetts to the United States Senate. On the opening day of Congress in 1967 the former attorney general walked down the multicarpeted aisle of the Senate chamber escorted by his senior colleague, Senator Edward Kennedy. As the tall and courtly newcomer approached the president of the Senate, Democrats and Republicans, Northerners and Southerners, liberals and conservatives gave him a standing ovation.

After being sworn in by Vice-President Hubert Humphrey, Brooke was warmly congratulated by Democratic Senator Harry Byrd of Virginia, whose father had been a segregationist and a bitter foe of civil rights. Moved by the reception, Brooke walked outside and saw across the Capitol grounds a thousand black demonstrators waiting for Adam Clayton Powell, who was in the House of Representatives weeping, "his huge frame bent and his face distorted by the shock of senseless defeat." He had just been expelled from the House and stripped of the chairmanship of the Education and Labor Committee, the most powerful post held by a Negro on Capitol Hill. House Speaker John McCormack, shaken, walked out of the caucus predicting to a bystander that every Negro would walk out of the Democratic party.

Responding to shouts of "Bring out Adam," the Harlem leader, puffing on a dead cigar butt, called his expulsion "a lynching, Northern style." Shouting that God would fight his battle because he was right and his colleagues were wrong, Powell told the crowd they no longer had to pay taxes, because Harlem no longer had a leader. Arms flailing in the glare of television camera lights, he screamed that he was a man of God whom the evil of racism had toppled from office. Steeped in a cynicism which led him to call himself "just a poor, humble parish priest," he prided himself on his service to constituents since he first went to Congress in 1944, when he had braved the establishment by storming into the House barbershop to demand a haircut, thus ending a discriminatory custom stretching from the Civil War.

On the House steps as Congress reconvened in 1967, two black women fumed. "Goddamn it," one said, "I'm coming back here and blow it [the Capitol] up." Tears streamed down the face of the other, who yelled: "The damn sons of bitches!" Powell supporters chanted, "Keep the faith, Reverend. Keep the faith, Adam." They cleared a path as he went down the steps.

"Get out of the way, get out of the way! Don't touch our leader! You get that goddamn camera away from our Adam!" A bearded black shrieked, "Bring out the Southerners and we'll kill them," while 20 young Negroes burned their draft cards, defying arrest as white policemen two rows deep nervously watched and listened to the cursing and threats that broke the normal brooding calm of Capitol Hill. The air hung heavy with the rumble of mutiny as irate blacks threatened to burn the town down, while Powell prophesied the end of the nation as the land of the free and the home of the brave. "This building [the House of Representatives] houses the biggest bunch of hypocrites in the world," he yelled. Black Panther leader Eldridge Cleaver later called Powell "that jackal from Harlem, when he came under attack by his brother jackals in Congress." One of Powell's aides summed things up: "Adam never believed his colleagues would take such a firm action against him, a Negro, with so much evidence of looseness in so many other areas of Capitol Hill. Adam stuck his neck out and they chopped off his head."

Brooke was back in the new Senate Office Building greeting a line of well-wishers that took hours to pass him. One Negro woman said she had waited 27 years for someone like him to come to Washington. Another said she would have walked to the Capitol to see him if she had to. "You don't know what this means to us." A white woman shook Brooke's hand. "I'm very proud today. God bless you." There was pride in some misty eyes, a glint of anger in others. A Harlemite who had just heard Powell screaming congratulated Brooke, muttering: "If we can't beat them one way, we can beat them another way."

"I guess you get more attention when you're going out than when you're coming in," Brooke said later, recalling the Powell demonstration. There was more to the going and coming than met the eye.

Powell, who based his power on a segregated society, taught his followers to "think black." To them he was high dice, with his flashy clothes, jauntiness, glamor-girl friends, cabin cruisers, Bimini junkets and disdain—not only for whitey, but also for such middle-class blacks as engineers, politicians, lawyers, doctors and ministers—"the man who owned a home, had a sizable income and an automobile, and lived in a hill overlooking the ghetto," as Jim Bishop wrote in his biography of Martin Luther King, Jr. "Negro clerics decried the efforts of . . . King and some ran to the white mayor to denounce King to the press. The middle-class black had something to project, something his brethren did not have, and he had no intention of risking it to fight for equality for all." It was Adam Clayton Powell who said: "The white man is finished and the day of . . . King has come to end." He called the Negro crusader Martin "Loser" King and was pleased when Harlem blacks pelted the minister's limousine with eggs.

Powell was a shrewd politician with magnetism, intelligence and a big potential to help his people. Then, out of arrogance and self-seeking, he betrayed a flock who had loved and trusted him.

At the other pole was the black's dream of equality with whites in terms of dignity. Brooke—conscientious, dependable and handsome —embodied that vision of a brighter tomorrow. He personally desegregated the Senate when the civil-rights thrust was deadlocked by militants such as Stokely Carmichael, who preached the kind of black power which, said Roy Wilkins, leads only to black death.

Brooke is no militant and, unlike King, is not a symbol of Negritude in the quickening drive for equality. He refuses to be identified as black, though he is proud of his heritage, primarily because he thinks himself as much a part of society as anyone else. Asked how he—as a "black leader"—reacted to the ousting of Powell, he said: "I don't qualify as that." Though he is a rallying point for a race of which he is proud, he is a man, an American and a Negro in that order.

Noting that racial distinctions, no matter how odious, are a fact of life in the United States, black columnist William Raspberry wrote that, while Brooke may consider himself primarily a Republican, "It is a safe bet that among the most influential members of his party, he is considered primarily a Negro." *The Washington Post* writer added: "My quarrel with Brooke is not over the fact that he is working toward the creation of an America where black men's first loyalties can be to country and party. I simply believe that for black people to act as though racism is dead is not necessarily the best way to kill it." Brooke agrees.

Most blacks are elected by and for blacks: Powell in Harlem, William Dawson in Chicago, Carl Stokes in Cleveland, Charles Diggs in Detroit. Responsible Negro leaders, knowing that whites elected Brooke, understand why he rejects the Powell approach. Raspberry does not fully understand this.

A black leader said: "Ed will never be an Adam Powell, neither as loud about civil-rights trumpeting, nor as wrong in trying to duplicate the faults of his white colleagues. Ed first and foremost will want everyone—black and white—to be proud of him." Although Brooke has never walked a picket line* and is at odds with black-power merchants, he has helped the cause more than most civil-rightists. Kenneth I. Guscott, when president of the Boston branch of the NAACP, said: "We're not stupid enough to think he should be marching in the streets." Brooke himself said: "I have not participated in a riot in my life. I reject them. I deplore them."

Brooke is a Republican who happens to be black, just as Jack Kennedy was a Democrat who happened to be Catholic. Though *Time* said, "Brooke found himself in a nebulous no-man's-land between the white and Negro worlds," his followers don't think of him in terms of color. Writers sometimes try to picture him as being confused between being "blue-eyed and five-fourths white," or "49 percent black." He sidesteps such trivia. What irks him, however, is the comment that he *thinks* he is white.

"This exasperates him to the point of bitter, shrugging laughter," *Life* reported, "—a rare lapse in the reporter-proof self-containment that seals off the private man from the public person."

Chancellor of the Old North Church (whose lantern gave Paul Revere the signal for his ride), a member of Trinity (Episcopal) Church in Boston, and president of the Boston Opera Company when the Brahmin John Cabot was vice-president, Brooke over the years has been called a Communist, a NASP (Negro counterpart of the WASP), an elitist, fence-sitter, formidable ladies' man, playboy, witch doctor, income-tax evader, damned idealist, slick pol, publicity hound, enemy of his people, an Uncle Tom, and, according to James

---

* On Boston Common on Good Friday in April 1971 Brooke carried a banner and walked in a Quaker-sponsored antiwar line.

Baldwin, "one of the innocents who are bringing about the ruination of the country."

To others he is a dedicated reformer, tough crime fighter, sincere truth seeker and a political genius with a sense of timing unmatched by any politician since Franklin Delano Roosevelt. Soon after his election to the United States Senate he became the hottest name on the speaking circuit and was tabbed "one of the most valuable pieces of political property in the U.S."

"And he still is," says Remigia, his Italian wife.

One thing is sure. In the incredibly crooked, sleazy world of Massachusetts politics Brooke is a welcome change from the machine politicans. "He inspires near-deification from his supporters, and even his detractors search for points to belabor," a reporter wrote. Newsmen who follow him agree that he is charismatic—the word crops up again and again—and that he charms men as well as women. "And magnetism?" a writer asked in *Harper's Magazine*. "He invented it." Another put it simply. "Class. The guy's class." Brooke can tend the shop 16 hours a day seven days a week. And he has the political aplomb, an observer noted, to "shake hands for three hours, take a ten-minute shower, lie down for ten minutes, and emerge for an important dinner engagement, appearing completely refreshed."

Unlike many black leaders, Brooke has a power base in every state in the Union because he is a temperate spokesman for both blacks and whites. Intent on winning allies rather than conquering enemies, he warns against violence while demanding constitutional rights through legislative and judicial process. Like the late Whitney M. Young, with whom he had much in common, Brooke believes "you can holler, protest, march, picket, demonstrate, but somebody must be able to sit in on strategy conferences and plot a course." Blacks bolster the opposition, Brooke says, if they reject the legal road and use fire and sword.

"We confuse those we are trying to persuade, and destroy our own program."

Yet Brooke knows the hell and heartache that underprivileged and underpossessed blacks suffer. "The American Negro didn't come over on the *Mayflower*," he says, "but he was right behind it—in chains. And he rowed the boat to get here."

Brooke sees a glimmer of light in the tunnel. "Eventually, distinctions will disappear," he says. "We've seen it in sports, in the theater, and in the armed forces. . . . Fifty years ago, the Irish were in the same situation. So, too, have been the Jews and Italians and all immigrants." He grinned. "Even the Yankees, when they first came over. People thought these groups were inferior because they didn't talk or think the same, but they were able to overcome the prejudice in time. Negroes can do it, too, even though, as Whitney Young said, 'It is easier to desegregate a chorus line at a burlesque show than it is the choir of a church.' " Like Young, Brooke thinks the key to equality is in unlocking the white power structure, not in building a separate black society. "Are we really moving, as the Kerner Commission Report suggested, toward two societies, one black and one white?" Brooke asked. "Do we really want war between the races of this nation?" His own answer is no. Brooke thinks more like Congressman William L. Clay of St. Louis: "We have no permanent friends and no permanent enemies. Just permanent interests."

Like Roy Wilkins, Brooke sees the dawn of a new era. "This will be a period when the Negro will have to make readjustments," Wilkins said. "We must counsel our Negro population on induction into an integrated society, teach them that you can't blame all disabilities on race, because that is self-defeating." Both Brooke and Wilkins think many blacks are ready for all their rights now. But, as Wilkins said, "A great number are not fully aware of the competition and responsibility which await them in an unsegregated world."

What is needed is a viable formula such as the Irish had when they were a "downtrodden majority," as the late James Michael Curley put it. "When the Irish didn't like the way the [Yankee] police behaved," Whitney Young wrote, "they didn't revolt. They joined the force and took it over."

"By the same token," Brooke says, "blacks must become a part of America to be a part of it."

Brooke is as critical as any black ghetto messiah of a white society that allows dope pushers, white prostitutes or call-house madams to buy or rent houses in communities which bar law-abiding, respectable blacks. He is also sensitive enough to his people's needs to understand what Elma Lewis, a forceful black spokesman, meant when she said: "They won't let us be proud of Brooke. They take him away from us and make him theirs."*

Brooke is a political paradox whose role in the Senate is not always understood. He was twenty-six before he studied law, thirty before he

---

* Elma Lewis, who operates the Elma Lewis School of Fine Arts within the National Center of Afro-American Artists, is a fiery militant who admires Brooke.

voted (having come from Washington, D.C., where there was no vote), and thirty-one before he went into politics. He is a Republican, although most blacks have been Democrats since the New Deal. "Black Republicans are as rare these days as white whales," a reporter wrote in 1965. Brooke is rarer than a black Republican. He is a black Republican who is the most popular officeholder in a state that is 98 percent white and two-thirds Democratic. He is a black Republican who is an Episcopalian in a state that is overwhelmingly Roman Catholic.

In the pattern of the late Robert F. Kennedy, Brooke is a senatorial lone wolf. He is also an enigma whose privacy is almost impenetrable, even to intimates. "I know all there is to know about Ed Brooke," said a friend who asks to remain anonymous, "but I don't really know him." It is perhaps because Brooke is also an enigma to himself that he once said to the person closest to him: "Mother, I am one of the loneliest men in the world."

What is Senator Brooke's formula for his spectacular rise in politics? Neither he nor anyone else can give a pat answer, since there are too many shifting variables in the political equation. But occasionally he drops a hint.

"In 1960, after the Republican National Convention in Chicago, I sat beside the late Joe Martin [former Speaker of the House of Representatives] on the plane back to Boston. I have never forgotten a bit of practical advice Joe passed along to me. 'When I was a boy,' he said, 'my mother told me that if you want to fill your pail with huckleberries, you have to go where the huckleberries grow.' "

But where are the huckleberries growing?

"He won't be known for what he says, but for what he does," Richard Nixon said of Brooke during the presidential campaign of 1968. As Brooke campaigns this year for reelection to the United States Senate, he says he is content to remain a U.S. senator.

"If you have to sit somewhere, the Senate is a good place to sit," he said at a testimonial in his honor on his fifty-second birthday.

He knows, however, that an age summons the heroes it needs. He also inclines toward a belief in predestination. *"Que será, será."* The thought colors his mood as he moves up the ladder.

He has never boasted about the fact that he has turned down two Cabinet posts or that he could, if he wished, have become ambassador to the United Nations. Although he will not admit that he turned down a nomination to the United States Supreme Court not once but twice, veteran newsmen in Massachusetts know he did. If Governor George Romney of Michigan had been the successful Republican presidential candidate in 1968, Brooke was under consideration as his running mate. This is interesting to recall in light of a statement made in September 1971 by Senator Edmund Muskie of Maine, when as the leading contender for the Democratic nomination for President, he told the press he didn't think a ticket with a black candidate for Vice-President could be elected. He was thinking primarily of a black candidate on a Democratic ticket.

President Nixon had an immediate comment. "The example of Ed Brooke in Massachusetts is eloquent demonstration of the fact that the American people, when confronted with a superior man, will not vote against him because of his race."

Senate Republican leader Hugh Scott said two weeks later that Brooke would be an asset to the GOP national ticket. "I think Ed [Muskie] probably regrets that voyage: from his foot to his mouth," Scott told newsmen. ". . . It's like saying a Polish Catholic doesn't have a chance." (Muskie is a Roman Catholic of Polish descent.) "I really believe that if Ed Brooke were on a ticket, he would bring more votes to the ticket than he would cost." Scott added that Muskie had demonstrated the error of generalizing on such an issue.

In November 1971 *Time* magazine quoted Vice-President Spiro Agnew to the effect that Brooke could be elected Vice-President. A limited poll conducted by columnists Rowland Evans and Robert Novak showed that a Nixon-Brooke ticket would run better than a Nixon-Agnew or Nixon-Connally ticket.

Brooke, who said he was "flattered" and "honored" by Nixon's comment, was also of the opinion that Muskie had erred. He *says* he wants to serve another six-year term in the Senate, but he is in a unique position to accept other options, having established his competency to serve in any of the three branches of government: legislative, judicial and executive.

CHAPTER TWO

The Virginia Branches

E DWARD WILLIAM BROOKE III, grandson of a railroad trainman and son of a Veterans Administration attorney, is a product of the antebellum rural South and the modern urban North. He is uncertain of his distant ancestry. "We never knew what we were," his mother says. Traceable family roots go back to three Virginia farms in Falmouth, Fredericksburg and Petersburg. His genealogy, lost in the maze of African, Indian and English antecedents, cannot be written.

Emily Hills, born around 1835, was the daughter of a Negro couple whose first names are unknown. She lived with her family on a plantation in Falmouth until, in her early twenties, she married James Jefferson, a young black whose parents owned a neighboring farm. On the Jefferson land Emily and James reared their children: Thomas, Nannie and Dorothy, known as "Dolly." While James ran the farm, Emily, a skilled seamstress, took in sewing from both white and black families. In her twilight years Emily Jefferson made uniforms for American soldiers during the Spanish-American War.

Dolly Jefferson, who was slender and light-skinned, married Edward Wiliam Brooke, a Negro mason from Fredericksburg, a city across the Rappahannock from Falmouth. According to word handed down from generation to generation, he was the son of a slave who took the surname of his owner. Edward, the first of three successive Edward William Brookes, was the grandfather of the Senator.

Dolly, who was 19 years old when she was married in 1889, lived

9

with her husband on the Falmouth plantation until the end of Reconstruction and the uprisings of the secret societies which terrorized blacks. These hate groups included the Ku Klux Klan, the Pale Faces, the Black Horse Cavalry, the Jayhawkers and the Knights of the White Camellia. Any dream of black political power in the region where three-fourths of all blacks lived was dying and soon to be dead. Democratic Senator "Pitchfork" Ben Tillman of South Carolina told the U.S. Congress at the end of the nineteenth century how whites treated black voters in his state: "We have done our level best. We have scratched our heads to find out how we could eliminate the last one of them. We stuffed ballot boxes. We shot them. We are not ashamed of it."

Fearful of their safety, Dolly and Edward, who then had a son, Clarence, moved to Fredericksburg, settling first in the white Kenmore Hill section, where Edward William Brooke, Jr., the Senator's father, was born. Two years later the family moved to a less fashionable part of the city.

In 1879 approximately 40,000 Negroes left the South in the wake of mounting terror. Washington, D.C., a gateway to the South, became a way station for blacks enroute to Pennsylvania, New York and New Jersey. The migration of the Brooke family began in the late 1890s, when life was becoming grim for young blacks. Clarence, then ten years old, was the first to go to Washington, to live with relatives. Two years later his brother, Edward, also ten by then, joined him.

In 1965 Emily (Brooke) Woods, ten years younger than Edward, recalled their early life in Virginia: "Edward was an energetic and mischievous boy who was always getting into trouble with my parents. He and Clarence used to come back to Fredericksburg in the summertime, and I remember, for instance, that my mother would force him to take me out in the street to play with him. It always embarrassed him. He would take me around the corner—out of Mother's sight—then leave me and go play marbles with his friends. Then one of the kids—you know how kids are—would run and squeal on him and my mother would come running out and I'd be screaming and she'd chase him all the way home."

Slavery had lasted until the Civil War in Washington, which was psychologically as well as geographically a Southern city. As the capital of a salvaged Union, however—a Union dedicated to emancipation—Washington attracted many uprooted blacks, for whom it was more than a way station. City leaders felt obliged to project a picture of equality as a model for the rest of the nation.

According to Dr. Adelaide Hill, a second cousin of Senator Brooke, the black community which evolved, called "The Secret City," had its character determined by the larger Washington environment, which provided sufficiently varied opportunities to draw blacks from adjoining states.

A local newspaper described the situation in 1883: "The colored people of Washington enjoy all the social and political rights that law can give them, with protection and without annoyance. The public conveyances are open to them, the theatres, and the jury box, the spoils of party power are theirs. Many of these men are wealthy."

But Washington was no Eden for blacks, for the color line was rigidly drawn. Wealth, learning and official place gave no black family the right to enter the best of the commonest white society on terms of equality. "In this respect, the colored man lives as in the days of slavery, and as a drop of African blood was once held to make a man a Negro, so now it taints him and makes an immutable barrier against social recognition."

As late as 1889 the Washington police force had only one black officer, and there were no black firemen. Over the years, however, there was steady progress for blacks in more professional pursuits. By the turn of the century there were more than 400 school teachers, 50 qualified physicians, ten professionally trained dentists, over 90 ministers and about 30 lawyers.

Thus conditions by this time were promising enough to attract the two immediate branches of Brooke's forebears: the Brookes of Fredericksburg and the Seldons of Petersburg.

"I have little explicit evidence of our family background," Brooke says. "However, I am certain that the Brooke family came originally from the Brooke plantation (now the town of Brooke), which used to be near Fredericksburg."

Brooke liked his grandfather, the first Edward, and his grandmother, Dolly, whom he remembers as a wrinkled old woman who had frightening attacks of asthma. She was light-skinned with reddish hair. "My grandfather was one of my favorite relatives. When he came to Washington, he gave up working as a mason and became a trainman for the Pennsylvania Railroad. He was jovial and congenial. I remember his bringing me peppermint and ice cream. He was dark brown and had straight black hair and the keen features of

11

an Indian. I had always heard that he had a lot of Indian blood in him." The first Edward was the only grandfather the Senator knew.

Washington became the home for a growing number of Brookes and Seldons, the grandparents and parents of the Senator.

The central figure of the maternal branch was Adelaide Seldon, the oldest child in the family. After she and her husband, William Mavritte, came to Washington in the late 1880s from Richmond, Virginia, many of her brothers and sisters came to live with her. One younger sister, Helen, was three when, after both parents died, she came north to live with Adelaide, whom she called "Mama."

"Aunt Addie was a beautiful person," Dr. Hill recalls. "She was open and tolerant so long as you didn't cross her. Her hair was so long she could sit on it." Addie was matriarch of a clan which included her own six children, her grandchildren, her younger brothers and sisters and their children. The clan lived in modest, comfortable houses on two parallel unpaved streets in a rural section of the district that is now a black ghetto. Holidays and Sundays found as many as 40 relatives trooping through the six-room Mavritte house or roaming through the woods separating the two streets, where some families kept horses and cows. Addie, a strong, steadying influence, was so adored that even divorce never alienated her from her extended brood. In the clan exact relationship wasn't important. All shared a common feeling of identity.

Grandfather Will Mavritte, a carpenter, never drank, smoked or swore. When just before he died an old friend suggested that he get ready to meet the Lord, he said that if he wasn't already prepared, it was certainly too late to start (at the age of ninety).

In this congenial atmosphere Edward Brooke was reared in his early years. He remembers "Aunt" Addie as his mother's "mother." For young Edward this was an enriching experience—an opportunity to grow up in a family as diversified as it was warm. It gave him a feeling of security and stability. There was, of course, also a degree of poverty, unhappiness and pettiness, but all was minimized by the overall strength stemming from Addie.

Brooke recalls cookouts in the yard, berry picking, Easter egg hunts and romps through the woods. His aunts—Sadie and Katie, as well as Addie—doted on him, often giving him spending money. Their gentleness and love rubbed off on him, just as they had on his mother.

When Brooke was elected attorney general of Massachusetts, three generations of the clan held a "Welcome to Ed" party at the home of his cousin, Dr. Wilbur Jackson, Kate's son.

12

"Did you all know one another?" Dr. Hill remembers a reporter asking.

"So well that some of us hadn't been speaking to each other for years," a relative said.

"Aunt Addie had an infinite capacity for love, and no one was ever a failure in her eyes," Brooke said. "She never gauged success by achievement. As long as a child was good and loyal to the family, that child was a success." Under her guidance the clan thought little of color distinctions, though complexions in the families ranged from deep brown to white.

"Addie's attitude made Senator Brooke's outlook on life more egalitarian," Dr. Hill said.

Helen Seldon and Edward Brooke, Jr., met in their early teens. "I don't remember exactly," she recalls, "except that we were quite young." Referring to her husband in 1966 (two years after he died) as "Daddy," she said her "mother" (Aunt Addie) would not allow her to "take company," but when Edward came to Washington from Fredericksburg and moved into the neighborhood, they became friendly. "Because he was such a nice boy, my parents [the Mavrittes] let him take me to school dances." They soon became attached to each other. "He asked permission of my parents to marry me, and that was it." They were married when she was sixteen and he, at the age of twenty, was a freshman at Howard University.

After graduating from the Howard School of Law in 1918, Edward Brooke, Jr., became an attorney reviewer for the Veterans Administration, retiring after 50 years of service. Although many blacks had respectable Civil Service jobs later, an important post with the VA was not easily come by at the time. Mr. Brooke received a Distinguished Service Award for his work in reviewing and judging legal cases that came before him in his years on the job.

Although his wife had not completed her education, she encouraged him to complete his legal education. She and her daughter, Helene, attended his graduation exercises. Mr. Brooke never practiced law privately.

He left an imprint on his son. "My father set guidelines for my life. He told me to find out what is behind this or at the bottom of that. 'Search for the key, then build your detail around it.'"

Dr. Hill remembers the Senator's father as being quiet and retiring. "He always made it clear what his desires and advice were, but never forced them on Edward, or pushed hard. While he hoped his son

13

would study law, he let him select his own course. I think his method
—his demeanor—had a much more profound effect on Edward than
did his words alone.

Edward William Brooke III was born in Washington on October
26, 1919, on Northwest Third Street. A sister, Edwina, had died of
blood poisoning at the age of three before he was born. His other
sister, Helene,* was five when he was baptized in an Episcopal church.
Edward and Helene grew up in their second home, on First Street in
one of a row of identical red-brick three-story houses attached to one
another with no alleys in between. Windows were close-set at the
front and at the rear, which opened on a small yard.

Helene and Edward were reared in a middle-class milieu in a stable
integrated neighborhood. After Edward enrolled at Howard University, the family moved to a neat detached hillside home at 1262
Hamlin Street in the Brookland section of Washington. In this older
section of the city picket fences enclosed well-kept yards. Residents
prided themselves on their clean streets lined with towering oaks in
the well-to-do black enclave. According to Dr. Hill, the Senator's
father bore no visible bruises from his race, "but you never knew what
Negro men were thinking and what permanent scars had been made.
You never knew what was happening to people inside while they were
out there fighting for survival. In a way, all our families in Washington
who could do so closed a door on the outside world."

"We never let being Negroes affect our lives," Helen Brooke said.
"We never had any race problems here. People took you for what you
are. There was no racial thing with us. We never felt hated, and that's
why Edward is the way he is." The Senator agrees.

"I was a happy child. I was conscious of being a Negro, yes, but
I was not conscious of being underprivileged because of that." Another time he said, "It would make a better story if some white man
had kicked me or yelled 'nigger,' but it just never happened. I grew
up segregated, but there was not much feeling of being shut out of
anything."

"If he did have any shattering experiences through racial discrimi-

---

* Helene married Ernest R. Amos, Jr., of Washington, D.C., after receiving
her Bachelor of Arts degree in 1934, seven years before Edward received his
B.S. A retired school teacher, Mrs. Amos lives in a Washington apartment
complex (Tiber Island) where her mother and brother also have separate
apartments. Helene Amos' late husband was director of medical affairs of a
major pharmaceutical manufacturing firm.

nation, he wouldn't tell you about it," his mother said. "He must have had some hard knocks." Brooke's reactions are understandable, since he has always been able to rise above the pettiness of people around him. Lingering in his mind, however, was Aunt Addie's warning to "stay in his place."

Brooke spent his boyhood, schooling and military service after college with his own kind. "I knew the dreadful discrimination and bigotry which many Americans suffered, but cannot say this had any traumatic effect on me."

Even in government buildings blacks and whites were served meals at different times or used separate dining rooms and lavatories. Also segregated were amusement and public parks, restaurants, theaters, music halls and even churches. "Blacks could not sit down and eat at the counter in a ten-cent store, for example. They had one section of the counter where we could stand and buy hot dogs, hamburgers and soft drinks."

Black families, although apart, didn't feel excluded. Barred from most cultural events in a city that was split into two distinct and separate societies, blacks didn't particularly mind, since they had their own centers, like the Lincoln Colonnade, where they could socialize, insulated from the stings of racial bias. Charles L. Fisher, a family friend who lived near the Brookes in Washington and later on Martha's Vineyard during the summer, said: "We middle-class blacks lived in a secure little world when we were growing up. Secure, but unreal. There was no need to go downtown other than to work. We had our own nightclubs, schools, restaurants, stores—everything we wanted. Washington's so-called ghetto was different from other black ghettos in the size of its Negro class who had fairly good jobs. Even during the Depression, government employees kept their jobs."

As a child and through high school, Brooke spent time with relatives, including Aunt Ruth, Addie's youngest sister, who, after their mother died, lived with relatives in New York. Ruth married Alec Pompez, a congenial Cuban who owned the Cuban All Stars baseball team. Alec, who lived on Sugar Hill in a pleasant section of Harlem, built Dyckman Oval, a ball park in the Bronx, where his team played in fast competition. Later Pompez became a pioneer baseball scout who drafted the first Cubans and blacks into the major leagues, including Willie Mays, Roberto Clemente and Willie McCovey. Edward spent summers with his uncle at the ball park selling hot dogs and ice cream. Later, when he was fifteen and sixteen, he had the same job at Griffiths Stadium in Washington, then the home of the Washington Senators. When he was seventeen he waited on tables in the Chalfona Restaurant in Washington. He still keeps in touch with Uncle Alec, who now lives in Long Branch, New Jersey.

As a youngster Edward also visited the Mavrittes during some vacations and spent as much summer time as possible with Uncle Henry and Aunt Carrie Seldon on a peanut farm in Petersburg. There he explored the cavernous red barn with its mysterious lofts, and the stable in the barnyard, which housed four plow horses. Fascinating was the old icehouse, where he chipped ice in prerefrigeration days. He fed chickens, pigs and the kenneled hunting dogs. His favorite dog was Rinny, named for Hollywood's Rin Tin Tin. Edward hunted possum with Uncle Henry in the brush around the farm. "Uncle Henry was full of fun. He had a wonderful disposition, and worked hard. I remember breaking hay with him and helping out in the little roadside stand they had in front of the main house."

Henry's daughter, Leola Seldon, remembers Edward as one of some 30 sons and daughters of relatives who had moved to Washington. "He was playful, handsome, easy to love. Even today, they say anyone who does not like him does not know him." He followed her father all over the farm. There were chores to be done, but Henry had hired hands, so the children never had to work.

Uncle Henry was in his seventies when he died in 1955. During Reconstruction he was the first Negro to register to vote in Prince George County. He was responsible for the first school built for blacks in that county, according to Leola, who still lives on the farm with her brother, Raymond, and her mother, Mrs. Carrie Seldon. Never a fractious child, Brooke says his father spanked him only once. The family disciplinarian and the dominant force in his life was his mother, who imposed her strong personality on him. Also rubbing off was her abiding religious faith and her independent spirit and determination to rise above bigotry in any form.

"When I was a little boy, I was close to my mother," Brooke said in 1971. "She called me her little man. After losing my sister, Edwina, Mother prayed to have another child, and I came. I was really named after Edwina, rather than my father." Edward was close to his mother. "We talked to each other about the most personal things. Mother, who is an extrovert, has great energy, and I could never keep up with her. I had a happy youth, and Mother had a lot to do with it." Helen Brooke, warmhearted and outgoing, taught her children compassion and to "love thy neighbor." She convinced them that hate merely consumes the hater. "I have never been a hater, probably because my mother never hated anyone. The thing I can thank her for most is my love of people. That is probably responsible for getting me into politics," Brooke said.

Mrs. Brooke helped him stay in politics, too, campaigning in every election. She was effective on a speaker's platform, according to her son, and a good cook, but "a complete loss with needle and thread. The only time she tried to sew a costume for me in a school play, I couldn't get into it."

In 1966, when Helen Brooke was named Mother of the Year by the Washington Shriners, her son told a reporter she had always been "a buddy, a friend, a booster. She always managed to get to every play, every speech, every school activity in which I took part and where parents were invited. It was the same with my sister." She never took his side when he had trouble with friends or classmates. "She always said, 'Don't tell me what *they* did, tell me the whole story. What did *you* do?' Then she sat as sort of judge and explained to me how the whole situation looked from all sides. If she felt I needed it, she would spank me immediately. Then she would go into her bedroom and cry."

Brooke also credits her with teaching him the art of friendship and sharing. She shared family dinners with the less fortunate and made her home a meeting place for her children's friends. "While other children felt ashamed, or weren't permitted by their parents to bring their friends home, I was encouraged to do this by my mother. She taught me to be sympathetic and generous. I not only shared my home, cookies and snacks, but I shared Mother, too." The children's friends, who still call her "Aunt Helen," could always expect a warm welcome in the Brooke home.

The family attended St. Luke's Episcopal Church, where Edward didn't miss a Sunday service from the ages of seven to seventeen. During the later years he served as crucifer. One morning when the regular crossbearer was absent, Edward asked if he could take his place. "Can you manage it?" his father asked. "Yes sir," Edward said. He did well enough to carry the cross every Sunday thereafter.

"At this time I thought Edward would become a minister," Mrs. Brooke said. "One night members of our congregation joined another Episcopal church in a program to which crossbearers were invited. Edward, who took the cross to the church downtown, found the door locked when he went back to St. Luke's to return it, so he took the cross home and put it at the foot of his bed. 'This cross is going to do something wonderful for me, one of these days,' he said." She

17

smiled. "And he is just as religious today as he was then. He always says grace before meals, prays before an election, and do you know something else? He always consults the Man Upstairs before giving a speech."

Mrs. Brooke had other reasons for thinking he might join the ministry. When he was ten he held make-believe church services in the family dining room. As "pastor," he lectured to his young friends, who were lined up on chairs. Someone would even take up a collection from the "congregation." Mrs. Brooke laughed as she sifted through the past. "Edward also trained boys to be acolytes."

"I wasn't really lecturing," Brooke said. "I was preaching." During college he was a lay reader at St. Luke's, a stint that developed his oratory and capacity for public speaking. "He rarely writes a speech," his mother said after he became senator. "He speaks from his head and heart."

Edward first attended Minor Teachers' College in northwest Washington, a teacher-training laboratory school for black children. Later he enrolled at the William Lloyd Garrison and John F. Cook elementary schools, where his grades began to pick up. He spent the next three years at Robert Gould Shaw Junior High School. He has few memories of early school years, except for an incident in junior high. "The only thing I'd done was march in an inaugural parade as a cadet." This gave him a taste for military drill in high school.

In junior high and high school Brooke remembers his mother studying "right along" with Helene and him. "It made school exciting and ten times more interesting, because I could play student and teacher."

Edward was one of the "talented tenth" eligible for Dunbar High School, then the best public high school in the country for blacks. By the time Edward enrolled, Dunbar was an academic oasis, with a blue-ribbon faculty which encouraged cultural pursuits. To compensate for racial barriers existing in places of public accommodation, teachers sent students to libraries, art galleries and museums. Dunbar, the only classical high school in the city for Negroes, attracted top graduates of Ivy League colleges because they were unable to get good-paying jobs elsewhere, since the only other teaching opportunities were at Negro colleges, which did not pay Dunbar's high salaries. Thus Dunbar had teachers with doctorate as well as master's degrees. "They came back to Dunbar because they had nowhere else to go," Brooke said.

Sons and daughters of Washington's best black families, including

Helene and Edward Brooke and their cousin Adelaide, went to Dunbar.

"We sort of lived in a cocoon," Brooke recalls. "Dunbar had an intellectual elite who enjoyed their own company, and almost never got out of it. We were not aware of any stigma, or of missing anything because of segregation. Dunbar took the cream of the crop, and they did well wherever they went." The school drew students from the entire city as well as from surrounding states.

Disaster for Dunbar came in the wake of the 1954 U.S. Supreme Court decision to end segregation. In implementing the ruling, the District of Columbia school board lowered Dunbar's status as a strictly academic high school. Thus the turreted gray-brick building became a neighborhood school for hundreds of students living in slums who could not compete with the "talented tenth."

Mrs. Bertha MacNeill, who taught English at Dunbar for 46 years, remembers Brooke as "a manly boy" who had "a great deal of personal attractiveness and was extremely popular with other students. He did well in my class, and, if I recall correctly, was . . . full of pep outside of school."

Although a good student, Brooke didn't make the Honor Society. "It was very competitive," he said. "I was doing other things. Besides, most of those on the honor roll were girls." One was Adelaide Hill.

He swam, played basketball and captained the tennis team in his senior year. "I was not tall in high school, and did not have the build to play more than sandlot football."

While Edward was growing up, many blacks from comfortable families hoped to enter medicine, because physicians earned more than teachers and commanded more prestige in a white-dominated society. At the time, blacks could not enter such fields as architecture, aeronautics and engineering, or even professional athletics, to any great degree. They were limited to professions in which they could serve only the black community. These included teaching, the ministry and medicine. "There was also undertaking," Dr. Hill wryly observed. The federal government had openings, but here again there was undisguised discrimination. Unqualified whites were promoted ahead of competent blacks. Thus Brooke was drawn to medicine—not primarily, as he once put it, because he was "keenly interested in saving humanity," but rather because of the social pressure and prestige involved.

While at Dunbar he occasionally dressed up like a surgeon, donning

19

a mask and rubber gloves before "operating" on rodents and other animals. He set up a laboratory in the attic for his experiments and posted a sign on the door: "Dr. Brooke's Surgery." "I dissected rats and cats up there, and while a junior in high school I cut open a huge dog and preserved his heart in a bottle of formaldehyde." He also "operated" on snakes, turtles and tadpoles. His mother then thought he would go into medicine.

"He and his friends took over the attic. They'd be in and out of the house with their bottles. One day I went up there and found dead snakes and frogs all over the place, parts of them in bottles, and other parts on the floor." She shuddered at the thought.

In the class "will" the incoming freshman class received from Brooke the legacy of "friendliness." He belonged to the Rex Club, a social fellowship for boys, and the Lettermen's Club. In the yearbook, which predicted that he would become a surgeon, his motto was "Live and Learn."

After graduating from Dunbar in 1936, he enrolled at Howard University in Washington, D.C. Howard, then known as the "black Harvard," like Dunbar had an excellent faculty and distinguished alumni, including Thurgood Marshall, a justice of the U.S. Supreme Court. Brooke took a course in political science from the late Dr. Ralph Bunche,* who, after Brooke became senator, did not recall having had him in class.

As a freshman at the age of sixteen, Brooke still dreamed of becoming a great surgeon, especially because every coed he met wanted to marry a doctor. But science courses bored him and late-afternoon laboratories interfered with his social life. He skipped biology and zoology labs, finding them dull and "overly methodical." After flunking organic chemistry he went on probation for a semester. Finally he switched to social studies when he discovered that he liked history, economics, political science and literature.

Living in Brookland meant a two-mile commute by bus until his parents let him use the family Buick after his sophomore year. "I often have wished I had gone away to school," he says. "Commuting was a drag."

Dr. Percy Barnes had kind words for Brooke, even though he flunked him in chemistry. Recalling that Edward was always in such a hurry that he ran everywhere, Barnes said: "He was a very good-looking boy. Curly hair. Smiling. Affable and always humorous. He

---

* Bunche became a delegate to the UN and in 1930 won the Nobel Peace Prize.

was in a class of a hundred or so students, but always stood out. There was something about him."

Dr. Louis Hansborough, a zoology professor, rated Brooke average, but "lively and intelligent, bright and aware of his responsibility as a student." Colonel Hyman Chase, a professor of anatomy with a Ph.D., knew Brooke best. He was a battalion commander in Brooke's regiment during World War II and his mentor after the war. "I watched him in college, where the atmosphere was calm and comfortable, and he functioned well; and I watched him at the front, where he had a chance to be yellow, and I knew he was a man who could be relied on under any circumstances."

Chase called him a student "with great potential, and he has become a great man. Tell him . . . this is the first time I ever talked about a former student without first calling him an S.O.B." The colonel's students were less profane. They called him "Big Black Chase."

Brooke, elected president of Alpha Phi Alpha in his senior year, later became eastern national vice-president of the nation's oldest black fraternity. Otto Snowden, director of the Freedom House in Roxbury, Massachusetts, said everyone at Howard knew Brooke. "Ed was one of the most popular, really well-liked men on campus. An above-average student, he was conscientious, and had a certain bearing, even then. You couldn't keep the girls away from him, especially when he got a car." Snowden, who is two years older, said Brooke was a good-enough tennis player to win several trophies. Omega Psi Phi tried to pledge Brooke, but he chose the Alphas, who, according to Snowden, "prided themselves on being more selective, choosing the best-looking and best-dressed students."

Royal Bolling, now a state representative in Massachusetts, was a freshman at Howard when Brooke was a senior. "When Ed was president of Alpha, he made us freshman pledges feel important and part of the organization. We had great respect for him."

Although Edward was a big man on campus, he had a short tether at home. "Even when he was twenty-one or twenty-two, he had to be home by a certain time," Helen Brooke recalls. "If he wanted to stay out late, he always called me to ask. I was never one to spare the rod. I was brought up that way, in a very stern family."

Dr. Adelaide Hill, who was close to Brooke during these years, feels that the university made no particular impact on him. "It stretched his mind a bit, and kept him on track, but the most significant, important influences at this period of his life, besides his family, were Dunbar High School and St. Luke's Church." Edward was more social than political while at Howard University, and there was already evidence that for him race would never be a political determinant. He refused to march in a protest demonstration against segregation at a drugstore chain, though he spoke out against it.

Senator Brooke is the lengthened shadow of the boy reared in a secure, protective environment removed from the racial bias of the white world. Thus he escaped the trauma that many of his Negro contemporaries suffered. There is a parallel between Brooke and the late Whitney M. Young during their adolescence. What a biographer said of Young can be precisely applied to Brooke: "He himself says of this period, 'I led a protected life,' a fact that goes far to explain his willingness to face the black-white confrontation without demonstrable rancor." Early experience gave both temperate leaders of the black community a biracial flavor.

By World War II Brooke had a Bachelor of Science degree, but he was drifting. The war changed all that.

CHAPTER THREE

The Shaping Years

AFTER GRADUATING from Howard University in 1941, Brooke pondered the next step. He didn't have long to wait. He had taken ROTC in college, with summer training at Fort Howard, Maryland, and when the Japanese struck Pearl Harbor on December 7, 1941, Brooke was inducted into the all-black 366th Combat Infantry Regiment as a second lieutenant and was sent to Fort Devens, Massachusetts. Underweight at the time, he had expected trouble in passing the physical examination. "You were supposed to weigh 135 pounds to get a commission, and I weighed only 132. I remember drinking a lot of water and eating bananas to get the three additional pounds."

At Fort Devens one of his jobs as executive officer of Headquarters Company, Second Battalion, was to handle discipline. Alfred S. Brothers, who spent the war years with Brooke, recalls the rapport Brooke had with enlisted men: "There was no resentment when he laid down the law, since he made it clear that nothing personal was involved. Punishment followed broken rules, and that was it."

"You know you're going to the guardhouse," Brooke would tell a man, almost apologetically. One soldier came into his office and saluted.

"Private Benson reporting, sir."

"You mean yardbird Benson," the lieutenant said.

As Special Services office in charge of recreation for officers and men, he set up programs to ease ennui and tension. In lieu of tennis, he arranged Ping-Pong tournaments, taking time out to beat every-

23

one in sight. He organized a basketball team that competed with the St. Mark Cherokees in Roxbury, Boston's Harlem. In off hours he became fond of Boston while visting friends.

The routine at Fort Devens was dull and frustrating, and there, for the first time, Brooke saw blatant racial discrimination. Years later he said black GIs in Vietnam were treated better than the men in his unit. Black officers, barred from the regular officers' club, were segregated in their own club. (One USO matron there was Thelma Smith, whose brother, Herbert Tucker, was married to Mary Hill, a Howard University classmate of Brooke. While on leave, Brooke sometimes visited the Tuckers.)

The arrogance of white officers was sometimes vented in rigid if not brutal treatment of black enlisted men, who often received stiff sentences for minor infractions. One of the junior officers' assignments was to defend these men at courts-martial. Most officers, considering this a bore, handled the assignment ineptly. Brooke, boning up on military law, became the Fort's top "public defender," as he parried efforts of white officers who had been serving as prosecutors. Brooke, who never lost a case, became the most sought-after "lawyer" in the regiment after it was known that he would go the route to defend enlisted men. Clarence Elam, a noncommissioned officer who served as court stenographer during the trials, was so impressed by Brooke's courtroom technique that he kept in touch with him during and after the war, as did their mutual friend Alfred Brothers.

In 1942 Brooke took a contingent of 30 men to Onawa, Maine, for a few weeks to guard a Canadian Pacific trestle and bridges on the ragged edge of nowhere. They lived in a sidetracked sleeping car. Even today there are only two permanent residents in Onawa, although many summer visitors own cottages on Lake Onawa. When Brooke and his men went there in 1942 there were no roads or automobiles, and the only buildings were a small grocery store, a post office and a shanty that served as a baggage and freight room. Near the lake there was a wooden church that could accommodate about 40 parishioners. The only way communicants could get to this Roman Catholic church, which also served as a community church, was to walk or take the "scoot," a handcar that went back and forth on the double rails (which became a single track beyond the trestle Brooke and his men guarded).

"When the Bishop of Maine came to Onawa to confirm two persons, I served as acolyte," Brooke said. "The few people around Onawa had never seen Negroes before, and I remember a boy trying to rub the 'black' off the hand of one of my men. The bridges we guarded were over Ship Pond Stream, which empties into Lake Sebec. When the St. Lawrence River is frozen over, the railroad running up through Maine to Montreal and St. John's, New Brunswick, is the only transportation route. Thus the bridges and trestle in Onawa were vulnerable to sabotage during the war."

Mr. and Mrs. D. J. Gagnon, who then lived in Monson, a few miles from Onawa, recall pleasant hours spent with Brooke. "He would come to our house now and then to play the piano," Mrs. Gagnon remembers. "His favorite piece was 'Ave Maria.' He played the piano by ear, and would keep going for about an hour. One night he and a few enlisted men put on a show for the townspeople at Social Hall. I still have a willow cane he made for me. . . . One night it was so hot, Lieutenant Brooke took off his tie and draped it over the living-room door. Later he and a sergeant drove about ten miles to relieve a guard at the trestle. I don't really know why he needed to wear a tie, since he was in the Maine woods. I don't imagine he minded being out of uniform that night."

The lieutenant declared the little store in Onawa off limits. "It sold beer, and some of my men had a tendency to get loaded," Brooke recalls.

Brooke made other excursions out of Fort Devens. "As soon as they learned I could read and write," he quipped, "they sent me to every school in the Army. I took a combat training course, with emphasis on infiltration, at a bivouac in Sturbridge, Massachusetts. We used to have to crawl under an umbrella of gunfire. Later I was at Fort Benning, Georgia, for more infantry training. They made me take a course in motor maintenance, which included reassembling a two-and-a-half-ton Army truck after taking it apart, although I scarcely knew the difference between a manifold and a gasket."

When Brooke finished third in his class in an advanced infantry course at Fort Benning, a colonel suggested his promotion to captain, but the recommendation was tabled when he rejoined his regiment, which had moved to Camp Atterbury, Indiana. His outfit next spent a few weeks in maneuvers in the boondocks of Virginia, Brooke remembers, not far from his ancestral plantation in Fredericksburg. The final stop before sailing from Hampton Roads was a staging area at Fort Patrick Henry in Virginia.

"We could call home from the Fort, but we couldn't tell our destination, which we didn't know exactly. We simply knew we were going overseas," Brooke said.

Taking a zigzag route to avoid Nazi submarines, the U.S.N.S. *Billy Mitchell* landed at Casablanca in North Africa.

"I was seasick during most of the crossing," Brooke recalled. "Two things impressed me as we approached Casablanca: the modern construction in the city, and the poverty of the Moroccans who lined up at our ship to fill their pails with garbage from the galley. They had an unfriendly look in their eyes, as if they resented having to beg for swill. But that's how starved they were. Outside Casablanca we lived in tents. It was difficult to drive the wooden tent pegs into the baked, rocky ground. There was a stampede one night while we were watching an outdoor movie, when someone yelled 'Rattlesnake!' "

Except for some of the modern buildings, Brooke found conditions backward in Morocco. The narrow-gauge train had no washrooms and went so slowly that the troops could jump off, relieve themselves, and run and hop back aboard. "A few of us had a rare luxury on Easter Sunday when I served a can of fruit cocktail I had been saving in my duffel bag." The train's destination was Oran, a seaport in Algeria. Army brass, apparently not knowing what to do with a black regiment, sent it to southern Italy to guard 15th Air Force planes. Brooke got seasick again when the U.S.N.S. *Sam Livermore,* another Liberty ship, transported his unit to Naples, Italy. At a bivouac in Pisa, Brooke, Brothers and Elam met Royal Bolling, Brooke's fraternity mate. "They asked me what it was like at the front," Bolling recalls, "knowing I had just returned from combat in the Viareggio Mountains. There were a lot of Howard men in the 366th, which was the first all-black outfit to fight under the American flag."*

In the Army in Italy Brooke ran into the same racial discrimination as at Fort Devens, especially when his regiment came under the command of Brigadier General Almond of Virginia. (Almond was in command of the 92nd Division, to which the 366th Regiment was at one time attached.) *The Afro-American,* a black newspaper, had criticized the Army for using black troops for such noncombat duties as guarding bridges and Air Force bases. Brooke remembers the resentment of some of the men in his unit when the general, in a

---

* The 366th was not the only black outfit, however. Fighting units such as the 761st Tank Battalion and the 332nd Fighter Group were among black combat units. The 761st is remembered for its valor in the Battle of the Bulge. The 332nd Fighter Group was led by Colonel Benjamin O. Davis, who became the first black general in U.S. Air Force history. His father before him had attained that rank in the U.S. Army. In World War I, the 872nd and 369th Infantry Regiments, both black, fought under the French flag.

speech to the blacks, said: "All right, you fellows asked for combat duty. Let's see how you like it."

Morale was at a low ebb at this time, according to Brooke. "To liven things, we organized a chorus and a few skits and traveled through southern Italy entertaining troops before we went into combat. There were baseball games, and later Joe Louis visited some of the troops."

Brooke was struck by the vast difference between the friendly Italians, who paid no attention to color, and white Army officers. The double standard was so marked a black MP couldn't even arrest a white soldier, in some cases. A black GI who had an orientation lecture in the morning on wiping out Nazi racism was segregated that evening in the "colored" post exchange. Roy Wilkins, director of the NAACP, summed it up: "While we were making the world safe for democracy in one way, and destroying Hitler's master race theory in another, the Negro [at home] rode in the back of the bus, lived in a ghetto across the railroad tracks, sent his children to Jim Crow schools, endured daily humiliation and insult . . . and was the victim of violence." The war opened Brooke's eyes.

The Germans had been in Italy for five years, giving them time to prepare for almost any attack. Italian fields were strewn with mines, and concealed gun emplacements were scattered in strategic places. As the Americans inched their way up the west coast of the peninsula, these obstacles had to be removed before General Mark Clark's Fifth Army could advance. Someone fluent in Italian had to get behind enemy lines to gather information about troop movements. Brooke knew a little French and in off hours had taken a few Italian lessons from an elderly Neapolitan teacher. At this point he seemed the most qualified officer in his unit to serve as liaison officer in command of a special unit that included American soldiers and Italian Partisans, who operated in a cloak-and-dagger setting behind Nazi lines in the Po Valley. "I had always like Romance languages," Brooke said, "and after taking several lessons, I got an Italian grammar and studied it so I could communicate with the Partisans. Fascist Italians were still active, and Nazis were everywhere. My principal job was to map mine fields, supply roads, ammunition dumps, to locate concentration camps, and take prisoners for interrogation."

This espionage was dangerous. Partisans were found with their throats cut or bayoneted to death. There was sometimes close contact with the enemy. In one frenzied scramble to dive into a foxhole, a soldier who fell on Brooke had his back ripped open by shrapnel.

Brooke, whose code name was "Carlo," escaped unhurt. Once, while hiding in a farmhouse wine cellar in an Italian village, he could see rats scurrying around while Nazis were stomping overhead. He heard the housewife denying that she knew anything about Partisans being in the area.

"Things looked pretty bad for a few minutes," Brooke said after the war. "But I never really feared I'd be injured or killed."

On the firing line for 195 days, Brooke, who had been promoted to captain, distinguished himself as a combat officer, receiving the Bronze Star for leading a daylight attack on a heavily fortified artillery battery and observation post on Mount Fato in the Apennines. The capture of this strategic peak enabled the Allies to spot enemy positions.

As at Fort Devens, Brooke, between actions, served as defense counsel in military court cases. In one case, an enlisted man who had been charged with being drunk on guard duty requested Brooke as defense counsel. His plea was denied, since Brooke was not in the area. The GI received a ten-year sentence, loss of pay and a dishonorable discharge. An officer, feeling the man had been dealt with too severely, asked the divisional commander to review the case. This time, with Brooke serving as defense counsel, the soldier was found not guilty and was returned to duty with full back pay.

Just before he was scheduled to return to the States, Brooke learned that an enlisted man had been charged with stealing a blanket and with being AWOL. Brooke took the case, risking a possible delay in his return to the U.S. He argued that nobody had seen the soldier with a blanket; he had simply been seen leaving a tent from which it was alleged that a blanket had been taken. The company commander, not knowing the enlisted man was being held for stealing, had automatically filed an AWOL charge. The man went free. After the war Brooke received a crate of oranges and a note from the soldier, who was living in Tampa, Florida.

Bad news came after V-E Day, Brooke recalls. "We were at a staging area near Pisa, waiting to be sent home or possibly to the South Pacific in the war against Japan. Instead, we were converted into an engineering regiment and had to stay in Italy, while other companies in our regiment went to the Philippines. Our unglamorous job was to repair bridges and rebuild culverts." Clarence Elam shared the frustration. "It was a severe blow to the morale of the 366th to be converted from an infantry unit to engineering duties. Most of us had seen enough of war and wanted to go home before further assignment to combat duty."

There is a story that soon after the war ended, Brooke met Remigia Ferrari-Scacco, a dark-haired, olive-skinned signorina with dancing brown eyes and a puckish grin, while she was serving as a secret agent with the Partisans. The true story is more interesting.

Remigia was one of three children of a cultured Genoa family. Her father, who was prominent in the community, was a prosperous paper merchant. "Remigia was always the best-dressed, best-liked and prettiest girl in Genoa," Pat Collins wrote in *The Boston Record American*.

World War II forced the family to move to their smaller home in the country, where Remigia's mother became bed-ridden. Her only brother joined the Italian navy and Remigia served as a Partisan underground guerrilla worker during the war in Italy. Late one freezing night in a small town near Genoa, when Nazi SS troops were in the area, Remigia tapped on the door of a small house and warned the Jewish occupants that their teenage daughter was in danger of being killed by Nazi terrorists.

"Let me take your children to the country where they will be safe," Remigia whispered. That was her job: to protect young people from torture or slaughter by the Germans. Remigia, who seldom speaks of her war experiences, remembers a sixteen-year-old girl who was brutally tortured to force her to reveal the whereabouts of her brother. There was one terrible night in the little town of Benedicta when the Nazi SS gunned down 118 boys. The Germans dragged other teenagers off to concentration camps.

"It was very dangerous working in the underground, but we never thought about the danger we were living in," Remigia recalls. "They would have killed us—not only us, but our whole families if they caught us." She cannot explain why she left the comforts of home to work as an undercover agent. "I don't know. I guess it was just the feeling we all had for our country. We just could not stand to see young boys, women and children captured and murdered. . . . You have to live through this to get the feeling, but I'll never know why they did this. After it was over, I never discussed it or tried to find out why they did it." She wants to forget the war. "It is so sad what happened over there that I just want to forget."

Her brother, who was in submarine service, was reported lost at sea. Two years later, when he appeared at the door of the family home in Genoa wearing a British army uniform, Remigia didn't recognize him. "I guess it was because it was such a big shock to see him and because we had thought for so long that he was dead. He went upstairs, where my mother was sick in bed, and kissed her. They both cried."

After the war, Remigia had her first vacation in five years. She, her sister Mina, their cousin Maria Parodi and her three-year-old daughter went to Viareggio on the northwest coast of Italy between the Ligurian and Tyrrhenian seas, where they stayed in the Principe di Piemonte Hotel, an imposing, ornate white building with a sidewalk café on one side facing the sea. A popular seaside resort, Viareggio has a beautiful beach, and the seaside promenade is lined with villas and gardens.

Remigia and her group were lolling on the beach on a hot day when Brooke came along "and started to look at me. Afterwards, he told me why. He said I reminded him so much of his mother."*

Remigia, who had studied French at Immacolatta Concepzione for eight years, knew no English, but remembers that Brooke spoke "beautiful Italian." Remigia's progress in mastering English is reflected over the years by the various versions she gives of their first meeting. When he accosted her group, she said in an early interview, "I tell him, listen, this is a public sit, so you can stay. But if you don't want to go away, I move." By 1966 she was more fluent: "I was engaged three years at the time. I doubted I wanted to marry my [Italian] fiancé, but Mr. Brooke did not, how do you say, win me over right away. He was very intelligent, a perfect gentleman. . . . I was impressed, but not in love."

Brooke's first impression was that Remigia was much like his mother, who recalls one of many letters he wrote her from Italy. "One day, not long before he was supposed to get out of the Army, he wrote and said he had found a girl who looked very much like me, had a temperament like mine, and even a little of my fiery temper. He said he wanted to marry her. Remigia was already engaged at that time to a young man from Genoa, but that didn't stop Edward."

That evening Brooke saw Maria Parodi's tiny daughter on the promenade and asked where the old folks were. "What are you doing up so late?" he asked. Brooke talked to her mother and to the Ferrari-

---

* When they first met, Remigia thought Brooke was Spanish. At the time he had a neat mustache grown while he was at Fort Devens.

Scacco sisters that night. Remigia, who was reluctant to talk to Americans she had not been formally introduced to, told him he was wasting his time when he said he wanted to see her again. To get rid of him, she told him she was married. "Then he say he is a lawyer and can get a divorce for me. I tell him my mother is sick so he cannot come and visit me and he say he is a doctor, too, and he will make her well. I tell him he is too young to be both a lawyer and a doctor."

Next day Brooke found out where she was staying by sending her flowers and trailing the florist. She had refused to tell him she was staying at the Principe di Piemonte. After Remigia returned to her home in Genoa, Brooke, who had got her telephone number from Maria Parodi, called and asked if he could visit her. She consented.

Brooke, who took a GI with him, remembers driving to Genoa in a jeep when the roads were full of refugees. "I never met Remigia's father. He was at his country home during my visits." Remigia introduced him to her mother, who was in bed, while Nana, the maid, prepared a luncheon of spaghetti in tomato sauce. Remigia told Brooke, "In Italy we do not put officers and soldiers in the same place."

"Do what you do in Italy," he said. Nana served the GI first, in the kitchen. Half an hour later Brooke, who was eating slowly, savoring the dish, gave Remigia the impression he didn't like the spaghetti.

"I tell Nana to go fry two eggs, these Americans are all the same," she said. Nana told her her mother wanted to see her. Remigia recalls the unusual scene.

" 'What's the story?' my mother asks me. 'He ask me to marry you. He say he in love with you.' He don't ask me nothing."

Remigia's mother, who was not in favor of her marrying her fiancé, who was expected back from his army service in two months, liked Brooke. "He [my fiancé] was in the nightclub business and my parents did not want me to have that kind of life," Remigia recalls. "He was a very good person but not for me."

When Brooke formally proposed marriage at their first meeting in Genoa, Remigia didn't know what to say. "It was so quick and I explained about the engagement." He gave her a week to decide.

"Then ten days later—it was Sunday afternoon—someone rang the bell. 'I'm not home, Nana,' I say. She comes back and says, 'I am sorry, there is some blonde girl wants to see you. She say it is very important.' " It was Brooke and the same enlisted man he had brought before—Rinaldo, as Remigia knew him. It was the code name for Samuel Jackson, a friend of Brooke before and during the war.

A month after the second visit Remigia broke her engagement, and they planned to get married the following month. Then tragedy struck. Brooke's niece, Patsy, daughter of Hélène and "Bun" Amos, was run over and killed by an automobile in Washington, and Brooke was wanted home immediately.

After landing in New York, he was temporarily assigned to Camp Kilmer, New Jersey, and soon thereafter was released from active duty at Fort Meade, Maryland.

Brooke, who was twenty-six when he came home, had changed. "A person matures during five years spent in a war. There was a lot of self-discipline, since officers have heavy responsibilities. When I got out in 1946 I was almost a different person and, incidentally, was in first-rate physical condition." By this time he was six feet one inch tall, broad-shouldered and strong. The war had turned him against violence. "I can't stand any kind of violence. Not even two dogs across the street fighting. I can't stand explosions, either—fireworks or anything like that. There was too much blood and too many bodies and too many mortars and close calls."

He returned with a new set of values. "In a battle, money doesn't mean a thing. In the black market in Italy you could sell a carton of cigarettes for 45 dollars. I saw one British soldier exchange a fifth of Scotch for a can of beer. To this day I have no real zest for money and no desire to accumulate it." Dr. Adelaide Hill thinks his broadened outlook stemmed from the stabilizing effect of the war. "All of the forces—all of the influences that were germinating in him flowered during those years in Italy: the basic goodness and concern for others, the honesty, integrity, decency. It was partly due, of course, to the country and its people—a tolerant attitude he had rarely found in his own country. The rest was due to the hardening and toughening experience of the war itself."

Returning to Washington in the fall of 1945, he had trouble adjusting. He was bothered by claustrophobia. "In Italy we were outside for so long a time, living in tents or on the ground, sleeping under leaves in foxholes or in sleeping bags, that I couldn't stand being inside. I couldn't sleep in my room without the windows being all the way up and air blowing through. I guess you get like that—like an animal—from living that way. My parents felt as if I were a stranger to them, and I was, in a way. It took time for me to learn to feel comfortable again in a bed or a bathtub."

His first concern was a choice of profession. He consulted Colonel Chase about attending graduate school. "His was a young mind, seeking to piece together the bits of his past and future," Chase recalls. "It was a radical change for him, just as it was for many youngsters, to come out of college and go directly into the war." After the session with Chase, Brooke was still at sixes and sevens. Then he listened to his two war buddies.

"Clarance Elam and I talked Ed into coming to Boston after the war," Brothers said. "At first we thought about going into the construction business in a small way, after our experience with an engineering unit in Italy. Then Ed and I thought of getting a Howard Johnson's franchise in Roxbury, but there wasn't enough parking space at the site we had in mind."

Brooke enrolled at Boston University Law School in September 1946. When he first came to Boston he lived in Roxbury with his cousin, Dr. Hill, then a student at Smith College, and her husband, Henry, an organic chemist with a Ph.D. from MIT, before settling in a 25-dollar-a-month apartment in an Italian section within walking distance of the law school, then on Beacon Hill. Having become fond of Italians during the war, he liked the West End, which had a European flavor, as Dr. Hill notes. "The close, small quarters, narrow streets and outdoor shops. The smells and colors. And Edward could speak Italian like a native." His one-room apartment, with a fireplace in a corner, had a kitchenette and bath.

He kept thinking about Remigia, wondering whether their cultural differences would be a drawback when she came to a strange country. The difference in race was of no concern to the Ferrari-Scaccos. But Brooke's mother had some reservations about such a marriage.

"I thought it was too much of a burden for Remigia, a young girl, to come to an unfamiliar country and into marriage with a Negro."

Dr. Hill was less concerned, feeling that Brooke differed from most Americans who had fallen in love while in the service. "He didn't worry much about the question of intermarriage. Actually, Remigia is darker than Edward, so the daily problems associated with a white marrying a black were certainly not a supervening consideration. Also, Edward felt he should honor his promises. He had made a vow, after all, and he loved her enough to keep it. They had been exchanging letters for about two years."

"In each letter he was honest," Remigia recalls. "He told me he could not give me all the things I had, but hoped I would still marry him. I thought about it for two years and still wanted to marry him, so I knew that was it."

Remigia's sister Mina married a GI in April 1947.* When Brooke sent for Remigia, she told Mina to send him a telegram announcing her arrival in New York, but Mina forgot to do this. Remigia had left Genoa in haste. After finding a ship leaving for New York the day after she received Brooke's letter, she was told it would be a month before another ship would be available. She rushed home late that afternoon, packed and sailed the following morning. When she arrived, nobody was waiting on the dock to meet her. Remigia and 20 other unclaimed war brides were detained on the boat for 12 hours. "Then they took us to prison [Ellis Island], where we spent two nights in a dormitory." Remigia was the only one in the group who had American money. She divided the ten dollars so each girl could send a telegram for someone to meet her. Red Cross representatives helped with this detail. Remigia wired Brooke that she needed a 500-dollar deposit. Receiving the cable on a Saturday, he had to wait until the bank opened on Monday. Meanwhile, he arranged for "Rinaldo" to take her to his aunt's home, where she showered and changed her clothes for the first time in five days. Rinaldo also arranged for her flight to Boston—the first time she had even been in a plane. Mrs. Helen Brooke picks up the story:

"When Remigia came from Italy, Edward and I went to [Logan Airport in Boston] to meet her. I didn't know what she looked like. Every little girl that stepped off the plane, I said 'Is that her?' And he said, 'No, you'll see when she comes. She looks like you.' Then she came out, this little frisky thing with her hair to her waist, in a tailored gray suit and tan bag. She looked beautiful." It was an emotional moment. "My heart went out to her," Mrs. Brooke says. "I took her into my arms, and she was trembling. That is the thing that touched me so." Later Mrs. Brooke said Remigia reminded her of a grown-up Edwina, her daughter who had died as a child. She made the bewildered Remigia feel at home immediately. Two months after their marriage Mrs. Brooke gave a reception in Washington for "Migia" and Edward, and later she taught her daughter-in-law to cook and helped her learn English.

The young couple were married on June 7 in the Henry Hills' apartment in Roxbury.

"The people Edward invited to stand with him in our small apartment wedding reflect something in his character," Dr. Hill says. "Two

---

* Mina lives with her husband in Tacoma, Washington. Remigia visits them occasionally.

of the men were old friends. One was Raymond Savoy, whom he had known in his early days in New York. The other, Samuel Jackson [Rinaldo], grew up with Edward, attended Howard University, and fought with him in Italy. Neither of these men ever felt that Edward had outgrown them, even after he became senator. He has always had the ability to encompass the lives of friends whose aims and interests were not the same as his."

Remi Cynthia, the couple's first daughter, was born in the West End apartment just before the Brookes moved in with the Brothers family in an eight-room apartment in Roxbury. About a year later the Brookes settled in a three-decker at another Roxbury address, after Brooke bought the house under the GI Bill of Rights, the same bill which helped put him through law school. "A wonderful bill," he says, smiling.

In law school there was little trace of the playboy who had been so popular with coeds at Howard. "I never studied much at Howard, but at Boston University I didn't do much else *but* study." It was his first real experience with the white community on a competitive basis. "I realized that having attended segregated schools I had an inferiority complex, but I soon overcame it after having more communication with my classmates."

Two future associates who recognized him as a comer at Boston University were John Bottomly and Glendora McIlwain. Bottomly was the son of Robert Bottomly, a brilliant Boston attorney who, as the leading member of the Good Government Association, was a gadfly of the picaresque James Michael Curley, whom he called "an unconscious psychologist who always knows when to do the right thing at the right time."

"I could say the same thing about Ed Brooke," John Bottomly said. Coming from a politically oriented family, he was one of Brooke's first political advisers.

Glendora McIlwain, the vivacious and attractive daughter of a wealthy black pig farmer in Methuen, Massachusetts, who helped found the Crispus Attucks Club,* used to come to Boston on an early train, always arriving in time to choose her favorite seat at the end of the second row in her first class. Brooke sat directly behind her.

"How is the farmer's daughter this morning?" he would ask.

"Ed was a terrible tease," she recalls. "When he asked me whether

---

* Crispus Attucks was a black slave killed in the Boston Massacre.

I had fed the pigs, I used to tell him to mind his own business and leave me alone." Although annoyed by his flippancy at first, she was impressed by his scholarship, charm and especially his thoughtfulness.

"In my final year, the evidence examination at the end of the term was tough. I kept going back to the first question, the hardest. After the exam, I went to the lounge to make a phone call. Ed came over and asked how I answered the first question."

"I could tell you were worried by the way you kept shaking your head," he said. "I think you handled it right. I just didn't want you to go home feeling depressed."

In his senior year Brooke was editor of *The Law Review,* meaning he was one of the top students in his class with a talent for writing. He received an LL.B. degree and an LL.M. the following year. He and Endicott Peabody, a future political rival, were among the 197 persons who passed the bar examination, which 598 candidates took.

At this time, wartime buddies were in business in Roxbury. Royal Bolling, soon to enter politics, was a realtor, as was Alfred Brothers, who recalls: "When Ed finished at B.U. he and I shared a two-room suite in an old building on Humboldt Avenue owned by the company that manufactured Necco Wafers. We paid 50 dollars a month for rent, light and heat. I sold real estate and Ed practiced law, handling land conveyances, accident cases, divorces and, in one case, murder." Brooke had a private office. His first secretary, Margaret McKinney, shared the other small office with Brothers. (A reporter spread the false rumor that the sign on the front door read "Brooke Brothers.") Mrs. McKinney worked from nine until two during the week and later, when work piled up, came to the office Saturdays and even Sundays. Work was slow in piling.

"At the beginning of my practice," Brooke says, "I was always glad when Remigia called me. It was about the only time the phone rang. Not that we starved, of course. Remigia could always cook spaghetti."

"The first thing I noticed about Mr. Brooke was his neatness," Mrs. McKinney recalls. "Everything had to be just right." She smiled. "There was no need to empty ashtrays, however, since neither of us smoked and he tried to discourage others from smoking by making sure no ashtrays were around. I also remember that if I commented on his weight, he would go on a diet right away." She said he built up a good reputation a few months after hanging up his shingle, and never dunned clients too poor to pay bills she sent them.

Remigia, too, soon learned that her husband likes things just so.

When he comes into a room and finds she has moved an ornament or a bowl of flowers, he returns them to their usual place before he sits down. He empties ashtrays and straightens lampshades or a picture on the wall. Like his parents and sister, he never smokes. "But Remigia makes up for me," he says. "When I tell her she is smoking too much, she sometimes goes into the bathroom for a cigarette. I can see the smoke curling out from the door frame." In early Roxbury days Brooke sometimes put a long-stemmed pipe in his mouth. "I was so young-looking, people would come in and ask to see Attorney Brooke. 'You don't mean that *you* are a lawyer,' one client said. I bought a pipe, figuring it would make me look more mature."

Brooke was already showing signs of becoming a lone wolf. After deciding to stay in Boston, he turned down offers to join law firms or partnerships. His father, who had thought of a father-son partnership in Washington, declined an invitation to join Ed in Boston.

Brooke practiced law in his first office on Humboldt Avenue, a Roxbury thoroughfare, for a few years before moving to a busier address at the corner of Massachusetts and Columbus Avenues, the present headquarters of the Boston branch of the NAACP.

"I was supporting my family, but wanted to do better, so in 1957 I moved to Pemberton Square in downtown Boston, hoping I could develop a more lucrative practice. My earlier clients were all local Roxbury residents. Even in the new location, there were times when it was difficult to pay expenses. I used to get behind in the rent. I was never one to pay much attention to financial matters, since money has never meant much to me. This may sound ridiculous, but it's true."

He kept everything in a checking account, and when the balance got low, his secretary would tell him. Sometimes he had to borrow money from his father.

"I never ate high on the hog," he said. "I never really had any large sums of money."

During these early years in the Boston's Harlem, Brooke used to play poker with the Elams, Brothers, Bolling and Otto Snowden, whom he hadn't seen since college days. "We used to have long sessions after fraternity meetings," Bolling recalls. "When it got toward midnight, Remigia would call, and Ed would tell her in Italian he'd be home soon. Some nights she called three or four times. Those were carefree days."

Carefree, but serious, too. The Elams, Bolling and Brothers, who had definite political aspirations, tried to interest Brooke in politics.

37

They were making friends at a time when thousands of Negroes were moving north looking for jobs. Each of these new residents in Roxbury was a potential voter.

"In those days," said Bolling, "the ethnic issue was paramount. People in our ward would say, 'I think you're a great guy, but you won't get elected until your own people put you in.' That was Ed's problem when he first ran."

Helen Brooke thinks her son's acceptance at Boston University Law School shaped his career. "I don't know that he would have gone into politics anywhere else. Certainly not in Washington, where there is no vote."

Bottomly, who succeeded Brooke as editor of *The Law Review,* urged him to go into politics. "We knew he was going places. At first he didn't know whether he was a Democrat or a Republican, but in those days in Ward 12 you could run as both a Republican and a Democrat."

CHAPTER FOUR

Two-Time Loser

EXCEPT FOR a few weeks before elections, Boston's black voters had for the most part long been ignored by candidates for office, and political patronage meant only a few minor jobs for Negroes. The lowly status of blacks largely stemmed from their own apathy, for they tended to stay away from polling booths. In this drift-and-despair environment Brooke had begun to practice law.

Roxbury, which was rapidly turning into a miniature Harlem, was predominantly Jewish, with a small Irish district. In 1950 it was 65 percent white and 35 percent black. Brooke's law office was on the border of the black and white community, and most of his clients were black. Through them he learned of the social and economic problems, which were going from bad to worse as more and more blacks moved in. There were overcrowded schools, understaffed hospitals, dirty and dark streets, run-down housing and sloppy garbage collection. Brooke's friends asked him to do something about improving conditions, and the only effective way was by going into politics.

Clarence Elam, who had taught business administration at North Carolina College after serving as regimental sergeant major in the 366th Infantry, was at this time president of the Roxbury Citizens Club, a nonpartisan group dedicated to community betterment.

In the 1949 Boston mayoral election Elam and Brothers joined the New Boston Committee to help elect John B. Hynes, who was running against the redoubtable James Michael Curley. Hynes had been Curley's secretary for one term. Feeling that Brooke was good for

Boston and Boston good for Brooke, Elam and Brothers got him into state politics. "We were always discussing the need for better representation from our ward," Elam recalls, "so we decided one of us should run for office. We wanted Ed because we needed leadership in general in our community." Brooke had never shown any interest in politics, although his father, he said, "like any self-respecting Negro before the New Deal," was a Republican. In 1949 Brooke, still in law school, kept out of politics.

In 1950 his friends finally talked him into running. "Ed swung gently in an arc in his swivel chair for an hour and a half before we could convince him," Brothers recalls. Since he had never voted, he was not enrolled as either a Democrat or a Republican. Remigia didn't know he was running at first. "I did not know what he was doing, he was gone so much. Having European politics in mind, had I known he was campaigning, I should have been afraid he would be killed." When she realized he was running, she cried for days. "I tell him he will be killed. I know politics in Italy, believe me." Later she calmed down and became a campaign asset, after he told her: "Remigia, you are wrong. You live in the U.S.A. now. We do not kill each other in politics."

"But I do not believe him, I am so scared," she said.

Brooke cross-filed for state representative in Ward 12. Most of his original supporters were well under thirty-five, and despite the lack of funds and political obstacles thought to be insurmountable, they kept plugging, encouraged when older people joined them. Early in the campaign, at a luncheon, Elam and Brothers hosted Roxbury ministers, telling them of the political "renaissance" taking place in the city and reminding them of their potential role in getting citizens to register and vote. Citing the growing black population in Ward 12, they said the time was near when a Negro could be elected to the general court (i.e., the Massachusetts State Legislature). They chose Brooke, they said, because of his tremendous popularity in the district, along with his talent and oratorical skill. The president of the Ministerial Alliance of Boston urged his colleagues to back the candidate, and the late Arthur Williams, a black who had served his community well, graciously stepped aside to support Brooke. (His wife is still an ardent Brooke supporter.)

Brothers was campaign manager, and Elam served as treasurer and chief strategist.

"This is a time when men of action are needed," *The Roxbury Citizen* reported in the summer of 1950. "Members of the legislature are their district's voice in the Commonwealth's government. They must make their voices heard and their influence felt in cloakroom, caucus and debate . . . as well as in the ballot box." The paper cited Brooke's educational background and wartime decorations, adding that he was national president of the 366th Infantry Association. Also noted were Brooke's frequent appearances before the legislature for NAACP in antidiscrimination matters as legal counsel.

Brooke was committeeman for Cub Pack 12 and Troop 9 in Roxbury. Brothers, who was Cubmaster of Pack 12, which was sponsored by St. Mark Congregational Church, used to take his boys, who ranged in age from eight to ten, to Loon Pond in Lakeville, Massachusetts, usually accompanied by Brooke and the Elam brothers. Brooke made biscuits and apple pie for the boys, joined them in hiking, chopping wood and rope climbing, and played softball, volleyball and Ping-Pong with them. He sang, cooked and slept outdoors with the Scouts, getting all the exercise he needed.

Brooke had other workouts with a friend, James Mahone, who was in charge of the Roxbury Tech Basketball League at St. Mark Community Center. Mahone and Brooke played tennis at a community playground. Later Mahone, who in the early 1940s used to drive a Pierce Arrow for Adam Clayton Powell* both at Martha's Vineyard and in Harlem, was a tireless campaign worker for Brooke, driving around the state putting up posters on trees and buildings. In local campaigns he joined volunteers in ringing Roxbury doorbells. Margaret McKinney remembers the reception she got at one Roxbury house during the 1950 campaign.

"I asked an old woman to vote for Brooke, and just before she slammed the door in my face, she said: 'I don't vote for nobody but James Michael Curley.' Most folks in the neighborhood, however, were enthusiastic for the boss."

Brooke was well known as a member of St. Mark Brotherhood and as a basketball player in the church gymnasium. While stationed at Fort Devens early in the war he had brought service basketball teams to

---

* When Brooke was growing up in Brookland, a frequent guest at his home was a boy from Harlem named Adam Clayton Powell. "He is remembered as being even then the antithesis of Ed Brooke," James Doyle of *The Boston Globe* wrote in 1967. "Once, after his success in Harlem politics, he was scheduled to address a national fraternity that both men belonged to. He was the keynote speaker, yet he failed to make an appearance." Doyle adds that Brooke, contrariwise, "is remembered by teachers and family friends as having always been extremely conscientious and a boy they knew would go somewhere."

play against the St. Mark Cherokees, made up of local college players. Games were played in the gym on Saturday mornings. Brooke had further widened his acquaintance by speaking occasionally from the pulpit of the church. Mrs. Melnea Cass, still well known as "the first lady of Roxbury," used to call him "the young old man," adding that he was cut out to be a minister. "He had advice for everyone and was very civic-minded and helpful in so many ways. He wrote the charter for the Roxbury Citizens Club and other groups. We used to send poor people in the neighborhood to him for legal help. They might be school dropouts, kids in trouble, or tenants who were about to be evicted or have a mortgage foreclosed. Edward acted like a father to the children and was considered wise and thoughtful by adults. He charged a small fee or nothing at all, according to circumstances. He was especially active at St. Mark Center, which sent children to camp and was instrumental in having a local playground lit up so children could play at night. Sometimes he spoke to the United War Mothers Chapter which met at the center. We visited hospitals, staged benefits and cooked for Am Vet parties. We told Brooke he had to run for office in 1950. For one thing, he had the solid support of the Am Vets."

As he made his first bid for office, all neighborhood racial and religious groups, young and old, for the first time organized a door-to-door registration campaign. In less than 24 hours after he filed nomination papers, 50 young men and women of the Roxbury Citizens Club and other friends obtained 1,200 more than the required number of signatures. Brooke's headquarters were on the ground floor of the Humboldt Avenue building that housed his first law office (on the second floor). During the contest it buzzed with activity, with a steady stream of supporters trooping in and out.

"Women for Brooke" met in St. Mark's gymnasium to boost his candidacy. Fifteen hundred persons attended a rally at Roxbury Memorial High School after a torchlight parade, old Celtic style, with more than a hundred cars in the line of march. There were street-corner rallies, with tailgating by local Ciceros, who gave Brooke florid introductions. Volunteers sold buttons for 50 cents up to two dollars and rang the doorbell of every house in the ward. This was Brooke's method. He let other candidates pass out balloons to children who couldn't vote.

Brooke climbed flights of tenant stairs after hours, when bread-winners were home, lighting a match to see the names of tenants above the bells in the dimly lit halls. Residents were pleased that he knew their names. Housewives told him of their fear of walking alone on dark steets, complained of the high price of milk and absence of parking. "There are no garages available, yet the cops book us for illegal parking in the streets." Brooke, getting his first taste of politics, patiently listened to complaints of inadequate garbage disposal and learned the pressing need for low-income housing and equitable rent controls. In one block of a hundred houses, 37 had no bathroom, and he found as many as five persons living in one room in two-room rookeries that had leaky plumbing and portable oil burners.

Outside, children dodged cars as they romped in the streets. No effort was made to open schoolyards and gyms for children who, in their frustration, turned to petty crime and vandalized property. For excitement they formed gangs and fought one another. At rallies Brooke blasted incumbents for allowing such conditions to exist.

As Brooke canvassed, he and his campaign workers walked dozens of blocks from early afternoon to 11:00 P.M. Brooke jotted items in a notebook after each visit. "Well," he said on the way back to headquarters, "time to get back to the office and really go to work. See this little notebook? That's my gold mine. In here I have a list of every visit I've made—host, problems discussed, interests mentioned—everything we've said each time. Comes the time I'm in office, these are the problems I'll interest myself in, and these are the people I'll contact when progress is being made, information sought and help needed. You've only half-completed the job when you win an election. From then on, you've got to prove you've earned the votes. . . . My little notebook will help with that."

In the 1950 election Brooke, like all candidates in Ward 12, ran in both the Democratic and Republican primaries, and was nominated by the GOP. In the general election in November, Brooke, with 5,050 votes, trailed George Greene, a blind incumbent, who got the sympathy vote (7,888), and Louis K. Nathanson, another incumbent, who polled 6,987.

"It was a wild campaign," Elam said. "We had almost no money, but the way we campaigned you'd have thought we were running Ed for President. It was a moral victory. We scored well in a heavily Jewish ward, and, in general, did much better than we expected. Brooke received the largest vote ever given a black candidate from the ward."

Brooke's showing was remarkable under the circumstances of the statewide Republican debacle of 1950, when Paul Dever was re-

43

elected Democratic governor with the biggest majority in Bay State history. In defeat Brooke got more votes in 1950 than Alfred Brothers received in 1960 when he was elected state representative, the first Republican from Ward 12 in a dozen years.

Although Brooke said later that he "never lost the bug," he was for a time on the verge of quitting politics primarily because of the way Remigia reacted to nasty talk of their mixed marriage during the campaign. "That kind of talk hurt Ed ten times more than losing," Elam said. "He felt there was too much criticism. Besides, he was anxious to get back to his law practice." During the campaign there were also charges that Brooke was backed by Communists. At the time it was Communist strategy to automatically support any minority candidate. "And some of the foremost Commies in the city lived in Ward 12," Elam said. In any case, immediately after his defeat in 1950, Brooke told friends he would never again run for political office. "Politics is not my cup of tea."

In 1952, however, Brooke—"reluctantly," according to Clarence Elam—ran again for state representative, this time only as a Republican. Governor Paul Dever, who that year lost his bid for re-election to Christian A. Herter, in the spring of 1952 called Brooke into his office and told him he could have the Democratic nomination if he wished. There are various versions as to why Brooke became a Republican.

"When he first ran, he got more votes as a Republican than he did as a Democrat," Royal Bolling said. "That's why he is a Republican today." Cynics said he became a Republican not out of conviction, but because it was the most opportunistic thing to do. Harold Putnam, who in 1951 and 1952 was chairman of the speakers' bureau for the Republican State Committee, gives another explanation:

"I first met Ed at a meeting of the Crispus Attucks Club at an all-day workshop in Roxbury in the fall of 1951. I was attracted to Ed while I spoke, because he seemed so interested and so alert to what I was saying. My recollection is that he walked up to me after the meeting, and that we talked at length at the side of the room. I can remember encouraging him to stay in politics and urging him to run as a Republican in the next election, since I knew he would be a prize candidate for the party in any election.

"At that time the Democratic party was in considerable disrepute. I had just forced roll-call votes on a bill to end segregation in the National Guard, and a bill to end segregation in state-aided public housing. Neither had any enthusiastic support in either party, but even less among Democrats. Only the fact that members were being roll-called made success possible, and Ed knew this.

"I had just forced the attorney general [Francis E. Kelly] before the Supreme Judicial Court as the result of some questionable land transactions, and this led to the disbarment of a central Massachusetts judge. As a lawyer, Ed was well aware of these developments. His sense of public decency made him disinclined to side with such rascals. He began to see that there might be a future for him in the Republican party, and that he might help younger members like me to turn the party around from a stodgy group of special-interest servers to one truly dedicated to the public interest."

Glendora McIlwain recalls the pivotal meeting of the Crispus Attucks Club in 1951. "My mother and I attended the day-long session at the request of my father, Simon, who, with Joseph Williams, was a co-founder of the club. Late in the afternoon Ed Brooke came in and sat behind me. After Harold Putnam addressed the small meeting of blacks, Ed leaned forward. 'You can make a Republican out of me if you have more men like Putnam in the party,' he said. 'He makes sense, and I'd like to meet him.' Brooke was also impressed by Sumner Whittier, who later became lieutenant governor of Massachusetts. Although Ed was never a Democrat, he had wavered in his party affiliation since the 1950 election, but after hearing Putnam and Whittier speak, he was drawn to the GOP."

Putnam did not see Brooke again until January 1952, when the Boston Junior Chamber of Commerce included them among the "Ten Outstanding Young Men of 1951," along with a rising young politician, Congressman John F. Kennedy, and other distinguished Bostonians. Putnam mentioned the decidedly favorable impression the thirty-two-year-old Brooke made, even in such select company. Brooke's citation mentioned his success in advancing the cause of blacks as legal counsel for the NAACP.

"His legal talents have been successfully employed in convincing the state legislature to abolish segregation in the National Guard, in compelling the Springfield Railway System to hire Nero operators, and in aiding in the appeal before the United States Supreme Court in the case which outlawed segregation in dining cars on our U.S. railroads."

At the 1952 Republican Convention in Springfield, which Brooke attended, Glendora McIlwain was a delegate, and Putnam was sergeant-at-arms. Senator Henry Cabot Lodge chaired the convention. "Dad raved about Ed and wanted to know if he was for real," Glendora told a friend at the convention. Simon McIlwain nodded, mentioning how impressed he had been the first time he heard Brooke speak. "My daughter went to law school with Brooke and she was saying good things about him then," he said.

"This convention was Ed's first commitment to the Republican party," Putnam recalls. "He was interested enough to be there. He did not have to file papers for the Republican primary for the House until July 1952. This was the first primary in which candidates were not permitted to cross-file.

"Once Ed filed papers for the House nomination, Glendora and I went to work on his campaign in Roxbury. Glendora worked on the sound truck and accompanied him to street rallies on Saturdays. I attended many meetings with him, walked through scores of apartment houses and tenements and introduced him to several audiences. I was then a member of the House, so it may have been some help to him to have a current House member with him. I made the pitch that the progress we had made on state civil-rights legislation could not continue unless we added some Ed Brookes to our House membership.

"The most memorable part of that 1952 campaign was the torchlight parade through the streets of Roxbury the night before the election. I had never seen such neighborhood devotion. Hundreds of people were hanging out windows shouting encouragement. Everybody seemed to know Ed and to be solidly supporting him.

"Election night was an anxious time, because the vote was close all evening and into the night. It never quite looked as though Ed could make it, but it was close enough to be hopeful until around 5:00 A.M. Ed's wife, Mrs. Melnea Cass, one of his influential supporters, a few others and I stayed until the bitter end. I left when it was clear that Ed was not going to make it that time. It was a sad moment, yet I was practical enough as a politician to know that it was really a significant beginning."

During the election Putnam not only got grass-roots support for Brooke, but also persuaded the Republican State Committee to contribute campaign funds. He also arranged for John Roosevelt and Senators Henry Cabot Lodge* and Leverett Saltonstall to speak in his behalf.

"Never before had such an eloquent, intelligent and attractive Negro run for office in Massachusetts," Putnam said.

---

* In 1952 Lodge ran for reelection against John F. Kennedy and lost.

Glendora McIlwain had joined Brooke's Roxbury friends in urging him to run. Early in 1952 she dropped into his Massachusetts Avenue law office and told him he would do better than he had in 1950.

"There isn't going to be any next time," he said. Although convinced at the time that he really didn't want to run, she kept prodding him. "I would drop into his office and, if he was busy, would leave. One day I stuck my head in and told his secretary to tell him I would see him later. She said he wanted to talk to me. When she buzzed, he left a client and took me into an office across the hall. I convinced him that he had a good chance of winning this time." At street-corner rallies during the campaign, Glendora, who could turn on the charm, introduced him. "This is the Ed Brooke I know. Let me tell you what he will do for you."

One fund-raising vehicle during this more sophisticated campaign was *Musical Journey,* written and directed by Harry J. Elam.* Al Brothers, Melnea Cass and Adelaide Hill solicited ads for the program, lining up sponsors from Dunbar High School, Howard University, Alpha Phi Alpha, Am Vets and various churches. Henry Cabot Lodge was an anonymous donor, and State Senator John F. Collins, a Democrat who became mayor of Boston, put a 25-dollar ad in the souvenir program. Enough money was raised to cover costs of newspaper and transit ads, posters, car stickers, campaign buttons, political folders and incidental expenses at campaign headquarters, which was on the same store-front floor of the building used in the 1950 campaign.

Brooke, who had spoken before from the pulpit of St. Mark Church, gave a stirring talk at a Mother's Day service before a crowded congregation. He had the support of the Mothers' Club and the local chapter of War Mothers. The candidate was touching all bases. Besides running his own campaign, he was Roxbury coordinator for the campaign of Congressman Christian Herter, the Republican candidate for governor, who joined his list of speakers.

"If Congressman Herter and the entire Republican ticket will roll up their sleeves and bring the campaign right to the people, they will win the November 4 election," Brooke told his workers in mid-September. "The Republicans, to win, must bring forth a positive program free from their usual campaign platitudes." The soft-spoken candidate was learning to swing hard.

Once again there was muttering about his interracial marriage, and

---

* Elam is now a judge of the Municipal Court.

Remigia was still pressuring him to get out of politics. "He was doing well with the law, and I wanted him close," she said. His father also advised him to resume his law practice and "go make some money." There were further attempts to link him with Communists.

Remigia, however, who hated campaigning and being away from home, couldn't stand people at rallies who pumped his hand and talked so fast she couldn't understand what they were saying, and with her Old World upbringing, she was repelled by women who embraced her husband and tried to kiss him. "There was nothing like that in Italy," Mrs. Helen Brooke said. "I had to help her learn."

Remigia tells one story on herself: "In 1952, Mr. Brooke was campaigning for Henry Cabot Lodge. A friend came by and asked me to come to a tea for John Kennedy, who that year was running for the Senate against Mr. Lodge. I liked Mr. Kennedy very much, so why not go to his tea? When Mr. Lodge heard about it, Mr. Brooke said: 'That Remigia! She went to count Democrats for us Republicans!' Later, we saw Mr. Lodge and he laughed and asked me if I was still counting Democrats."

"It looks as if Eisenhower is winning," Glendora said early on election night.

"Yes, but he isn't taking me with him," Brooke said. The odds were still stacked against a black newcomer, despite his talent and energetic campaigning. He had, however, made another strong showing, losing by only 984 votes to Greene. While Brooke was piling up 6,647 votes in Ward 12, Eisenhower in the same ward received 5,021 and Herter 5,089 votes.

Herter offered him the job of executive secretary of the Governor's Council, a post traditionally given to blacks. "I didn't take it. I don't believe in Negro jobs. I wanted to be elected on my own ability," he said. "Only then do you have progress." There was a faraway look in his eyes. "People should not use race as a basis for labeling me. They may be disappointed."

When Representative Herbert Jackson of Malden, a black, declined the post, Herter gave it to Clarence Elam on Brooke's recommendation.

William R. Sims, publicity director of the Urban League of Greater New York, wired Brooke not to be discouraged: "Even in defeat, you have reached political heights unreached by any other Negro in the community. So stick it out. You've already carved a sizable niche for yourself."

Former Mayor and Governor James Michael Curley sent Brooke a copy of his biography, *The Purple Shamrock,* inscribed: "Don't get discouraged. You are destined for a successful career in politics."

In Brooke, Curley saw a persuasive spokesman for the GOP, and a shrewd politician who could win support from whites as well as blacks. Cool and unflappable, Brooke was easily the most articulate candidate from either party since Curley himself, the most silver-toned orator of his generation in the Commonwealth.

By this time Brooke was deeply involved in civic affairs. On the board of directors of the Greater Boston Urban League, he was Judge Advocate of Massachusetts and second vice-president and legislative chairman of the Boston branch of the NAACP. As legal counsel for the NAACP, he fought discrimination in business, social and military life. Locally he was a member of the St. Mark Community Forum, St. Mark Brotherhood, Roxbury Citizens Club and the Early Risers Club, an organization to help youth. He was on the endorsement committee of the New Boston Committee, a member of the Ward 12 Republican Committee, the Republican Club of Massachusetts and the Massachusetts Civic League. He belonged to the Boston, Massachusetts and American bar associations, and was a director of the Boston Council of the Boy Scouts of America. He was not merely a "joiner." He was active in almost every organization or cause dedicated to community betterment.

After losing the 1952 election, Brooke stayed out of politics for eight years, a move that helped him later, for at a time when most politicians were collecting enemies, he was out of target range. He remained on the fringe of politics, however, managing unsuccessful campaigns for Brothers and Harry Elam in their 1954 run for the House, and Elam's bid for the City Council in 1955 and 1957.

During these eight years Brooke rose in the hierarchy of the Am Vets (American Veterans of World War II). "In politics you know your enemies," he told Brothers. "In Am Vets politics you don't." In 1952 the Am Vets presented him with its Distinguished Service Award and later helped Brooke form the nucleus of a statewide "Know Ed Brooke" organization. Brooke, Brothers and Clarence Elam had been members of the 366th Infantry Veterans' Association, which met in a boiler room of a Roxbury housing project. Guest speaker one evening was George V. Medeiros, now national service officer of Am Vets. He told the group they would be more effective in promoting beneficial veterans' legislation if they joined the national organization. They applied for a charter and as 366th Infantry Post 128, Am Vets, bought land and a building in Roxbury.

Brooke, Brothers and Clarence Elam had earlier conferred in Washington with the national Am Vets commander, Harold Russell, star of the Academy Award–winning film *The Best Years of Our Lives*. Russell attended the charter dedication ceremony in June at St. Mark recreational center, installing Brooke as commander, Clarence Elam as first vice-commander and Brothers as third vice-commander.

Medeiros was impressed by Brooke, who had presided at the meeting at which he spoke. "This man will go places." he said. Brooke was elected state commander for 1954–55 at the tenth annual convention of Am Vets, held in Fall River, Massachusetts, in 1954. Almost 30,000 spectators lined the route as the convention closed after a two-and-a-half-hour parade featuring 40 bands. (In the line of march was Troop 9 of Roxbury, whose scoutmaster was James Mahone.) The motorcycle escort was so long some of the spectators thought President Eisenhower was coming to town.

In introducing Lieutenant Governor Sumner Whittier of Massachusetts, Commander Brooke said he was "a young man just about two or three years older than I am. I think he is thirty."

"Department Commander, my very good friend, Ed Brooke—sorry you made that mistake about my age," Whittier said. "I'm twenty-one." After the laughter, he brought greetings from Harold Russell. Brooke read a telegram from Melnea Cass, past department president of the United War Mothers of America. "May God bless all of you as you continue your work of service for the benefit of all veterans and their families." To Brooke it was like a letter from home, for to him the Roxbury leader, who has many of the looks and mannerisms of Helen Seldon Brooke, has always been "Mother Cass."*

Brooke was getting statewide and even national recognition by this time. In 1955, when the Am Vets convened in Philadelphia, he addressed several delegations, including Southern caucuses. In 1956, when he was elected National Judge Advocate of Am Vets, he carried every state in the South, including Mississippi. "You could see the emergence of a personality destined to a great future," Medeiros said.

---

* On her seventy-fifth birthday anniversary in 1971, Brooke sent her flowers and phoned her at the home of her daughter, who gave her a surprise party with over 100 guests present.

"This national post gave him his first real power base." At one meeting of the national group Brooke introduced Henry Cabot Lodge, then Ambassador to the United Nations. That same year (1956) Brooke was a platform guest when President Eisenhower came to Boston during his campaign for reelection. Such experiences were beginning to rekindle his political ambition.

When he became Massachusetts department commander of Am Vets he made Harold Putnam public relations chairman. "We attended many meetings around the state and in Washington, D.C.," Putnam said. "This helped Brooke become known favorably in the cities of the Commonwealth." Brooke visited more than 70 Am Vet posts in one year, installing officers, speaking and always winning more friends.

Brooke at this time was a member of 16 boards of trustees, including Boston University and the New England Hospital. A fellow trustee* at the hospital remembers Brooke coming in late at the annual board meeting. "As Brooke came in, the president beckoned for him to come to the seat reserved for him at the head table. He refused, and sat down with us 'ordinary mortals.' Years later, my husband, who had met him briefly only once, was impressed by his remarkable memory. We were attending a performance of the Boston Opera Company, of which Senator Brooke was president. After his opening speech, he passed us as he quickly walked down the aisle. My husband was amazed when he greeted him by name."

Brooke's ability to remember names is a continuing political asset. A former teacher at the Boston Industrial School for Crippled Children in Boston recalls occasional visits Brooke made years ago. "After retiring, I moved to Amherst and did not see Mr. Brooke again until the 1968 presidential campaign, when I was working at the Republican trailer on Amherst Green. One day who came streaming up to the trailer with all sorts of campaign workers but Edward Brooke, who with no hesitation said, 'How are you, Mrs. Sanderson?' He mentioned several of my former students by name. His last sally, as he left, leaning out his car window, was: 'Whatever happened to Jimmy Dawkins, Mrs. Sanderson?' Incidentally, you should have seen all the women grabbing him and kissing him, all trying to show how they love their black brothers. But Mr. Brooke and I are friends. We shook hands."

By 1956 Brooke was so well known his friends gave him a testi-

---

* Mrs. Charles H. Myers.

51

monial dinner at the John Hancock Building in Boston. He was better known as a lawyer than a politician at this time, however, for he had established himself as a match for top attorneys in the Bay State. One publicized case involved Daisy Richards, a professional dancer who was injured in an automobile accident in 1954 on the Worcester Turnpike. She brought suit for 150,000 dollars against the driver, Joe Benjamin, a bass violist for singer Sarah Vaughn, Miss Richards' traveling companion. Although opposed by Hubert Thompson, a prominent insurance trial lawyer, Brooke won the case. The verdict was the largest ever obtained in Massachusetts for a victim of gross negligence in a passenger versus operator case. It was not all collectible, however, as Brooke told a friend who congratulated him. "All we could get for Miss Richards was the proceeds of a 10,000-dollar insurance policy."

Brooke needed a good income, for now he had a family to fend for. He spent as much time as possible with his young daughters, Remi and Edwina, who, her mother said, smiling, was supposed to be a boy. "I was so sure she was going to be a boy, I bought everything in blue."

Meanwhile, Brooke found himself drifting back into the political mainstream. He was appalled by the corruption in Boston and state politics. The Democratic administration of Foster Furcolo, who had been elected governor in 1957, was shot through with corruption and was ripe for exposure.

CHAPTER FIVE

Off and Running

B Y 1960, Massachusetts Republicans had been humbled by Democrats in so many elections that the state was close to one-party rule. This forced the GOP to move away from its primary emphasis on WASP (white Anglo-Saxon Protestant) orientation and offer a statewide ticket with ethnic balance.

The Republican party had always been the preserve of old-line families and Yankee cliques who had over the years surrendered their power to rising ethnic groups such as the Irish, Italians and Jews. Snapping to, the Old Guard in recent years has tried to get back on the track by offering ethnic candidates who appeal to disenchanted Democrats and the growing ranks of independents. Thus in 1960 the GOP nominated John Volpe, an Italian-American Roman Catholic, for governor and Brooke for secretary of state, the first time in American history a Negro had been nominated by a major party for statewide office. The Democrats called it a "United Nations ticket." It was a Republican concession to the theory that, ethnically speaking, a statewide slate should include something for everyone.

Ethnic ticket-balancing was nothing new in 1960, as David Broder noted in *The Washington Post*. "When voters lose the habit of identifying themselves as Republicans or Democrats, they may not, as the reformers hoped, begin to think of themselves as conservatives or liberals, or even hawks or doves. They may instead view electoral politics as a power struggle between Italians and Irish, Catholics and Yankees, or blacks and whites."

From this point of view, Brooke's prospects seemed hopeless in 1960, since he had liabilities candidates are not supposed to have in the Commonwealth. Not only was he a Negro, Republican, Episcopalian with a Virginia accent (was this an asset or a liability?), but he was also broke. When his ardent supporters, more convinced than ever that he could walk on water, urged him to run for secretary of state, the state's third highest office, he consulted GOP soothsayers.

Joseph Fitzgerald, now Election Commissioner for the City of Boston, had been Suffolk County coordinator for Christian A. Herter in 1952. He reminded Herter about the ability of the energetic group of young blacks in Roxbury to get votes for Republicans in a Democratic ward. "It was a district where voters crossed party lines," Fitzgerald explained. "The upper part of the ward was Jewish, the middle black, the lower Irish." Fitzgerald, who was Brooke's campaign manager in 1960, had also noted that Brooke appealed to whites in the Am Vets. Like Glendora McIlwain, John Bottomly, Harold Putnam and James Michael Curley, Fitzgerald saw Brooke's catch-fire potential. Fitzgerald talked to GOP leaders, who agreed that Brooke's candidacy could deal a severe blow to bigotry and, in a year when the Democrats were running an "all green" (i.e., Irish) ticket, that Brooke would give the Republicans a chance to show they were for the new races.

Remigia did not stand in her husband's way. "I stopped him for eight years. . . . I kept him away for a long time. But after so many years, I saw that there was no danger really when I saw that so many people in politics were safe. I thought when I married him he was a quiet, home type. But he was in everything, this man. Never keeping still."

The Boston Globe, in announcing that the former Massachusetts commander of Am Vets and ex-vice-president of the NAACP was running for the office, quoted him as urging a clean sweep to replace "the hopelessly befuddled Democratic administration, which has made a political playground of the State House."

In his secondhand Buick Brooke drove around the state to talk to delegates. In 1960, when there were only 93,000 blacks in Massachusetts, it was considered unusual for a Negro to woo the support of an overwhelmingly white electorate, but Brooke campaigned as an American, not as a black, feeling his qualifications would get him by. He used the same technique as another 1960 candidate. John F. Kennedy, while running for President, repeatedly said: "I am not the Catholic candidate for President; I am the Democratic candidate." Just as Kennedy drew votes from hard-shell Baptists and Southern Democrats, Brooke siphoned off votes from whites, Catholics and Democrats.

It was a bold move in Bay State politics, and an indication that Brooke could, like James Michael Curley, "think ahead of the mob." Said Joseph Fitzgerald: "As my wife, Brooke and I drove to the Worcester primary convention in my creaky Chevrolet, it seemed odd that without any machinations by the party stalwarts we were backing a relatively unknown black from the Sugar Hill section of Roxbury as a Republican standard bearer."

Brooke's room at the Bancroft Hotel in Worcester was too small to accommodate well-wishers. "So many delegates wanted to meet him," Fitzgerald said, "my wife and I turned over our two-room suite to Brooke after having the beds and furniture taken out to make more room. Delegates stretched all the way down the corridor, waiting to shake his hand. I recall that the switchboard operator at the convention called him 'captivating.' " Mayor Durbin H. Wells of Northampton, who gave the nominating speech at the primary at which Henry Cabot Lodge, Jr., served as convention chairman, spoke of Brooke as "a real sweet guy." Newspapers were already calling "charm" one of his best assets.

Glendora McIlwain, a delegate and a member of the Republican State Committee, placed Brooke's name in nomination. "At least 20 delegates had to stand to second the nomination," she recalls. "Almost every delegate stood. I remember breaking into tears. Yes, he really captivated them." In seconding the nomination Elizabeth McSherry of Milton said: "Massachusetts has a great heritage in equal rights that started before the Civil War, but that was over a hundred years ago and we need to be reminded that we are still in the forefront of civil rights and must practice what we preach in Massachusetts."

UN Ambassador Lodge then recognized Brooke.

"Our own Henry Cabot Lodge, the man who tells the Russians where to go and how to get there and is doing a great job. . . ." Brooke ticked off the names of other notables present. "In 1960 we will show the people of Massachusetts that we are a united party and that we will destroy the myths of class, race, creed, wealth, antilabor, suburbia, which the Democratic party has attempted to shackle us with. It is not the Democratic party—it is the Republican party which is truly the party of the people, the party of Lincoln, the party of Eisenhower, the party of Saltonstall, and the party of John Volpe. I will be proud to be on that team."

Brooke was beginning to sound more like a politician.

"The ballots rolled," Miss McIlwain said, "and he ran away." The balloting in the five-way secretary-of-state race had covered only ten of the state's 40 districts when Brooke had piled up such a top-heavy margin that his four opponents conceded.

Campaign money was hard to come by in 1960. When Brooke's Democratic opponent, Kevin White, who spent 33,000 dollars in the campaign, held his first fund-raising party in the grand ballroom of the Sheraton Plaza Hotel, fewer than 50 persons showed up. To spur Brooke's campaign, Fitzgerald and others arranged a 100-dollar-a-plate dinner at a Masonic temple in Roxbury and raised about 5,000 dollars. When Brooke opened headquarters in downtown Boston, volunteers poured in to type, file, handle telephone calls and stuff envelopes. One was the charming, tall and tweedy Sally Brooks Saltonstall, niece of Senator Leverett Saltonstall, who sought reelection in 1960. Sally, who had met Brooke while serving as a page at the 1960 GOP convention in Chicago, was one of the original quartet who in the 1964 New Hampshire presidential primary masterminded the unexpected victory of Henry Cabot Lodge. During the 1960 campaign a friend asked whether she was helping Saltonstall.

"Oh, no," she said. "I'm working for Mr. Brooke. But I hope Uncle Lev wins, of course." She also helped the Nixon-Lodge ticket in 1960, spending part of her time on the street soliciting campaign funds. One day she came into the Brooke headquarters with a canful of money for the presidential fund. "One person also donated 13 cents for our campaign," she told Brooke.

Brooke said the odds were 150 to one against him when he was nominated. "Now they're much better," he told a women's group late in the campaign.

In a Channel 2 TV show sponsored by the League of Women Voters, a reporter asked Kevin White whether a black could win a statewide election in Massachusetts. Before he could say yes, Salvatore J. Micchiche, a *Boston Globe* reporter who was a panelist, cut in: "Sure he can win. If he's a Democrat." After Brooke had been nominated, some of White's advisers told him it would be a breeze, running against an unknown, and a black at that. White, who had been assistant district attorney under Garrett Byrne, had seen Brooke in action in the courtroom, and he knew otherwise.

"He made his presence felt in the courtroom and he will make his presence felt in the campaign," he correctly predicted.

While it was a clean campaign, the "Vote White" slogan used by the Democrats early in the fight (without White's permission) carried an obvious innuendo. It meant "Don't vote black." White ordered the slogan removed.

"Normally," he said, "I would have passed out bumper stickers saying, 'Vote White.' But, knowing this could be misinterpreted, we made them read, 'Vote Kevin White.' "

A Brooke worker showed a campaign leaflet to a passerby, saying, "Your vote for secretary of state is very important."

"I hope so," the man said. "I'm Kevin White."

In what was to become a typical, tireless pattern of campaigning, Brooke took in a scallop festival, clambakes, countless Kiwanis, Rotary, Lions, Elks and American Legion meetings, county fairs and many a kaffeeklatsch. He knew when to speak and when to remain silent. In North Adams he admired Mt. Greylock Bowl, but refused to campaign among the bowlers.

"They're here for fun," he said. "They don't want to stop just to shake hands with a candidate."

Brooke campaigned across the state. "Ed was often late on his rounds," Glendora recalls. "But usually nobody would leave. At first some of the people were unreceptive, but he always won them over." Voters who worried about his color were more relaxed after meeting him. Some, said Brooke, had never seen a Negro and wanted to be sure he wasn't an ogre. He generally warmed up with a wheeze before giving a vibrant, factual speech appropriate to each region. He told audiences he enjoyed suppers in asparagus country, "but I sure hate to visit the onion districts." This became known as his "onion speech." He often wound up by quoting from a favorite hymn:

> God of justice, save the people
> From the war of race and creed,
> From the strife of class and faction,
> Make our nation free indeed;
> Keep her faith in simple manhood
> Strong as when her life began,
> Till it finds its full fruition
> In the brotherhood of man!

As he made the rounds, Brooke explained the functions of the office he sought: the secretary of state handles vital statistics, prepares the ballots for elections, handles state archives. Although the office was anything but glamorous or dramatic, Brooke said it was a job that calls for integrity and conscientious attention to duty. In Winchendon he laughed when asked if he thought people knew what office he was running for. Once, while he was addressing a group of women, an old lady said she liked him and thought he would certainly do an excellent job. But, she added, Christian Herter (Eisenhower's Secretary of State) had also been doing a good job. Brooke told her Herter dealt with people like Khrushchev, while he, if elected, would be taking care of the interests of people in the Bay State.

"The present secretary of state [Joseph D. Ward of Fitchburg] has said the office of secretary of state in Massachusetts is nothing more than that of a glorified office boy," Brooke told a Springfield audience. "The other day Lieutenant Governor [Robert] Murphy was named chairman of the Metropolitan District Commission, and if Governor [Foster] Furcolo resigns, that would leave Ward as acting governor with power to name Furcolo either to the vacancy on the Supreme Judicial Court of the state or to the U.S. Senate if Senator Kennedy wins the presidency. I think this is a lot of power for an office boy."

While he was campaigning in Springfield a woman asked Brooke how good the secretary of state had to be at taking dictation and queried him about his typing speed.

"The office may go to the man who wakes up first and puts out a leaflet proclaiming: 'I can type!' " a newspaper reported. "About the only counteraction available to the opposition would then be another leaflet saying: 'I can type faster *and* use shorthand!' "

In Haverhill, Brooke, besides "pressing the flesh," handed out what at first glance looked like business cards. They were carefully designed brochures, not much larger than regular business cards, telling his complete history and qualifications. Brooke introduced new techniques during the contest. He admitted he was taking a gamble with public reaction to his campaign literature and pins which referred to him as "Mr. Brooke." He did so to raise the prestige and respect for the office he was seeking, and to call attention to his campaign, since he knew that a public whose interest was taken up so much by the Kennedy-Nixon, Saltonstall-O'Connor, and Volpe-Ward contests probably were not watching the Brooke-White battle too closely.

In Boston, Republicans laughed during a big Nixon dinner in Commonwealth Armory when the toastmaster, trying to get the crowd away from the head table where everyone was eyeing Vice-President Nixon, said: "I hope you crowd up to the polls in November like you are doing now. If you do, we're in." At this big rally, according to a newspaper, "One of the biggest 'hands' was given to

Edward Brooke . . . who was introduced as the first Negro to be nominated for high state office anywhere in the United States."

This reminded Brooke of an unpublicized incident that happened at the Republican National Convention in Chicago, where he led the delegates in the salute to the flag. Brooke, who was the only Massachusetts delegate whom the Brahmin Congressman Lawrence Curtis did not invite to a cocktail party, was asked whether he was willing to nominate an unqualified black from Indiana* who wanted to be the first Negro in American history to run for the presidency. Brooke refused. He also refused to appear on the *Today* television show with this candidate, even though the exposure from an interview with Dave Garroway would have given his candidacy in Massachusetts a big boost. Thus, as early as 1960, Brooke rejected the notion that he was a symbol of Negritude.

While in Chicago Brooke told the press the GOP should include a strong civil-rights plank in the platform: "It is unfortunate in 1960 that so much time must be spent in a fight for a strong civil-rights plank, when civil rights are guaranteed by the Constitution . . . and the platform is merely a reaffirmation of our principles of equality and justice for all men. . . . In our Pledge of Allegiance are contained the words 'with liberty and justice for all.' No platform can be acceptable to the American people which does not give meaning to those words."

At the end of September the "Youth for Brooke" truck of Boston area college cheerleaders led by Sally Saltonstall, along with a "Volpe for Governor" float, were part of a 50-car motorcade in western Massachusetts climaxed by a "Salty in 60" rally in the Leominster state armory. There was music for dancing, a free reception and a receiving line. The reception was open to the public, regardless of party affiliation. Brooke picked up a few Democratic votes that evening. Next day Brooke, in a white Cadillac convertible, led another motorcade from East Longmeadow to Wilbraham, where he and other GOP candidates spoke at a rally at the high school. The big parade, however, was on Columbus Day in East Boston, when 250,000 persons turned out along a seven-mile route from the Suffolk Downs open-air theater to the reviewing stand in Brophy Square.

---

* According to Donald Whitehead, who accompanied Brooke to the Chicago convention, this Negro importuned Congressman Charles Halleck of Indiana in his abortive bid to run for the presidency. "There were many ambitious blacks in Indiana at the time," Halleck recalls. Neither he nor Whitehead can remember the black's name.

The last person to reach the reviewing stand was Brooke, still looking fresh and vigorous after traveling the entire route on foot, zigzagging from one side of the street to the other, shaking hands. At the reviewing stand he shook hands with his friend Mayor John Collins, honorary marshal.

Handshaking his way around the state and looking straight into people's eyes, Brooke told everyone he needed his vote. He pinched little girls on the cheek, asking them to remind their parents to go to the polls.

"Of course, the job pays less than I earn now," he said at rallies. Warm receptions hiked his confidence. "People may come to listen because they're curious, but they remain because they become interested in what I have to say."

By 1960 Brooke's ability to field tough questions or blunt barbs was well known.

"You've got your nerve coming in here," a Cambridge factory worker told him. "We're all Democrats."

Brooke grinned. "I won't hold it against you." A worker returned his smile. "You've got courage, fellow; I'll give you a vote."

In Holyoke Brooke commented on Henry Cabot Lodge's promise made late in October that a new Republican administration would appoint a Negro to the Cabinet.

"Why not promise an Indian, too?" Brooke said. "Lodge's statement only makes the issue more pointed." Brooke said Lodge had been carried away by his liberal-mindedness. "Any man or woman with the proper qualifications should be eligible. In that way there could be more than one black in the Cabinet," Brooke said.

On October 18 in Springfield, when a debate between Brooke and White was scheduled, Brooke charged that it was the third time White had failed to show up for a confrontation on the same platform. Carl M. Sapers, White's campaign director, said both candidates were well qualified, but that since there would be a Democratic legislature, it would make sense to vote for White. Brooke disagreed:

"Only the Man Upstairs knows that. But if there is a Democratic legislature, that is all the more reason we should have a Republican secretary of state. Somebody has to mind the store."

Sally Saltonstall, chairman of the youth group supporting Brooke, with her brigade drove a sound truck during rush hours in downtown Boston and all over the state, broadcasting a Brooke song. Patricia Beck rode the sound truck playing a record, "Look for Brooke on Your Ballot," and when the record broke, she sang the song herself. Getting a leave of absence with pay, Patricia worked full time late in the campaign after learning the routine by working evenings and weekends. She recalls one rally held on Boston Common, to which all candidates were invited with little warning. Brooke, who was scheduled to speak at a small gathering in Weston, planned to keep his appointment until the local chairman, hearing of the big rally, released him from the commitment.

When Patricia married Vincent Caroleo, Brooke was invited to a simple ceremony when Caroleo was sworn in as a member of a state board by Governor Volpe.

"All I have to say, Vincent, is that your wife worked in my first campaign and I lost. Later she worked for John Volpe and he lost. When you ran for state senator she campaigned for you, and you lost. It's a good thing she had nothing to do with your appointment, or you wouldn't have gotten it." His workers knew he teased only people he liked.

Sally Saltonstall introduced Brooke at some rallies, and Remigia made the circuit. Her English, acquired by "osmosis," was getting better as she campaigned, but she was most effective when speaking Italian in Italian districts. Brooke himself, at the Italian-American Social Club in Watertown, wowed his audience when he broke into fluent Italian. In Italian neighborhoods he rushed onto stoops to converse with old folks in their native language.

Late in October, wives of the Republican and Democratic candidates buried the hatchet and attended a tea at the Harvard Club in Boston as guests of the nonpartisan State Club. Remigia, who was one of the first to arrive, thought it was "fun to meet the opposition." Mrs. Vincent Greene, co-chairman, summed things up: "I like this idea—it got Republicans and Democrats together as Americans." The other co-chairman, Miss Sybil Holmes, had a comment: "Politicians are certainly marrying good looking women these days."

Communists again endorsed Brooke, hoping to defeat him for propaganda purposes. Brooke rejected their support, ideals, aims, godlessness. He sent a registered letter to Premier Khrushchev, then touring the U.S., asking him to quit endorsing American minority candidates "when your obvious intent is to insure their defeat." More than once he told audiences that Communist endorsement "sounds like the purr of a pussycat, but leaves the smell of a skunk."

Brooke was ired by a brochure put out by the New England Communist party which said: "Negro people have less representation in government than most people on this globe. Massachusetts citizens who believe in Negro liberation may well cast a vote for one Republican even though they skip the rest of the ticket." Brooke resented the suggestion that he should be supported on racial grounds. A Sunday newspaper noted that he was the target of false and vicious reports circulated by both Democrats and Republicans. One rumor was that he was denied a federal post (U.S. Attorney) because of lack of security clearance by the FBI. "This whispering campaign can be regarded only as the most deplorable kind of political undercover maneuvering." In later campaigns political enemies passed the word that Brooke belonged to a Communist group while in college. His classmates called the charge ridiculous.

In one slur, a Marine who cited his service in the Pacific charged: "While you were safe at home in Boston in 1951, speaking in favor of keeping the Communist party on the ballot in Massachusetts, the war in Korea was in full blast with Communists pouring into North Korea to slaughter American soldiers." The writer apparently didn't know that Brooke had spent most of his five Army years in combat.

Another undercurrent worried Brooke. Negro dissidents took a dim view of his marriage to a white woman, and some Roxbury mothers complained that he had become too "uppity" to attend their daughters' weddings. Others said he stayed away from their silver or golden anniversaries. Then, too, he had moved his law office out of Roxbury to downtown Boston. To quell the mutiny, on the Sunday before the Tuesday election, Georgia Ireland and other Brooke strategists arranged an afternoon tea for Remigia at the Women's Service Club on Massachusetts Avenue, on the fringe of Roxbury. Mrs. Ireland, then vice-chairman of the Republican State Committee, turned the tea into a solidarity session, warning the blacks in a hard-line speech to stick together, jut as the Irish and other ethnic blocs had always done in politics. Former Representative Herbert Jackson also urged unity and loyalty. The grumbling slacked off.

A week earlier Remigia was a guest of honor at a reception for candidate wives at the Professional and Businessmen's Club. Mrs. (Emory) Ireland was the main speaker, and Mrs. Melnea Cass told a big turnout why they should vote for Brooke.

On election eve William Jackson, Brooke's old friend and body-guard-chauffeur, drove Brooke and a few campaign workers, including Sally Saltonstall and Patricia Beck, junior national committeewoman from Massachusetts, from headquarters at 6 Beacon Street after a busy day.

"I'm hungry," Sally said. Brooke told Jackson to stop at the nearest Howard Johnson's restaurant.

"I'm tired of eating at Howard Johnson's," Patricia said. "This is the night before election. Can't we try some fancier place?"

In the dead silence Jackson waited for "the boss" to speak.

"Take the next right," Brooke said. Jackson asked whether they were stopping at Howard Johnson's.

"Yes, we are. All except Pat. She is eating at a place of her own choosing and is getting there under her own power."

On election night Brooke awaited returns in his suite at the Somerset Hotel in Boston, while his followers swarmed through the lobby and sat in the lounge. The elevators were so crowded that some of the faithful walked several flights of stairs to Brooke's suite. He came into the hall to greet his tearful workers, who had heard the bad news.

"Cheer up," Brooke said. "There's always tomorrow."

John F. Kennedy, leading a Democratic sweep, knocked out every Massachusetts Republican except Saltonstall and Volpe, who became the first Roman Catholic Republican governor in Massachusetts history. Brooke, who ran well ahead of Nixon in the Bay State, lost by 112,000 votes, but polled more votes than anyone else on the ticket except Saltonstall and Volpe—an impressive 1,095,054.

Brooke's person-to-person approach carried him so far ahead of his party that Kevin White won only by the lowest plurality. White, who admits he avoided debating with Brooke during the campaign "because Ed is more intelligent and a better speaker," said he would have lost if the contest had lasted two more weeks. "Ed was gaining all the time. Of course he had a few things going for him. *The Boston Herald* endorsed him on the grounds that his election would show Massachusetts voters were not bigoted. Where did that leave me?"

Brooke didn't blame prejudice for his defeat. "I was a victim of the Kennedy landslide," he told UPI the day after the election. "I do not think that my race had anything to do with the outcome." In his first television appearance he was grim-faced and wore a tight smile when he conceded to White.

"A friend who saw me on television said, 'Why didn't you tell me you were running for secretary of state? If I had known, I would have voted for you.'"

This writer asked Brooke how his career would have been affected if he had won the election. "It's hard to say. The office can be a graveyard, and a successful candidate can be buried there throughout his political career. After losing the election, I became chairman of the Boston Finance Commission, and that gave me an opportunity to show any investigative talent I had, as well as legal talent."

Thus, although now a three-time loser, he had shown his political clout. In losing he had really won, since the office he sought usually lead nowhere except to reelection.* "The job," noted *The Saturday Evening Post,* "has a reputation as a prestigious dead end, because it offers no way, short of stealing the office stamp money, to get your name in the paper."

Kevin White read the message. "Ed Brooke without doubt has a first-class mind. His success is due in large measure to his own personal magnetism, his voter appeal. As a campaigner he has no faults. He knows when to say the right things and never went overboard on the civil-rights question." White said Brooke would be around politics for a long time.

By this time puzzled cynics were offering private reasons for Brooke's ballot magic. He was just what white voters wanted, some said—a respectable black who opposed violence and favored lawful procedure in gaining civil rights. After 1960, however, the cynics were less sure of the reasons for Brooke's success. He was a "natural-born winner—the kind of man catastrophes ignore and handicaps merely ignite," *Newsweek* would conclude later. Ask ten persons why they voted for Brooke and you would get ten reasons. The late Calvin Brumley, then writing for *The Wall Street Journal,* said Brooke "exudes a masculine charm that appeals to men as well as women, and he doesn't look much like a Negro." Hardy Nathan, his executive assistant, who left a lucrative insurance job to join him, calls his boss "the most impressive man I've ever met." The devotion of Brooke's hardworking staff put muscle in the 1960 campaign.

"I wish I could get campaign workers in my district to work for me like they do for Brooke," one politician said.

As in his two earlier defeats, Brooke's mother told him to try harder next time. Brooke, who doesn't worry if he sometimes sounds like "Mama's boy," told one reporter that his mother had always taught him to think there was nothing he couldn't do "if I prepared properly for it, and she told me this so many times I believed her. Somehow, Mother has always been right. Today, no matter how tired or discouraged I may become, I can always hear her voice saying, 'You've got to keep fighting.' "

After 1960, political plums beckoned. His old Roxbury friend, the able and affable John Collins, a Democrat who had just been elected

---

* Kevin White was an exception. He later was twice elected mayor of Boston, but lost to Francis Sargent in the gubernatorial contest. "Ed Brooke has not yet peaked," he told this writer in December 1971. "I seem to move laterally while he moves vertically."

mayor of Boston by besting the heavy favorite, John Powers, who had been backed by such leaders as John F. Kennedy and Richard Cardinal Cushing of Boston, had first met Brooke in 1952 at an Am Vets meeting and "liked him immediately." Collins, who then lived in an adjacent ward, smiled as he spoke of Brooke:

"He still kids me about his souvenir book in which I placed an ad endorsing him in the 1952 campaign, even though I was a Democrat. When I ran for mayor in 1959, Brooke signed my billboard advertising. Later he told me I was so short of supportive leaders my top backer was 'a former commander of Am Vets, and black at that.' Early in 1960, I offered Ed the post of election commissioner for the City of Boston. He leaned toward the assignment at first, but, because of its better visibility, changed his mind and accepted an appointment to the Boston Finance Commission."

Once settled in the State House, Governor John Volpe wanted to reward Brooke for helping him in the 1960 campaign. As Herter had in 1952, Volpe offered Brooke the post of secretary of the Governor's Council, and again Brooke shook his head. Volpe then suggested various judicial appointments, which Brooke also declined, not because he wanted to get out of politics, but because he wanted to get in deeper.

John Bottomly and Joseph Fitzgerald had told him the best available political springboard would be the Boston Finance Commission. Bottomly had heard his father speak of the commission, popularly known as the "Fin Com," after it had been set up in 1909 by the Republican state administration to probe Mayor John F. Fitzgerald's conniving palace guard and to curb the power of rising Irish politicos such as the irrepressible James Michael Curley, who would add credence to the legendary shenanigans and skulduggery of Celtic chieftains during an era when it was said that Boston mayors could not be bought, but they certainly could be rented.

For most of its 52 years this watchdog agency had snoozed. As *Time* magazine noted, it "had not barked in years." The commission was notably ineffective under Republican governors and virtually nonexistent when Democrats took over the State House. Joseph Fitzgerald, like Bottomly, told Brooke he could bring the tiger to life. For one thing, they said, the Fin Com had subpoena power. Fitzgerald, knowing there was a vacancy on the commission and that nobody seemed to want the job, told Brooke the post of elections commissioner was a dead end. "You wouldn't have time to practice law. On the commission you can get far more public exposure and still continue your practice. It's a potentially powerful instrument." Brooke said he would look into the matter. A few days later he talked to Fitzgerald again

"It's twice as powerful as you said, Joe."

When Volpe offered him the job, Brooke took it. Bottomly was delighted. "With your talent and skill, you've got it made."

Although Volpe won't admit it, political pundits are sure the Governor would never have given him the post had he realized what a launching pad it would be. Brooke had ideas that Volpe didn't suspect.

"Let's face it," a GOP leader said. "If they'd thought Ed was going to do anything with this post, he damn sure wouldn't have gotten it."

Volpe reasoned that whatever scandals Brooke might uncover would probably involve Democrats, since they controlled the city and legislature. Mayor Collins, although a Democrat, said, "I am looking forward to working with Mr. Brooke."

As he pored over financial records in city departments in his sparsely furnished office on the seventh floor of a bank building overlooking City Hall, Brooke was appalled by the patent corruption. In the summer of 1961 the Boston Finance Commission accused a fireman named O'Banion of being a $50-a-day consultant for a Dorchester company installing fire alarm systems in Boston schools. After several hearings the commission recommended to the fire department that O'Banion be fired for violating department rules and regulations. After launching the probe that led to O'Banion's dismissal, Brooke's commission established new protective procedures for the safety of school children. Although O'Banion admitted the charges, he eventually obtained a court order directing that he be reinstated with back pay. The order issued by a municipal court judge said O'Banion's civil rights had been violated at the original Fin Com hearing when he was not advised of his right to counsel. He returned to his job early in 1963.

One of the first newsmen to appreciate Brooke's investigative talent was Al Benjamin, a commentator on WNAC, the first radio and television station to spotlight the new Fin Com chairman. Benjamin invited Frank Bucci, then a reporter for *The Boston Traveler,* to attend sessions in Brooke's office. "Almost every night we had something newsy to report from Brooke's office," Benjamin said. "The guy was just beginning to get into orbit. One day, while questioning a witness who couldn't understand English, Brooke broke into Italian.

Reporters who didn't know him were stunned. The amusing part was that the Italian had trouble understanding Brooke, who apparently used a dialect that was unfamiliar to him. Anyway, he kept saying, 'Me no capisco.' From then on, Brooke got plenty of coverage from the media," Benjamin said.

Calling the new chairman "a young Republican with the toughness of a bulldog and the tenacity of a terrier," *The Boston Herald* said he "restored to vigorous life an agency which many had thought moribund." As a result of the publicity, the Fin Com telephone rang more and more often with tips of corruption. Brooke made headlines almost daily as he exposed scandals in city agencies, all the while competing with some of the sharpest legal minds in the Commonwealth. He shook off the suggestion that he was a crusader. "I'm not a do-gooder or a Goody Two-Shoes. I like to go to the racetrack and bet the horses. But our present laws state there can be no off-track betting. If that is the law, then we live by it. If we don't like the law, then we can change it. But while it exists on the books, that's it. And the same thing applies to any case of malfeasance or misfeasance brought to our attention."

Brooke's most spectacular probe was triggered by a CBS-TV documentary, *Biography of a Bookie Joint,* which showed traffic parading in and out of a well-known bookie joint in a small key shop on Massachusetts Avenue. Leaving their cruisers double-parked while other police officers directed traffic past the horse parlor, cops were seen going in and out of the shop. The camera showed gambling stubs being burned in a metal barrel on a sidewalk while a cop watched.

In Washington, D.C., Brooke conferred with Quinn Tamm, field-service director of the International Association of Police Chiefs. Tamm, who had probed the Chicago Police Department when it was hit by scandal in 1960 and later investigated the Denver police after 47 cops were indicted for burglary, called the Boston scandal shocking, after Brooke brought him to Boston to make a thorough study of the administrative and fiscal practice of the Boston Police Department.

In the summer of 1961 Justice Department officials saw the documentary in Washington, and in December of that year the film was shown on a national hook-up. Fred Friendly, head of CBS, told Governor Volpe the film was blacked out in Boston because of cases pending against men booked on gambling charges, but he invited Volpe, his legal staff and Frank Giles, Commissioner of Public Safety, to a private viewing. "We have a real problem here," Volpe told his staff. A month before seeing the film, Volpe was a guest of the MIT Faculty Club in Cambridge. In the parking lot after the meeting he collared Police Commissioner Leo Sullivan and told him to clean up gambling in Boston. After privately viewing the film and watching Boston cops directing traffic in front of the bookie joint, Volpe was stunned. "Now I know we have a major problem," he told his legal aides, "but first we must check the authenticity of the film." Early in 1962 he told his aides to open an investigation. Then he left for a ten-day vacation in Palm Springs, California.

While he was away, Brooke told Volpe's staff he was probing the police.

"Wait a minute, Ed," a Volpe attorney said. "This comes within the purview of the Governor. He appoints the police commissioner. This case needs expert police personnel, which we have, and you don't." The lawyer called Volpe, who was irritated when summoned off the golf course to answer the telephone.

"Tell Brooke to stay out," he said. "Tell him we are conducting the investigation."

When Brooke insisted on talking to Volpe right away, the lawyer warned that the Governor would not see him in California. That afternoon, *The Boston Record American* ran a photo showing Brooke boarding a plane at Logan Airport on his way to California. There were complications when Brooke was refused admission to the club. If the story leaked, Volpe might be asked why he frequented a lily-white club so discriminatory that even one of his political appointees couldn't reach him. Volpe avoided an embarrassing situation by escorting Brooke onto the premises.

"The matter could have been handled over the telephone, but I could understand Ed's reasons for coming to California. He felt a responsibility in the bookie-joint issue. We sat around the swimming pool and discussed the problem. Before this meeting, I had called Leo Sullivan into my office and confronted him with information I had on the documentary. I told him it would be in his interest to resign. When he refused, I was forced to press for his removal, which had to be approved by the Governor's Council. We hired James St. Clair to conduct the removal hearing, then sent the removal order to the Council. At this point, Sullivan resigned."

Volpe, after his return from California, consulted Brooke about the best way to handle the police commissioner.

"Send Sullivan a letter requesting his resignation, Your Excellency,"* Brooke said. "Make a simple statement. Don't assume what his answer will be."

"Ed, will you prepare the press release?" Volpe asked.

"You have a competent staff," Brooke said, whereupon Volpe took action.

There was an odd twist. During the removal proceedings Volpe sent an attorney to New York to see how the film had been made and to be sure there were no "reenactments." The attorney viewed 14 hours of footage that had not been shown in the documentary. In one scene, he thought he recognized a man who walked into the shop and came out shaking his head. The attorney asked a technician for a close-up of this section. The familiar person was the sedate editor of a Boston newspaper who had gone into the horse parlor to have a key made!

Biography of a Bookie Joint was not shown in Boston until 1964. By then the Boston press, which had criticized CBS for producing the film, was defending the network. There was a sad sequel. Volpe, who hates personal vendettas, was crushed in 1962 when, at the wake of Leo Sullivan, who had died bitter and disillusioned, one of his relatives handed Volpe the flowers he had sent.

Although burdened with a busy law practice and a heavy workload with the Finance Commission, Brooke spent a few weekends in New York seeing plays on Broadway or watching professional football games, and took a brief vacation with Remigia in Mexico. When he returned he had luncheon with another foe of corruption, Representative Francis Perry of Duxbury. Brooke was toying with the idea of running for attorney general, and Perry was thinking of running for lieutenant governor. With Volpe and Brooke giving ethnic balance to the GOP ticket, a Yankee like Perry might satisfy some of the GOP stalwarts who were plumping for Elliot Richardson.

"That's a nice tan you have, Mr. Brooke," the headwaiter at Locke-Ober's said. "Have you been south lately?"

Brooke grinned. "Yes, I just came back from Acapulco."

In the fall of 1962 *The Boston Herald* said it would be hard to name two men in Massachusetts public life who have done a better job of fighting corruption than Brooke and Perry. The paper also

---

* Brooke used this formal term not out of subservience, but because it was obvious that Volpe at this time liked to be addressed as "Your Excellency."

praised Governor Volpe for removing a police commissioner who refused to sweep the stables, for promoting the passage of the conflict-of-interest law and creating a crime commission. "Yet Perry and Brooke have seemed especially effective—each in his particular sphere of activity." (Perry, also with the "toughness of a bulldog" and the "tenacity of a terrier," had almost single-handedly and without benefit of investigative powers exposed "sweetheart" parking-lot rental arrangements in the Department of Public Works and later the even more venal contract irregularities and land schemes in the Division of Waterways.)

By the spring of 1962 Brooke's visibility had risen. In view of his successful prosecutions, the other members of the Finance Commission voted to recommend that his salary be doubled to 10,000 dollars a year. He said no. "I'm certainly not anti-money; I do feel, however, that once the salary for this job gets larger and larger, the entire purpose of the commission will be subverted and the post will degenerate into just another political plum."

Brooke, while proud of his record in weeding out graft, knew much remained to be done. He saw an opportunity when Governor John Volpe established the Massachusetts Crime Commission, which had broad investigative powers, including the right to subpoena private citizens, public officials and confidential records. To head the commission, Volpe chose Alfred Gardner, a respected if not scintillating Boston attorney whose flinty austerity became anathema to sinners. To help his probes, Gardner had a bipartisan committee of six prominent citizens, a general counsel, several attorneys, a staff of stenographers and bookkeepers and 25 special investigators.

While the Commonwealth had long been shot through with corruption, matters had worsened during the administration (1957–61) of Governor Foster Furcolo, Volpe's predecessor.

The most headlined scandal involved the building of an underground garage on Boston Common. Another headliner starred John "Mucker" McGrath, the city auctioneer, who allegedly bought municipal property at bargain prices he set, then sold it to the state for a big profit.

Brooke felt the time had come to clean out the stables. He announced his candidacy for the office of attorney general.

CHAPTER SIX

The Turning Point

"**I**F THIS GUY doesn't run for attorney general, I'll write him in," a Brooke fan said early in 1962. "So he's colored. I wouldn't give a damn if he was plaid. The only thing I can say against him is that he's better-looking than I am."

Brooke's loyal backers by this time were saying, "Ed can walk on water." Soon after his 1960 defeat, Brooke told Lionel Lindsay, a former president of the Boston branch of the NAACP, that Attorney General Edward McCormack would run against Edward Kennedy for the U.S. Senate in 1962, and that he (Brooke) would seek McCormack's seat.

After his 1960 showing, Brooke felt he would do well in the race for attorney general, and his confidence got a boost early in 1962 when Opinion Research, a national survey organization, said he was "the party's strongest candidate for attorney general." Encouraged, he met at the Parker House in Boston to block out assignments with John Bottomly, Harold Putnam, Georgia Ireland, Roger Woodworth, Alfred Brothers, Clarence Elam and Gael Mahony.

Brooke knew he was in for the toughest fight of his career, because GOP leaders opposed his candidacy. In 1960 they had accepted him as a candidate for a minor position, but they balked at backing him for the number-two post in the Commonwealth, and there was snide talk of his being "a pushy nigger." Party chieftains tried to derail him by offering him a judgeship or their endorsement for lieutenant governor. Their solid choice for attorney general was Elliot Richardson, a

71

Boston Brahmin millionaire with blue-ribbon credentials. He was a partner in the prestigious Boston law firm of Ropes and Gray.

After graduating from Harvard, where he was middleweight boxing champion, and Harvard Law School, Richardson had clerked for Judge Learned Hand and Justice Felix Frankfurter, and served as aide to Governor Christian Herter and Senator Leverett Saltonstall. In the Eisenhower administration he had served as Assistant Secretary for Health, Education and Welfare. Returning to Boston as U.S. Attorney for Massachusetts, he made repeated headlines through his successful prosecution of Bernard Goldfine in a case that enhanced his image as a crime buster. More headlines came when he exposed federal highway scandals, angering William F. Callahan, chairman of the Massachusetts Turnpike Authority, who for more than a decade had been more powerful than any governor. Known as "the shadow governor of Massachusetts," Callahan could swing votes in the legislature any time he wished. "His influence extended into every nook and cranny of state government, large segments of the business world, and even into banks and newspapers," *The Saturday Evening Post* reported. Brooke later probed his ties to John F. Thompson, Speaker of the House, and came to know intimately of his power over the legislature. According to one story, "a number of lawmakers were once said to have genuflected when he walked into the room." Scores of relatives of Massachusetts legislators were on Callahan's payroll, and not until a year before his death did the state auditor have the authority to examine his turnpike records, although he spent "sums of money that exceeded the entire budgets of many a foreign government." Callahan and his cronies were in a large measure responsible for the increase in corruption in the Commonwealth, an issue that favored both Richardson and Brooke in the campaign. Although Richardson honestly believed he had the experience necessary to lead the fight against crooks, by the spring of 1962 Brooke was better known all over the Commonwealth as a no-compromise crime fighter. "As supporters observe him in his investigative action or read about it in the press," an editor wrote, "they probably regret that his talent and integrity have not been used on a statewide basis."

GOP kingmakers did not share this opinion. "Let's face it," one said when Brooke refused to step aside to leave the field clear for Richardson. "Everybody who is anybody in the party is against you. You can't possibly win an election. You've already been defeated three times. You have none of the assets and all of the liabilities." He repeated the old admonition: "You're a Republican in a Democratic state, a Protestant in a Catholic state, and a colored man in a Caucasian state—and besides, you're poor." Richardson himself, sure that Brooke could not overcome the odds of family, position, race and money, talked things over at a private luncheon.

"This campaign will cost a lot of money, and you don't have it. Why don't you run for lieutenant governor?"

"You may have money," Brooke said. "I may have the people." One of his people was Harcourt Wood, a Richardson backer before he met Brooke. When Richardson asked Wood to help him in the 1962 campaign the answer was no. "Sorry, Elliot, but I'm with Brooke."

Wood, treasurer of the 1962 campaign, raised the first of the 200,000 dollars spent by taking 20 of his affluent friends to a Locke-Ober luncheon and persuading them, after the second convivial round of drinks, to kick in.

Ignoring party brass, Brooke mounted a statewide search for delegate support at the Republican preprimary convention to be held at the Worcester Memorial Auditorium on June 16. A Committee to Elect Edward Brooke sent letters to delegates: "Please be assured that in 1962 Ed Brooke will be a candidate for the Republican nomination for attorney general and will not be a candidate nor will he accept the nomination for any other office." (Volpe and other GOP bigwigs hoped to push Brooke into the fight for secretary of state.) "We believe that not only should you know that irrevocable decision now, but also the major consideration upon which it is based. . . . He wants to use his talents to serve . . . in the most effective manner available. He is not the sort of person who will be a candidate for any office simply to supply the ticket with so-called balance."

Brooke, feeling that Richardson gave the impression of being too much of a "cop" interested in putting malefactors behind bars rather than in reforming a system that made their dereliction possible, told audiences that he (Brooke) was no knight on a white horse*—that he was more interested in the corrective part of the attorney general's job than in jailing people.

Nevertheless, he campaigned chiefly on the corruption issue. "I am convinced," he told voters, "that if you assert the power that is

---

* At the Worcester convention Georgia Ireland told Brooke a delegate had just called him "the white knight of the contest." Said Brooke: "He must be color-blind."

rightfully yours in our democratic system, the cynics, the self-servers, the corruptors and the corruptibles need no longer make a mockery of justice.

By the time he had revved up the motors for the attorney general race, Brooke had a sophisticated staff. John Bottomly, who had no official title during the campaign, was known as "chairman of the board." He told a reporter after the election: "Just the two of us started together last fall, and it grew from there." During the 1961 professional football season Brooke and Bottomly spent a few Saturday afternoons watching the New York Giants play. After the game they dropped into the Waldorf Restaurant opposite City Hall, a political pad, to talk politics with Roger Woodworth and State Representative Mary Newman. When Brooke invited Mrs. Newman to join his staff, she said she had never been with a winner.*

"Well, be with one for a change," he said. Woodworth, who had helped Mrs. Newman in a special election, was campaign manager for Brooke's 1962 contest. Another member of the steering committee was the personable Attorney Gael Mahony, one of the top young lawyers of the Commonwealth, who had been counsel for the Boston Finance Commission when Brooke was chairman. Mahony made several substitute appearances for Brooke during the campaign. After one grueling day during which he addressed workers in a spaghetti factory, members of a women's club and a Rotary Club, he marveled all the more at Brooke's ability to shift gears to the needs of special audiences. Brooke's team of political amateurs had more energy and political savvy than a corps of hardheaded politicos.

Another important member of the team was Nancy Porter, who had been president of her senior class at Bryn Mawr, where she, like other future Brooke staffers, majored in political science. Late in 1961 she saw an ad in *The Boston Herald:* "Are you interested in politics? Good offer. Shorthand & typing required." In January 1962, after a preliminary screening at a luncheon with Bottomly, she had a two-hour interview with Brooke in Bottomly's State Street law office. She convinced the candidate that she was well qualified for the assignment, taking pains not to mention that she knew no shorthand.

"I really want to work for you, and I'm the best gal you can get." Brooke thought she had the right background to help win women's

---

* Other members of the steering committee were Albert Gammal, Clarence Elam, Georgia Ireland, Harcourt Wood, Jerry Sadow, Harriet Wittenborg and Attorney Benjamin Gargill.

votes. She joined the office staff three days later, living at the YWCA until she found an apartment.

While waiting for telephones to be installed, and typewriters, office furniture and draperies to be brought into an office at 6 Beacon Street, Nancy and Glendora McIlwain went over the delegate list after towns and cities elected delegates in April and May. They had separate labels for the three candidates running for attorney general: green for Brooke, red for Richardson, yellow for Arlyne F. Hassett, a former Assistant U.S. Attorney under Richardson. After Bottomly, Woodworth or Nancy Porter arranged meetings where he could meet delegates and their friends, Brooke would sometimes spend an entire evening with groups ranging in number from 6 to 60. He and Miss Hassett at one session in Framingham talked to 35 delegates.

Brooke formally announced his candidacy in April, first at a breakfast press conference at the Parker House in Boston, later in the day in Springfield. Accompanying Brooke were Nancy Porter, Roger Woodworth, and Jerry Sadow, a former WBZ news editor who had joined the staff as press secretary. Brooke held a press conference in the dimly lit Cheshire Room in the basement of the Sheraton Hotel, where he met reporters, delegates and workers of the 1960 campaign. After cocktails and a steak dinner in the function room, the Brooke party left a stack of releases to be distributed in the Springfield area. Harold Putnam prepared campaign literature, and Albert Gammal, Jr., was field director. Brooke had first met Gammal in 1961 when, as chairman of the Finance Commission, Brooke spoke at the Worcester Chamber of Commerce. Following Gammal from the hall, Brooke collared him on the sidewalk in a chill drizzle and said he would run for attorney general in 1962.

"You don't have a chance against Richardson," Gammal said. "Why don't you run for lieutenant governor?" When Brooke insisted he had a good chance, Gammal nodded. "All right, I'll get you the eight votes in my ward."

As the 1962 campaign went into orbit, Gammal found himself in a squeeze. The Richardson camp, out to crush Brooke, also went after Gammal, who, realizing his House seat was in peril, fought back. A Brooke victory for him became a matter of personal survival. He organized a network of statewide coordinators down to the ward and sometimes even at precinct level, who still form the base of Brooke's political organization, which Gammal considers as efficient as the Kennedy machine. "And it's strictly a volunteer organization. This is the significant thing."

In May and June the staff made a more intensive analysis of the delegate situation. Going through a stack of cards, Brooke spent hours on the telephone talking to delegates and was encouraged by the response. Some delegates gave him names of other key persons to contact. "The boss would often open the door after a successful call in our Beacon Street office and tell us what a delegate said," Miss Porter recalled. Meanwhile, Glendora McIlwain kept changing the color of the tabs as delegates were realigned. The Brooke file grew thicker and thicker. By the time of the Worcester convention, he had talked to most of the delegates, and his staff had written thousands of letters to persons who required special attention, including some who had reservations about supporting Brooke.

"It was an effective way of canvassing," Miss Porter said. "A single phone call could lead to a dozen useful contacts."

Two weeks before the convention, Thomas Nash of Brockton, an unpledged delegate, wrote a note to Brooke: "I have decided to cast my ballot for you. I realize this means only one vote for you, but I want you to know about my decision."

A few days later Nash received a reply from Brooke: "Please don't say 'it's only one vote.' Every vote counts." In view of what happened at the Worcester convention these were historic words.

"If only I had kept Brooke's letter," Nash said.

Harold Appleton, whose advertising firm handled Brooke's 1962 campaign, noted in a campaign folder that Christian Herter, an old friend of Brooke who had been Secretary of State under President Dwight Eisenhower, was backing Richardson. Appleton phoned Herter at his North Shore residence to ask about the endorsement.

"I admire both Richardson and Brooke," Herter said. "When Elliot asked me to support him, I didn't know Ed Brooke was in the race."

A week before the primary, in a weekly column he wrote on Tuesdays for the *The Natick Herald,* Appleton told of his telephone interview. "Richardson called the following day," Appleton recalls, "and accused me of denigrating his role at the coming convention. I told him his argument was with Secretary Herter, who was equivocating. Following my suggestion, Richardson wrote an answer that appeared in *The Natick Bulletin,* which came out on Thursday, two days after my column appeared, and just a few days before the convention."

Richardson, once regarded as a sure winner at the convention, was getting worried.

"Brooke had a lot going for him," Al Benjamin said. "The working press loved him. He also had the advantage of being the underdog."

On June 15, the day before the preprimary, Brooke and his staff were in the city attending meetings, banquets, caucuses and suite parties, as well as a big cocktail party and banquet given by the Young Republicans. In the convention area on Saturday, Sally Saltonstall and the "Brooke Girls" manned booths, passing out campaign material. At a press conference at the Bancroft Hotel, Richardson was parrying questions when Cornelius Owens of *The Boston Globe* suddenly asked: "Would you prefer your opponent in another race?" Richardson, momentarily nonplussed, recovered in time to say any qualified candidate had a right to run regardless of creed or color.

"Picking winners at a Republican state convention is as easy as making a pennant choice between the Yanks and the Red Sox," a veteran political observer said on the eve of the convention, "and on occasion the selection of a nominee for the ticket was made at a conference that could have moved into a phone booth. But things are changing." They were indeed. The Red Sox were gaining on the Yanks and minority candidates were gaining on GOP stalwarts.

Realizing that the endorsement of the GOP convention was critical, the two leading candidates made guarded statements. Richardson said he would abide by the convention's choice "unless the delegates are influenced by some last-minute factors that do not reflect the genuine views of most Republicans." Brooke already was known as a man who could not be rushed into a decision. "Caution has always been my fault or my strength—I don't know which. I don't like to leap. I like to get all the facts even before I make minor decisions, and that's sort of conservative." He refused to commit himself. "I'm not the kind of Republican who thinks a primary fight is generally bad for the party. But I'll make that decision if and when I come to it."

Brooke and his camp went into the convention with guarded optimism. In the delegate roundup Woodworth claimed a whopping success in wooing former Richardson adherents, including many top-drawer delegates. He was fairly sure that Fall River, Worcester (the city), Pittsfield and Gloucester would be solid for Brooke, whose partisans also claimed Essex, Middlesex, Bristol and Suffolk. The bellwether ward in Mattapan was 100 percent for Brooke. It seemed that efforts to recruit Democrats, independents, young people and some Richardson backers were about to pay off. Meanwhile, neither Governor Volpe nor Senator Saltonstall, who chaired the convention, had put an arm around Brooke or Richardson to say, "He is my boy."

Successful politicians need luck, and Brooke had it in the closing phase of the preprimary convention when he hit front pages in the city-auctioneer case, which involved John "Mucker" McGrath. Frank Bucci of *The Boston Traveler* had stumbled onto the story one morning when he walked into the office of the Metropolitan District Commission (MDC) near the State House. On the wall calendar he saw a "Hold" notation on a 25,000-dollar item beside McGrath's name. Bucci mentioned this to the general counsel for the MDC. The two men, consulting a file on land taken in Hyde Park, a section of Boston, discovered in the title search that the plat had been auctioned off to a person named Shea, then conveyed over to McGrath at a higher price.

"At the time the sale looked legitimate," Bucci said. "I gave the information to Paul Costello, a colleague on *The Boston Herald,* and he asked MDC Commissioner Robert Murphy whether any irregularity was involved. Murphy, who called the plat 'mystery land,' didn't suspect anything devious, but I was getting more and more suspicious.

"I went to Brooke's Fin Com office one Friday afternoon just as he was slipping into an overcoat to fly to New York to see a professional football game. Glancing at his watch, he said he could give me only ten minutes. In that time he absorbed all the facts we had uncovered and promised a probe. I learned later that his commission had been getting complaints from people who had been bilked at auctions. One beef was that an auction had been held at 5:00 A.M. Another opened and closed in two minutes—just enough action to make the thing legal.

"Costello and I spent months tracking down the McGrath story, which was often headlined, and during that time we saw a lot of Brooke and Maxwell Grossman, a member of the Fin Com who had previously been state penal commissioner. After morning sessions, which reporters attended, Grossman invited all of us, including Fin Com members, to lunch at Locke-Ober's."

Brooke had a subpoena drawn up for McGrath, who never appeared. Later the Supreme Judicial Court ordered McGrath to appear before the commission. Brooke, charging McGrath with conflict of interest, proved he had been fleecing taxpayers by buying land through straws at low prices before palming them off on the state. When McGrath was found guilty on four counts, James J. Sullivan, head of the Boston Real Property Department, accepted the Finance Commission's recommendation and fired McGrath on Friday, June 15. The firing, which climaxed a long, well-publicized investigation by the commission, was front page news on the day of the Republican preprimary at Worcester and hot news on radio and television. Thus it lifted Brooke's hopes after the late State Senator Leslie Cutler of Needham placed his name in nomination.

On that sweltering day in Worcester the hall hummed with excitement as tension peaked. The contest turned out to be one of the most dramatic seat squirmers in political history, according to veteran observers. It was also one of the dirtiest.

"Despite an oath which both candidates had pledged before witnesses to refrain from rumor-mongering, the convention floor was electric with whispering campaigns." Richardson partisans, accusing Brooke of improprieties in his private life, even said he beat his wife. Delegates heard out-of-the-side-of-the-mouth talk that his Communist activities had kept him out of a federal post.

"Before the convention," Woodworth said, "we had several meetings with, Philip K. Allen, a national committeeman, and Ralph Brownell, another top GOP leader, to work out ground rules and stop rumors, realizing that Richardson had guns for hire. Mary Newman, Georgia Ireland and I met with Allen and Brownell ten days before the convention to warn we would go to the press unless Richardson called off the dogs. Richardson then wrote Brooke an 'of course, Ed,' letter in which he said he had nothing to do with the Communist charges."

"Richardson didn't merely want to defeat Brooke," an aide said. "He wanted to *destroy* the boss." It was rumored that Robert F. Kennedy, seeing Brooke a threat to the Kennedy dynasty in Massachusetts, had the same ambition.

In any case, Brooke's opponents brought racism into the campaign, as well as communism. A circular passed around at the convention read: "Negroes voted against the Republican party in 1960. Negroes will vote against the Republican party again this year. Why should Republicans vote for Negroes? It is respectfully requested that you leave a blank beside the name of Edward W. Brooke, a Negro who is running for attorney general. Kindly mail this to another Republican voter."

To counter the rumors, some Brooke backers circulated reports about Richardson's drunken-driving record when he was young.

At a last-minute conference, with aides sitting on twin beds in Brooke's Bancroft suite, the brain trust told him to ignore the gossip. But as the day wore on, they glumly saw many of their delegates switching to Richardson under pressure from GOP leaders, including Elmer Nelson, former chairman of the Republican State Committee, and Winfield Shuster, the wealthy boss of Blackstone Valley who owned Shuster Woolens.

The first fight at the Worcester convention was between George Lodge and Congressman Lawrence Curtis, a conservative. Governor Volpe and one of his powerful lieutenants in Worcester County— Albert ("Toots") Manzi—were committed to Lodge. Gammal promised to stay neutral in the Lodge-Curtis contest if Toots stayed out of the Brooke-Richardson fight. But after Volpe and Manzi locked up delegates in Worcester County for Lodge, they gave their blessing to Richardson. When Gammal blasted Manzi for breaking his pledge, he blurted: "Win Shuster has been my friend longer than you have."

Gammal quotes an Arab proverb: "Fear your enemy once. Fear your friends a thousand times."

"We didn't realize the erosion at first," Woodworth says (he was floor manager). "We had come to the convention thinking we had a bulge of 150 to 200 delegate votes, but when the roll call started, the fight was much closer than we had figured." Brooke himself later said he thought he had enough votes to win by at least 200, only to see the margin dwindle on the floor.

Some Richardson delegates were counted after they left the hall, according to Woodworth. "When I tried to move in to challenge the vote in one delegation, I was strong-armed and couldn't push close enough to get to the monitor. Hardy Nathan and I went from delegate to delegate, as did others on our staff. The boss himself was outraged when he saw Congressman Bradford Morse, who had no business on the floor, since he wasn't a delegate, twisting arms in the first Middlesex district and pleading for delegates in his own congressional district to switch from Brooke to Richardson, 'just for me.' The boss went down on the floor and told Morse to get back to the platform. Some of our people could hear Morse using threats of jobs to sway delegates. He called the boss next day and apologized for his conduct."

Harold Appleton heard one Republican leader promise one Brooke delegate a job and threaten another with the loss of his job if he didn't vote for Richardson. The latter told the GOP leader to mind his "goddamn business." Another well-known Republican leader gave a delegate a 100-dollar bill to switch to Richardson. Cornelius Dalton, political editor of *The Boston Traveler,* although neutral, was incensed by the tactics of the Richardson camp and went to the floor to protest.

Meanwhile, other Brooke friends swung into action. After George

Lodge, for whom she had been working, won the nomination, Sally Saltonstall told Joseph Fitzgerald that Brooke needed his help in the floor battle for delegates. Fitzgerald told his three coordinators to circulate in the Essex and Middlesex delegations to win back support. Delegates from the Middlesex district had passed on the first balloting, and some strategists thought they would determine the winner.

For Brooke, Gammal was the right man in the right spot, when Brooke's career was at a turning point. Votes of the Worcester area delegates could also spell the difference between victory and defeat. Gammal's frenzied efforts among the Worcester delegation were primarily responsible for stemming the Richardson surge.

Senator Leverett Saltonstall, shirt-sleeved and perspiring in the steamy atmosphere, was in sharp contrast with Brooke, who, as usual, was dressed to the nines, looking relatively cool. On the first ballot Richardson got 854 votes to 845 for Brooke and nine for Hassett, who had withdrawn her candidacy halfway through the balloting. Crushed by the thought of losing, Brooke, running his tongue over parched lips, sat morosely on the platform on one side of Saltonstall. Bill Jackson, who was looking down from the gallery, wept inconsolably, and the Brooke camp was thick with gloom. Hardy Nathan recalls the scene:

"As the balloting neared the end, Richardson came out and sat to the right of the chairman, with people swarming all over him, in the glare of television cameras, which focused on him as he shook hands with Volpe and Morse, who never looked more jubilant. Brooke sat alone. Richardson rose from his chair, walked over and extended his hand.

"Tough fight," he said.

"You bet."

Then it happened.

Pounding the gavel, Saltonstall, trying to raise his voice above the din, ruled there would be a second ballot, since Richardson was one vote short of a simple majority. From the floor Richardson's angry partisans screamed that since the Hassett votes were void, because she had dropped out of the race, the necessary majority figure should have been lower than 855. Saltonstall was still pounding the gavel when another Richardson delegate, shouting for recognition, tried to shift his vote from Hassett to Richardson. Saltonstall ruled that delegation chairmen could make changes in the vote totals of their delegations, but that individual delegates could change their votes only by following that procedure.

That precise moment was the turning point in Brooke's political career. Woodworth, foot-weary after spending all day feverishly bouncing around the hall, mustered his co-workers and they stormed through delegations, shouting, "Get back, get back! It isn't over yet!" Meanwhile, Brooke, in a radio appeal, urged his delegates to return. "Wherever you are—in the street or in your automobiles—I need you. I need you now. There's going to be a second ballot."

Brooke supporters charged later that several GOP leaders, pretending to be neutral, had urged pro-Brooke delegates to go home as the second balloting began, assuring them that Brooke would easily win. Meanwhile, scores of Richardson delegates, with cocktail and dinner parties beckoning, were rolling down the Massachusetts Turnpike, with the Myopia Hunt Club one destination. Many, already home, were irretrievable. Some Brooke delegates who had left the hall later, had time to return when they heard Brooke's radio plea. Judge Alfred Podolski was in a car with five other delegates when, about halfway home, they returned in time to be polled.

In the interim, Governor Volpe, standing next to George Lodge, said he would support all convention-endorsed candidates in the September primary. Mary Newman, the convention parliamentarian, was numb with tension. "I was sitting on the platform next to Mrs. Helen Brooke and Georgia Ireland when someone tapped me on the shoulder. 'Don't interrupt me,' I said, 'I'm praying.' But even at that moment, I was sure Brooke would win on the second ballot."

Remi Brooke had slipped away during the uproar, and everyone—especially Remigia and Mrs. Helen Brooke—was worried about her except her father. Brooke aides sent policemen around the convention area to look for her. Remi finally turned up in a ballroom on the first floor, where she was doing the Twist, after crashing a bar mitzvah.* Less nonchalant was her grandfather, Edward Brooke, who, convinced that his son had no chance to win, had left the platform after telling his wife, "I can't watch him get licked again." Harold Putnam found him sitting dejectedly in the balcony.

"This is no time to be crying," Putnam said. "The reporters want to see you. Ed is going to win."

---

* Remi pulled another disappearing act during the 1962 campaign when she went to a tea at Divine Word Seminary at Miramar, in Duxbury. Remi, who was fourteen, met a girl the same age—Margaret Dickow, who lived across the road. Remi was delighted when Margaret invited her to ride her horse. The Brooke departure was delayed until an aide found her riding around the pasture on the horse.

Delegates who had been pressured to vote for Richardson on the first ballot switched back to Brooke on the second; he also picked up Hassett votes. "I chased one of Arlyne's delegates down an aisle, pleading for her to vote for Brooke," Mary Newman said. "And she did."

Brooke slid to victory on the second ballot, 792 to 673. In the climax of the stirring convention, his father was back on the platform amid the cheering and the clicking of TV camera shutters, watching the crowd mob his son. "Mr. Brooke just stood there, weeping," Putnam said. "He couldn't believe that white people could warm up to his son that way."

More than one delegate took credit for putting Brooke in orbit. One with a valid claim is Francis Alden Wood of Dracut, an original Richardson supporter who, since the Worcester convention, has been Middlesex County coordinator for Brooke. *The Lowell Sun* told the story after the convention: "The Middlesex delegation was an acknowledged Richardson group in the battle [between Richardson and Brooke]. . . . Internal arguments among the delegates caused them to pass on the first ballot, and when all others had been polled, the vote was deadlocked at 839. Lowell City Councilor Ellen Simpson announced the district vote as twenty-two for Richardson and eight for Brooke, which would have given Richardson the number needed for nomination."

It was at this instant that pandemonium broke loose. Photographers rushed to take Richardson's picture as he was announced the winner. "Meanwhile," *The Lowell Sun* reported, "Francis Wood also knew how the vote went. The last to vote in the delegation because of his alphabetical standing, he knew he had voted for Brooke, a man whom he had not known prior to the convention but who had so impressed him as to warrant his instant support. What's more, he knew his one vote left Richardson short of the one needed for victory."

The flashbulbs were popping when Wood headed for the microphone. When he reached it, he said, "I wish to challenge that vote." His statement stopped the convention. Chairman Saltonstall ordered a poll of the delegation, and the resulting figures showed Richardson shy of the number needed for nomination. While some Richardson backers ranted about the chairman's fast gavel, a second ballot was taken. "The rest is history," the newspaper concluded.

Mrs. Gael Mahony, the lovely, vivacious wife of one of Brooke's strongest supporters, recalls a poignant moment in the flush of victory. Attorney Roger H. Moore, who had been keeping tally for

Richardson, told her: "This breaks my heart. But, goddamn it, you people deserve the victory, because you cared."

One person who only half jokingly took credit for Brooke's triumph was Attorney George McLaughlin, the defender of John McGrath in the city auction scandal. Meeting Brooke on State Street after the Worcester preprimary, the Democrat grinned. "I'm the one man who elected you attorney general," he said. "It wasn't my intention."

The contest wasn't over, however. After the Worcester convention Richardson told the press he would run in the September primary because "the outcome of the preprimary convention did not reflect the judgment of the majority of delegates." He contended that many of his delegates had left the hall at the end of the first ballot after being assured their votes would be counted, only to have them erased during challenges of delegations. He also charged that a "technical ruling" by Saltonstall had cost him victory on the first ballot, when two votes cast for Hassett (after she had withdrawn from the race) should have been treated as blanks. He added that delegates who had tried to switch votes from her to him were stymied. Thus he concluded that the second ballot did not mirror the will of the convention, because 233 delegates had left the hall to go home.

Brooke countered that Richardson was "a poor loser and a crybaby" for claiming he was a victim of a short count. "Many people had to leave, and all were not Richardson people. Over 80 percent of the delegates remained. It's ridiculous for him to holler foul."

Brooke also said Richardson had fallen into a trap set for him by former Attorney General Francis Kelly, who sought the Democratic nomination for the office of attorney general. Goading Richardson, Kelly charged he would be afraid to run in the primary because of his record of court convictions for motor-vehicle law violations. "Kelly baited him into running, using the divide-and-conquer theory. And Elliot took the bait." Finally, Brooke said, his second-ballot win was clear-cut and decisive because so many delegates switched from Richardson to him. "You cannot hold votes out of fear and intimidation."

Two weeks after the convention Brooke told newsmen that if he revealed the dirty tactics used against him, it would "rock the Republican party in Massachusetts." During their heated exchange, he said Richardson belonged to a GOP clique who were more interested in bossing the party than in winning elections, a paraphrase of an earlier statement: "Some Republican leaders are more interested in who is pitching than in winning the ball game." He was thinking of GOP leaders such as Elmer Nelson and Winfield Shuster.

When the storm cleared, the Republican State Committee ruled that Brooke was the official Republican nominee and that the Worcester convention was a closed book. Thus Brooke would carry after his name on the primary ballot the prized words "endorsed by the Republican preprimary convention."

Still sure he could beat Brooke, Richardson entered the September primary.

GOP diehards were still licking their wounds 12 days after the Worcester convention, when the Republican State Committee invited Governor Nelson Rockefeller of New York to address a fund-raising gathering at the Boston Garden. George Murphy, the Hollywood actor who later became a U.S. senator from California, served as master of ceremonies, introducing an all-star cast of entertainers that included Jane Powell, who sang; Edgar Bergen and his puppet; the Kingston Trio; and the then relatively unknown comedy tandem of Rowan and Martin. Advance publicity gave Rockefeller and Volpe a big play, but little attention was paid to Brooke, although he was one of the speakers. Harold Appleton, whose advertising agency handled Brooke's campaign in 1962, got little cooperation from the sponsors of the program.

"We could get no instructions on the kind of signs we could hang for Brooke in the Garden. Finally, three hours before the rally, we got permission to mount a 12-foot-long banner for Brooke high over the stage. The problem was how to get the sign up there. I stripped down to the waist, hung my clothes on a steam pipe under the eaves, and, with the aid of a roustabout whom I paid ten dollars, crawled onto a catwalk about 60 feet above the floor to rig up the banner."

In ensuing weeks Brooke overshadowed Richardson, gaining solid support after he was seen on the platform or on television. Former State Senator William Weeks, one of "the young Turks" who had sided with Richardson during the 1962 campaign, was at the exclusive Union Club when Brooke, along with Richardson, was invited to address about 50 prominent Boston lawyers, businessmen and civil leaders.

"Ed spoke and discussed some of the legal problems the next attorney general would face. I was as impressed—perhaps 'astounded' would be a better word—as any of the men present by the ease and lucidity with which Brooke handled the most complicated questions."

Always well dressed, smooth, engaging, and in complete command of his audiences, "he [Brooke] was easily the most eloquent candidate from either party in many a year," according to *Harper's Magazine* George Frazier, a student of Bay State politics since the days of Curley and usually a persistent gadfly of Massachusetts politicians, spoke of Brooke's grace and style, matched only by Jack Kennedy's. "To see him (his sad, handsome face without visible trace of guile), to hear him (his voice soft and deep) you would not believe that this man could have an enemy in the world. . . . In a world of ward politics and atrocious taste, he is strictly gentlemanly charm." Frazier overworks a word he owns—"duende," which he defines, in lieu of help from lexicographers, as "charisma to the nth power, heightened panache, or overpowering presence." Writing in *The Boston Globe,* Frazier gave what he considered an apt appraisal of the candidate. "Senator Edward Brooke has duende, but not Senator Edward Kennedy."

Brooke's budget was pared by appearances on the Jerry Williams talk show, where some of the questions were barbed. "Why did you marry a white woman?" a caller asked.

"Because I loved her," Brooke casually answered.

Much to Roger Woodworth's surprise, Brooke blew the circuits in afternoon television programs beamed to shut-ins. "The response was just as favorable as on prime time," Woodworth said. "He picked up a lot of Democratic and independent converts on the Williams show. Housewives often called to say they had changed their mind and would vote for him."

A big payoff came when Harcourt Wood told Nancy Porter and Sally Saltonstall he had just received a campaign contribution that would finance a television spot that was to follow a half-hour show on which Richardson, his wife, Ann, and their children were to appear. Mary Newman was at campaign headquarters when Wood brought the good news.

"Courty [Wood], Jack Bottomly, Gael Mahony and I sat around discussing the format of the show, while Nancy and Sally primped at the hairdresser and slipped into chic ensembles, since they, along with Gael, were to handle incoming calls during this first telethon. Richardson gave a sober, well-prepared fireside-chat kind of speech, but Ed was dazzlingly good—exciting and alive. Brooke sat at the far end of a long, narrow table, with Gael Mahony at his left. Nancy and Sally sat on the same side of the table as Gael, with telephones in front of them. They jotted down questions and passed them to

Mahony, who checked them only to be sure there was no repetition, before dropping them into a slot. Then Brooke picked up each card (four by eight inches) and read the question before giving his reply. The girls had several prepared questions to be used until calls came in, but Ed didn't see them. The idea was to make the show as spontaneous as possible, and it worked. Just before the opening I gave Ed a paper cup of champagne to clear his throat. He answered 17 questions, smoothly and without hesitation." According to aides who monitored them, calls poured in after the telecast. "The gist was, 'I saw Brooke and he was terrific,' " Mrs. Newman said. "We were so pleased we finished the bottle of champagne and wished we had another. The program was so successful it was repeated by Brooke in later campaigns."

Brooke beat Richardson by more than 42,000 votes. Edwina Brooke, Remi's younger sister, was then ten years old and a student at William Lloyd Garrison School. "It was just wonderful," she said when she heard the good news, adding that after the primary returns came in, they went to the Parker House, where "my father went to his office upstairs, and then we went to his room and listened to the radio and watched television. . . . And then Governor Volpe came up to shake hands with my father and congratulate him." Edwina conceded that her dad was "the best in the world."

With victory assured, Brooke took his family to Ward 12 in Roxbury to thank his original supporters.

Then came Brooke's first real test against a seasoned machine politician of the rowdy and raucous era of Hibernian politics. Brooke's Democratic opponent was Francis "Sweepstakes" Kelly, a former attorney general of Massachusetts and the only Democrat to defeat Leverett Saltonstall in a political contest (in the 1936 race for lieutenant governor). An old war-horse, Kelly for years had advocated a state lottery as the cure for the Commonwealth's fiscal problems.

Kelly was favored to beat Brooke in the 1962 election. Using the same strategy as in 1960, the 1962 GOP ticket for statewide offices offered three Yankees, an Italian-American, an Irishman, a Jew and a young black. In the contest for attorney general Brooke faced a wily campaigner who was popular in the many poor wards in Boston. Brooke hoped to carry the "egghead belt" of Brookline, Newton and the inner suburbs, but to win he also had to carry "bedroom" towns on the North and South Shores of Boston. He hoped to put together an unusual coalition of right-wing groups such as the Young Americans for Freedom, locals of the International Ladies' Garment

Workers Union, and other liberal groups, including the Americans for Democratic Action (ADA).

"When Al Gammal heard the ADA was supporting Ed, he almost jumped out the window," Jack Bottomly said.

One night at the end of October, at the Sheraton Plaza, more than a thousand Republicans gathered to honor Brooke, and GOP chiefs who had once tried to hand Brooke the hot end of the poker were fulsome in their praise. Richardson, in announcing his support for his former rival, stole the show when he ridiculed the entire Democratic ticket, after strongly endorsing Brooke: "The last time I shared a platform with Ed Brooke, I was rooting for a loser—myself. This time I am sharing the platform with a winner and the big winner."

Richardson called Ted Kennedy, who was running against George Lodge for the U.S. Senate, "a man who served for a few months as a part-time district attorney for a dollar a year," adding, "That's just about all he was worth, and like other members of his family he is bent on getting out of Massachusetts as quick as he can." Richardson said Endicott Peabody, the Democratic candidate for governor, was "chiefly known as a former football player and that's the way he is still known today." Heady talk from one Brahmin about another! Then Richardson drew a bead on Kelly: "He is trying to draw attention away from the issue of corruption in the state by having us admire his children. It is a frightening prospect indeed, this willingness of Democrats to let Frankie Kelly mind the store."

Roland Hayes, the seventy-five-year-old Negro tenor, capped the evening by singing "The Battle Hymn of the Republic," changing the words "to die to make men free" to "to vote to make men free" to fit a tribute to Brooke.

Until that fund-raising event, Brooke had few campaign funds. Appeals to prosperous blacks across the nation were disappointing. "Negroes historically have not recognized the responsibility of contributing to election-campaign expenses," Brooke explained. To him this reflected a basic problem—that there is little that unites Negroes. "Take the Greeks: at least Greece is the common denominator. Take the Jews: religion is the common denominator. But there are Negro Jews, Negro Protestants, Negro Catholics, Negroes more Nordic-looking than Germans. The only thing that unites them is civil rights." The word "minority," he said, refers to numbers, not discrimination. "The Yankee is becoming the minority in Massachusetts."

Although Brooke had never run as a racial candidate, he knew that race was a factor in the fight against Kelly, since the Irish, as well as

WASPS, took a dim view of black militants and their clamor. Late in the campaign some Kelly cohorts tried to smear Brooke as a subversive, a freethinker and a "pushy nigger." Kelly himself denied sending a dilapidated car plastered with Brooke stickers and filled with flamboyantly dressed, half-drunk, cursing blacks into fashionable suburbs, boisterously inquiring about houses for sale. They loudly and obscenely told realtors they had been sent to find a suitable house for Ed Brooke, the next attorney general. This clumsy ploy backfired, as did an attempt by State Representative William F. Keenan to link Brooke with the Communist apparatus. As chief puncher for the Kelly camp, Keenan based his ridiculous charge on an incident that had occurred in 1951 when Brooke, as NAACP legislative chairman, recorded the NAACP in opposition to the McCarthy-Dorgan bill. This unconstitutional measure was designed to outlaw not only the Communist party in Massachusetts, but also any organization which the attorney general might determine to be subversive. The bill was so defective that the legislature, despite the hysteria on subversion prevailing at the time, substituted a sound bill aimed specifically at Communists, while denying the attorney general the right to outlaw whatever organizations he wished. Among groups opposing the McCarthy-Dorgan bill were the League of Women Voters, the American Civil Rights Union and the Massachusetts Council of Churches, as well as all Boston newspapers. In 1962 Endicott Peabody ran against Governor John Volpe. A reporter asked why Keenan didn't attack Peabody, who nine years earlier had assailed congressional investigations of communism as "intimidating public thought, discouraging disagreement on public policies, and damaging reputations." Peabody viewed this as "a danger to our security and our liberty far greater than the public exposure of Communists."

A newspaper dismissed Kelly as "a discredited political hack with a record and a platform so bad that his embarrassed colleagues on the Democratic ticket are trying to pretend he doesn't exist." Another paper noted that Kelly's "eye-catching advocacy of a state lottery has diverted attention from the far more important fact—that the conditions that have so beset Massachusetts in recent years took root while Kelly was attorney general. However urgent it is to keep Frankie Kelly out of office as attorney general, it is the positive assets of Ed Brooke that recommend him to the voters."

Throughout the campaign most of the media boosted Brooke's candidacy. *The Boston Herald* predicted that as attorney general Brooke would be in a position to fight corruption on two broad fronts—directly in his capacity as the state's chief law-enforcement official and indirectly through the recommendation and promotion of corrective legislation. "His opponent, whose public record is long but unappetizing, has campaigned mainly on the spurious issue of reducing taxes by means of a state sweepstakes."

Scurrilous charges spread by Kelly cohorts actually helped Brooke as the campaign wore on, since they were so patently trumped up. Brooke received much of his 200,000-dollar campaign fund from affluent society, including the most proper Bostonians. "A great many of them were purging themselves of guilt when they financed Ed," a reporter wrote. "They were expiating all the sins of prejudice they had committed not only against Negroes, but against the Irish, the Italians, and the Jews as well."

Brooke crisscrossed the state in a white station wagon carrying the slogan "Brooke Attorney General." He circulated postcards with a photograph of the Brooke family on one side. Set in bold type on the other side were the words, "You can BELIEVE in Brooke." Remigia was not merely seen on a postcard. She was one of the speakers. "I remember the first time they asked to make a speech in 1962," she recalls. "I was scared to death. My friend said, 'Remigia, tomorrow we go to lunch with 200 ladies and you have to speak.' I went back and called up Carlo [he calls her "Remigia" or "baby"] and say, 'Write something for me.' He said, 'Be yourself, say what you feel.' Now it doesn't bother me to speak."

Brooke ran hard, "like a Democrat," *Time* reported. "He was at factory gates by 5:30 A.M., waiting to shake hands, and he won support from Boston bankers and Beacon Hill matrons." After one long day in Springfield, Brooke and his workers toured a casket factory near dusk. Albert Gammal, Jr., motioned toward a baby's coffin. "If it was larger, I think I'd crawl in and take a nap," he said.

Brooke concentrated on garment industries, where female employees are clustered. "In one factory," Gammal recalls, "hundreds of girls were working at machines in rows, and they fell all over Ed. Many of them, after shaking hands with him, ran to the end of the next row for a repeat performance."

During the campaign Roger Woodworth heard of a meeting to be held at the home of Mrs. Stephen Courtney Gale, chairman of Ward 6 in Cambridge. He arranged for Brooke to attend and sent a photographer.

"I was pleased, with a few reservations, knowing my neighbors," Mrs. Gale said. "In the details of getting a good group together to hear Brooke, I phoned a neighbor, a very up-and-coming lady of seventy who went everywhere. However, it seemed she had her limits. When she met me in the street the next day, she said in a piercing whisper, looking around, 'But a *colored* man, Mrs. Gale!' I reassured her, and she promised to come to the meeting. The best picture was taken while Brooke was speaking. Seated near him was my friend Mrs. Ralston, her face uplifted, completely absorbed, and her mouth *wide open*."

During the contest, Brooke's telethons were not pretaped but live and unrehearsed, since by this time it was obvious that he functioned best when on the hot seat, "when there is no second chance," as Georgia Ireland put it. "He is more comfortable and can communicate better when he is talking freely and spontaneously, rather than be tethered to a script. In answering questions, he always preferred the toughest."

The telethon was his most effective vehicle in 1962, when he appeared on 16 half-hour segments on seven of the eight channels in Massachusetts. As in his battle with Richardson, he got good mileage out of radio spots. One ally on the Jerry Williams radio talk show was Charlotte Yaffe, a secretary at the studio, who arranged programs. When possible, she booked Brooke to follow Kelly's radiocasts. Then, while Kelly was on the air answering questions phoned in, she jotted down notes in the control room. Thus Brooke was better able to refute some of the points made by Kelly.

Noticing her wearing a Brooke button, Kelly said, "You're quite anti-Kelly. And by the way, why does Brooke always seem to follow me on the air?"

"I'm not anti-Kelly," Miss Yaffe said. "I'm pro-Brooke. And I don't believe in tearing down the opposition."

In the final days of the campaign the Kelly smear squad slipped nasty anonymous notes under the studio door.

"Do you want a nigger as your next governor?" one note read. There were also obscene telephone calls. Mrs. Helen Brooke told Miss Yaffe that during a bus ride one woman said to another, "There's a rumor going around that Brooke is colored." Mrs. Brooke chuckled at the memory.

"We never knew what kind of crank would pester us," Miss Yaffe said. "One night a drunken Kelly supporter barged in demanding to see the Brooke files. One of our newsmen had to push him out of the studio." Kelly himself denied any connection with these incidents.

"I never mentioned these things to Mr. Brooke, feeling it might upset him," Miss Yaffe added.

While on Jerry Williams' talk show on Brooke's birthday (October

26), Miss Yaffe interrupted by bringing in a birthday cake inscribed by a Democrat (Julius Ansel, known as "the Jewish Curley"), a Republican (Mary Newman), and an independent (Miss Yaffe).

"What's going on here?" Williams said. "It's not my birthday."

"Shut up," Charlotte whispered. "It's not for you."

After the show the group sampled the cake and the inevitable champagne, which Mary Newman had hidden in Charlotte's desk.

"I never knew people could be so nice," Brooke said.

"If my son considers you a friend, it's for life," Mrs. Helen Brooke told Miss Yaffe. Charlotte, who had a cancer operation early in 1971, received flowers and a note from Brooke: "Your letters lift my heart and bring back wonderful memories of those first talk-show appearances with Jerry Williams," Brooke wrote. "That was our toughest campaign, Charlotte."

On the night of the election President Kennedy called a *Boston Globe* reporter to ask how his brother Ted was doing in the Senate race against George Lodge.

"He's ahead, Mr. President. By the way, Brooke is way ahead. He's practically in."

"My God," Kennedy said, "that's the biggest news in the country."

Earlier in the evening at Brooke's headquarters in downtown Boston, his supporters were glum as early figures dribbled in from Democratic areas with voting machines.

"He's trailing," Lionel Lindsay said. "What do you think, Roger?"

"Don't worry about it." After phoning six key precincts and learning that Brooke was running ahead in three, Roger turned to Lindsay. "Everything is all right." Hours later, when Brooke was running more than 30,000 behind Kelly, Woodworth remained unruffled. "Wellesley isn't in yet," he said shortly before one o'clock in the morning. Minutes later he flashed a victory sign and suggested that "the boss" make a victory statement. As Brooke adjusted the microphone he paused dramatically, to the delight of the crowd in the room. "Wait a minute, Roger, are you *sure* I have won?"

"Perfectly sure."

"Well, I can't believe it," Brooke said.

Political professionals also found it hard to believe. By all accepted rules of Bay State politics Brooke couldn't win, yet he had won big. While every other Republican, including Volpe, went down to defeat in a Democratic landslide, Brooke crushed Kelly under a plurality of almost 260,000 votes to become the first Negro in the nation to be popularly elected to a major statewide office. And of the

1,143,065 votes cast for him, fewer than 25,000 came from blacks. Most of these were Democrats.

"Now," he said, smiling, "I have to prove I can do the job."

Kelly congratulated him. "I really have no alibi for not winning. . . . That Brooke is a popular vote getter. He has a nice personality, is a good campaigner and makes a good appearance. He's easy to talk to and has had a good press throughout his political career."

Refreshed after a steam bath and a rubdown, Brooke greeted well-wishers on his fifth-floor headquarters at Court Square, one floor above Volpe's.

"I'm very happy, my wife is happy, my children are happy, and I hope the people of Massachusetts are happy. My mother and sister are here, and I know they are happy, too." Mrs. Brooke said her husband was too ill to come to Boston. "But he is recovering, and I'm sure this news will hasten him on his road to recovery."

Never were Brooke backers so jubilant. "We want Brooke, we want Brooke," some chanted in the long, narrow room.

"We *got* Brooke!" the gathering roared. "We believed *first!*" one man yelled. Albert Gammal told a reporter: "To us he is ten feet tall, and he always will be ten feet tall, and we will work for him again, for governor, senator or anything he wants to do."

In one of the Boston newspaper offices he toured in the wee hours of the morning, Brooke met Ted Kennedy, Chub Peabody and Francis Bellotti (the Democratic candidate for lieutenant governor), all successful in their campaigns.

"Congratulations to you and the best of luck to you," Kennedy said, extending his hand.

Brooke thanked him and nodded when Peabody said he hoped they could work together. "I hope so."

"We can work together," Bellotti said.

Brooke smiled. "We'll have to."

From what he told the press, Brooke was unaware of some of the smear tactics used during the spirited contest. "Hardly anyone even mentions I'm a Negro anymore," he said. "I think it's progress. . . . Massachusetts is not without its racial problems, but we have far fewer than most other states. I didn't hear any racial epithets during the whole campaign nor did I even receive any crank mail. I don't think I was asked more than five questions on civil rights in the last two months."

The morning after his election he had a breakfast meeting at Hotel Madison in Boston. "I want to try the job on for size, for a while, before I make any drastic decisions," he told his workers. "But the one thing I want to do is live up to my campaign promises—and I intend to. I'll rest a few days, then talk with Attorney General McCormack to work out a transition of powers." He said he would seek the best possible assistants, choosing them on a nonpartisan basis.

He put his arm around his wife, calling her "a wonderful, wonderful woman." Remigia said Massachusetts would benefit because "Carlo" was "an honest man, a good man." She had a faraway look in her eyes as she shook her head. "I couldn't understand last night how Carlo could feel so sure he would win when he was running behind Mr. Kelly. I thought I knew something about politics. I campaigned the entire state for him, but last night I was all mixed up at how he could look at the figures and be so certain of winning."

During the session a woman praised Brooke for having overcome such great obstacles in winning the election. Assuming she meant Protestant-Republican-Negro problems, he thanked her. Then, realizing she was referring to a background of poverty, poor education and racial bias, he took her aside and told her of his middle-class background and sound education. He said that, like most blacks in America, he had seen discrimination and segregation, but because of his family's socioeconomic status, he had suffered little. In later interviews he often elaborated on this. "When we couldn't buy tickets for a concert or the opera in the segregated theaters of Washington, my mother simply took us to New York to Carnegie Hall or the Metropolitan."

Brooke's election, a landmark in American political history, made him the second most important leader in a Commonwealth of what had been a dying and predominantly white Anglo-Saxon party. Hardy Nathan wrote a letter to the editors of *Time:* "With all the space you've given to Massachusetts politics, you might have mentioned that we did elect Ed Brooke attorney general. This Negro Republican is a man to keep your eye on. He just might wind up being the first Negro governor anywhere."

There was time to think of that later. Meanwhile, exhausted from the grinding campaign, Brooke flew to San Juan, Puerto Rico, with Remigia for a few days in the sun.

CHAPTER SEVEN

A Den of Thieves

THE ATTORNEY GENERAL has the potential of being the most powerful officeholder in the Commonwealth next to the governor. As
the thirty-fifth attorney general of the state, Brooke kept six of the
staff of 200 inherited from Edward McCormack, who cooperated
with him during the transition period before Brooke took office on
January 16, 1963. On that day House Speaker John Thompson gave
Brooke the use of the House chamber, where he greeted thousands
of well-wishers.

Hundreds of applicants sought appointment as assistant attorneys
general. Unlike his predecessors, who had personally made staff
choices, Brooke named Gael Mahony chairman of a screening committee that included John Bottomly, Roger Woodworth, Albert Gammal, Clarence Elam, Mary Newman, Harcourt Wood and Benjamin
("Papa") Gargill, whom Brooke called the "mature member" of the
group. Before being interviewed by this committee, each candidate
submitted a résumé. While a secretary took notes, candidates answered
questions about their political background, the nature of their practice—whether civil or criminal—and the number of years they had
practiced law. After the interview, Mahony presided at a post mortem
during which there was a lively exchange of views. From late November 1962, the screening committee, which went over almost 700 appli-
cations, interviewed several persons a day, working even on New
Year's Eve. After the committee narrowed the field to about 140 applicants, Brooke studied the synopses of applicants whom he had not

95

previously seen (after they were approved by the Bar Association and checked out by Republican town and ward committees) and completed staffing a few weeks before he took office. Brooke also went to prestigious law firms in Boston to ask for the loan of top lawyers who would lose no status while they served in the office of the attorney general.

Brooke wound up with a top-flight team.

"You have to work with Ed to realize just how good a lawyer he is," one assistant said. "He has a dazzling grasp of legal complexity, and is a glutton for homework. Whenever he enters a courtroom you know he has surrounded the case from every possible perspective."

Edward T. Martin, now a judge of Probate Court for Middlesex, was a specialist in state and federal tax problems whom Brooke named first assistant attorney general. As deputy attorney general, Martin had argued several important cases before the Supreme Judicial Court of Massachusetts, including the Teachers' Oath case and the so-called Blue Shield case. Another appointee was Lee Kozol, an expert in cases involving civil liberties and discriminatory procedures who had written articles on fair housing practices.

Dividing the office into 13 units, Brooke put a chief in command of each, leaving day-to-day operations in their hands after outlining departmental policy. Knowing the tremendous abuses in eminent-domain procedures, Brooke put John Bottomly in charge of this division, assigning him nine attorneys to help handle a backlog of almost 4,000 cases and setting guidelines for Bottomly to follow. Since this division handled millions of dollars annually, Brooke set up more efficient procedures with the Department of Public Works, where Perry had uncovered "sweetheart" deals, and the U.S. Bureau of Public Roads. As a special assistant, Perry brought irregularities in this field to his attention.

"I particularly want top people for this division," Brooke said. "I want to improve land-taking procedure and the awarding of land damages, because the state has lost much money in that field. The homeowner must receive promptly a fair price for the taking of his land by the state, but we must always remember that it is the taxpayer's money we are spending."

During the first few months in office Brooke received many calls from attorneys who said something to the effect of, "I have talked to Jack Bottomly, who offered us 32,000 dollars. I think we should get at least 45,000 dollars."

"Sorry, but I won't second-guess Jack," Brooke would say. After a while, as word got around, the telephone calls stopped. It was great for team morale.

Herbert E. Travers, later U.S. Attorney and now Superior Court Judge, who had been an assistant district attorney in Worcester County, headed the complaint section in the criminal division before becoming chief of the criminal division itself. He took the job "because it was clear that Ed was trying to create a professional legal staff, as opposed to one colored by political considerations." Since many legislators and other Bay State politicians were as crooked as a snake track, Brooke wanted a complaint section to which taxpayers could come without fear of disclosure or threat. But he wanted more than "tips," noting that his office could not proceed with mere rumor or hearsay or anonymous letters. "My office wants information. We want people to . . . give evidence of wrongdoing."

He said the complaint section could curb corruption. "It is unfortunate that we had public officials who were taking money out of the public till. I have never said Republicans had a monopoly on virtue, but . . . there were fewer Republicans around."

He said graft had no geographical boundaries. "Every state that has contracts and is spending a lot of money is going to have someone with his hand out, reaching for an easy dollar," he told *Newsweek*. "The only difference is that here . . . we have brought scandals out into the open and have tried to do something about them." Former Governor Foster Furcolo was cynical: "Listen, if you put a man in charge of a big department with a lot of money passing in and out, I don't care WHO he is, he'll eventually start helping himself. That's an occupational hazard of modern government."

A busy member of Brooke's team was Attorney Edward M. Swartz, later author of the book *Toys That Don't Care*. Swartz, who had never been in politics, was top editor of the *Law Review* at Boston University. He headed the advisory council on conflicts of interest and chaired Brooke's legislative committee, which drafted bills through which Brooke strengthened law-enforcement officials' hand in chasing down crime and corruption.

According to Swartz, Massachusetts was the first state to try to legislate morality in government. "The Conflict of Interest Law falls like rain on both the just and the unjust," he says. "I will be the first to admit that the statute hurt some town officials. But public servants have to learn to live with the law." Since the law went into effect in May 1963, 440 opinions have been written on the statute by the attorney general's office. "What this statute did, among other things," he adds, "was to focus the searchlight of scrutiny on all public officials. Big city politics had long been suspicious, but now the small towns found their officials were guilty of some of the same things."

He gives Brooke credit for following through with this prototype legislation. After Swartz gave a speech on the measure at the 1963 Eastern Regional Conference of Attorneys General at Newport, Rhode Island, the delegates voted to recommend similar legislation to their legislatures. Swartz finds it dismaying that while Massachusetts has a national reputation for political shenanigans, little attention has been given its leadership in reform. He mentions a case on which the State Supreme Court ruled while he was serving under Brooke. It involved an Ipswich selectman who owned a drugstore which filled about 90 percent of the prescriptions paid for with public funds for people on welfare. When a vacancy came on the Public Welfare Board, the board of selectmen, with the drugstore owner serving on it, named as the successor a clerk in the drugstore owned by the selectman.

Another case involved a police chief who was paid for mowing lawns on town-owned property. An unpaid tree warden in another community saw that his tree-surgeon company got all town contracts. There was a selectman whose oil company sold fuel to the town's schools. Credit for ending such practices goes to McCormack, and especially to Brooke.

Old associates appointed to Brooke's staff were Glendora McIlwain, Roger Woodworth, Harold Putnam (whom Miss McIlwain married in 1964) and Herbert E. Tucker, Jr. Brooke also named Harcourt Wood, who is not a lawyer, to the seven-man Committee of the Permanent Charity Fund. An experienced investment counselor, Wood was adviser to American and Canadian investment funds and a member of the Boston Security Analysts' Society and the Business Associates Club of Boston. His wide acquaintance was a big asset to Brooke in his campaigns.

Putnam had been an assistant attorney general under Attorney General George Fingold, McCormack's predecessor, and had served as legislative counsel to the U.S. Senate Small Business Committee. Brooke named him chief of the Consumer Council and Antitrust Division.

Tucker, who had headed the Finance Division under McCormack, retained the post. He was once associated with the Bureau of Internal

Revenue and later used his knowledge of that bureau to help Brooke out of a tax dilemma. Tucker, an old friend of Brooke, recalls the day Nancy Porter ushered him into Brooke's private office at the State House. Brooke was standing, hands in pocket, back turned.

"I've studied your record," he said, still looking out the window with no trace of recognition. "I am considering reappointing you as chief of the Finance Division."

"I am honored, and will do my best if you look favorably on my application."

Brooke walked over and shuffled some papers on his desk, still unsmiling. "Miss Porter, my secretary, will let you know of my decision," he said.

On the staff of John E. Sullivan, who headed the administrative division before he took over eminent domain, was Nelson Crowther, a devout Christian Scientist. In action against Grove Press, publisher of the allegedly pornographic novel *Fanny Hill,* Crowther researched the legal aspects of the case, but was so straitlaced he refused to read the naughty book! He understood it was too prurient.

Robert DeGiacomo, an assistant attorney general in McCormack's office, charged that in the early 1960s "power in Massachusetts is held by such an interlocking combine that one almost gets the feeling of a giant conspiracy."* The scandal of the week in the state involved consultants and engineers who wangled contracts by bribing highway officials and legislators. Probate judges gave trusteeships to relatives and friends, and realtors doubled as official assessors. A state representative was reelected while in jail following a conviction of larceny. Crooks conspired with big businessmen and prominent public officials to cheat the state, with huge sums of money "passing illicitly from schemer to schemer sometimes through complicated bookkeeping devices and sometimes almost openly, from pocket to pocket or briefcase to paper bag."

Patrick M. (Sonny) McDonough, as the uncrowned king of the Governor's Executive Council and an old-line politician, Curley style, is equally critical of proper Bostonians, reformers and WASP financial barons. "I know a lot of ditchdiggers who never lifted anything heavier than a paycheck," he told a political writer. "I men-

---

* DeGiacomo told this to a *Boston Globe* reporter on October 9, 1971. Under Attorney General Edward McCormack he was chief investigator of the Boston Common Garage scandal, a case which Gael Mahony under Brooke brought to a successful conclusion.

tion no names, but under one governor [Furcolo] we had, they stole things wholesale, while they might have gotten away with it if they had stolen them retail. They dredged out everything but the frog pond on Boston Common." McDonough said there were more thieves on State Street, Boston's financial district, than he ever found in the State House.

Because of Furcolo's venal administration, his successor, Volpe, persuaded a reluctant legislature to establish the Massachusetts Crime Commission and give it sweeping investigative powers. The commission cited William Callahan as a chief source of corruption. At this czar's request, legislators on Beacon Hill were put on the payroll of an engineering firm and were paid huge sums for doing little if anything. According to the commission, this arrangement and payments they received on performance bonds "were the principal means by which [Callahan] influenced the passage or defeat of legislation. . . . The commission has found a connection between the times when the payments were heaviest and the presence in the legislature of bills with which the chairman was concerned." At one time 54 of the 280 members of the legislature were serving as insurance brokers, and eight drew salaries from an engineering firm with a turnpike maintenance contract. The commission concluded that the methods Callahan used to get results played a large part in ruining the moral climate of the state government.

The Crime Commission gave Brooke much of the evidence needed to secure indictments. The commission was created by the legislature to identify problems and make changes in the law, and Brooke never forfeited his decision-making power in connection with the recommendations and evidence which the Crime Commission brought to his attention. The commission and Brooke's office worked effectively in tandem, especially after the legislature, with help from Governor Endicott Peabody, gave 639,000 dollars to the commission to finance a one-year crash probe corruption in state government.

"I knew what the Crime Commission would find within the Democratic party," Peabody said, "but I went ahead, because we had to do away with corruption wherever it festered."

Meanwhile, Brooke's problem was to attract and keep lawyers capable of dealing with crack defense attorneys. He conferred with House Speaker John F. Thompson, known as the "Iron Duke," and Senate President John Powers, both powerful Democrats. How, he asked, could he maintain a competent staff on a maximum salary of 8,000 dollars a year? He wasn't interested in part-time assistant attorneys general, and knew he couldn't ask top lawyers from leading firms to work 40 hours a week at small salaries. He had been getting by because he had hired fewer attorneys at higher pay. A few bureau chiefs were getting 18,000 dollars and 19,000 dollars a year—several thousand dollars more than their predecessors had received.

Thompson and Powers agreed with Brooke's arguments, confident that he would be impartial enough to prosecute Republicans as well as Democrats. Thompson, in giving Brooke what he wanted, did not realize he was signing his own political death warrant.

Brooke also asked for an appropriation to provide additional special assistant attorneys general to prosecute cases developed through Crime Commission evidence, pointing out that the nonpartisan commission had the advantage of secret operations so essential to successful investigations. This protected the rights of persons being investigated. The attorney general, on the other hand, was elected with a party label and could conceivably become partisan during a probe. The Crime Commission had to be neutral,* Brooke said, "since corruption had no party label."

The autonomous power of the attorney general is unique. Brooke, the only Republican in a Democratic state administration, was accountable for his actions neither to the governor, the legislature nor the executive council. Yet he had a lot of people over him, he said— "the electorate." He considered himself the protector of the rights of the accused, the innocent and even the guilty. "I am a prosecutor, not a persecutor. I abhor any act by a prosecutor who goes beyond his constitutional powers. I get no glee out of prosecutions. I don't need them for political purposes. It is not a sound basis for politicking. So far as this office goes, no one will trespass on the rights of any person."

Nevertheless, with help from television, the press and the Crime Commission, Brooke's repute as a crime buster grew, a role that disturbed him. "I don't like presenting evidence that puts people in jail. But if corruption is uncovered, I can't ignore it. Actually the picture of me as a crusading reformer is wrong. If there is any credit due for exposing malfeasance in Massachusetts, the Crime Commission deserves it. . . . The evidence is handed to me and I merely present it to the grand jury."

Four days after he took office, when a banquet at the Sheraton Plaza was planned for Eugene Farnum, the Republican insurance com-

---

* Actually the Crime Commission was dominated by Republicans.

missioner of Massachusetts, Brooke made a ground-breaking decision by interpreting for the first time a statute that banned testimonial dinners for officials in law enforcement and regulatory and investigative agencies, knowing that these arms around affairs were primarily intended to compromise the guest. Farnum was furious and columnists astounded, realizing that Brooke could have construed the legislation in favor of the dinner. It was a clear signal that the new attorney general would indeed call them as he saw them, regardless of where the political chips fell. This was step one in rooting out corruption. Before he left office, he had indicted more violators of the public trust (mostly Democrats) than any man in Bay State history. According to Peter Lucas of *The Boston Herald Traveler,* some cases were thrown out of court, the defendants found innocent, or the charges dropped because of lack of evidence. While acquittals and directed verdicts of innocence brought stinging criticism of him, Massachusetts voters, according to *The Boston Globe,* clearly found his ferreting out of political corruption satisfying, although Brooke never posed as society's avenger.

The Massachusetts press missed a significant incident early in Brooke's career. A few weeks after taking office, he was invited to be the principal speaker at a Lincoln Day observance at the St. George Hotel in Brooklyn. Governor Nelson Rockefeller of New York, whom Brooke had known for some time, was also scheduled to talk. When flights were canceled because of a blizzard, Brooke drove to Brooklyn over sleety roads at a speed of 80 to 90 miles an hour, according to Bill Jackson, who can drive a car as expertly as moonshiners used to do without lights at night on mountain roads. During the trip Jackson recalls seeing about 20 cars off the road. Sitting in the back seat were Assistant Attorney General Donald Whitehead and Detective Sergeant Leo Martin of the Massachusetts State Police. Three New York state troopers ushered them into the St. George.

"This is the way we were meant to live," Brooke told the group as they went up in the elevator. After taking a shower and slipping into a tuxedo, Brooke told Whitehead he would not go down to the head table until Rockefeller arrived. An hour passed, and no Governor. The party ordered drinks and chicken-salad sandwiches. By this time Whitehead was glued to the room telephone asking the reception committee to be patient. As dinner was about to be served in the ballroom, indignant delegations pounded the door, saying the guests were getting restless. Whitehead told them to go ahead with the dinner. Rockefeller hadn't arrived even after coffee and dessert were served. Whitehead, exasperated, told the toastmaster to kill more time by having head-table guests speak. After everyone had spoken, he suggested that the emcee introduce distinguished members of the audience.

"It was really excruciating," Whitehead recalls. "Finally, about ten past ten, Rockefeller breezed in and jauntily suggested that we join the assembly. 'Let's go, let's go.' As we left, he turned to Martin and Jackson. 'Gentlemen, just press that button on the wall if there's anything you want.' "

The audience, according to Whitehead, was sullen and hostile to the point of being bristling, even after Rockefeller's brief talk. "Then Brooke took the microphone, and it was a caution to see the way the assembly simmered down. By the end of his talk, Ed had them in the palm of his hand. Rockefeller was obviously impressed. And that's just how Ed planned it. He wanted Rockefeller to hear him speak."

That evening Bill Jackson drove Brooke to the elegant Fifth Avenue home of Laurance Rockefeller, where the attorney general chatted with the Rockefeller brothers over a late snack. Brooke breakfasted with them the next morning before driving back to Boston.

Leo Martin recalls another incident that occurred soon after this trip. Learning that a wild-eyed man was handing out two mimeographed sheets to commuters at South Station accusing Brooke of heading a gigantic conspiracy to block construction of an inner belt highway, Brooke sent Whitehead and Martin over to check.

"The man was standing beside an easel handing out sheets of paper while shouting that Attorney General Brooke was guilty of embezzlement and conspiracy," Martin recalls. After reading the message, he confiscated the rest of the mimeographs and warned the man he would be arrested the next time he was caught. "The poor guy was terrified. He folded up his easel after giving us his name and disappeared into the crowd. We learned he had recently escaped from a mental institution."

One morning at the Sheraton Plaza, where Saltonstall, Volpe, Brooke and Richardson were closeted, Jackson and Martin waited in an anteroom for Brooke to come out. An hour passed. They finally called the attorney general's office to say the boss would be later than expected.

"He's right here," Nancy Porter said. "After the conference he couldn't find you, so after looking around the lobby, he took a taxi." Brooke had left by a different door.

By the end of his first year in office, Brooke had an extensive program of reforms ready for the consideration of the 1964 legislature, further proof that he was more concerned with correcting flaws in a system which permits abuses than in getting convictions. He had curbed some of the shenanigans that had made state politics squalid as he teamed with the Crime Commission. Like some of Boston's mayors, there were legislators who could be rented, if not bought.

On May 7, 1964, 26 persons and ten corporations were charged on 217 counts ranging from bribery, larceny, and perjury to conspiracy in state contract negotiations and conflict of interest. Among high officials fingered were two former Speakers of the House of Representatives, a judge, two members of the Executive Council, the former head of the State Police (Frank Giles), and former governor Foster Furcolo. One official was John Thompson, who eventually was indicted on 60 counts of conspiracy and of soliciting and accepting bribes from loan companies. Thompson was Speaker of the House until January 1965.

Governor Peabody was stymied by the "machine" in the Democratic legislature when he tried to oust Thompson. Failing, he had to come to terms with the Iron Duke. The Speaker, whose days were numbered because of failing health, told Brooke: "You will never convict me." When the grand jury returned its verdict, it was the end of the line for Thompson. Brooke phoned him.

"I'm sorry, John," he said. A ruined man, Thompson died a year later before his case came to trial.

Another official indicted was Charles Gibbons, former Republican Speaker of the House who had run unsuccessfully for governor in 1958. When indicted on 23 counts of bribery and one of conspiracy, he was chairman of a special commission supervising the construction of a 40-million-dollar government center in Boston. It was also the last stop for Gibbons. Also caught in the web was Frank S. Giles, state commissioner of public safety, who was convicted of perjury. Furcolo was indicted on charges of "conspiring to arrange a bribe," in trying to get Anthony DeNatale reappointed as commissioner of public works. The Governor's Council held up the reappointment when the Crime Commission charged there had been a bribe offer of 25,000 dollars. When it was further charged that Furcolo knew of the bribe, Elwood McKenney, a black who had been Furcolo's chief secretary and confidant,* went to see Brooke.

---

* Elwood McKenney is presently judge of the Roxbury District Court.

"You and I have known each other during the Crime Commission's investigations, when allegations were thrown about freely," McKenney said. "This indictment looks trumped up. Please keep the doors open as you probe the case."

"Of course," Brooke said. "The door is always open and I'll do what is right."

Furcolo's indictment was returned on the eve of the 1964 election, leading to the charge that Brooke and the Crime Commission were bent on defeating the Democratic ticket in the upcoming election. Superior Court Eugene Hudson ultimately threw out of court the charge against Furcolo as totally lacking in substantiating evidence. Meanwhile, four of the governor's councilors were found guilty of conspiracy and bribery.

Also caught in Brooke's dragnet were out-of-state officials employed by national small-loan finance chains. These officials connived with Massachusetts officials to victimize Massachusetts borrowers. Brooke assigned Herbert Travers to prosecute them and the ten corporations involved.

Travers found that the loan companies, through agents, had used bribes to hike interest rates. One culprit was Morris Garfinkle, a wholesale dealer in secondhand automobiles and a former member of the Massachusetts Small Loans Regulatory Board, which set the minimum interest rate on loans. Another was Martin J. Hanley, supervisor of the Small Loans Bureau in the Department of Banking and Insurance, which gave investigators much of the evidence. I recall sitting in the attorney general's office with Brooke, discussing Hanley and the trial of persons in high places," Travers said. "He was always interested in the right thing to do, regardless of a person's status."

All defendants were convicted. The loan firms were fined a maximum of 3,000 dollars, and five persons went to state prison for terms ranging from two to five years. In a second trial, which lasted almost 11 months—the longest in Massachusetts history—Hanley, the loan companies and their executives were convicted.

The Boston Common Underground Garage scandal was one of the most grandiose and bizarre cases of grand larceny ever uncovered in Massachusetts. This involved and protracted case had all the ingredients of a contrived Perry Mason television drama, including trumped-up engineering and finder's fees, a massive falsification of official records, the founding of a fake corporation and the mysterious disappearance of a defendant, one of four principals who stole almost 800,000 dollars from the state till.

In the fall of 1958 the legislature, prodded by Governor Furcolo, set up the Massachusetts Parking Authority and empowered it to build a garage under Boston Common. The Authority, which financed itself by floating a municipal-bond issue, was not bound by laws of competitive bidding, nor were its records examined by the state auditor. Furcolo named William F. Callahan chairman of the Authority and appointed, as an associate member, George L. Brady, a former editorial writer of *The Boston Record American* Brady, who had long recommended the garage, was an affable person who wore colored wigs, cowboy boots, a rodeo jacket and sombrero. In the spring of 1959, when Callahan unexpectedly resigned from the parking authority, Furcolo put Brady in his place and appointed Joseph W. Monahan, Jr., an insurance salesman and son of a probate judge, to fill the remaining vacancy. Young Monahan was one of the five principal conspirators in the scandal.

In 1959, according to Gael Mahony, who prosecuted the case, Brady looked for a bonding company to underwrite the cost of the garage and a contractor to build it. He told certain local contractors they would have to fork over several hundred thousand dollars in cash if they wanted the contract. There were no takers until The Foundation Company of New York City accepted what seemed to be a legitimate contract.

Then came falsifications involving attorney Richard Simmers and Judge Richard Gordon, who got 100,000 dollars for imaginary legal work. The fifth conspirator was the jaunty Francis W. Kiernan, "an engineer of sorts," who received 344,468 dollars for doing practically nothing. His services were limited to visting the premises 13 times in two years, usually keeping his taxi waiting. He seemed almost to enjoy the trial which sent him to prison. Once, on leaving the courtroom, he turned to Mrs. Gael Mahony. "Let's all smile," he said. "We're on *Candid Camera*." During a recess on a sweltering day, the Gael Mahonys went to an air-conditioned theater to see *Cleopatra*. Sitting a few rows down front were Kiernan and his wife. During the 11 hours the jury was out, Gael Mahony was sitting in a courthouse chamber when Kiernan popped his head in.

"It's a hung jury," he said, smiling. "Ten to two against me. The two women are for me."

Brooke had entered the case while chairman of the Finance Commission, according to Mahony, who succeeded him as chairman. "Ed engaged law-school students from Harvard, Boston University and

106

Boston College to prepare reports in the spring of 1962, when Brooke was opening his drive for attorney general. In May the garage scandal broke when Attorney General McCormack released statements to the press. At my request, Brooke secured the services of William Docksen after talking to the senior partners of Choate, Hall and Stewart. Docksen was a brilliant young lawyer. So many records were involved, Brooke, with his usual thoroughness, got the best certified public accountant—Seth Armen—who worked 50 hours a week sifting evidence. His hard work paid off." Mahony brilliantly prosecuted the cases in Suffolk Superior Court after they were meticulously prepared in the attorney general's office. Simmers, Gordon, Kiernan and Monahan went to jail. Brady was declared mentally incompetent to stand trial, although there were hopes of prosecuting him later. In September 1963 he vanished from his suburban home and was missing until late 1969, when the FBI nabbed him in Atlantic City. He promised to "name every name" in the garage scandal after his capture, while seeking dismissal of the indictment charging him with conspiracy to steal 400,000 dollars in garage construction funds.

Brady's bid to dismiss the indictment was based on his wife Lucy's allegation that she had placed him under guardianship in 1963 with the understanding that Attorney General Brooke would "nol pross" the case. She said Burton L. Williams, her husband's attorney at the time, had so informed her. "Why else would I take out a guardianship on my husband?" she asked Judge Edward F. Hennessey, who issued an order prohibiting all witnesses and attorneys from making out-of-court statements on the Brady case.

Brooke denied her charge, saying he had done everything possible to find Brady with the intention of bringing him to trial. "I'm not saying that Mrs. Brady is lying, but she is mistaken. If she believes what she says, she has been misinformed by Brady's lawyer." Attorney Williams testified that in August 1963, when Judge Francis J. Quirico had declared Brady incompetent to stand trial, Brooke had suggested that the defendant be put under guardianship, but never agreed to drop indictments or even "let them gather dust in a drawer."

Brady, who was ill when captured, was released from custody after serving less than three years.

Brooke's most sensational case involved "the Boston Strangler." "It is inconceivable," a biographer wrote, "that anything could ever match for sheer horror the series of grossly grotesque stranglings by

107

a sexual psychopath who made fiendish assaults on his victims—all women—and then left them in obscene positions, shockingly exposed as though to debase and degrade them."

Between June 1962, when a fifty-five-year-old housewife was found strangled with her bathrobe sash, and January 1964, when an eighteen-year-old woman was murdered, 11 women had been strangled. One person, presumably, had garroted with a stocking, scarf or other ligature and left bound and gagged all the victims, while a terrified populace waited for the next assault. Jack the Ripper, who murdered only seven persons, had never caused such panic. "Strangers on legitimate business found it impossible to gain entrance to buildings," a Boston newspaper reported. During the mounting terror, law-enforcement agencies launched a manhunt that may not have been the longest or most intensive, "but it was one of the most obsessive—and most bizarre," *Newsweek* reported.

The death of the Strangler's last victim, eighteen-year-old Mary Sullivan, aroused such a furore that the attorney general's office stepped in and took over the investigation, to the scorn and annoyance of some Greater Boston police who had been working on the case. Brooke's office had been flooded with letters and telephone calls from frantic and terrified persons—most of them women, young and old.

"Normally," Brooke explained, "the attorney general does not get involved in the investigation of rape, robbery and crimes of this nature. But the attorney general is the chief law-enforcement officer of the Commonwealth. . . . When these stranglings occurred in five different communities and across the borders of three different counties, no one was left to step in but the attorney general."

After consulting with law-enforcement officials, Brooke created a special Strangler Investigation Bureau and named John Bottomly coordinator of all police efforts to track down the maniac. Broadening the manhunt, Brooke brought into the case psychiatrists, psychologists, pathologists, sociologists, anthropologists, hypnoanalysts, and truth-serum experts in an effort to project the probable character of the Strangler. Meanwhile, the strangulations got so much publicity that Erle Stanley Gardner, the modern master of whodunits, came to Boston to discuss the case with Bottomly.

After another conference with police chiefs and other law-enforcement agents, Brooke asked Governor Peabody to offer a 5,000-dollar reward for information leading to the arrest of the person or persons who had committed one or more of the murders. Later the state posted a 10,000-dollar reward, which was never paid.

Brooke and Bottomly screened every tip, clue and lead, no matter how fanciful, that might point to the killer. Finally, a group of concerned citizens headed by Kivvie Kaplan, a philanthropist, came to Brooke. They said the situation had got so out of hand, with so much fear and trepidation in the community, that Brooke could not be faulted for trying a long shot. Bring in the Dutch medium, Peter Hurkos, Kaplan said, and his group—anonymously—would pay the fee.

On a dreary Friday afternoon in January 1964 Brooke called in newsmen to say that Hurkos, a "sensitive," had been asked to help find the Strangler. Brooke was ready to take Kaplan's advice after two veteran reporters—Jean Cole and Loretta McLaughlin—commented on the lack of coordination among police departments around the state. According to Deputy Attorney General Martin, "Miss McLaughlin was so upset when she came to the attorney general's office, she cried."

Hurkos joined the case in January after the eleventh woman had been murdered over a 20-month period. By this time homeowners were putting locks and chains on their doors, and taxi drivers were tipped extra for walking women passengers to their doors. Brooke was even more frustrated than the police, who had to no avail put thousands of bits of information into computers to establish a syndrome.

Hurkos, who had described people and places he had never seen, had gained notoriety after finding the missing Stone of Scone in an obscure church in England after it had been stolen from Westminster Abbey and had used his supranormal powers to solve crimes and locate missing persons in 17 countries before he came to Boston. At his news conference Brooke, over strong protests, convinced reporters of the need for a total news blackout, explaining that Hurkos (whom he has never personally met) would act only if the media, including wire services and broadcasters, honored the blackout.

"When I took over the coordination of this investigation, I said I would use all possible means," Brooke said. "I can see no harm in consulting this individual." Brooke's aides thought his use of a clairvoyant might later be used as an issue against him, but he kept his cool. "We have everything to gain and nothing to lose. A group of private citizens gambled and brought him here." (Kivvie Kaplan donated a thousand dollars for the psychic's six-day investigation.)

Some law officials sneered that this showed how ignorant Brooke was of police methods. "The epitome of rationale, logic and method put his faith in a questionable psychic," a critic said. Others, realizing it would cost the state nothing, felt that anything was worth a try.

Bottomly had read about Hurkos in Jess Stearn's book *The Door to the Future* before checking with police in cities where the seer had worked. All praised him. Bottomly then called Hurkos in Beverly Hills, where he was staying with actor Glenn Ford in preparation for a possible TV documentary to be titled *One Step Beyond*. Hurkos didn't want the assignment, but friends convinced him it would be a humane act to step in.

"So I tell Mr. Bottomly, I cannot promise anything, but I will try."

To avoid publicity if Hurkos landed at Logan Airport, Bottomly arranged for the psychic and his towering bodyguard (James Crane) to land at Providence, Rhode Island. Bottomly and Leo Martin drove them to a motel in Lexington near Boston, where both registered under false names. Hurkos gave an inkling of his supranormal powers during the ride to Lexington when he told Martin about his mother's varicose veins, asked how her eye was, and whether she had got the glasses she needed. Martin was amazed. But he shook his head when Hurkos told him his wife had fallen down a flight of stairs when she was a child and had as a result a slight curvature of the spine. When Martin got home around 3:00 A.M. after this first meeting with the psychic, he woke his wife and she verified the story about her.

On the way to the motel Hurkos also gave a strikingly accurate description of Julian Soshnick, an assistant attorney general who worked with Bottomly on the case. He asked Bottomly where the chain to the gold watch in his drawer was. Smiling nervously, Bottomly said his brother Bob had it. Later Edward Martin was astounded when Hurkos described the duplex house where he had lived as a boy, but was puzzled when Hurkos mentioned an "explosion" which had occurred when Martin was twelve. He phoned his sister and she verified the incident, which involved "things flying around," according to the mystic. She reminded Martin that at the age of twelve he was sound asleep when an incubator blew up.

"The guy is fabulous," Martin told Brooke later. "He can touch part of your clothing and tell you all kinds of things about yourself." He picked up one of Brooke's gloves and turned to go. "Let's see what he can do with this," he said.

Grinning, Brooke walked over and grabbed the glove. "Oh, no, you don't," he said.

During the drive to Lexington Hurkos had blurted out to Martin: "You think me a kook, ja?"

"And that's just what I was thinking," Martin said. But by the end of that ride he was a believer. The hard-boiled detective Jim Glynn was skeptical until he met Hurkos. Noticing that Glynn had his right hand in the pocket of his trench coat, Hurkos said: "You have rosary beads in your hand, ja?" Glynn blinked in disbelief.

On the afternoon of January 30 Soshnick and his aides took a stack of large sealed envelopes, each containing scores of photographs and ligatures, for Hurkos to psychometrize. Soshnick took the photos out of the manila envelopes and laid them face down on the bed. The psychic ran his fingertips over the photographs as he concentrated. Suddenly he stiffened. "Phony baloney! This one not belong!" he said.

Soshnick's jaw fell. He had included one photograph from another murder case to test Peter's psychic powers.

"You want to play tricks, ja?" he asked angrily. "I fly all the way here to help you, and you think Peter is a faker?" He fingered the back of another picture. "This is a dead woman, legs apart, here, I show you." He dropped to the floor and assumed the grotesque posture of the victim. Then, to the bewildered onlookers, he told unpublicized details of every Boston strangling. That same night, when a detective joined the group, apologizing for being late, Hurkos told him he wasn't late because, as he said, his car had broken down or because of heavy traffic.

"You took time and stop by your girl friend's apartment and did a quickie one, huly-buly, hanky-panky. Am I right, sir? And then you come here."

The embarrassed detective shook his head in disbelief when the psychic, who was right, minutely described his girl friend's apartment.

Hurkos then pointed, on a map of Boston, to the exact location where he thought the Strangler could be found.

"Here . . . here . . . you find the killer. He talks like a girl. He's no good, he's a pervert." The psychic correctly described the murderer as a puny male with a mark on his left arm and "something wrong with his thumb." He had a French accent, "was a woman-hating homosexual who had something to do with a hospital." He went on to say the Strangler's hair was "thin, he has a sharp, pointed, spitzy nose and a big Adams's apple." Hurkos gave an incredibly accurate description of his cluttered room on the third floor of a shabby rooming house near Boston College. The man slept on a spring that had no mattress, and took showers downstairs with his shoes on, a habit his landlady admitted later was rather odd.

111

Next day Hurkos led Bottomly's detectives to the apartment, and the man inside, who slammed the door in their face, fitted Peter's description exactly.

On their next visit, the detectives, armed with a search warrant, got inside. When they saw the man's beaked nose, the scar on his left arm and the deformed thumb on his right hand, the detectives felt that the gnome of a man was indeed the Boston Strangler.

But Thomas P. O'Brien, as he is known to conceal his true identity for reasons that don't satisfy all authorities, has never confessed to being the Strangler, when cross-examined. Confronted with photographs of the victims, he said, "I must have done a bad thing, a very bad thing," or "Yes, I have done a wrong thing, very wrong. I was very bad."

He escaped trial by voluntarily committing himself to a mental hospital, where he still is. Some of his revelations there (Bridgewater State Hospital, Massachusetts) to other inmates compounded confusion to an extent not realized until Norma Lee Browning wrote a book, *The Psychic World of Peter Hurkos.*

There were many bizarre developments during the secret investigation by the Dutch sensitive. George Frazier, then writing for *The Boston Herald,* was among those who had advised Brooke to give ESP (extrasensory perception) a try, after other methods had failed. "Nor was Hurkos the only psychic I had look into the matter," Frazier said, "for, at a certain expense, I brought Gerard Croiset to Boston from Utrecht, Holland, but without the authority of the attorney general, who by then had been pilloried in a cartoon depicting him as a witch doctor." As the case wore on, some investigators had no idea whether they were looking for one strangler or 11. According to *Newsweek,* one psychic became a suspect himself. This was Croiset, who gave Frazier "such presumably accurate information about one strangling that Bottomly, who saw possibilities in ESP, persuaded him to submit to a truth-serum or be booked as a suspect."

When the role of Peter Hurkos was revealed, the mail was overwhelmingly in favor of Brooke's decision to use him in the investigation. "*The Pilot,* the Catholics' spokesman, gave the lie to certain politicians who tried to discredit me by saying religion and extrasensory perception are inimical to each other," Brooke said. As time passed, the detectives who worked with Bottomly and Soshnick were not the only persons who professed respect for Hurkos' psychic talent. Edward Sheehan wrote in *Harper's Magazine:* "It is a fact . . . that, though he may not have picked the proper Boston Strangler, he

[Hurkos] did precede his actual investigation by astounding several detectives on the case with the accuracy of his revelations about their own private lives." The most hardheaded detectives were impressed by the psychic's "uncanny divinations in which he accurately reconstructed the crimes simply by touching objects associated with them."

During the probe the police quizzed two shoe salesmen who fit the Hurkos description of the Boston Strangler: "a slight man with a sharp nose, a scar on his left arm and a deformed thumb." Both were eliminated. By 1966 the police had questioned other suspects, including a schizophrenic with a history of rape who had escaped from an institution at times matching the dates of the murders. Another suspect was a physician on the staff of the U.S. Immigration Service who called immigrant girls just off ships and "examined" them over the telephone. The chief suspect, however, except for the religious fanatic with an obsession about shoes and nurses (Thomas P. O'Brien), was Albert DeSalvo, who boasted about almost a thousand rapes. Neither clairvoyant had fingered him as the Boston Strangler, since he did not fit the pattern.

A few weeks after his arrest for a series of rapes, DeSalvo told Bottomly he was the Strangler. He could give no valid reasons for the killings. "I just go here and there. I don't know why. . . . Whoever came to the door first, that was it." Bottomly, who heard DeSalvo's unofficial confession, believed him.

In May 1965 *The Boston Traveler* said Brooke sought a petition of guardianship for a strangler suspect under observation at Bridgewater State Hospital. Earlier that year the suspect had told a fellow inmate at Bridgewater that he had strangled 11 women and killed two others. All 13 had died between June 1962 and January 1964. This thirty-two-year-old man, whom Brooke called a prime suspect, gave minute details of the murders, some of them unprintable, according to *The Boston Traveler*. He said he plunged a carving knife into the breast of one elderly woman after beating her, the method detailed by the autopsy report. Many details he outlined were never published. He also sketched details he recalled at the scenes of his confessed crimes—sketches that tallied with physical evidence.

This "prime suspect" turned out to be the man known as Thomas P. O'Brien. Was the "fellow inmate at Bridgewater," to whom he had told his story, Albert DeSalvo? According to a story carried in Boston newspapers on February 28, 1968, George W. Harrison, a convict, charged that DeSalvo was not the real Boston Strangler, but that he had learned the role from a roommate at Bridgewater State Hospital.

113

Harrison said he had overheard many conversations between DeSalvo and the inmate, who apparently was the real Strangler. According to Harrison, who was one of two inmates who had escaped with DeSalvo from the mental hospital, the other inmate had been the number one suspect during the investigation of the stranglings. He was eliminated as a suspect, Harrison went on, after DeSalvo "confessed" his crimes. Harrison did not know that the other inmate was "O'Brien."

In a brief trial that ended on January 10, 1967, DeSalvo faced charges of breaking and entering, assault and battery, armed burglary and "unnatural and lascivious acts" against four women. His attorney, F. Lee Bailey, had hoped for a verdict of not guilty by reason of insanity, but was not allowed to introduce as evidence DeSalvo's confession of 13 murders. Refusing to allow any evidence relating to the stranglings, or any testimony from Bottomly or his assistants, the judge said: "He is not on trial in this court for homicide." DeSalvo was sentenced to life imprisonment for armed robbery, to be served after he completed a nine-to-ten-year sentence on other charges. After returning to Bridgewater State Hospital, and escaping five weeks later, he returned to custody and was later transferred to the prison infirmary at Walpole State Prison.

In 1967 Brooke rejected an offer of 50,000 dollars to play himself in a film based on Gerold Frank's book *The Strangler*. The following year he was offered almost twice that amount, but again declined, primarily because the script pointed to DeSalvo as the murderer. The first script clearly identified DeSalvo as the Strangler. Brooke argued that the film was prejudicial to DeSalvo's pending trial.

When the film, starring Henry Fonda as Bottomly and Tony Curtis as DeSalvo, was shown, Brooke was displeased by the way he was depicted. The producer had him saying and doing things that were completely out of character. In one scene he and Bottomly at day's end are relaxing in the attorney general's office. Brooke walks to a cabinet and pours himself a jigger of Scotch, while Bottomly sips a cup of tea. Brooke drinks only tea in his office and sips Scotch elsewhere sparingly.

Throughout the entire proceedings Brooke had refused to talk to Gerold Frank, also for fear of prejudicing a subsequent trial. Elliot Richardson, who succeeded Brooke as attorney general in 1966, also refused to let his office be filmed as part of the movie, complaining that the script "departs in many respects from actual facts."*

---

* Six months after DeSalvo's long confessions ended, Bottomly resigned as assistant attorney general "over matters unrelated to the stranglings."

Peter Hurkos was fired as consultant on the movie because he insisted DeSalvo was the wrong "guy." Asked whether he had ever met DeSalvo, he said, "No, no, never. He was picked up a month later, after I left.* But he roommated with O'Brien. . . . Oh, yes, they roommated together in the same mental hospital. That is how DeSalvo knows everything to confess."

Hurkos knows that few persons agree with him. The public is convinced that DeSalvo told the truth when he confessed, and after the film *Boston Strangler* was shown, the person in the street was surer than ever, despite new evidence, that the rapist was not the Strangler.

"Remember," writes Hurkos' biographer, "the movie cameras were just beginning to roll in Boston in February 1968 when the Strangler probe was reopened. But with ten million dollars at stake and Tony Curtis as their Strangler, you certainly cannot expect the moviemakers to admit they've got the wrong guy, now, can you?"

The case was unsolved long after Brooke left the attorney general's office. On February 16, 1968, Boston newspapers reported that Attorney General Richardson had reopened the special bureau investigating the Boston stranglings of 1962–64 because of "new information." It developed that DeSalvo, serving a life sentence at Walpole on other charges, was then "ready to talk" further about the stranglings and might confess his guilt to a grand jury.

District Attorney John J. Droney was against kicking a dead horse.

"It's incredible how this man can dictate to the Commonwealth. He's now complaining he doesn't like it at Walpole, and he's masterminding another trial. He would hope to be found not guilty by reason of insanity, and then make a quick recovery."

Droney changed his mind, however, after the revelations of Harrison. Droney interviewed Harrison in prison and prepared to let him take a lie-detector test to back his allegations. Droney released a statement: "We have information from authentic sources that before all the television, the movies and the books came out about the Boston Strangler, DeSalvo said he had never hurt anyone." Droney, changing his opinion, said he was certain that DeSalvo was not the Strangler and that he was "play-acting." Psychiatrists and correctional officials at Bridgewater agreed.

Then, abruptly, the picture again changed. On April 25, 1968, Richardson said the probe was being officially closed permanently be-

---

* During the six days he worked on the Strangler case, Hurkos lost 15 pounds, and it took him several months to get over the ordeal, he said. "I was a broken wreck," he told Norma Lee Browning, his biographer.

cause of the inability of psychiatrists to agree on whether DeSalvo was competent to undergo lie-detector tests and interrogation.

Stories about the case still circulate in the State House. In August 1971 Senate President Kevin B. Harrington, recalling that Republican attorneys general in the past have been given extra money for new programs, added: "When Edward Brooke was attorney general the Republicans kept asking Democrats what they had to hide in not approving more money for the attorney general's office. So we appropriated more money for the attorney general, and do you know what he did? Remember when there was a fellow known as the Boston Strangler running around? The attorney general went out and hired a mystic. He hired a soothsayer and drove him around to soak up the vibrations. And do you know what he discovered?

"He said there was crime in Boston."

This drew laughter on the floor of the Senate. Then the Republican minority leader, Senator John Parker, took the floor.

"Attorney General Brooke did get good advice from the mystic," Parker said. "He told him to run for the Senate."

CHAPTER EIGHT

On the Firing Line

O N A WINTRY day early in 1964 Attorney General Brooke stood at the window of his elegant, spacious office on the third floor of the State House overlooking snow-covered Boston Common. For a moment, hands in his trouser pockets, he watched a civil-rights parade sloshing up Beacon Hill. A group of blacks, carrying mud-splattered banners and placards, were on their way to City Hall to protest conditions in Boston schools. At this time, the city had 49 racially imbalanced public schools, ranging from 35- to 100-percent black.

Brooke turned to a magazine writer who was interviewing him. "You know, I sympathize with them, but I'm convinced that nothing I could do would harm the cause more than to conduct myself as a civil-rights leader while I hold this office. I'm the lawyer for the five million citizens of Massachusetts, not for its 50,000 Negroes."*

Brooke was thinking of the charge that because he was a Negro and did not want to seem overzealous in the civil-rights movement, his administration was less liberal than that of his predecessor, Edward McCormack, who had taken a strong civil-rights stand.

Roger Woodworth succinctly put his "boss" in perspective. "Look, it's all very well to march around in parades, preside at sit-ins and write angry articles denouncing the white establishment. Unfortu-

---

* Brooke was mistaken. According to the federal census, there were 111,842 blacks in Massachusetts in 1960. By 1970, there were 175,817.

nately, however, if Brooke had taken this route, he couldn't possibly have got himself to the office of attorney general, and most people agree that his election represented a real shot in the arm for the Negro cause. Let's face it. Brooke is a Negro politician in a white society. This means one thing—it's white votes that elect him to office."

Woodworth added that Brooke's mandate as attorney general required him to respect the rights of all citizens, to enforce the law fairly for the protection of all. "The attorney general isn't supposed to make decisions on the basis of pro-white or pro-Negro, pro-Republican or pro-Democrat, pro-civil rights or anti-civil rights. If the law is on the books, he has to read it the way it's written."

Unlike most Negro leaders, Brooke refused to be identified as black. He was not ashamed of his heritage, but he argued that he should be taken as anyone else in American society. He has always ringingly called for rejection of black and white separatism, whether in ghetto or swank suburb, in urging the GOP to pursue as its goal "an integrated society of magnificent pluralism." Overall, his relationship with the black community has been good. Negroes were proud when he was elected attorney general. That was progress. Few intelligent blacks criticized him when he moved from Roxbury to a "styleless split-level [house] with no virtue greater than a sufficiency of bathrooms" in Newton, an expensive suburb. Although the house is in a fashionable neighborhood, Brooke thinks the location is better suited for a gasoline station. Nor was he criticized when he sent his two teenage daughters to private schools.

"Wouldn't you give your child the best education you could afford?" he asked a reporter.

In Massachusetts the thrust of blacks for equality showed concrete results by 1963. Brooke's election had raised the hopes of blacks, who also took pride in the consecration of the Right Reverend John M. Burgess as the first Negro bishop in the history of the Episcopal Church in America. Both offices carried serious responsibilities, and Brooke, because he was a politician rather than a churchman, from the beginning of his administration was busy putting out brush fires.

In 1963 he clashed with the NAACP and other civil-rights groups when he ruled against a plan for a student hooky-for-a-day demonstration on *de facto* segregation. Brooke knew of the *de facto* segregation in Boston schools and had tried to mediate a long-standing dispute between the Boston School Committee and civil-rights leaders, but the committee rejected his offer. He also made it clear during the controversy that he valued demonstrations in dramatizing problems but only if they were properly controlled and legal.

One morning Louise Day Hicks, chairman of the Boston School Committee, slipped past newsmen into Brooke's office and tearfully asked for his help. It would be terrible to have kids running around the streets, she said. Couldn't he appeal to black community leaders as the highest elected Negro official and most powerful member of his race in the Commonwealth? She thought he could do more than anyone else to persuade black militants to call off the boycott. Brooke said he would meet with black leaders provided she kept his role from the press.

"Brooke and I picked up an evening *Boston Traveler* shortly after six o'clock just before we drove to St. Mark Community Center, where the meeting was to be held in a basement hall," Donald Whitehead recalls. "There, right on the front pages, was an account of Mrs. Hicks' session with Brooke. Hicks quoted the boss saying he opposed the boycott. He was furious and terribly embarrassed."

Harry and Clarence Elam, Herbert Tucker, Kenneth Guscott, Melvin King, Canon James Breedon and Hubert Jones, executive secretary of the Roxbury Multiservice Center, along with other community leaders such as Mrs. Melnea Cass, attended the meeting. Some rebuked Brooke, asking what right he had to speak for them. Before the meeting, which lasted until almost 3:00 A.M., was over, Brooke brought some of the black leaders to their senses. He brought out the weakness of Melvin King's proposal to have black Metropolitan Transit Authority employees stay away from their jobs.

"If you do that," Brooke said, "you will penalize all employers who hire blacks." He urged peaceful means to avoid the rioting which came later over the administration of welfare in Roxbury. When Melnea Cass had said Brooke would come to the community meeting, King, who was director of the Urban League, scoffed, saying the attorney general was too busy to come to a private session. By the end of the meeting he was willing to adopt a more temperate policy.

"I think Ed prevented a violent confrontation," Mrs. Cass said.

Brooke, who tends toward gradualism, is a pragmatist who recognized the difference between theory and practice and understood that the aim of racial balancing in schools was to end the heritage of fear that has divided mankind for so long on the basis of surface differences such as language, religion and color. He was as anxious as black militants to have an America where human beings of varying color and creed can enrich one another's lives "rather than pinching them into artificially limited horizons," as a writer said. This is no visionary goal. It is the law. According to the U.S. Supreme Court ruling of 1954, separate education is not equal education. Massachusetts endorsed this view with its imbalance law in 1965, and since it would take a four-fifths vote of the State Senate to repeal that law, racial balancing in the schools is here to stay.

One primary concern of the black community leaders at the St. Mark meeting was that the Boston School Committee recognize the existence of *de facto* segregation in Boston schools, and to that end they sent Clarence Elam and other soft-spoken moderates to reason with Mrs. Hicks and her committee. When the mediators' offer was rejected, black militants took action.

Brooke knew, better than some of the activists, that in an imperfect world, the concept of racial balancing is not always easy to implement.

In Boston the basic reason for racial imbalance was economic, not social. Blacks were clustered in schools because they were clustered in ghettos. The real issue was to solve housing, economic and social problems. Novelist James Baldwin, who does not always agree with Brooke, wrote that the best schools cannot help black children enough if they continue to be ill-fed, ill-housed and imprisoned in unsavory, crowded ghettos.

Brooke became involved when the NAACP–School Committee dispute erupted into protest picket lines in front of School Committee headquarters near the State House. Louise Day Hicks, a foe of integration, as chairman of the committee ignored racial imbalance, and when her board backed her, black activists told pupils to boycott schools. Brooke said that such action, however morally justified, was illegal. His ruling on "Freedom Stayout" followed questions sent him by Owen B. Kiernan, educational commissioner. Brooke said state law requires children aged five to sixteen to attend school unless they suffer a mental or physical impairment. "The School Committee can direct truant officers to retrieve absent pupils and where necessary seek their attendance through the district or juvenile courts."

His decision drew flak from black militants. Cornell Eaton, chairman of the Boston Action Group, said: "Brooke ain't nothin' but an Uncle Tom, man. That cat can't help us. He's too involved with the white power structure." The Uncle Tom label comes easily to militant lips. As a black member of the Illinois legislature said, "Now, just by making a sober, honest judgment on how civil rights should be won, you can be called an Uncle Tom by anyone who disagrees. What does this do to Negro leadership? It demolishes it." He adds that Brooke made black enemies because, "even going all out for civil rights, he argues that the Negro, too, has obligations to uphold." He argued that blacks had to demonstrate respectability; they had to demonstrate their wares in the marketplace for impartial judgment, like all other citizens. Commenting on housing projects he had inspected, Brooke said: "There's writing all over the walls, and children defecate right in the halls when there's a bathroom a few feet away. You can't just offer people opportunities; you have to show them what to do with those opportunities." He was talking about underprivileged people in general.

Brooke's ruling on the proposed boycott as being illegal drew fire from Kenneth Guscott, president of the Boston chapter of the NAACP. "There is no law in Massachusetts which provides for criminal action against a child, or against a parent or guardian who keeps a child out for any reason up to seven days in a six-month period." Lawyers denied that the proposed stayout was even a technical violation of the law. In any case, Negro leaders threatened to "physically defy" any truant officers who tried to remove children from freedom classes during the first boycott.

"To get the children attending freedom classes in my church," a Negro minister said, "the truant officers will have to remove me physically. I will give sanctuary to the children in the church." Brooke's friends the Otto Snowdens, as directors of Freedom House, backed the minister, calling the boycott "the same type of civil disobedience employed by the early American patriots in the Boston Tea Party."

Ignoring Brooke's warning, blacks kept their children out of school for two separate days in June 1963 and February 1964. Mrs. Hicks charged the parents with contributing to truancy.

In the first boycott the children heard lectures on Negro history and racial problems at the freedom schools. Brooke, on vacation in the Virgin Islands at the time, was accused of dodging the problem, and when he was away during the second stayout, he again drew static. Actually, speaking engagements and other commitments kept him on the move. In mid-June 1964 he attended a four-day convention of the National Association of Attorneys General in Honolulu. He worked under such pressure he had to unwind now and then, and when Al Benjamin on WNAC-TV once said he was in the Virgin Islands "again," Jerry Sadow exploded.

"What do you mean, *again*?"

Thereafter at news conferences, according to Benjamin, when Brooke didn't like a comment, he would say, "Again?"

121

(Benjamin added that when Bill Jackson drove Brooke to the airport in the winter, he wore a heavy overcoat, then slipped into a light coat before boarding the plane. "He often flew tourist in the front seat next to first class, and after the plane took off, the stewardess invited him into first class. We used to refer to the 'Brooke Airlines.'" "That happened once in a while," Brooke said, smiling. "But you must remember that we senators don't make much money." Once at Logan Airport, when Brooke was talking to one of the airport cleaning women in a VIP room, Jackson neglected to tell him his plane was about to take off. It was moving down the runway when a receptionist told the gateman Brooke wasn't aboard. The gateman signaled for the plane to back into position so Brooke could board it.)

Cardinal Cushing, agreeing with Brooke that boycotts were wrong, warned against breaking the law while endangering the community by sending upset children through the streets. This surprised the embattled black comedian Dick Gregory, who came to Boston in February 1964 to back the second boycott. Cushing above all others, he said, was the one person blacks could completely trust.

Before the second stayout, Brooke said the action could result in fines up to 50 dollars for each pupil induced to stay away from school. Realizing that this decision further alienated him from the black power structure, he added: "Boycotts, sit-ins, and demonstrations don't achieve the desired consequences in this Commonwealth. On the contrary, they merely intensify the resentment of the population . . . and undermine the best interests of the Negro community."

It was his first strong statement on civil rights. Brooke could see definite signs of progress being made by blacks, and he didn't want to jeopardize it. He warned against lingering recriminations. "You can't curse the white man for cursing you for a hundred or 200 years. What are you going to do, curse the darkness for another hundred years, or strike that match and get out of the hole?"

As abuse rained on him, Brooke repeated that he was the attorney general of *all* the people, that the civil-rights division in his office was merely one of 13. "The minute I become a specifically Negro attorney general, I cease to do justice to my office, and, in fact, I squander whatever effectiveness I might have in advancing civil rights." This was his rationale. In a speech in Seattle he repeated: "Those who participate in peaceful, nonviolent demonstrations are marching along the right road. . . . The only real progress toward civil rights in this country has been made by the judiciary. The need is for progress at the local level."

122

The heated controversy over racial imbalance in public schools brought Representative Albert A. Gammal, Jr., into the picture. To legislation designed to correct imbalance he attached an amendment precluding mandatory busing of pupils from one school to another, whereupon Ruth Babson, a black militant, charged that he was worse than a Mississippi racist. This put Brooke in an embarrassing position, since Gammal, who had sponsored legislation for Brooke in the past, was, as a reporter wrote, "looked upon as the attorney general's spokesman in the Legislature's lower branch." Cynics even suggested that Gammal was fronting for Brooke when he offered the anti-busing amendment as a means of watering down the imbalance proposal and possibly killing it. Snipers on Beacon Hill called the anti-busing measure the "Brooke amendment." Brooke made it clear that Gammal was operating solo. "I'm sorry if he harbors those thoughts. I certainly disagree with him." Brooke said he endorsed the findings of the Kiernan Commission, recognizing the need of action by the School Committee to correct the imbalance. He said he did not oppose busing "per se," adding that "in any busing program, no parent, black or white, is going to want to bus children from a superior . . . to an inferior school." Describing Gammal as "a very good friend" but a "very independent thinker," he said he hoped they could come to some agreement. Jerry Sadow, however, was furious at Gammal's amendment.

During the furore Gammal captained the Republican legislative baseball team, which beat the Democratic senators and representatives in a game played at Fenway Park. With Representative Michael Dukakis blocking the plate, Gammal snapped his ankle sliding home and was taken to nearby Beth Israel Hospital, where Brooke visited him. According to Gammal, Brooke made no effort to get him to change his mind about the amendment. Recalling that Governor Peabody had pleaded with the Senator to persuade him (Gammal) to vote to abolish capital punishment, which Brooke opposed, he quoted Brooke's answer to Peabody: "I would never ask a man to vote against his convictions."

Gammal's opposition to the racial imbalance bill's inclusion of busing was based on the theory that "you don't strengthen the weak by weakening the strong." But when he realized how strongly the black community felt about the matter, after his own proposal was beaten he voted in favor of the Racial Imbalance Bill of 1965, which passed.

By this time, within the limits of his authority, Brooke had a strong record on civil rights. He not only backed the Racial Imbalance Bill but also favored abolishing literacy tests as a voting requirement long before the issue went to the U.S. Congress. One of his first acts as attorney general was to file a brief in support of the Fair Housing Law, which banned discrimination in renting procedures in the Commonwealth. When he took office, the so-called all-out fair housing practices bill was before the Legislature, and Brooke was the only person to file a brief supporting this legislation and placing it in proper context both legally and morally. After negotiations for integrating public housing in Boston among the Boston Housing Authority, the Commission Against Discrimination, the NAACP and CORE stalled, Brooke drafted an agreement that was signed by all parties. He also helped draft legislation which sought to bar discrimination by unions and businesses in the state. Finally he drafted the Massachusetts brief in support of the 1965 Voting Rights Bill, to which 19 other states added their signatures. Brooke, more than any other attorney general of Massachusetts, was the author of prototype legislation.

He fished in troubled waters when he ruled that Massachusetts must respect the U.S. Supreme Court's decision against public classroom prayers. He said teachers could schedule periods of "reverent silence" at the opening of the school day, but it was illegal to schedule prayer sessions, even including grace at lunch. Vocal prayers were permissible at graduations and baccalaureate exercises, since attendance was optional and ceremonies were not part of the educational process. Pageants were lawful in connection with Thanksgiving, Patriots' Day and Memorial Day, because they were historical rather than religious. Religious holy days (Christmas, Easter, Passover) could be observed if no one faith or orthodoxy was stressed.

The Boston Pilot, the Roman Catholic oracle, approved Brooke's understanding of the traditional role played by religion in the educational life of the nation, conceding that "his opinion respects the U.S. Supreme Court decision, but carefully exempts those areas not included in it."

When Education Commissioner Kiernan asked for a ruling about North Brookfield, where prayers continued despite the Supreme Court edict, Brooke asked the local school committee to "immediately cease and desist your defiance of the supreme law of the land—the Constitution of the United States as interpreted by the Supreme Court."

The issue came before the Supreme Judicial Court of Massachusetts. In his finding, Justice Paul C. Reardon said in part: "An ordered society cannot tolerate the disposition to resistance made manifest by the School Committee of North Brookfield, no matter how high the motives which may have animated it. To hold otherwise would be an invitation to anarchy. . . . Let a writ issue permanently enjoining and restraining the respondent School Committee . . . from ordering the continuation of Bible reading and prayer in North Brookfield public schools." The court handed down its decision on December 17, 1963.

Brooke seldom receives hate mail, despite his controversial stands, not even on the prayer issue. "I got many letters disagreeing with my decision, but that would have been true no matter who was in office."

Brooke, whose skin is "the color of an early summer sunburn," has penetrating, coolly appraising hazel eyes and black wavy hair combed in a pompadour. He looks even more dashing these days with touches of gray hair at his temples. Brooke was well known to the public while attorney general because of his constant television exposure and public appearances. Weighing a well-distributed 175 pounds, he stood six feet one in the leather slippers he sometimes wore behind his office desk before the day's business began. He looks like a matinee idol, even with Richard Nixon's nose, as a writer noted; "it is uncanny to see it sitting there on Brooke's face, but his grin is of Kennedy quality. It throws out enough wattage to charm a vote out of a Democratic alderman at 30 paces and Brooke uses it shamelessly."

An early riser, Brooke had a cup of tea and a light breakfast with Remigia before slipping into the front seat of S-4, a black limousine driven by Captain William Jackson, an old faithful who has worked for Brooke since the doorbell-ringing days of 1950 and 1952. Using a permissible amount of political muscle, Brooke took Jackson off the rolls of a housing-authority job and made him the first black on the State Police. Massachusetts law requires an attorney general's body guard-chauffeur to be a state trooper. The rapport between Brooke and Jackson, as between Brooke and his other bodyguard-chauffeur, Leo J. Martin (now a retired captain of the State Police), is a study in congenial dignity. Jackson, who has driven the boss hundreds of thousands of miles and has followed him in and out of barrooms during vote hunts and along campaign trails that led to every corner of Massachusetts, will yield to no one in his admiration for Brooke. Jackson, who is also retired from the State Police, cannot remember a single ugly incident during all the turmoil of campaign years.

"I have been everywhere with the boss and never once heard him hissed or booed, even by drunks. I never heard him tell a dirty joke, swear, or say anything mean about an opponent or about a man's race. He is easy to work for, but once, when I pressed too hard on the accelerator, he told me to slow down. 'Now, listen, boss,' I said, 'I don't tell you how to run the attorney general's office, do I?' "

Jackson, who would never step inside the attorney general's office for fear of interrupting something, said Brooke is the only person in the world for whom he would drive 15 hours a day, day after day, if necessary. He is torn between getting the boss to appointments on time without exceeding speed limits *too* much and respecting Brooke's aversion to high speed. One day on the Worcester Turnpike Gammal sped past them.

"He must be going at least 90," Brooke said. Minutes later Jackson drove past Gammal, who had been stopped by a state trooper. Brooke shrugged and said nothing. Meanwhile, the trooper, recognizing Gammal, wished him good evening. "Sorry, Rep," he said.

Brooke, who sits in the front seat with his drivers, gets restless in slow traffic. Evan Dobelle, who took over the Boston office after Mrs. Ireland was promoted to the Bicentennial regional directorship, was driving him to the Court House in January 1972 when traffic got snarled. Brooke put on his gloves and jogged six blocks to get to a swearing-in ceremony on time.

During the 30-minute ride to the State House from his Newton home when he was attorney general, Brooke skimmed through *The Boston Herald, Globe* and *American* and, when possible, *The New York Times,* but only when the car was moving. At red lights he turned to smile and wave to traffic cops and commuters waiting for buses. Even without recognizing the black limousine, they knew who he was.

"How *are* you! Good to *see* you!" Brooke flashed his grin at the delighted people, who would have a candidate to remember at the polls.

Warm and gregarious as a politician, he can quickly shift moods. By the time he reached his office—usually by eight—he was more businesslike. He is a fiend for punctuality. Office personnel who reported for work a few ticks after nine might find him casually stationed as they rounded the first "buoy," a water cooler near the entrance. He would bid them a frosty "good afternoon" until they got the message. Once Jerome Sadow protested, saying that since he often worked overtime, why couldn't he come in a few minutes late once in a while?

"That's a reason," Brooke said, "but not an excuse."

Nancy Porter, delayed by bumper-to-bumper traffic now and then, said: "You want to fight back, to say it wasn't your fault, but you can't; he hasn't actually scolded you."

Even after moving to Washington, Brooke checked his aides at his political offices in Springfield and Boston. At 9:05 one morning he called his office in the JFK building and asked for Georgia Ireland, his administrative assistant in Massachusetts.

"I think I can hear her footsteps coming down the corridor," Claire Alfano, a secretary, said.

Brooke then asked for Maura O'Shaughnessy, second in command, who came in with Georgia a few minutes after Brooke called. "Well, tell Maura to call me the minute she gets in." At 4:50 that afternoon Sally Saltonstall called Maura from Washington on other business. At the end of the conversation Maura said, "Tell the boss I just got in." Tardy staffers who lack Maura's Celtic aplomb accept Brooke's "time-clockery as the eccentricity of a hero," a writer said. "And," says Roger Woodworth, "after all, punctuality is the etiquette of kings."

Woodworth isn't the only devoted member of a talented staff whose morale is consistently high, in contrast with the staff of a Massachusetts congressman who had a following known as "the Keith Alumni."* Brooke's team functions smoothly, with no feeling of oppressive discipline, although conscious always of Brooke's low-key authority. One morning Nancy Porter, tanned after a holiday in the Barbados, came in just before nine.

"Good morning," Brooke quipped. "I'm glad to see you have integrated our office." He told another secretary who returned from a vacation with a deep tan: "Imitation is the sincerest form of flattery."

When word came of Albert DeSalvo's arrest, the premises became a madhouse as telephones jangled and reporters swarmed in. Brooke, amid the bedlam, kept his cool. Only once did he lose his temper, to the extent of getting into a shouting match with an assistant attorney general who had leaked information about DeSalvo to the media. Brooke, who never lets the sun set on his anger, apologized moments later. "I'm sorry I lost my temper. When you lose your temper, you lose your case."

In a rare disgruntled mood** Brooke can be captious. One morning

---

* The reference is to Congressman Hastings Keith of Massachusetts.
** "When he gets angry, he bites his lower lip," Remi Brooke told the writer. "He used to punish Edwina and me by making us sit on a chair in the dark for a half hour or so." Remi, admitting she is the family "rebel," once had to sit tight for an hour.

an assistant attorney general took Maura O'Shaughnessy and two other secretaries on a tour of state prisons. Brooke, who had not been told, was annoyed when they returned in midafternoon. He told Maura to bring in three cartons of unanswered mail on Woodworth's desk.

"Look at these," he said, scooping up handfuls of letters. It seemed that Roger, who can dictate nonstop for several hours over Brooke's signature, knowing about what he would say in any situation, was behind in his correspondence. "You could have been answering these letters instead of going sightseeing," Brooke said. Before day's end he told Maura he didn't mean to be harsh. His staff know when they get out of line. On their desk they find a note: "See me. EWB."

Although some of the girls think he is vain, he is no dandy. During working hours he is always impeccably tailored, usually wearing a dark, conservative suit. No one has ever seen him on the job in a wrinkled suit or, in recent years, when he has added a sharkskin suit and brighter ties to his conservative wardrobe, in the same suit more than twice in one week.

While attorney general, he took an occasional breather in an apartment at 21 Beacon Street, where he had a two-room office, kitchenette and bath. Here Mrs. Helen Cavelle presided as den mother.

"I have just gone on Social Security and am going crazy," she wrote Brooke in 1962. "I have admired you from a distance for a long time. I am a registered nurse and a widow, and if you will pay my carfare from Allston, I'll work for you full time for nothing." Mrs. Cavelle, who is 25 years older than Brooke, handled the mail and the telephone calls, did some hunt-and-peck typing, and made sure he had spare suits and clean linen ready for a quick change. She also cooked for him, after getting his favorite recipes from his mother. "At that time he really loved kidney stew," she recalls. For in-between snacks Brooke during one spell liked oatmeal cookies and a glass of skimmed milk. It became a ritual to have them on hand after he went to Washington and returned to his Boston office for one of his frequent visits. One morning, while looking for a document, Claire Alfano found seven unopened packages of oatmeal cookies in his desk drawer.

Like Miss O'Shaughnessy, Mrs. Cavelle knew when to humor the boss. When he refused to install an air conditioner in the inner office, she and two other office workers pinned on placards that read: "Don't Be a Simon Legree. Agree to an Air Conditioner. Unfair to Workers at EWB Political Office, 21 Beacon Street, April 7, 1965." They paraded up and down the hall and refused to let Brooke into the office until he met their demands. Another stunt had Brooke thinking he had been drinking. While he was out on an appointment, Nurse Cavelle bought three five-dollar wigs for herself and the girls. They rearranged the furniture and donned the wigs. When Brooke opened the door, he raised his hands to his head with a "Where-am-I?" look.

Another loyal supporter was Wendy Dewire, a school teacher who was on Brooke's campaign staff for both attorney general and Senate campaigns. In 1962 she called to say she would work for him as soon as she got over the measles. Wendy got her political baptism at 6 Beacon Street, where all by herself for ten days she handled five telephones. Miss Dewire grew up politically with the "gang," retiring reluctantly from the scene when Brooke went to Washington. She recalls Roger Woodworth, coatless and shoeless, writing letters and speeches on his Corona. When really concentrating, he told Wendy, he didn't want to be disturbed. "If anyone asks for me, say I'm out of town." One morning a caller, anxious to see him, was about to leave after being told Woodworth was in Washington. As he reached for the doorknob, Woodworth, in his stocking feet, walked in eating an apple.

"Oh, hi, George," he said. "I just got back."

When the workload got heavy, Woodworth, as he did later in Washington, slept on an office sofa, and after washing his socks and underwear, hung them up to dry in a lavatory.

When Brooke left his State House office, often well into the evening, he took home a briefcase full of documents and went over them in his den against a backdrop of operatic selections. He worked about 15 hours a day, counting speaking engagements. Exclusive of political campaigning, in the early 1960s he addressed meetings about three times a week. Occasionally a member of his staff substituted for him. Edward Swartz recalls the night Brooke told him to speak at an Episcopal church meeting. The title? "A Christian Role in a Changing Society." Ten days later Swartz gave the same speech in a synagogue, changing the word "Christian" to "Jew."

In rare moments of relaxation Brooke went to Suffolk Downs to bet on the races, occasionally taking a flyer at the 50-dollar-a-ticket window. He also liked prizefights, as well as professional and college football games. One night he took Donald Whitehead and Leo Martin to watch Tom McNeely, a local heavyweight with a good punch and an inviting chin, knock out Tommy Hunsaker, a Southerner, so quickly that ringside cynics yelled fake. After the fight Brooke and his friends congratulated the winner, then dropped by to comfort Hunsaker, who, when he realized he was in the presence of the attorney general, his assistant and a state trooper, thought he was headed for jail. Later, while in the Senate, last-minute business kept Brooke from flying out of Logan Airport in a helicopter with his daughter Remi to see the Sonny Liston–Cassius Clay fight in Maine. "Even if we had left the airport on schedule, we would have arrived too late for the fight, it was over so quickly," Remi said.

Brooke also squeezed in time to attend the theater and opera and at least once a year took Remigia to New York to see Broadway hits. He had little time for his hobbies—tennis, swimming and bicycle riding—except when at Oak Bluffs.

Brooke never neglected his Christmas stint, when Marines ("Nick") Nikitis, a former deputy sheriff who served Brooke as a jack-of-all-trades, took toys supplied by a plastics manufacturer to orphanages, and handed out gift certificates to the needy who came to the office the week before Christmas. Nikitis also handled patronage. When a Brooke fan wanted a low-number license plate, it was Nick who called the right man at the Governor's office.

During his first term there was a dramatic confrontation when Governor Ross Barnett of Mississippi, a racist, came to speak at Harvard Medical School. When Barnett paid a courtesy call to Governor Peabody, Brooke was invited to meet him, knowing Barnett had tried to bar James Meredith, a black, from the University of Mississippi. Barnett was sitting with his back turned when Brooke entered Peabody's office.

"I would like you to meet our attorney general," Peabody said to Barnett, who rose and turned as Brooke, extending his hand, grinned. "Nice to meet you, Governor."

Adjusting his glasses and clearing his throat, Barnett, shaking hands briskly, managed a "Hi." Then, the ice broken, the three men settled down for a friendly chat. Later Brooke declined an invitation to visit Governor Barnett in his executive mansion in Jackson, wryly explaining that he preferred to visit the University of Mississippi.

One of two framed documents on the walls of Brooke's State House office was a silhouette of Abraham Lincoln over the familiar words: "If I were to try and read, much less answer, all the attacks made on me, this shop might as well be closed for any other business. I do the very best I can, and I mean to keep doing so until the end." On another wall, near a ship model and tokens of esteem from B'nai B'rith and the Knights of Columbus, hangs a diploma pronouncing

Brooke an honorary attorney general of Georgia. Asked about it, Brooke said, "with canary feathers sticking to his smile," that the great state of Georgia had honored him when he attended an attorneys general convention in Atlanta. "They couldn't overlook me," he said. "In his cool, inward way Brooke enjoys that diploma," a writer said.

As attorney general Brooke upstaged Governor Peabody. "Hardly a day passes but that Brooke's handsome countenance appears on the television screen, as he gently announces some new indictment or launches some new phase of his investigation into the Commonwealth's diseased civic life," *Harper's Magazine* reported. Tips on corruption were still pouring into the complaints section, and monumental evidence coming from the Crime Commission led to a backlog of indictments that would take years to prosecute. The scandals remaining to be exposed would make the underground-garage case look like a Kiwanis Club luncheon, Woodworth said. "The magnitude of them suggests a moral cesspool which even the most decent people in Massachusetts don't care to admit exists—they simply don't want to face the fact that the situation is as bad as it has become." The effect on Brooke, who didn't want to be remembered as another crusading Tom Dewey, became depressing toward the end of his first term.

"He's no longer simply disturbed—he's jaded," Woodworth said. "And he's already suffering from a nervous stomach."

Brooke had other problems. Political opponents who considered him a burr under their saddle wanted to get rid of him. Soon after his election in 1962 federal authorities had begun an audit of his income-tax returns for 1959, 1960 and 1961. When the federal government waited until the day before Brooke announced the indictment of House Speaker John Thompson to say the IRS was checking Brooke's tax returns, political motives were suspected. There was a strong feeling that U.S. Attorney General Robert Kennedy wanted to liquidate him, seeing him as a potential threat to his brother. There was, in any case, no doubt that the reasons for the audit were political.

The IRS found that for one of the three years he had overpaid his tax; in another year he had failed to report a fee of 13,000 dollars, part of the 15,000 dollars he had received as conservator for a state hospital patient. When Brooke explained that his secretary had made a clerical error, the matter was dropped. Then, just as suddenly, it was revived. On May 7, 1964, Herbert Tucker, Brooke's lawyer, charged that the investigation had become a "harassment." Brooke's tax problems, *The Boston Globe* reported, had "become the best-known secret in Boston. Rumors about the tax investigation have been circulating in political circles for many months."

Brooke's tax records," Tucker said, were a hodgepodge of poorly drawn documents describing the flow of cash from a checking account that Brooke used for both his legal and his household business. They had been kept by a part-time secretary whose job included answering the telephone, typing wills and legal briefs, writing out checks for Brooke to sign and making bank deposits.

Ernest Nasif of the IRS and Tucker went over the records. Then in June, Nasif asked Tucker to have Brooke prepare a net-worth statement, the first sign that the heat was on. Net-worth statements are often required in fraud cases.

Tucker told Nasif of a 1957 venture in which Brooke had lost heavily. He had bought the former *Morning Star* estate on Oak Bluffs, Martha's Vineyard, as a summer home, partly with money given him by his father. Connected to the residence was a six-room party house which Brooke had tried to turn into a clubhouse for people unable to join exclusive clubs on the island. When he failed to get a zoning waiver after investing heavily in remodeling the guest house, Brooke was in a financial squeeze. Much of the loss from this project was recorded on the 1959 tax return.

In August Tucker turned over to the IRS all of Brooke's canceled checks for the three years in question, then advised Brooke to hire a tax expert with more knowledge of the IRS Intelligence Division's operation, since his (Tucker's) tax experience while with the IRS had been mostly on the civil side. At this point James M. Kendrick, a tax lawyer, entered the case.

Although a Democrat, Kendrick thought his Republican client was being used as a pawn in a political gambit. "Is it anything to worry about when a man whose professional future depends on his public reputation cannot get his tax case settled in 16 months, or more, despite the rumors that are destroying him?"

Kendrick gave the IRS an analysis of Brooke's finances and tax returns, including an itemized expense account across or out of the country between 1958 and 1962. Brooke had made eight trips, in-

---

* While attorney general, Brooke won a far-reaching Supreme Judicial Court decision which established the right of law-enforcement agencies to obtain individual copies of federal income-tax returns when relevant to the subject matter under investigation.

cluding one to speak at Florida A and M in 1958, when the college paid his expenses. He paid his way to Madrid in 1960, and that same year the GOP National Committee financed his trip to the Republican Convention in Chicago.

At his own expense he went to Acapulco, Mexico, in 1961, as National Judge Advocate of Am Vets. In 1961 the Boston Finance Commission paid his fare to Seattle, Washington. In 1962 he went again to Acapulco at his own expense, and also went to San Juan, Puerto Rico.

At a hearing at the end of November an IRS agent asked Brooke whether it struck him odd that the amount of his adjusted gross income (5,600 dollars) for 1959 was almost 10,000 dollars less than a single fee he had received during that year. Kendrick explained that the transaction reflected a loss from other sources. It turned out that Brooke, after taking a loss on the guest house at Oak Bluffs, had borrowed money from his father, who, by the time of the IRS investigation, was retired and in a terminal illness. When the IRS demanded an interview with the elder Brooke in Washington, Tucker and Brooke objected, arguing that after suffering a stroke, Mr. Brooke was bedridden and that his mind was not active and his speech was slurred.

"The mere fact that you say you are from the IRS is going to disturb him and perhaps permanently damage his spirit," Tucker said, asking the IRS to limit their interview with Mr. Brooke. It was no use. On November 7, 1963, IRS agents interviewed the elder Brooke in his bedroom, two months before he died.

"We arrived at the Brooke home around 10:30 in a taxi," Tucker said. "Mrs. Brooke offered us coffee and doughnuts in the living room and we talked informally there for a half hour. Then Mrs. Brooke said, 'Well, I suppose you want to see Dad. I'll get him ready. You better come up alone first, Herb, and try to explain this to him.' "

All loans from the elder Brooke to his son had been detailed in an analysis given to the IRS, and thus in the 90-minute interview no new facts emerged. Mrs. Brooke sat on the edge of the bed during this time, comforting her distraught husband.

"The trip proved nothing," Tucker said later, "and the agent who was there knew it."

During the long investigation the IRS had checked oil companies, butcher shops, department stores and organizations to which Brooke had contributed. They had subpoenaed friends, neighbors, shopkeepers and relatives. *The Boston Globe,* after a conference in a private room at Locke-Ober's restaurant between Brooke and top *Globe* editors who knew the story but wanted more background information on it, aired the full details, and the investigation slacked off and was soon forgotten.

Having survived the crisis, Brooke pondered his next political move.

CHAPTER NINE

Brooke and Volpe

B ROOKE FACED a tough decision in 1964. Some advisers told him to run for reelection as attorney general to continue rooting out corruption, arguing that a two-year term had not given him enough time to complete the job. Others told him to swim with the current that was propelling him and run for governor. Brooke wavered, cautious as usual.

For one thing, he knew that if voters ratified a constitutional amendment in the 1964 election, the governor's term would span four years beginning in 1966. There was a chance that Robert F. Kennedy—one candidate whom Brooke probably could not defeat—might run for governor in 1966. But Brooke had a more immediate obstacle in Governor John Volpe.

By 1964 Brooke and Volpe were eyeing each other with a suspicion that Boston newsmen felt was "entirely justified." According to a political columnist, Brooke had "played showcase Negro for Volpe and the GOP on the Finance Commission and as candidate for secretary of state in 1960. In 1962 he boldly ran for attorney general and was on his way, on his own. He made more hay of Volpe's Crime Commission than Volpe did." In 1966, when reminded how a once-obscure state officer had become a major candidate for the Senate, Volpe said, "I know it only too well." By that time, the two men had exchanged quiet insults. Brooke complained that Volpe's overdeveloped ego made him hard to work with, and Volpe called Brooke "a man consumed with his own ambition." According to *The Catholic*

Digest, Volpe managed "to be humble and cocky at the same time." A reporter snidely remarked: "Both men are usually considered good judges of character.

There were neutral observers who agreed that both men are consumed with ambition, as what politician isn't? Francis Perry, who was overwhelmingly endorsed as the GOP candidate for lieutenant governor at Worcester in 1962, didn't always get a fair shake from Volpe, then running for governor. The Democratic candidate for lieutenant governor was Francis X. Bellotti, who, like Volpe, is an Italian-American. During a swing through the Berkshires Volpe and Perry found themselves sharing a platform with Bellotti in North Adams, where the Italian-American population in the factory town is high. Perry shook his head when Volpe, well within view of several hundred persons, warmly embraced Bellotti, who was running with Endicott Peabody. The Peabody-Bellotti team won.

In 1964 Brooke hedged when asked whether he would oppose Volpe in the GOP gubernatorial contest.

"Normally, I would have to say I wouldn't oppose him." Advisers warned Brooke he might come a cropper if he did. "I told the boss he might not be able to beat Volpe at the Republican Convention, and warned that a bruising interparty fight could ruin both candidates," Hardy Nathan said. "There had been some talk by this time about the boss being too pushy."

To win the gubernatorial endorsement Brooke would have to defeat three prominent Republicans who, by the spring of 1964, were actively campaigning for the nomination: Volpe, State Senator Philip A. Graham and former Representative Francis W. Perry. Perry at that time was getting mileage out of his series of position papers which attacked both Volpe and Peabody. Peabody advisers suspected that Perry, who had worked for Brooke as a dollar-a-year consultant while exposing "sweetheart" deals which resulted in major convictions, was in the race as a stalking horse for Brooke. "One thing is certain about Perry's candidacy for the governorship: the former lawmaker is bent on destroying former Governor Volpe's image before Republican delegates convene in Boston this summer to make their decision on the GOP standard bearer for 1964," a columnist wrote.

The Peabody camp was also concerned over the constant publicity Brooke was getting as he went before the grand jury to prosecute both Republicans and Democrats. More Democrats were involved because, in Brooke's opinion, Massachusetts was fast becoming a one-party (Democratic) state. In simple terms, "Members of a party enjoying a lopsided majority become arrogant and lazy," Brooke said. Thus more of the malefactors were Democrats.

Volpe also had cause to worry, especially if Brooke indicted any officials appointed by the former governor (Volpe) who had created the Crime Commission. In 1944 the commission was threatening literally hundreds "of people in and on the fringe of state politics." Brooke was himself in a delicate position, as a reporter noted: "Before the Crime Commission has completed its probe of politics in Massachusetts, Brooke will be faced with the unpleasant task of prosecuting many individuals, including some who are friendly to him."

The overall picture was rosy, however, for by the time of the pre-primary convention in June, Brooke could be in a position so commanding he might win the nomination if an early ballot deadlock developed among the three candidates.

Peabody considered Brooke more formidable than Volpe, knowing the attorney general's voter appeal had peaked by 1964. There was another factor. The racial crisis sweeping the country, though mounting, might not have gained enough momentum by voting time to hurt Brooke in the general elections in November. It was more likely that Brooke would be more vulnerable in the 1966 elections if the racial crisis deepened in 1965 and 1966, as political prophets predicted. As governor of Massachusetts, Brooke would be in a strong position to solve some of the pressing problems involved. The Peabody assessment was logical.

Brooke knew that color prejudice was rampant in 1964 because of the growing backlash against Negro militants. The Boston Irish voting bloc highlighted the danger during the St. Patrick's Day parade in South Boston in March 1964, when an angry mob in the Celtic citadel pelted an NAACP float with beer cans and ripe vegetables.

Brooke was warned that if he won the nomination, he would be running against a well-known Yankee (Peabody) who could get votes (Republican included) in a state that might not be ready for a Negro governor. He had a far better chance of being reelected attorney general and, as an incumbent, would have a good chance to run for the Senate in 1966 if Leverett Saltonstall retired. A loss to Peabody, on the other hand, might be a fade into the sunset.

Despite all arguments, Brooke was ready to run for governor if a deadlock froze party machinery at the Boston Arena convention in June. According to Perry, Brooke had telephones set up all over the arena and was set to move fast to corral delegates.

In an April speech at the Statler Hilton Brooke's criticism of the GOP was taken as a trial balloon for his candidacy. "Some day, some time, someone in this Commonwealth is going to have to stand up and do the things which need to be done . . . and he cannot be primarily concerned with winning the next election," he said, as Volpe, Perry and Graham listened. The 900 Republicans at the ninety-seventh annual dinner of the Middlesex Club were startled when Brooke suggested that the GOP would benefit from a hot primary battle to get rid of bad losers "who take their ball and go home." He compared this petulant attitude with that of Democrats who kiss and make up after mauling one another in primary battles. When the dust settles, "they do not sulk, but join together and march on to victory."

Brooke grinned when a newsman said his speech sounded like an announcement for governor. "Oh, boy," Brooke said.

"Do you have anything to say on that, sir?"

"No, that's your business." Brooke was still smiling. Executive Councilor Margaret M. Heckler, a Republican, was asked her opinion.

"It certainly sounded like a candidate's speech," she said.

According to Brooke, Perry congratulated him after the address. "The speech is tremendous," Perry said. Brooke added that Perry "would not say that if he didn't mean it." Brooke had chuckled during the evening when Perry referred to the President as "Light Bulb Johnson," a phrase coined by Goldwater to needle the President for saying he had shut off lights in White House closets to save taxpayer money.

This speech was the strongest sounding board for Brooke's candidacy. When Volpe won the nomination at the June convention, however, Brooke announced that he would seek reelection as attorney general.

At the Republican Convention at the Cow Palace in San Francisco in the summer of 1964 Republican liberals gloomily watched their choice, Governor Nelson A. Rockefeller, give way to Barry Goldwater, and most of them accepted defeat. At the convention Brooke was the only state or national official to give three addresses to the nation. He presented former President Eisenhower with the Gold Convention Badge in view of a national TV audience on July

14, giving a five-minute tribute to Ike, who spoke at the convention. The presentation came immediately after his speech. Brooke was the only New Englander besides former UN Ambassador Henry Cabot Lodge to play a major role at the convention. He and Senator Saltonstall headed the 34-member Massachusetts delegation at a conference with the GOP National Committee at which he (Brooke) urged a strong civil-rights plank in the GOP platform.

After Rockefeller was eliminated, the liberals in a frenzied last-minute drive rallied behind Governor William W. Scranton of Pennsylvania. "In deep, well-modulated tones," Brooke seconded Scranton's nomination.

"Let's not fool ourselves," Brooke said. "The Republican party faces a crisis." In the din few listened to him. The reason was pure cynicism, according to a magazine writer. Any Negro who could be lured to a Goldwater convention must be tame. "How like political leaders—Democratic or Republican . . . but particularly Republican —to produce an exhibition Negro who was five-fourths white. So much, amid the anger and the earache, for Edward W. Brooke."

Even as an organization man Brooke could not accept Goldwater's view. In this case his instinctive feeling of politics was evident, as implied by Richard Fleming, formerly research director of the Massachusetts Republican State Committee, who said conservatives felt "Brooke as a Negro had to take liberal stands [in 1964], including not endorsing Goldwater—stands that they would not readily accept if they had been taken by a white candidate."

Brooke said he would not campaign for Goldwater unless he clarified his views on civil rights, extremism and control of nuclear arms. This he failed to do, and Brooke, risking his future in the party, refused to support him.

He ran his own campaign as a Republican who did not back the national ticket. "I'm Ed Brooke, the Republican candidate for attorney general," he told groups. "I would like to have your vote."

Harcourt Wood, Brooke's campaign manager in 1964, predicted rough going because of the Goldwater problem, increasing indications of a Democratic sweep, underestimating the Democratic opponent and the feeling that Brooke was an odds-on favorite.

"I didn't leave my job for four months because I thought Brooke was a shoo-in," Wood said.

There was also some flak from blacks, still smarting because of Brooke's 1963 opinion that school stayouts were illegal, making parents criminally guilty. Roxbury constituents were talking about his

139

unfulfilled 1962 campaign promise to clean prostitutes off a street corner in Boston's Harlem. Brooke's 1963 stance on school boycotts was likened to John F. Kennedy's stance in opposition to federal aid to parochial schools.

Brooke's statement that there were unspannable gaps between his and Goldwater's political philosophies did, however, come at the right time. A new Committee Against Political Extremism (CAPE) was circulating 5,000 postcards designed to force GOP candidates to say whether they denounced Goldwater. (CAPE was an adjunct of the Massachusetts Freedom Movement, then emerging as the strongest activist civil-rights organization in New England.)

"Canon Breedon . . . will soon come to speak with you about your relationship to the Goldwater candidacy," the postcard read. "I want you to know that he brings with him my concert and support." Civil-rights organizations distributed the cards to be signed by anti-Goldwater voters and mailed to Brooke. "If we can show there is a substantial frontlash on pro–civil-rights sentiment here," a CAPE spokesman said, "perhaps the Republicans will be less leery of speaking out against Goldwater."

Brooke aides answered each card with a personal note explaining his position. Tired of answering questions about Goldwater, Brooke would go no further.

When Goldwater came to Boston during the 1964 campaign, Volpe met him at Logan Airport. Brooke stayed away.

Pollsters could find no clear-cut trend early in the campaign. A taxi driver who said he would vote for Goldwater because he resented black militants added: "I'll vote for Brooke because he does a good job and is honest."

Fund-raising for Brooke's campaign had begun in February, with 3,500 persons attending a party at the Donnelly Memorial Theatre in Boston. Tickets were scaled from a hundred to ten dollars to make it a popular affair. Victor Borge, with Leonid Hambro, a pianist, was featured in *Comedy in Music,* along with Miriam Makeba, whose parents were members of the Swazi and Xosa African tribes. Late in October Brooke was again feted at a 100-dollar-a-plate dinner, at the Sheraton Plaza, with Gael Mahony the toastmaster. Senator Saltonstall introduced Brooke, and Governor George Romney of Michigan was a guest. Earlier in the month Senator Jacob Javits had come to Boston to endorse Brooke at a Parker House luncheon. Dinner parties, champagne receptions, regional gatherings and luncheons gave Brooke more exposure than in previous campaigns. Giulio Mastrangelo, a famed baritone, attracted a big crowd at a "Friendship Dinner" in Framingham.

Brooke went after the Democratic votes he needed to win. He invaded a veterans' post in Worcester even though he knew he could count on few votes, since most of the members were Democrats. Nevertheless he walked around shaking hands with everyone, and stayed longer than most politicians, a member said. "He was a hit, too. I'm not sure he didn't pick up a few votes."

During the campaign Brooke wrote a letter endorsing the candidacy of Jack E. Molesworth for the U.S. House. He was running against House Speaker John W. McCormack, the incumbent, and Noel Day, a black independent who was co-chairman of CAPE. Molesworth had backed Goldwater. When Molesworth added Brooke's name (the only Republican) to his endorsers, he included additional material in his campaign literature that was factually suspect and inflammatory, as well as in bad taste, whereupon Brooke was besieged by telephone calls from liberals accusing him of favoring an anti–civil-rights candidate.

"We had a session one night with Brooke," Harcourt Wood recalls. "We decided to send out postcards repudiating Molesworth's implications. We got our material to the *Minute Man's Press* around 3:00 A.M. and set type with the aid of a flashlight. The next night [Saturday] about 50 volunteers addressed over 15,000 cards. We worked from Friday night until 3:30 A.M. Sunday. The cards said Brooke's letter had been used without his approval."

Molesworth fumed. "I was a strong supporter of Ed Brooke," he told reporters. "In 1964 I spent a great deal of time talking Goldwater Republicans out of cutting him." He accused Brooke of being expedient, as if this were sinful for a politician. "On civil rights . . . he was conveniently out of town during the two school boycotts when Louise Day Hicks was looking for him."

By 1964, Brooke was aware of the devious ways of Bay State politics. One night in Wellesley, GOP State Committee Chairman Frederick C. ("Buck") Dumaine, former president of the New Haven Railroad and now chairman of Amoskeag Company, in a bumbling introduction said: "It is my pleasure to introduce you to Ed Brooke. And just because he's a Negro doesn't mean he isn't as good an American as any of us." A reporter reminded him that Negroes had been in America since 1513.

Brooke, responsive to the tides of change, originally had wanted

Francis W. Perry of Duxbury to succeed Philip K. Allen as chairman of the state Republican committee in 1964, and was upset when Dumaine was elected by a four-vote margin over Donald Whitehead at the Hotel Bellevue in Boston. Accosting Lloyd Waring, a former GOP state chairman of the Republican state committee and of the GOP finance committee, in the lobby after the vote, Brooke said he had no confidence in Dumaine's ability to bring harmony to Republican ranks. "You don't know what you've done to me and the party," he added.

When Allen resigned and GOP leaders realized that Perry was not cold and mean enough to take over, Saltonstall, Volpe and Brooke sent a telegram to all state committeemen endorsing Donald Whitehead, an assistant attorney general in Brooke's office in charge of veterans' affairs, as Allen's successor. (Whitehead would resign as assistant attorney general if he took the post.) Whitehead, who had rejected the job earlier, changed his mind when Waring offered it to Dumaine, and asked Waring to get Dumaine out of the picture. Like Brooke, GOP brass felt Dumaine was a publicity seeker, a novice and a political amateur who didn't have enough rank-and-file Republican support to get the party back on the track. Arguing that Dumaine had never been intimately involved in GOP affairs, they felt he wouldn't do the nuts-and-bolts job needed—that he would consider the assignment a hobby. They were also warned by big-money men on State Street, who recalled the ill fate of the New Haven Railroad under Dumaine's management, not to expect sizable donations to the GOP treasury. Others thought Buck was too tactless and flamboyant for the job, and there were remarks that Dumaine, who still speaks admiringly of certain John Birch Society members, was lukewarm in the field of civil rights. Brooke aides recall his reference to the boss as "that inkspot."

Actually, Dumaine is a jovial, jaunty and outgoing, if foot-in-mouth, tycoon who tried to build up the state Republican organization according to the conservative gospel of Lloyd Waring and Elmer Nelson. He has the saving grace of not taking himself too seriously. "After that close vote at the Bellevue," he grins, "about 95 percent of the state committeemen assured me they had voted for me." He was less amused, however, when, after failing to call Brooke's office for a fence-mending appointment, he was kept waiting for over two hours. "He came unannounced and the boss was busy," Roger Woodworth said. "It was that simple."

As was feared, Dumaine showed a yen for pontificating on policy matters, instead of acting as an agent or lightning rod for GOP office-holders. He leaked information to favorite columnists, and took un-deserved credit for masterminding the 1964 electoral victories of Volpe, Brooke and Richardson. Once, instead of raising campaign funds, he loaned the state GOP 180,000 dollars.

In the summer of 1965 Brooke met with Volpe and Richardson in the Governor's office to discuss a replacement for Dumaine as state chairman. Later, in a private session with Governor Volpe, Senator Saltonstall agreed that Buck must go. Volpe's chief secretary, Tony DeFalco, who gave Dumaine the bad news, recalls that in his farewell speech to the state committee Dumaine gave such an emo-tional talk some of the ladies wept. State Senator John Parker suc-ceeded him.

Brooke's opponent, former State Senator James W. Hennigan, Jr., who comes from a politically oriented family (he is now chairman of the Boston School Committee), still had his sound trucks and workers on the street when the polls closed. Though handicapped by little money, he staged a hard-hitting campaign. Touring every part of the state, and realizing that the Crime Commission was the top issue during the contest, he charged that it was a partisan exposé of corrup-tion at the state level, especially after the indictment on a charge of conspiring to arrange a bribe came down against Furcolo. Brooke, who ran a soft-sell campaign from the attorney general's office, letting his work with the commission speak for itself, disagreed, as he scored on his radio and TV appearances and toured the state evenings and weekends.

"The presentation of evidence from the Crime Commission and our cooperation . . . were never political. . . . I believe the voters agreed with us and have endorsed the work of the . . . commission and our effort to cooperate." Brooke said he would continue to pre-sent evidence to a special grand jury. "We still haven't seen all the evidence uncovered by the . . . commission."

Remigia, no longer hesitant about campaigning, often pinch-hit for him, touring the state with Leo Martin. At factories she greeted em-ployees as they left work and passed out campaign literature. She was a guest at dozens of receptions and spoke at scores of rallies. In the city room of *The Salem News* a reporter asked what she thought of her husband's indicting Furcolo for taking a bribe.

"I think that is very good," she said. "It makes me so happy."

Noticing the puzzled look on the reporter's face, she asked: "Well, so then it is not good? What is not so good about a man taking a bride if he is single?"

In 1960 Brooke hadn't asked her to campaign. "You have the house on your shoulders; you take good care of the girls; you have enough to worry about." In 1962, when Brooke was nominated, she had been bewildered by all the scurrying around and was often confused during the ensuing campaign. "It was all so new and mysterious to me." In 1964 she found the tour exhilarating but was always thankful to get home where politics could be forgotten.

Brooke's popularity was mushrooming. One unique headquarters was a 200-year-old home in Westminster whose owners invited anyone interested in the reelection of Brooke to a warm welcome. "Ed Brooke is a favorite of both Democrats and Republicans," they said, "and has been considered to be way out in front in the current battle for ballots. But therein lies possibly the greatest danger to his candidacy—complacency, or overconfidence. His friends take nothing for granted." There is a poem about the historic house:

> "Too old-fashioned," I've heard say,
> I like a house which is built that way,
> Heavily timbered, with lots of room,
> Fireplaces—for cold and gloom—
> Knocker and latches and narrow stairs,
> And one or two high-backed rocking chairs.

"Yes," said the master of the house, "and many are they who like a man's record built that way, built in the way Brooke has built his, sturdy, and true, with distinguished service in war and peace, in keeping with the best traditions of our Commonwealth."

Brooke, who is sentimental, was pleased.

Sensing defeat, Furcolo and Gerard F. Doherty, Democratic state committee chairman, charged that Alfred Gardner, as chairman of the Crime Commission, had violated the Corrupt Practices Act by contributing 100 dollars to Brooke's campaign. Furcolo had been indicted by a grand jury under Brooke which heard evidence collected by the commission. Doherty and Furcolo demanded that Brooke either resign or disqualify himself. Brooke told 1,100 supporters at his 100-dollar-a-plate birthday banquet at the Sheraton Plaza that he would not "shirk my responsibility" in ruling whether the donation was illegal. He ruled it was not in a ten-page decision which read in part: "In my opinion, the General Court never intended to enact a law which would make it a criminal offense to contribute to political committees legally constituted in behalf of incumbent officeholders while permitting contributions to all other candidates." He said the provision of the election law cited in the Gardner case was intended to protect public employees and officials from solicitations, not to prevent them from donating.

In the closing week Remigia took a tour in Volpe's bus with the wives of other GOP candidates, including Jenny Volpe, Ann Richardson and Jessie Sargent, with one stop at Boston's Faneuil Hall for a rally sponsored by the Massachusetts Federation of Women Republicans. In a self-service cafeteria at an insurance company in Worcester, the bus driver fretted because he was dropping behind schedule. This was because Remigia, after the other wives had left, took her scarcely touched tray to the return slot and stuck her arm through to shake hands with the kitchen help whom she couldn't see. She would have walked into the galley if she had had time, having learned the trick from her husband, who always visited barbershops and kitchens in hotels and inns during campaigns, shaking hands with barbers, busboys, waiters and chefs.

As returns trickled in on election night, results were never in doubt. By nine o'clock victory was assured for Brooke, and his headquarters at the Sheraton Plaza was bedlam as bands struck up victory songs and hundreds of supporters whooped it up. Hennigan conceded two hours later.

In the lopsided win Brooke took communities by larger margins than in 1962 and carried all the state's 351 cities and towns except two towns on the Rhode Island border (Blackstone and Millville). In 1962 he had beaten a Yankee Republican for the nomination and trounced an old club fighter in the Democratic arena in the general election. In 1964, in the face of a million-vote landslide by President Johnson, he whipped another Boston Democrat of Irish descent, piling up 1,543,900 votes and a plurality of almost 800,000. It was otherwise a disastrous election for the GOP. "The racial issue has been beaten, beaten, beaten," Brooke said.

In an interview with a *Life* writer he had other comments: "There's no one Negro leader. Negroes are proud of a Martin Luther King or a Marian Anderson—they identify. But there is no one who can speak for the Negro people." He said he liked street campaigning. "There's a bit of ham in all lawyers and politicians. People buoy me up. . . .

145

Television freezes me." During spot TV interviews in his office Brooke surrounds himself with his staff to rid himself of a feeling of isolation.

His prospects in the GOP picture were brighter than ever.

A gracious loser, Hennigan said most of his fellow Irishmen voted for Brooke. "The Irish are the most liberally minded people in the world. They're sensitive and sympathize with the minority group—maybe because they were once discriminated against." Hennigan compared Brooke to another glamor politician: "He's almost like Eisenhower—he has a special attraction for voters. It's a certain quality that is hard to describe."

Even after this landslide, diehards said he was twice elected attorney general because Democrats ran creampuffs against him. Kelly and Hennigan were hacks: "The people weren't voting for Brooke [in 1962], they were voting *against* Frankie Kelly," a Democrat said. "In fact, five percent of the electorate—105,000 voters, most of them from Democratic areas—left their ballots blank in that contest. Registered Democrats outnumber registered Republicans nearly two to one in this state, and all we need is a palatable, clean-cut candidate to rally the Democratic majority and turn Brooke out." Democrats further noted that Kelly and Hennigan had scanty funds, little TV time, few newspaper ads or the overall exposure Brooke had. "When he runs up against a Democratic candidate of stature equal to his," repeated Gerard Doherty in 1966, "then you'll see him tumble." The problem was finding a candidate "of equal stature."

Self-styled pundits said voters who gave Brooke whopping majorities in the two contests didn't know he was black, but an Opinion Research Corporation poll just after the election found that 76 percent of its sample Massachusetts voters could pick Brooke's name as that of a Negro from a list of public figures both black and white. Other observers dredged up an old argument. Apart from his ability and integrity, they said, Brooke profits from a guilt factor. "A lot of people are for him *because* he's a Negro," a reporter said. "It salves their consciences." Carl Rowan, himself a highly intelligent black, has his version of the "expiation of sin" concept: "For a lot of proper Bostonians, being able to vote for an articulate Negro is the cheapest kind of conscience-clearer. Electing Brooke is a much easier way to wipe out guilt feelings about race than letting a Negro family into the neighborhood or shaking up a Jim Crow school setup."

Certain voters do support Brooke because they want to compensate for a guilt feeling over their desire to keep schools and neighborhoods segregated. Brooke gets big majorities in the same districts that give big majorities to Louise Day Hicks, anathema to blacks. Her political strength stems from racial resentments of lower middle-class whites.

The basic fact is that Brooke is a magical vote getter primarily because he has tremendous ability, is honest, sincere, and, with his personal magnetism, able to captivate even hostile audiences. "He could not only charm a nightingale out of a tree," one admirer said extravagantly, "he could bring a dog down off a meat wagon." Despite the fact that virtue is not always rewarded in Bay State politics, class often counts in the voting pattern. This explains why the "classy James Michael Curley" was elected to Congress while indicted for mail fraud. "A private suspicion is that Brooke owes much of his success to the voters' simple fascination with watching politics practiced by a master," a writer observed. "There has not been much class in Massachusetts public life since they caught the Brinks robbers. (Except for the Kennedys, of course. But the Kennedys have been primarily national politicians.)"

Asked whether being a Negro helped a candidate in a statewide election in Massachusetts, Brooke shrugged. "I think it balances."

As he began his second term as attorney general, Brooke said it would take up to four years for his office to complete prosecution of pending cases on evidence supplied by the Crime Commission, which was to expire on June 30, 1965. Brooke hailed the commission's final report and its effective work through the preceding few years. "It has shown that no matter how high a man may sit or how powerful he might be, he is still subject to investigation, indictment, prosecution, sentencing, and jail." Thanks to Volpe, Peabody and Brooke, new Massachusetts laws curbed many temptations which lead to corruption. They put a strong conflict-of-interest law on the books. Scandals such as the underground-garage case had far less chance of success after severe penalties for falsification of official reports put teeth in the law, which also requires independent authorities to open their meetings to the public and their books to the state auditor. The Crime Commission* recognized the traditional fragmentation of power as a primary cause of corruption. Brooke placed the responsibility for eliminating corruption in state government on elected officials, however, not on his office or on a citizens' crime commission.

---

* When the Crime Commission died on June 30, 1965, it was replaced by a beefed-up Criminal Division in the attorney general's office.

147

"If elected officials can't do it, we should get rid of them," he said on a panel discussion of the Crime Commission report. He called for more funds from the legislature to enable his office and the offices of district attorneys to hire investigative staffs to curb graft. District attorneys at the county level, he said, needed funds and personnel to provide aggressive law enforcement.

To replace the Crime Commission, Brooke favored a state FBI or some sort of state-level investigative force to root out crimes such as loan sharking, gambling, murder for hire and hijacking. He said an agency could ferret out criminal elements normally bypassed by regular enforcement agencies.

In his second term Brooke championed legislation to protect borrowers from unscrupulous loan companies, to reduce air pollution and to improve election procedures that were unfair to blacks. When more criticism arose about his not using his office to advance the cause of civil rights, he repeated: "If I did confine myself to Negro problems alone, there would hardly ever be another Negro elected to public office except from the ghetto, and justifiably so."

If Brooke's progress was any criterion, Negroes had come a long way, as a national magazine noted in a comment on Volpe's inauguration as governor in January 1965, an occasion that was "pregnant with historic irony."

On the walls of the Massachusetts House of Representatives are murals commemorating the eminent Yankee statesmen-scholars who have been the founders and custodians of the Commonwealth. Among those sharing the platform with Volpe in this august setting were Brooke and Henry Cabot Lodge, Volpe's personal guest. Ambassador Lodge, after giving his chair on the dais to the Roman Catholic Bishop of Springfield, during the entire ceremony sat on the floor, "never quite deciding where to rest his very long legs." It was a memorable moment.

"Here was Henry Cabot Lodge, of the Cabots who talked only to the Lowells and to God, literally at the feet of the colored lawyer and the erstwhile hod carrier [Volpe] who were now the leaders of his party. Massachusetts had turned its history inside out."

The day after his reelection Brooke launched a campaign to revitalize the GOP by suggesting a national conference to articulate a constructive program. A few days later, on the nationally televised *Meet the Press,* he asked the GOP to hold a special convention in 1965 to enunciate a new program. In December 1964 he had written

Republican governors, urging them to unite on a cohesive policy. Republicans, he said, "should face the plain and grim fact that our party's candidate for President and the platform on which he campaigned were overwhelmingly rejected by the voters of the country." The appeal fell on deaf ears.

In February 1965 the Young Republicans attended a four-day leadership training school at the Sheraton Park Hotel in Washington. One night the 500 Young Republicans gave Goldwater, whom they considered a fallen idol, a standing ovation when he blamed his defeat on gross distortions of his position on two issues: that he would "risk war too easily," and that he would "destroy the Social Security system. They were . . . the biggest political lies ever told in this campaign."

On the following night the same group sat stunned as Brooke told them that Goldwater's bid for a white backlash vote was mainly responsible for the crushing defeat in November. The GOP, he said, must attract votes of minorities by opening doors to the sons and grandsons of immigrants, the great-grandchildren of slaves. Brooke had anticipated a cool reception. Instead, he drew cheers as he pressed his attack. "We gave the voters a wrong choice when we had an obligation to give them a constructive alternative. We joined in an 'Operation Dixie' that was based on a gamble for white backlash. . . . As a consequence we lost millions of votes."

At a press conference at the hotel Brooke said GOP leaders should open all committees, North and South, to blacks. They should, by integrating their Southern clubs, gain control of the South.

After his reelection, a *U.S. News and World Report* correspondent asked Brooke whether he sought a higher office.

"I guess I wouldn't be a politician if I didn't," he said, "and I certainly plead guilty to being a politician."

"What office? Governor? Senator?"

"Frankly, I don't know at this point. I find both offices very challenging goals, of course. This year probably will be the year of decision for me. You know, in this business you either go up or out."

Brooke recalls conversations he had with John F. Kennedy when the late President was Senator. "John F. Kennedy used to say to me, 'Ed, you ought to be a Democrat,' and I said, 'Jack, you should be a Republican.' " Brooke added that Kennedy "had a truly unusual mind, and was unquestionably an intellect. He had great integrity, charm and warmth and seemed to me a man of destiny." In another conversation, Kennedy told Brooke: "In my opinion, Ed, there are only two public offices worth having: U.S. Senator and President of the United States."

"You notice that Kennedy bypassed the governorship," Brooke said.

As early as 1962 Brooke's mother dropped a hint to Charlotte Yaffe: "Someday, I feel Edward will come back to Washington. Lev Saltonstall isn't going to stay in the Senate forever, you know." In the summer of 1965 Brooke told Volpe in a telephone conversation that he was interested in the Senate, and a few weeks later he floated "one of those trial balloons all politicians have in their back pockets to test public reaction and support: 'I may not run for anything. Perhaps I'll just take up private law practice,' he said. He didn't expect anyone to believe him."

At his glittering forty-sixth birthday fete on October 26, 1965, a thousand couples paid 25 dollars each to fill his political war chest with 50,000 dollars. A reporter at the party at the new Sheraton Boston Hotel guessed where the money would go: "It's headed toward some good hard campaigning," he grinned. "I'll tell you that much."

Before the dancing began in the grand ballroom Brooke posed for pictures with Saltonstall, then with Volpe, then with Margaret Heckler, the only woman on the Governor's Council. A reporter wondered whether Margaret would run for governor while Brooke and Volpe vied for the Senate. "Then he [Brooke] started to pose with Tom McNeely, a heavyweight fighter from Arlington; would McNeeley challenge Volpe for governor, while Brooke ran for . . ." Newsmen were having a field day guessing. It was obvious that Brooke had his sights raised on some political office; among those he kept guessing were Saltonstall, Volpe, Lieutenant Governor Richardson and Senator John Parker, chairman of the state Republican committee, all of whom were at the ball.

Saltonstall told the gathering he would not announce his reelection plans until the summer state convention. "I have many things to consider before I make an announcement."

Brooke's relations with Volpe were then cordial, as was evident when they chatted amiably at the VIP reception before the ball. Saltonstall glanced at two giant birthday cakes which were inscribed: "Happy Birthday to General Ed Brooke from the staff."

"You won't be around in 1966 if you eat half of that big birthday cake," he said.

150

Late in 1965, when asked whether he would run against Saltonstall in 1966, Brooke hedged, quipping that the Senator looked healthier than he did.

A feature of the banquet was a massive scroll attached to an easel which rolled on and on so everyone could sign a birthday remembrance. "The size of the cakes was unbelievable," a woman said. "Proof of the love for Brooke that night was the way people waited hours in line to have their programs autographed."

In the fall of 1965 Brooke, learning that Volpe was thinking of running for the Senate, told Volpe and Richardson he would like to be a candidate for the seat if Saltonstall retired. Brooke banked on polls that showed him stronger than Volpe for either the Senate or governorship. Party leaders considered both front-liners for the possible vacancy. The matter was again discussed, during the 1965 summer when Brooke met with Volpe and Richardson to discuss a replacement for Dumaine.

If Saltonstall sought reelection, Brooke would find himself between a sword and a wall. He would have either to seek a third term as attorney general or to oppose Volpe in a fight for governor, a dangerous choice, since Volpe had strong backing from liberals because of his vigorous stand on civil rights. This group, along with the Italian-American bloc, was one from which Brooke had always drawn strong support.

Of the six constitutional officers serving in the Commonwealth in 1965, Brooke and Secretary of State Kevin White had the best press relations, according to Al Benjamin. "The press respected Brooke for his fluency and candor, as much as for his honesty. Yet he was the least accessible of the men holding office. He refused to give out his home telephone number to reporters and was the most difficult official to reach evenings and weekends for statements. Even close associates such as Roger Woodworth and Georgia Ireland well know the line that separates the public servant from the private person, beyond which few ever penetrate."

"Brooke has a certain aloofness or veneer that allows him to remain distant from us and at the same time appear warm, relaxed and personal," a reporter said. "He has an odd combination of naïveté and political savvy that is disarming at the least and suspect at the most. One moment he is the humble public servant; the next, the wily, polished politician."

Over the years the news media, recognizing him as a superfluent straight shooter who could be counted upon for succinct and often newsworthy appraisals and quotable one-liners, built him up, and he helped his own cause by learning not to alienate newsmen. Although he generally answers questions directly, he will, when necessary, look a questioner in the eye and tell him he cannot discuss the issue at the moment. "If the interrogator tries to rephrase the question, he will look into space and repeat his refusal with a quiet finality," John H. Fenton wrote in *The New York Times*.

Brooke, with a good change of pace, puts out verbal brush fires with a needling humor, mild sarcasm or gentle admonishment which sometimes makes bumptious reporters feel as if he had told them to pull in their ears. Three reporters who occasionally badgered him during press conferences while he was attorney general were Al Benjamin, Frank Bucci of *The Boston Traveler* and Salvatore J. Micchiche of *The Boston Globe*. Bucci and Micchiche had studied law and, when the mood was upon them, tried to paint Brooke into a corner.

"Boss, you've got to break those guys up," Jerry Sadow told Brooke. "Don't let them sit together at press sessions." Brooke dubbed the trio the "law firm of Benjamin, Bucci and Micchiche," and was usually able deftly to field their hot-line shots.

"Remember, Sal," he would say, "you're only a second-year student. You haven't passed the bar exam yet."

Brooke is at his best when a reporter tries to snow him with a double-loaded question, as when one asked whether he considered the opposition to his candidacy by conservatives the result of the support he had from the ADA-Communist sector. In a soothing, judicial monotone Brooke said he did not associate his adversaries with responsible conservatism, adding that he had always been supported by responsible conservatives and expected them to back him in his next campaign. He noted that Americans for Democratic Action (ADA) are responsible liberals, not Communists, and he welcomes their support.

"The TV cameraman shuts off his machine, and Brooke turns, laughing amusedly, to the interviewer who tried to torpedo him," John Skow wrote in *The Saturday Evening Post*. "He pats the man on the shoulder." Noting further that Brooke told interviewers he has never classed himself as a liberal, moderate or conservative, Skow added: "This became known as 'taking a Brooke.'"

During interviews, Brooke may break into a brief and sometimes bitter laugh at a probing or tasteless question, or don a furrowed look. Then, suddenly, he turns on the charm, as if on cue. He has well-defined mannerisms. He may greet an old friend or a reporter whom he trusts with a quick affectionate hug. During a conversation he nods briskly. "Yeah, yeah—that's right, that's right," he may say when he is "on." He smiles and gestures frequently when he talks, and standing behind a lectern at a press conference he may jingle coins in his trouser pockets or tug at the side pockets of his jacket, especially when the questioning gets sharp. He uses his hands to bring out a routine point, with a casual wave, but in a more serious, analytical mood, he thrusts out both hands, fingers curled up, according to one observer, as if he were cupping an imaginary object. Judge Benjamin Gargill notes an idiosyncrasy: "When an interview is over, he crosses his legs and twitches his big toe. At least, he *seems* to be twitching his big toe."

Cornelius R. Owens, then a *Boston Globe* reporter, said Brooke "would write you a personal note if you wrote anything nice about him, and sometimes—when you criticized him—he would thank you for your interpretation. He had a clever way of making you feel like a heel. And he had an uncanny knack of buttering up newsmen." Owens recalls an embarrassing incident involving Remigia Brooke.

On a freezing night in January 1965, when Brooke was visiting his sister, Helene Amos, in St. Croix, the Virgin Islands, Remigia used a state automobile because the family car* had broken down at a time when she had to rush to her daughter Remi,** who was ill at a private school (Wykem Rise) in Washington, Connecticut. Normally, state-owned cars could not leave the state without permission of the executive department, but since 1958 this rule had not been applied to cars used by constitutional officers. The Dodge Remigia was driving—registered to the Commonwealth—was assigned to the attorney general.

As she made a wide turn in Route 47 in Connecticut, her car col-

---

* Brooke now keeps one car at his summer home in Oak Bluffs, another at his residence in St. Martin, and a third in Washington. Remigia and Edwina each have a car. "I have the best car in the family," the nineteen-year-old Edwina smiled. It is a 1972 Oldsmobile. Edwina graduated from Pine Manor Junior College in June and expects to continue her education. Remi, who is engaged to John J. Coyle, vice-president of Alpine Chalet, Inc., needs a few more credits at Northeastern University for a B.S. degree.
** After attending public schools in Roxbury and Newton, Remi attended Ursuline Academy in Dedham for a year before enrolling at Wykem Rise. Later she was at Beaver Country Day School for a year (as was Edwina) before graduating from Newton High School and going on to college.

lided with another vehicle, and state troopers and firemen were called to the scene. Firemen gave a sedative to Remigia's mother, Teresa Ferrari-Scacco, and took her to Waterbury General Hospital, where she was treated for a back injury and cut forehead.* Remigia posted a 25-dollar bond which was declared forfeited on January 29, and the case was closed on April 6. Then, according to Brooke's office, a personal injury and damage suit was filed in the amount of 790 dollars. When it was learned that the Dodge was uninsured, the Connecticut traffic commissioner notified Registrar Richard E. McLaughlin of Massachusetts that all cars owned by the Commonwealth would be barred from Connecticut highways. McLaughlin called Brooke, and an insurance company assumed the risk of all financial responsibility. McLaughlin then called the Connecticut commissioner, who lifted the ban after one day. Both cars in the accident, according to Connecticut State Police, were traveling "at a low rate of speed."

Tongue in cheek, Owens wrote in *The Globe:* "The sympathy of mothers across the state went out to Mrs. Remigia Brooke when it was learned that in the rush to reach the bedside of her child, who was stricken with a virus infection, the state car was involved in a collision." Owens said the state used to provide only the governor with a car, but that currently four cars were available for the governor—two for the attorney general. "It would be more efficient if the legislature established a special 'employee' status for the wives to permit them to drive the publicly owned limousines placed at the disposal of their husbands," Owens wrote sarcastically. "With such an arrangement, embarrassing situations could be avoided, and in a few years, it might be possible to further liberalize the program so children of the constitutional officers, as they reach driving age, might be permitted to use the vehicles assigned to their parents, thus relieving the older folk of the necessity of acting as chauffeurs for their offspring."

Not realizing she was being ribbed, Remigia wrote a note to Owens, thanking him for his consideration.

In an exclusive in *The Boston Herald* in September 1965, David Farrell wrote that Brooke was seriously considering retiring from office at the end of his second term as attorney general. "Unless an opening occurs at the top of the GOP ticket via retirement of Senator Saltonstall, Brooke in all probability will finish his present term and

---

* The ailing Mrs. Ferrari-Scacco now lives in a hospital in Framingham.

accept one of the many positions which are or will be available to him."

Actually, at that time Brooke hoped circumstances would warrant his running for the Senate. But to keep from being too pushy after Farrell's piece appeared, Brooke publicly wrote the Senator urging him to continue his distinguished service. Jerry Sadow, however, in a transparent effort to build up Brooke as a potential successor to Saltonstall, sent the article to Washington columnists. Robert Healy, political editor of *The Boston Globe,* then embarrassed Brooke by writing: "The effect of such circulation of [the retirement story] would be that the Republican party in Massachusetts was holding back one of its brightest stars and the highest elected Negro official in the country."

Finally, on December 29, 1965, Saltonstall invited the press to a federal courtroom in Boston and read a statement: "After painstaking thought and consultation with my family and friends, I have reached the decision that I will not be a candidate to the U.S. Senate in 1966." It was the end of a 45-year-long career for Saltonstall, who was seventy-three. "It's not easy for me to leave the Senate after 22 years," he said months later, "but I feel a great deal better about it, knowing I will likely be succeeded by a man like Brooke."

There was no hint at the time of his announcement, however, that he favored Brooke. There was widespread speculation about his successor. *Time* reported that among hopefuls "Brooke was first off the pad—and promptly became the favorite in informed speculation. In a press conference that followed Saltonstall's by only 24 hours, Brooke declared his candidacy and program in appropriate sonorous senatorial generalities."

Much has been written about Brooke's scooping up the ball and making an end run around Volpe. Actually, after Volpe, Brooke and Richardson were elected in 1964, they often met at 21 Beacon Street for a chat over a snack, as the three constitutional officeholders of the state. According to Donald Whitehead, one of Brooke's political advisers at the time, Brooke often talked candidly about the situation, but Volpe and Richardson refused to reveal their own political ambitions.

"John, you are, as governor, head of our party, and I respect that. If Salty doesn't run again, and you want to, I'll defer to you and support you. If not, I will run."

Volpe, confident that Saltonstall would seek reelection, said there was nothing to discuss. "Old soldiers never die," he said. Two of his closest advisers, Tony DeFalco and Attorney Joseph Tauro, Jr., who in 1971, on Brooke's recommendation, was named U.S. Attorney to succeed Herbert Travers, confirm Volpe's attitude.

Both were with Volpe the day before Saltonstall announced he would not run, and they heard Volpe's conversation with Brooke, who had called to say he had a premonition that Saltonstall wouldn't run. Again Brooke told Volpe he would run unless he (Volpe) announced. Brooke felt that either Volpe or he should move fast, since other possible candidates, such as Bradford Morse or Silvio Conte, might announce their candidacy if there was an opening. That night DeFalco got a tip from Charles Colson, a White House aide to Nixon and a former Volpe assistant, that Saltonstall would not seek reelection. He told Volpe, who was still not ready to make up his mind.

Meanwhile, as Buck Dumaine points out, GOP leaders who favored Volpe wanted Saltonstall to run, then resign, since he could easily be reelected without spending much money, leaving the field open for Volpe to appoint himself or some other Republican as Saltonstall's successor. According to DeFalco and Elmer Nelson, Saltonstall was too honest and honorable to stoop to such a tactic. They say the Senator decided not to seek reelection because of his wife's ill health.

In any case, Saltonstall phoned Brooke at the attorney general's office a few minutes after his press conference. "I immediately called Volpe and told him Saltonstall was not going to run," Brooke says. "There was a long, dead silence." It meant that Saltonstall had not notified Volpe, who recovered to say he would get back to Brooke. Volpe, who was again with DeFalco and Tauro, called Brooke back within ten minutes.

"I repeated to Volpe what I had said so many times before—that I would run if he didn't. He asked me to wait a month or so before reaching a decision—to leave the situation fluid. 'Let's get together and discuss it.' I told him I wouldn't wait a month, a week or even a day."

According to Woodworth, with the Saltonstall crunch imminent, Brooke prepared two game plans. If the Senator ran, he would hold a press conference and pledge full support for Saltonstall. "If he decided not to run," said Woodworth, "we planned to call every Republican of consequence in Massachusetts, starting with congressmen, senators, representatives, and state committee members." Brooke called a friend, the manager of the Sheraton Plaza, and ordered orange juice, coffee, tea and Danish pastry for those he invited to the Oval Room. "I need your support," he told each one. "I want your support. Please come."

After the second telephone call, Brooke and his staff spent seven solid hours calling Republicans. While Jerry Sadow, Jan Sjoland and Nancy Porter took turns manning telephones in Nancy's outer office, which was next to Brooke's private sanctum, Woodworth briefed the boss on who was being called so he could have a greeting ready. Woodworth dictated phone numbers from a master list. The staff was encouraged by the enthusiastic response of Richard Treadway, a former state senator and national committeeman who had been a strong Volpe supporter. It was a good augury. Later, John Powers, former president of the state senate and a Democratic national committeeman, told Brooke: "I don't understand how you did it. It was a masterful example of jumping the gun." By the end of the day Brooke aides had called almost 500 Republicans.

Volpe insists he was not miffed because Brooke beat him to the punch to stake out a claim on the Senate seat. In a telephone interview with this writer in June 1971 Volpe, then Secretary of Transportation, gave his version of the events: "I was thinking of my political future late in 1965, aware that Saltonstall might not seek reelection. I planned to run as governor or senator. Brooke told me he would like to run for one of these offices. . . . 'You're governor, and you have first choice,' he said. 'I appreciate it, Ed,' I said. 'Give me 30 days to decide.' "

Then, forced to make a quick decision, Volpe felt that since his primary background was on the executive level, he would seek reelection as governor. Volpe said it was "poppycock" that he was angry and upset when Brooke announced his candidacy, adding that he had admired Brooke for years. "We worked together. Ed is aware that he is a politician, as I am, and we can both take a joke. You have to get a laugh out of life or you won't last long in politics. Ed and I are kindred spirits."

Actually, Volpe was on the spot. As the top Republican in Massachusetts, he felt his credentials were superior to Brooke's. He had never announced his intention of running for the Senate, however, fearing that "any overture might stimulate unwanted political comments." Brooke was also treading on eggshells, but he was encouraged by polls. At the moment of decision, knowing that Brooke would run for governor if he ran for senator, Volpe was painted into a corner, for, as Woodworth said, "A good number of white Yankees in this party would not look with favor on Ed as head of the state party." So Volpe stood pat.

Remigia and her daughters were with Brooke when he formally announced his candidacy on December 30 as over 500 supporters applauded. Magazine writers and newsmen from New York and Washington were on hand to spread the word.

"I'm sure today's announcement won't be as much of a surprise as yesterday's," Brooke said.

Among those who had urged him to run for the Senate were Senator Jacob Javits of New York and Governors George Romney of Michigan and William Scranton of Pennsylvania. A reporter asked if Brooke would seek the help of individual Republicans or groups outside Massachusetts to advance his candidacy.

"My fight is local . . . and I intend to keep it in Massachusetts." Noting that his campaign might cost up to a million dollars, he said he hoped to raise all the money in the Bay State.

A newsman rephrased the question about soliciting outside help, and Brooke smiled. "Some names come to mind and some don't." This obvious reference to Barry Goldwater drew a laugh.

Asked when the campaign would begin, Brooke said, "It started yesterday. I don't expect it to stop until November 1966." Another reporter asked whom he expected his Republican opponent to be. "I would hope there would be none." Then, more seriously, he said there seemed to be only two other possible GOP contenders: Congressmen Silvio Conte and F. Bradford Morse. He had phoned both men within an hour after Saltonstall had made his announcement on December 29. "Sil Conte said he was undecided and Morse said he might run, but had not made up his mind. Hasty Keith [U.S. Congressman Hastings Keith] said he definitely would not run."

During the calls, Brooke had also phoned former House Speaker Joe Martin, then in Florida. Martin encouraged him to run. Brooke told the gathering in the Oval Room that Governor Volpe had told him he expected to run for reelection and that Lieutenant Governor Elliot Richardson would either seek that post again or run for attorney general. He said he had made no choice as to his successor as attorney general and would "not make any or dictate who my successor should be."

The questions kept coming. Would he abide by the Republican Convention choice of a candidate, if he was not chosen? "I'll cross that bridge when I get to it—and I don't expect to get to it," he said.

158

Did he expect race to be a problem in the senatorial campaign? "It hasn't been a major factor in any of the other campaigns. If the people of this state are so racially blind as to elect me by 800,000 votes, that's good enough for me."

He refused to compare his qualifications with those of Mayor John F. Collins, who had said he would run for the Senate, and when asked about another possible candidate—former Governor Endicott Peabody—he smiled.

"I don't want to say anything good about Mr. Peabody, because that's bad politics, and I don't want to say anything bad about him, because I don't know anything bad about him."

In answer to another query he said, "I don't like debates. They don't really help. If anything, they hurt." He added that he would campaign strictly on the issues, which he expected to be peace and the preservation of freedom. He implied he would continue to be a loner. "I'm a pretty independent fellow. I will do first what is in the best interest of the nation and second what is in the best interest of Massachusetts. I won't let a minority of my party dictate what I should do." In a parting shot he said he would serve out his full term as attorney general to January 1967. "I love that office."

Three days after Brooke announced his candidacy *The Boston Herald* said Volpe was not out of the Senate race. "Anything can happen in the next several months." The same newspaper a few weeks later said Volpe would seek reelection as governor, "but Brooke's adversaries in the GOP harbor hopes that the Governor can be persuaded to change his mind." Brooke said, "I would consider him [Volpe] a very serious opponent if he runs for the Senate." At this time Brooke served notice that he was "in all the way" and would go into the September GOP primary if he didn't get the nod at the June GOP convention.

Polls influenced Brooke more than the wishful thinking of the conservative wing of his party. Three days after Saltonstall bowed out a poll showed Brooke had nearly as much strength as Saltonstall, with Volpe ten percent behind. Brooke also ran well in a poll for governor.

Although Brooke had said earlier that color would not be a campaign issue, he touched off a furore when he told a national television audience on the *Today* show that his opponents "always saw to it" that voters were informed he was a Negro.

"I wouldn't dignify it with comment," Secretary of State Kevin H. White snapped. "Any campaign I have run has been at the highest level, and if anyone should know this, it should be Attorney General Brooke."

Kelly flatly denied the allegation. "I have never referred to Mr. Brooke as a Negro and I just don't believe in referring to people by race, creed or color. I can also say that at no time whatever in the campaign, to my knowledge, was there ever a reference to Mr. Brooke's race directly or indirectly by any of my followers."

Former State Senator James W. Hennigan, Jr., said he had never referred to a man's race in his life. In an earlier television interview Brooke had said the 1964 contest against Hennigan had been clean, adding that being a Negro "certainly didn't hurt me" during the campaign, since he had carried Boston and practically every city and town in the state.

People outside Massachusetts—even the most competent observers—could not understand Brooke in the context of the color issue. Marianne Means, writing in *The Washington Post,* thought it "inescapable" that race would be a real issue in the campaign. In a letter to the editor of *Life* magazine a local supporter objected to the media's constant identification of Brooke as a Negro. "We don't think of him in terms of his skin color. Rather we think of him as a man of sound judgment and great heart, and wish the best for him."

While civil-rights activists had no love for Brooke, some Southern editors had surprisingly kind words to say about his candidacy. *The Norfolk* (Virginia) *Pilot,* noting that most Negro candidacies were from "safe" black constituencies or were mere protests without hope of victory, added that Brooke's career fitted neither pattern. "He is a candidate in the mold of postwar political success: active, attractive, articulate, young (forty-six), who also happens to be a Negro. . . . Win or lose, Mr. Brooke's candidacy is in the great and honorable melting-pot political tradition."

Just before leaving for a Caribbean holiday Brooke had a few words for reporters. "In my concept of government, great improvements can be achieved in the legislative halls. That is where the real responsibilities lie. That is where social changes are taking place, and I want to have a part in those changes." He said he had launched his political career as a candidate for state representative and that he had long wanted to be a U.S. senator. "It offers great opportunities to make important contributions to Massachusetts and to the country. I think my experience as attorney general, in researching facts and making decisions based upon facts, is a good foundation for my Senate candidacy."

He returned from the Virgin Islands at the end of January to find his personal mail had more than doubled—much of it from Massachusetts, but some from around the country. An Illinois Republican (white) sent him a five-hundred-dollar check for his campaign chest. *"Life, Coronet, Newsweek, The Saturday Evening Post* and *The Reader's Digest* have been around,"* writes a *Globe* reporter, "festooned with Leicas and Hasselblads and speaking accents strange to Beacon Hill."

On February 6, 1966, *The [New York] Sunday News* reported that the "GOP current champion vote getter has bolted away first from the starter's gate and is running 'hard and scared' for U.S. Senator." Meanwhile, Goldwater disciples and GOP diehards who, like the Bourbons, never learn and never forget were looking around for a more representative candidate.

CHAPTER TEN

Brooke and Peabody

THERE WAS mutiny in Massachusetts Republican ranks in 1966. Ruffled young GOP militants, cringing at the thought that the ADA had twice endorsed Brooke for political office, joined other dissidents who hoped to come up with a conservative candidate to oppose Brooke at the June preprimary convention. Congressman Bradford Morse was one possibility. Most anti-Brooke conservatives planned to limit their campaign to the fight for the convention endorsement, which was believed to represent over 100,000 votes, but some diehards talked about organizing Republicans to work for Brooke's Democratic opponent if he was the GOP nominee. There was also talk of fielding an independent in the preprimary.

Coming to Brooke's defense was Lloyd B. Waring, even though he had been an ardent supporter and was a personal friend of Barry Goldwater. Waring had headed Goldwater's Massachusetts organization and served as his New England coordinator at the San Francisco national convention. Waring, who had also been chairman of the Massachusetts Republican state committee and chairman of the state finance committee, called Brooke "a very attractive candidate" who was sincere and honest and dedicated to advancing the cause of the GOP. He promised to help in every way, including raising money. He said he was also speaking for leaders of the Goldwater campaign.

The pendulum took a swing when Brooke on a nationally televised interview inflamed the GOP's far right and angered the more moderate conservatives by opposing the Vietnam war and advocating social-welfare programs which put him on the left of President Lyndon Johnson. Brooke called for a hike in the minimum wage, more money for the poverty program and greatly expanded Medicare coverage. He praised Mayor John V. Lindsay of New York, who had virtually disassociated himself from the Republican party to get elected and who already, before switching to the Democratic party, was bad news to many GOP partisans. Brooke suggested another liberal— Governor Nelson Rockefeller—as presidential timber in 1968, while ignoring former Vice-President Richard M. Nixon, considered the front runner.

Annoyed because of the TV interview, militant conservatives bombarded Goldwater with letters and telegrams demanding that he at least clarify, if not withdraw, his endorsement of Brooke, who, after announcing for the Senate, had received a warm note from Goldwater saying his election would be "good for the country" and offering help—financial and otherwise. When Goldwater, who had not forgiven other 1964 renegades, sent Brooke a 100-dollar contribution in 1966, the candidate said: "I only hope I would be as big under the same circumstances."

In their letters and telegrams Goldwaterites said the endorsement, "premature and unwarranted," boiled down to "intervention in the internal affairs of Massachusetts politics." Some partisans said Brooke was *not* the nominee and would not be unless he was endorsed by the preprimary. They argued that in endorsing Brooke, Goldwater was undercutting candidates such as Volpe, who, although opposing Goldwater's nomination in 1944, had worked for his election.

There was an overt anti-Brooke incident in April, when 3,500 persons attended a 100-dollar-a-plate farewell dinner for Leverett Saltonstall at the Commonwealth Armory in Boston. Although Saltonstall in his speech praised Volpe, Richardson and Brooke, what he said about the attorney general was interpreted as faint praise. While Saltonstall was speaking, the Massachusetts Committee to Preserve the Two-Party System was picketing outside the armory, distributing anti-Brooke literature. This disenchanted group of young conservatives, after scouring ranks for a candidate to oppose Brooke, disbanded in June after a leader, Daniel J. Carmen, urged them to back the GOP choice. "I am very tired of hollow and wasteful efforts within the party that can lead only to self-defeat," Carmen said. "There comes a time when one has to be absolutely realistic. If the party is going to work effectively, the two percent of extremists on either wing should either quit or come aboard." Carmen changed his tune later.

The trumpet of dissent continued to be heard, however. Brooke fueled flames when he said: "There is such great political imbalance in Massachusetts that the nation feels it is a one-party state." Said a critic: "Brooke's brand of apologetic Republicanism is philosophically anemic. It's as trite, worn and rejected as Thomas E. Dewey. Brooke is wrong. Our two-party tradition is not in danger. It's vigorous now because tireless Republican statesmen are providing alternative . . . programs."

It was Brooke who provided alternative programs. He trod on corns in the spring of 1966 when his book *The Challenge of Change* was published a few weeks before the GOP preprimary. His thesis was clear: "As the Republican party goes, so goes the nation." By that he meant to stress the grave danger to a viable two-party system posed by the current Republican sickness which was not so much caused by the Goldwater infection, *America* magazine noted, "as one that enabled the 1964 debacle to come about; it revealed itself in the ominous trend toward departure from the Lincoln and T. Roosevelt tradition of the Grand Old Party." Brooke felt that if two-party politics is to function meaningfully, something must be done to improve the *substance* of GOP proposals, not merely the party's image. The basic principle, Brooke wrote, is to "help the people to help themselves."

He said the GOP, which had lost touch with people, was negative and anti-intellectual; it talked slogans rather than issues. He advocated massive federal spending for health, education, transportation and beautification. In the March 1966 issue of *The Atlantic Monthly* Brooke had recommended a reverse, or negative, income tax as a means of raising the income of the poor to an established minimum level.

"This idea," he said, "was once considered revolutionary, but now, based on the fact that the potential exemptions of many poor families exceed their incomes, it appears more and more logical." Thus a family of six with an income of 3,000 dollars has exemptions totaling 3,600 dollars, thereby incurring no tax liability. Brooke felt the 600-dollar difference should be paid by a federal appropriation or from "found money"—that is, money collected by the Internal Revenue Service in interest and penalties for late payment of taxes. "If this sounds like outlandish charity," Brooke wrote, "it ought to be remembered that such a family often costs the local, state, and federal government far more than 600 dollars a year in terms of welfare services. Such a direct payment might be simpler, more effective, and more economical."

"His proposals make LBJ's Great Society look as stodgy and unimaginative as pre-Bastille France," wrote Carl Rowan. Brooke's stance was so un-Republican, Rowan said, the GOP could probably name a hundred Democrats whom they would rather see carrying the Republican standard.

In *The Challenge of Change* Brooke points out that if the GOP is to be rejuvenated and win more than isolated elections, it must welcome into its fold minority groups, most of whom live in low-income areas, where the votes are. Remembering what Joe Martin had said about filling a pail with huckleberries, Brooke in his campaigns often gave his "highways and byways" speech. "We must go out to the highways and byways, down to the docks and fish piers, and not just to the country clubs, if we want to win." If Republicans did not do this, he said in his book, they would risk letting control of local, state and national government go to the Democrats by default. He said the GOP, to win elections, must look to all ethnic groups for qualified candidates:

"In the last decade in Massachusetts, for example, John Volpe, the son of an Italian immigrant, was three times nominated by the Republican party for the governorship, and twice elected.

"George Fingold, a Jew, was three times elected a Republican attorney general, then nominated by the Republican party for the governorship, an office he doubtless would have won had he not suffered an untimely death.

"And I, a Negro, have been three times nominated for statewide office by the Republican party, and elected twice."

He pointed out in his book that the GOP refuses to face up to the political facts of life: "In 1960 and 1964 we lost some 85 percent of the Catholic vote, and from 75 to 95 percent of the Negro vote. Our support among Irish-Americans, Italian-Americans, Polish-Americans is slim."

He tells how former Republican National Chairman Leonard Hall, while attending a meeting of GOP leaders, noted that no Polish-Americans, Italian-Americans, Negroes or Jews were present. Hall said the situation dramatized what was wrong with the Republican party.

Brooke could snub Goldwater and Governor Ronald Reagan of California, two arch conservatives, and get away with it. GOP leaders

165

could stomach his overt contempt for Goldwater in 1964, when Brooke refused even to be photographed with the Arizona Senator. Nobody winced when Brooke refused to attend a luncheon in Reagan's honor in 1965, when, as a countermeasure, Reagan had sailed into Brooke's attorney general's office, trailing cameramen, to chat with him for an hour. "It was all vague and hazy," Brooke recalls. "I don't think he thinks very well. I couldn't always make out what he was driving at, except that he was trying to tell me that, although he wouldn't have signed the civil-rights bill, he was a friend of Negroes. He seemed embarrassed, and I didn't help him any." Brooke was independent, if not a loner, and could be excused for a few party digressions. But the ideology in *The Challenge of Change?*

Waring defected when he read the book, which had been proofread by John Bottomly and Mary Newman (who said some of Bottomly's insertions were longer than the paragraphs in which they were inserted). "I cannot go along with his thinking and philosophy," Waring said.

Combing the brush for an alternate candidate, the right wing chose J. Alan MacKay, a young lawyer who was national vice-president of the Young Americans for Freedom, Tories who idolized Goldwater. Ignoring MacKay, Brooke spoke of "responsible conservatives" whom he trusted. Then, almost as if further to estrange far-righters, he told the press a week before the June convention that he endorsed the Supreme Court's Medina decision, which gave suspects questioned by the police the right to prior counsel to avoid self-incrimination. Conservatives thought the decision weakened police power.

MacKay counted on Brooke's statement as a deficit which, with his New Dealish comments in his book, would sap his strength at the convention. On the eve of the convention MacKay forces circulated emotional literature that included a newspaper photograph of Brooke speaking at the Community Church of Boston in juxtaposition with an old report branding the church "the most active center of Communist party activity in Boston." The ploy was guilt by association.

Attention to detail is a mark of every Brooke campaign. A week before the convention, at a staff meeting, Brooke's nerves were frayed. According to John Skow, "The energy-draining grin has been turned off, and he is tapping irritably with a pencil as he checks arrangements [at the convention]." He wanted letters thanking his nominating speakers mailed before the convention ended and told his staff to have speeches, which he had spent the afternoon writing, checked with nominators "to make sure there are no awkward words." He asked aides what would be on the wall behind him when he shook hands at the delegates' reception. "It's important; it will show in the photographs."

The opening of Senate nominations at the convention was delayed because of a platform row that saw Chairman Sidney Q. Curtiss blasted for gag rule. The GOP leadership controlling the machinery vetoed a test vote to insert a Vietnam policy plank backed by Mac-Kay calling for the bombing of Hanoi and blockading Haiphong. MacKay felt any war worth fighting was worth winning. The platform adopted called for support of the war, further U.S. commitment of troops and free and legitimate elections in Vietnam. Curtiss deftly derailed the MacKay proposal by referring the amendment to the platform committee, which tied it up indefinitely, since the committee would dissolve at the end of the convention. Former GOP State Committeeman Jack Molesworth, as a platform committee member, strenuously objected to the "jobbing" of the amendment by Curtiss and the co-chairmen of the platform committee (Senator William F. Weeks and Representative Mary B. Newman).

The convention keynoter Senator Thruston Morton of Kentucky, with Saltonstall, solidly supported Brooke before the convention. State Senator Leslie B. Cutler of Needham put Brooke's name before the convention. Giving seconding speeches were George C. Lodge, son of Henry Cabot Lodge, and Sally Saltonstall, who had taken several elocution lessons to hone her speech. Gael Mahony and Mayor Francis Florini of Northampton also gave seconding speeches for Brooke, who thanked them all and lauded his campaign managers, Albert Gammal, Jr., and Roger Woodworth. Referring to charges that he was not a Republican, Brooke said the GOP "believes in helping people to help themselves, and I believe in that principle. . . . I want you to know that I want conservatives, moderates, liberals, all in this election to join with me in a victorious fight." He said he did not want his party to live in the past. "I want to see it profit from the past. I want to see it recognize that changes have been taking place in this world and in this nation and in our state." He reminded the convention that when he took office as attorney general the Commonwealth "was plagued with graft and corruption" and "the political climate was such that industry did not want to come to Massachusetts" and "people were ashamed of being Massachusetts residents."

Daniel J. Carmen, in entering MacKay's name, said: "We hope to prove to the discerning voter who views these proceedings today that a highly honed intellect and Massachusetts politics are not necessarily incompatible." In his speech MacKay said, "I am not running against anyone. I am running for certain things which to me are Republicanism." Although his words were temperate, a small group paraded through the hall with hawkish placards: "Curb Defeat in South Vietnam" and "Keep Red China Out of the UN."

Lodge said the crises facing the nation were "Vietnam, the explosion of the political, economic and social revolutions sweeping the underdeveloped world, the tensions of race relations at home and abroad, and the massive problems of our cities." In seconding the nomination, he asked delegates to "stand up proudly for a man destined for national leadership." At this point delegates gave Brooke a standing ovation.

He swept to a 1,485-to-215 first-ballot win. While the seven-to-one vote was a solid victory for the liberal-moderate wing of the party, the votes polled by an unknown politician warned that some Goldwater shock troops were still licking their wounds.

Flanked by his wife, mother and daughters, and visibly moved, Brooke was held up for seven minutes by newsmen and photographers before he gave his acceptance speech in which he asked the assembly to join with him "in the return to a two-party system of government." During the Brooke demonstration a band featuring bagpipes drowned everyone out, as balloons floated above cheering supporters and others, tied to chairs, bobbed about while a boy dressed as an elephant paraded down the aisle. Brooke aides, with the help of a special rented pump, had worked for hours, beginning at 5:00 A.M., blowing up about 2,000 balloons.

Early in 1966 there had been talk that Saltonstall favored Elliot Richardson as his successor, but by the time of the convention he was strong for Brooke. In a session in his Washington office he had promised Brooke all-out support, a big plus, since the Senator's prestige would blunt opposition from the conservatives. In the flush of victory Brooke brushed aside the threat that his adversaries might launch a campaign for a write-in vote for Saltonstall in the September primary. Countering rumors that he was lukewarm for the candidate, Saltonstall in August accepted an invitation to be keynote speaker at Brooke's forty-seventh birthday dinner in October and signed up to appear with him on radio and television, while promising to stump the state after the primary. Saltonstall's son William, who ran a winning fight for a state senate seat, also actively campaigned for Brooke.

In August Saltonstall arranged a fund-raising function for Brooke at the Capitol Hill Club in Washington. Among the 250 guests were former Vice-President Nixon, 20 GOP senators and many Republican congressional leaders. A Brooke aide has a vivid memory of Senator Everett Dirksen on crutches, balancing a glass of bourbon in one hand, while kissing lovely ladies who came within range.

The Democratic contenders for the Senate nomination were Mayor John Collins and former Governor Endicott Peabody. Collins, who had been reelected by wide margin in 1963, considered himself brighter and more experienced than Brooke or Peabody, whom he called "a lightweight and a charm merchant." He also considered Brooke a charm merchant. Collins scoffed when polls reported by *The Boston Globe* in January 1966 had given Brooke a two-to-one lead over him. This was a source of both comfort and concern to Brooke supporters, who wondered whether their man had peaked too early. Brooke had no place to go but down, and three factors could push him down.

One was the possibility of widespread civil-rights agitation in the summer of 1966. A second factor was his heavy schedule as attorney general, which would limit his campaigning. "Finally," David Wilson wrote in *The Boston Globe,* "there is the factor that might as well be known as 'the latest Brooke story.' These fabrications, based unequally on Brooke's personal magnetism and a peculiar sort of malice, could cause trouble should they be widely believed. He has lived with them in every campaign." After some television appearances, Brooke found women whom he had never seen before "waiting" for him in the lobby.

In January Brooke was the target of Mayor Collins' gibes. "Look, I've got nothing against Brooke personally, but let's be clear that the Republicans only want him so they can wear him like a fob on their watch chain." Later that month Collins was even cockier. "He [Brooke] has done nothing. He is going nowhere. My position is that Massachusetts is under no obligation to send Brooke to the Senate merely because he is a Negro. I'll win by 250,000 votes."

Collins was apparently unimpressed by the publicity Brooke had been getting. In the 18-month period before the November elections Brooke was featured or discussed in virtually every major news magazine and newspaper in the country. He attracted worldwide attention in news journals of London, Paris and Rome, and on the *Voice of America.* He had been profiled in widely distributed national magazines, including *Ebony.* "We were really beginning to think the boss *could* walk on water," Roger Woodworth said. "Except for Ted Kennedy, and we no longer except him, Brooke was the most appealing and glamorous figure in Massachusetts politics. And by early 1966 he was a national figure, as the GOP predicted that he was the one person who could restore the image of the party of Lincoln in the eyes of blacks, whom it had alienated. Brooke was considered the most promising bonus baby of the 1966 election."

Newsmen agreed. If elected senator, he would "be one of the Republican 400 hitters by the time of the 1968 presidential and congressional campaign elections," *The Boston Herald* prophesied. Late in January 1966 Mary McGrory, the syndicated columnist, wrote in *The Washington Star:* "The national Republican party is totally turned on at the thought of electing Brooke. The day he takes the oath could wipe out the disastrous 1964 campaign with its unfortunate 'minority-be-damned' overtones."

Carl Rowan said Brooke might be "the first man to ride to the U.S. Senate on the hopelessness of his party, the guilt feelings of his constituents." Rowan warned that anyone in the GOP hierarchy who was tempted to stop Brooke would be "quickly reminded that he is a liberal and a Negro, both of which are in short supply in the Republican party. It is especially unusual for the Republicans to get both in one man; they tend to prefer their Negroes more on the nineteenth-century side."

Republicans in Washington counted on his election. U.S. Representative Gerald R. Ford of Michigan predicted that Brooke would be "a shot in the arm" for the GOP. "He makes a great impression," Ford told reporters in Boston.

In the Democratic preprimary Collins faced Endicott Peabody, the underdog. After defeating Volpe for governor in 1962, Peabody was often lampooned as a bumbling executive with little political finesse. He had, for example, let himself be photographed serving his wife, Toni, breakfast in bed, pushing an old woman's car out of a ditch—dubious duties for a governor, according to public reaction. There were uncharitable remarks that he had played football too long without a helmet* and that the two towns in the Commonwealth named after him were Peabody and Marblehead. "Chub [Peabody] is by no means stupid," a Harvard professor said. "He's morally inhibited. His mind is constantly preoccupied with ethical judgments. His extreme Puritanism is the key to his character."

---

* Patrick ("Sonny") McDonough said this.

During his administration, Peabody, like the man from Jericho, fell in among thieves. A conspiracy against him began in 1964 when William F. Callahan, chairman of the Massachusetts Turnpike Authority, died. Edward J. McCormack, Jr., Brooke's predecessor as attorney general and the nephew of House Speaker John W. McCormack, wanted the job as a launching pad for his future political career, which he had bitterly renounced temporarily after losing the Senate race to Ted Kennedy in 1962. Kennedy persuaded Peabody to give the vacancy to State Treasurer John R. Driscoll, mentioned as a Democratic opponent of Brooke in the 1966 Senate race. An angry McCormack then plotted to get rid of Peabody, figuring that if Peabody was reelected in 1964, he could team with Kennedy to blunt McCormack's 1966 aspirations. McCormack and Secretary of State Kevin White persuaded Lieutenant Governor Francis Bellotti to oppose Peabody in the 1964 primary. This was a double cross, since only once in this century had an incumbent governor been opposed for reelection by a member of his own party, "and for a lieutenant governor to attempt this mutiny against his own governor was even more preposterous." Bellotti beat Peabody in the primary, and his betrayal further divided Democratic ranks.

Peabody, as a victim of an unpardonable political sin, gained enough sympathy votes at the Democratic preprimary to get the nomination. Incredulous, Collins—his voice trembling with anger—told a statewide television audience he had been jobbed. The Judas was Senate President John Powers, still smarting from his humiliating defeat by Collins in the 1959 Boston mayoral race.

"The voice is the voice of Chub Peabody," Collins roared into the microphone, "but the hand is the hand of John Powers. Peabody got his revenge tonight." Collins has a version of the upset: "I was mayor for six years. I made enemies. My sales tax was unpopular. The Boston Redevelopment Authority tore down the city. I was considered a strong guy, always lecturing people. Smilers don't make enemies, but I'm no smiler. Also, Chub was the underdog, so he got the sympathy vote because of Bellotti's betrayal in 1964." Collins correctly assessed Powers as the mini-Machiavelli who had engineered the convention endorsement of Peabody.

In *The Saturday Evening Post* John Skow wrote that "the most fascinating eye-gouging has occurred between former Governor Peabody, the convention choice for the Senate, and Boston's Mayor Collins." While they mauled each other in the summer of 1966 in the primary contest, Brooke, who had no primary opponent, campaigned against the state's big small-loan companies, whose officers he accused of conspiring with state officials to keep loan rates high.

"It was a winner's kind of luck that brought the loan case to trial in July, when Brooke needed publicity," Skow wrote; "any politician who can make a loan company bleed in court has half the state's votes right there."

In the GOP primary Brooke ran behind four members of the slate. Although all candidates for the top offices were unopposed, Brooke received less of a vote of confidence. There were many blanks. Volpe led the field, with Francis Sargent, his running mate for lieutenant governor, runner-up, trailed by Richardson, the candidate for attorney general, and John Buckley, who was running for auditor. The conservative wing's defection was apparent. In the November election Brooke would have to trade hard-right votes for the independent-Democratic vote, as in past campaigns.

When Peabody won the Democratic primary, Brooke sensed victory, according to Collins. "I know that Brooke doesn't drink much, but I was told that when he heard Peabody won, he turned to an aide and said: 'Pour me a double Scotch. I have just been elected Senator.'"

Nevertheless, Peabody was the toughest opponent Brooke ever faced. A popular member of a ducal family, he could wean votes from Republicans and independents. A former All-American guard at Harvard, Peabody, like Brooke, was a forty-six-year-old Episcopalian, handsome, affable, liberal and an aggressive campaigner. Both ran a driving, person-to-person campaign, getting up as early as five to shake hands with factory workers before attending socials and rallies all over the state. According to *Newsweek,* "The similarities between the two men tend to obscure their differences—all but the obvious one."

On July 19 Brooke reactivated his old "21 Club" headquarters at 21 Beacon Street. His campaign would focus on young people. He would appear at colleges, universities, secretarial schools, technical institutes—anywhere he could expect an enthusiastic audience. Some young people would vote; others could ring doorbells, stuff envelopes and otherwise serve as the infantry of the campaign, which saw increased participation by Remigia and her daughters. Remi put on bumper stickers and during the summer handled the switchboard, well qualified because of her pleasing voice. At this time Remi was seventeen, Edwina fourteen. When a reporter dropped by their Newton home for an interview, the brown-eyed, raven-haired Edwina was writing "gum" a few hundred times, having been caught chewing at Newton's Weeks Junior High, where she was in the ninth grade.

Remi, blonde with green eyes, told the reporter her classmates called her "Rem" or "Do-Re-Mi." Her parents came home just as her boyfriend called, and it became "the shortest phone call in history." Taking care of the girls while their parents were campaigning was Mara Cochetto of Genoa, who came to the U.S. to keep the house in order during the contest. "I talk to my mother by phone last night," Mara said, "and she said if he [Brooke] needs help, we'll all be over." Remi and Edwina told the reporter their mother spoke to them in Italian often, especially "when she's mad at us."

Sally Saltonstall had left her job in Washington in March 1965 to join the Brooke camp as a volunteer, and because of the involvement of youth, Sally, who was in her mid-twenties, became one of the key campaign workers. When she first joined the staff in 1960 she had written in a letter to Brooke: "I can't type and I can't spell, but I can *yell!*" Sally and the "Brooke Girls" would do a lot of yelling in the fall of 1966.

After meeting in Brooke's office on July 19 for shrimp and champagne, Brooke and the rest of the GOP ticket marched down the State House steps as a baby elephant flopped off a trailer to join the parade past several dozen Brooke Girls snappily dressed in uniform green skirts, white jackets and plastic bowlers emblazoned with "Proudly for Brooke" stickers. Senator John F. Parker, GOP state chairman, introduced Brooke, Volpe and other candidates, who spoke from a stand in front of Brooke's Beacon Street headquarters under darkening skies as about 500 partisans and passersby, who clogged the street for over an hour, cheered.

Volpe, who said he ordered a tornado to "facilitate" the rally, added he would bet a million dollars "that Ed Brooke would win this election—if it were up to Ed Brooke alone." But he needed support, as did the other candidates.

Richardson called the ticket as strong as the GOP had ever offered and predicted that Brooke would make "a great senator." Handsome former Public Works Commissioner Francis W. Sargent, a candidate for lieutenant governor, said, "We're going to miss Ed Brooke in Massachusetts, but in November he's going to be more than a Massachusetts senator—he's going to be a national figure." Parker read telegrams from Governors William Scranton of Pennsylvania and Robert E. Smilie of Idaho. Brooke, surrounded as usual by his mother, wife and daughters, thanked the crowd for turning out despite the

173

tornado scare, just as rain began to fall, forcing the crowd into head-quarters. He said he would start his campaign in Blackstone and Millville, the only two towns he had lost in 1964.

The old-fashioned street-corner rally was festive with a six-man band, a sound truck and floodlights shining on the chic Brooke Girls.

Brooke traveled all over the state, shaking a thousand hands a day to keep up with his athletic opponent. As he and his aides went through shopping plazas, each would collar a pedestrian "Good afternoon. I want you to meet Attorney General Brooke, who is running for the Senate." Most people jumped at the chance to shake hands with the candidate, but a man in Springfield balked. "I don't want to meet Brooke," he grunted.

Brooke was at his side in a twinkling. "But I want to meet *you*." He probably made another quick convert.

There were rumbles of discord in Republican ranks, and the media spoke of frosty relations between Brooke and Volpe, who by this time had become so popular in the Commonwealth it was thought that he, too, could tread water. "Whatever happened to Horatio Alger?" a little joke went. "He changed his name to John A. Volpe." On October 10 *The Washington Post* reported friction between the two Bay State warriors: "The two men have not appeared on the same platform since the campaign began." Syndicated columnist Marianne Means wrote that their relations had reached a point where "tempers flared over such a simple joint decision as when the two candidates should appear before a GOP clambake," and two other syndicated columnists, in their book *The Republican Establishment,* noted that "The Democratic state chairman had a moment of radiant amusement during an otherwise gloomy fall when he issued a two-page press release chiding the Republican leaders for their apparent disunity."

Nothing could have been further from the truth. Anthony DeFalco, one of Volpe's most trusted lieutenants, sacked a Brockton campaign worker for failing to cooperate with Brooke campaign workers. "Volpe, Brooke and Richardson all worked hand in hand," he said. "If there was any friction, it's news to me."

Roger Woodworth agreed. He mentioned the stupidity of putting all the eggs in one basket. "When you have three men of star quality you don't put them on the same platform," he said. "While Richardson was speaking in Pittsfield, Volpe should be speaking in Lynn and Brooke down in Provincetown. The three men worked as a team in 1966."

Brooke had breezed through the summer and into September as a sure bet to win. "By then," according to *Newsweek,* "a mystique had built up around the gregarious, poised and articulate Brooke; he was, his growing legions of admirers said, unbeatable." By the first week in October, however, Brooke seemed in trouble as the backlash caught up with him. Woodworth, sensing that Brooke, caught in an ethnic squeeze because of the violence of black militants during the 1966 summer, was facing a surge of anti-civil-rights, anti-Negro sentiment, predicted that Brooke would lose the big bloc of Irish votes. An astute Boston Catholic priest had an assessment: "I think Brooke would get all the Irish vote if they really knew what Peabody and his family stood for in civil rights."

Brooke's patience wore thin as the campaign progressed. "I'm so tired of hearing about 'backlash' and 'sidelash' and every other kind of lash. I'm not running as a Negro. . . . I'm trying to show that people can be elected on the basis of their qualifications and not their race." Nonetheless, the "lash" issue haunted him throughout the campaign.

He was in double jeopardy. He was up against a blacklash to the backlash, as *Newsweek* noted. Some liberals felt he was not so strong on civil rights as his white opponent. Peabody's patrician seventy-four-year-old mother had made headlines in 1964 when she was arrested during a civil-rights march in Florida while trying to desegregate a motel. A Harvard professor who backed Brooke said his wife, "who's an NAACP-er, is voting for Chub. Brooke's not Negro enough for her." And once again voters were reminded that Brooke as attorney general had made rulings that roiled civil-righters.

The Brooke camp was jolted when *The New York Times* sent a reporter into the white ghetto of Reading (population 20,000) to sample sentiment believed to reflect the thinking of Boston's 78 "bedroom" communities. The reporter collected comments heard in car pools and on commuter trains: "It's nothing personal, but if Brooke got in, there would be no holding 'them' [blacks] down; we'd have a Negro President and you've got to believe it." Other comments were along similar lines.

The civil-rights picture was confused to the point of being unfathomable. According to Carl Rowan, who knows the ways of his "soul brothers," most black Democrats "and a lot of white ones will be secretly pulling and praying for Brooke's victory. . . . A lot of Negroes and liberals, in fact, regard Brooke as one of their own, infiltrating the enemy camp—and making the enemy like it." Others said Brooke was just what the whites wanted—a respected black who opposes violent demonstrations and favors lawful procedure in obtaining civil rights.

Some observers thought Brooke would do better in the 1966 campaign if he were white. From random observations heard during the contest, the pattern was blurred. An Edward Kennedy fan, knowing the Senator backed Peabody, voted for Brooke, calling him "a really solid guy. If he doesn't get elected, it will be a tragedy. It's all terribly sad," he said early in October. A cabbie tried to sum things up: "We vote for the best man here [in Massachusetts]. I guess we're more broadminded than anywhere else. Brooke will represent all the people. This may make a lot of these civil-rights people angry, but that's the way it should be. You can't say a bad thing about Ed Brooke." James Hennigan, Brooke's 1964 opponent, had this to say: "If you said you were going to vote for Peabody, your friends immediately would accuse you of being prejudiced. Pretty soon this had you thinking that maybe you were, and you'd vote for Brooke out of conscience."

Brooke compared his situation and John F. Kennedy's in 1960: "He did not run as the Catholic candidate for President and I do not run as the Negro candidate for the Senate. But his election did help improve relations between the religions in this country and helped unify it in a difficult time. I hope mine will do the same."

Fed up with being called "the first Negro this" or "the highest Negro that," since it clouded his reasons for running, Brooke put his case another way. "I discuss civil rights as an issue, that's all. It's just like . . . Kennedy had trouble with his religion, and if I'm elected, it will merely prove that a man can be elected to office in spite of his race or religion."

Brooke hoped voters wouldn't hold him responsible for the violence and rioting in San Francisco and Atlanta. Peabody, who came from a family of civil-rights militants, agreed, discounting the backlash issue. "It's never been a factor against Brooke before. My opponent [Mayor Collins] tried to use my support of civil rights against me in the primary, and it didn't work. I just don't think the backlash is there."

Nevertheless, the Brooke forces were worried after *The Boston Traveler* reported early in October: "The biggest political mystery in Massachusetts today is why so many politicians and political experts think John Volpe will win and Ed Brooke will lose in November." The paper recalled Brooke's landslide victory in 1964 amid a Democratic avalanche, which Volpe barely squeaked by in the contest for governor that same year. *The Traveler* thought Brooke would win the election. But the political soothsayers?

The Brooke camp glumly noted the way Democratic leaders, fragmented only weeks before, had united behind Peabody—a bothersome item in a state with two registered Democrats for every Republican. It was a jolt to have Senator Ted Kennedy plumping for Peabody, who was getting good receptions as he handshook his way around the state with "on-the-hoof assistance from the Kennedys and Postmaster General Lawrence O'Brien." Brooke's camp took some comfort in mid-October when Saltonstall, who had rarely campaigned for other candidates, made an unexpected appearance at a Harvard rally for Brooke, obviously to offset fellow Harvarder Kennedy's support for Peabody.

In view of the changing picture, Brooke in the first week in October changed his mind and challenged Peabody to a television debate. By this time Peabody, who on September 20 had told the press he would accept any reasonable proposal to debate with Brooke—at a time when Brooke said he didn't want to get in a name-calling contest with Peabody—knew he was no match for Brooke, who had a deft way of parrying criticism. "My opponent says I've been on both sides of the issues. Well, that's better than not knowing what the issue is." After reading of Democratic leaders scheduled to speak for Peabody, Brooke said: "They cannot think for you in the U.S. Senate." Brooke wouldn't let Nixon and Javits stump for him during the campaign.

Peabody feared debating with Brooke partly because he was an inept speaker, even after taking voice lessons from Professor David Blair McClosky, who had coached John F. Kennedy during the 1960 presidential campaign, doing some tutoring while enthroned in hotel bathrooms as Kennedy soaked in hot suds.

Brooke strategists used bumper stickers and billboard advertising ("Proudly for Brooke") early in the campaign. They made the mistake of not renewing the slogan when the supply of stickers ran out and the billboards were repainted. The new slogan was simply "Edward W. Brooke for U.S. Senator." As the campaign peaked, Brooke used radio, a half-hour film showing his achievements as attorney general, and effective telethons during which he again sparkled while answering telephoned questions. Brooke strategists expected Peabody to gain on Brooke in polls after Peabody won the primary. Nevertheless, Brooke was worried when a Becker poll in mid-October showed slippage. One of his advisers was Paul Grindle, a political entrepreneur who (with David Goldberg, Sally Saltonstall and Caroline Williams) was one of the four original "Lodge-for-President" promotors in 1964, when Goldberg operated Campaign Consultants, Inc. (CCI), and Miss Williams was his secretary. Grindle, overly concerned about white backlash, wanted Brooke to hit the civil-rights issue head on at a televised appearance at Boston College, a Jesuit institution, but Brooke's other advisers vetoed the idea. Stokely Carmichael's Boston appearance, on the other hand, gave Brooke a chance to label black power as extremist. He also denounced Georgia's Lester Maddox as an extremist of white power. At every opportunity Brooke denounced violence, and when Peabody refused his offer to debate, he concentrated on TV with audience participation as the best vehicle for the closing weeks of the contest.

Money for the television slots took a big chunk out of the campaign budget, since it was on prime evening time for half-hour shows, but they paid off. Brooke used the question-and-answer format eight times in October to counter backlash or whatever had swung the pendulum toward Peabody. "We have to reverse to trend," he told his advisers, who stuck to their campaign plan with no basic changes.

"The longer we campaign," Peabody told Mt. Holyoke College students, "the fewer issues there seem to be between my opponent and me." One issue was Vietnam. It was Brooke the dove versus Peabody the hawk. Brooke went after the peace vote by recommending new peace initiatives, while Peabody backed President Johnson at every turn. As early as February, on the *Meet the Press,* Brooke said peace would be the most important campaign issue. He said the GOP could make an issue of Vietnam unless something were done quickly. On Vietnam, Brooke asked for a full congressional debate, adding that the war should be contained rather than escalated in the interests of "an honorable peace." He proposed direct peace negotiations with the Vietcong, a reassessment of the air war in the North and a two-China policy in the UN.

"The trouble is, you're far ahead of the average American," a Newton neighbor told him at a World Affairs Council meeting held in that city.

On October 9 Peabody and Brooke walked in the Golden Jubliee Parade in Peabody, a leather center.

"How's Peabody?" someone yelled. Brooke, grinning, pointed to the pavement.

"Peabody's wonderful—the town, that is."

Brooke knew he was "running" for office that day as he crisscrossed the street shaking hands while trying to keep up with Peabody, who was about 200 yards ahead. The march was five miles long, but Brooke covered almost twice that distance as he zigzagged, greeting spectators. At every street corner a Sally Saltonstall claque squealed with soprano delight to spur applause. After generating enthusiasm at one corner, the girls rushed to the next. They were perhaps the most vocal portable cheering section ever seen in a political campaign.

If there was any backlash in the city that Sunday afternoon, Brooke missed it in the deafening ovation along the route. Yet this was a Democratic city, where registrations ran almost five to one against Republicans. In 1962 Brooke had carried the city by almost a thousand votes. Two years later he doubled Hennigan's vote.

Roger Woodworth, walking about a quarter of a block behind Brooke, listened for backlash comments. "There were none," he said. "It made us breathe a lot easier."

Peabody's mayor had advertised the parade as "nonpolitical," with all officeholders marching together in a bipartisan tribute to the city's fiftieth anniversary. Brooke, Volpe, Richardson and other candidates went along with the idea until they heard Peabody was marching in "solitary prominence" in front of the Boston Police Department band. Farther up was Senator Ted Kennedy, flanked by Edward McCormack, the Democratic candidate for governor, and Joseph McGuire, the Democratic choice for lieutenant governor.

"I had to grab the ball and run with it," Brooke said.

He dropped back into a strategic position between his group and a formation of Peabody city councilors, to the cadence of the Tufts University band blaring the "Washington Post March." When not shaking hands, he was waving to the left with one hand, to the right with the other, greeting the cheering throng that was 20 deep in places, making it difficult for Sally's cheering squads to maneuver. The Democratic candidates were not amused.

When the Democratic city councilors tried to close the gap on Brooke, he spent the next three miles weaving in and out of the line of march. "Brooke managed to hold onto the ball most of the way," a reporter said. After one of the best workouts in the marathon against Endicott Peabody, he sipped ice water and relaxed in his limousine on the drive to a strategy meeting in Boston.

It had been an encouraging day, begun with a speech at Faneuil Hall at a meeting sponsored by the Massachusetts Political Action for Peace Committee (PAX). Brooke was interrupted by sustained applause as he outlined his Vietnam views. He called UN Ambassador

179

Arthur Goldberg's bid for negotiations aimed at ending the war a step in the right direction and warned that further escalation of the war might invite a conflict with Red China and the possibility of a nuclear holocaust.

On his way out of Faneuil Hall he paused to chat with Peabody. They shook hands for photographers. It was, a newspaper reported, "a momentary, sportsmanlike time out in a bruising contest. There won't be many of these for these two men in the next 30 days."

In Attleboro, Joe Martin's home town, Brooke stepped out of an elevator at City Hall. "I'm Ed Brooke." The woman he spoke to smiled. Brooke swept the town with the impact of a film celebrity. "Tony Curtis wouldn't have received a more enthusiastic greeting," a reporter said. "The crowds mobbed him."

When Brooke visited the town's Republican headquarters just before noon, his photographer pocketed a handful of cookies against the day's schedule. "I've missed too many lunches on this campaign," he said. Just after noon it took Brooke ten minutes to push through a crowd at a downtown intersection. He finally made it to the limousine with the S-4 number plate and reached a Fall River radio station just as the announcer, glancing nervously about, was saying, "And our guest this afternoon is Edward Brooke." After the show a listener called to say the local newspaper had endorsed Peabody the day before. (In Fall River the Democratic-Republican ratio was the same as in Peabody, yet Brooke carried the city in 1964.) Other callers on the telephone show referred to him as "Mr. Brookes." He still had work to do.

He got a standing ovation at Attleboro High School. "Those kids can't vote," Jerry Sadow said, "but they have parents at home who *can* vote."

Brooke signed autographs in a bank and a newspaper office, where he "handshook" his way through the city and composing rooms. Back on the street, he introduced himself to passersby. "I hope I'm not interrupting you, ladies, but I'm Ed Brooke and I'd like to say hello." One pedestrian said, "Well, I'd like to say goodbye." At a fire station Brooke donned a helmet, a gimmick he had learned from Cardinal Cushing, who was known as a "man of all hats."

Meanwhile, Sally Saltonstall and the Brooke Girls were passing out bumper stickers, brochures and campaign buttons. A woman told Brooke to go to a nearby restaurant, which would be packed with voters waiting for the 99-cent special. Brooke went.

By sunset Brooke, who had had raw hamburger for lunch, had visited every newspaper plant and appeared on several radio and TV slots. With his birthday party scheduled in New Bedford that night, his aides advised him to rest in a motel. Instead he toured factories in New Bedford, answering questions on Vietnam and civil rights. An old woman grabbed his arm on the street.

"Oh, Mr. Brooke, I've been looking forward to this." She tiptoed within reach to buss him on the cheek.

"Thank you," Brooke said. "Remember me on election day."

"Oh, I will, you can count on it. You're going to be our next governor."

"Well, at least she didn't call me 'Mr. *Brookes,*'" he said.

It was a rugged campaign for both sides. Toni and Chub Peabody, saying it was their last time around, admitted after the election that it was the most arduous campaign they had ever been in.

Since April Remigia had been scorching the campaign trail, encouraged by warm receptions everywhere. Once on the campaign trail, she didn't spare the horses. "Yes, she loves politicking, and at a pace that matches that of her energetic husband," a magazine reported. "Usually, when everyone else is exhausted and worn out and ready to give up, she'll just shower and change her makeup and keep going."*

Her method, aided by disarming candor, a dazzling smile and fetching accent, was charmingly unorthodox. She talked to cops on the square, fish handlers on wharves, dockers and truck drivers. Asked how her husband felt about blockading Haiphong or ending the war in Vietnam, she switched the conversation to her recipe for baked lasagne. "I can't answer this question. I could mess it up. Write it on a piece of paper. I will get my husband to answer it." He always did. A cop asked her about Brooke's views on a pay raise for Boston policemen. "Write it down and I will get my husband to answer you tonight on TV," she said.

That night, within hours of the interview, Brooke answered the question on his telethon. What floored the cop was that Remigia phoned him the following day to ask how he liked the answer. If he didn't vote for Brooke, he was an anarchist.

In another encounter, Remigia raged when a fisherman on the

---

* To help her husband, Remigia, although a "home body," became a joiner. She is a member of the Boston Opera Company, the Boston Am Vets Post Auxiliary, the Massachusetts Federation of Republican Women, the Newton Parent-Teachers' Association, and the Boston Association for Retarded Children.

wharf said he didn't like her husband. Violating more verb tenses than usual, Remigia spent several minutes telling him why he should vote for Brooke. She looked at him in disbelief when he laughed.

"Ed Brooke has been my man for six years. I just like to hear you talk," he said.

By this time Remigia was a political buff. She had come into her own as a chattery, informal speaker. "Oh, I've been asked about the white and back lash, or whatever you call it," she said, "but I personally have never felt it." Neither had her daughters. She was asked whether the fact that she was white might cause difficulty for her husband if he was elected.

"I don't think so. Nothing could change me. Nobody could change me. I love my husband and my girls. What else is there?" Her non sequiturs were part of her total charm, which was enhanced when she smiled. Even *The London Times* took note of her campaigning: "Remigia's old-fashioned Italian warmth appealed to the women of Massachusetts during her husband's . . . campaign. . . . She makes no speeches in English [*sic*], but in Italian communities, particularly in Boston, she is effective. 'Then I spoke about politics. In English I never could give any answer. I can twist a question very badly in English.' "

Much of her campaigning consisted of meeting thousands of women through hundreds of women's organizations. She spoke at morning coffees, met with dozens of Italian clubs and was a "smash" in Italian districts where white prejudice against her husband might have been strongest. Thus Brooke, instead of downplaying her in backlash areas, used her to good advantage. She even campaigned while buying groceries. "Come to visit me," she told fellow shoppers, and many, taking her at her word, did just that.

At factory gates or inside, where many workers were of Italian extraction, she set the mood with a *"Buon giorno,"* then talked in suitable dialects. She told voters it was in their interest to vote for her husband, especially if they were not citizens. "If anything happens, you have rights if you are naturalized." She helped Italian immigrants become citizens, and for this they were grateful. She said her husband, when elected, would encourage people to attend night school to make it easier for them to be naturalized.

Remigia, who pretends she is displeased with her Italian accent, said: "I should have gone to school when I first came to this country. Now it's too late." She knew, however, that she was picking up votes. She had no formula for success: "I love people, that's all. I talk to them as if I were interested in their lives, and I am." Reporters trailing her liked her sincerity. "She is concerned with the individual dignity and sensitivity of everyone she meets," a reporter wrote, "and it comes through in a way that most vote-getting wives of candidates would envy."

When factory workers asked, "Are your doors closed to us now you are successful?" she said: "If you are honest, my doors are always open." She meant she is faithful to old friends. In a shoe factory in Cambridge a young worker said he was about to be drafted. "What can your husband do about Vietnam?"

Though unable to tell him, she gave him the feeling she cared. "This [being drafted] is a very hard thing for our young people. It is a big issue, but my husband understands and I hope everything will come out all right for you."

Remigia and her mother-in-law often substituted for the candidate when he couldn't attend outings and socials. Brooke had to miss rallies scheduled one day in western Massachusetts. Remigia, with a temperature of 102, filled in, moving from one engagement to another in one of the two helicopters Brooke used in the campaign. In one landing, on the outskirts of Fitchburg, a helicopter burned a circular patch of alfalfa. Remigia pacified the irate farmer, assuring him that her husband would pay for the damage.

"Look at her," a Brooke aide said after a long day on the circuit. "She's been up and out since dawn and she still looks radiant."

Mrs. Helen Brooke, who filled in for Remigia at some Washington socials, had been commuting to Boston for 20 years to see her son and family, and was usually on hand to help in campaigns. In this race she worried about results because of the militancy of Stokely Carmichael and the braying of Adam Clayton Powell, recalling his visits to her home in Washington when he was a boy.

"I don't know what happened to Adam," she said. "He used to be such a nice boy."

Brooke asked his mother how she would feel if he lost the election.

"I would be proud whether you won or not." She remembered the time just before a TV appearance when he disappeared into a side room. "He will be out in a minute," she said. "He's praying."

Like Remigia, Mrs. Brooke enjoyed campaigning "because everyone was so nice." Remigia was more relaxed than during earlier campaigns because people gave her confidence.

In Washington Mrs. Helen Brooke raised campaign funds by selling more than 3,000 dollars' worth of tickets for a benefit birthday party held for her son at International Inn, a social sponsored by Washington Friends of Brooke. His old friend Charles Fisher handled the affair. A retired warden of St. Luke's Church raised a few hundred dollars by asking parishioners to donate to the "Eddie Brooke Campaign."

Late in the fight Brooke aides worked almost around the clock trying, by telephone, to canvass every voter through the county, city, town and ward chairman. Sally Saltonstall and about 120 girls, many from Wheaton College, Smith and Mt. Holyoke, escorted the boss to college campuses. "Whenever he spoke, students came running out to meet him," Sally says. "He was especially good in answering questions on issues like Vietnam. He never gave a pat speech. Really interested in students, he always wowed them."

Contrasting campaign tactics between Richardson and Brooke were marked during the 1966 campaign. Richardson, running for attorney general, was a frost when it came to mingling with people. Before a Boston College football game he stood outside the stadium, shaking hands and introducing himself as fans approached the turnstiles. All friendly and folksy, according to a reporter. But when the crowd thinned out, Richardson's press aide suggested that the reporter ride to the next appointment in Malden so he could interview the candidate on the way.

"But it didn't work out that way, because Richardson got into the front seat and said, 'Hey, the game's on.' " He concentrated on the action and there was no interview. The reporter wasn't surprised at his role as silent chauffeur, since it was *the* Princeton game, and because he always voted for Richardson as "the Stuffed Shirt of the Year."

Brooke attended games in Massachusetts when there was a big turnout. Evan Dobelle, who succeeded Georgia Ireland as Brooke's Boston administrative assistant, was field coordinator for five western counties. Dobelle, who has a doctorate in education and public policy, attended the Boston University–University of Massachusetts game in 1966 with Brooke and the Hardy Nathans, after joining the party too late to enjoy the tailgate picnic.

"I wound up with a hard-boiled egg and a third of a glass of sauterne," he said. "Hardy told me the Cornish game hen was yummy."

They sat in row N on the 50-yard line of the U. Mass. side during the first half. As they slowly climbed to their seats, students cheered, while Brooke signed programs.

"The boss doesn't simply sign his name," Nathan said. "On each program he wrote something like, 'To Dave, with best wishes for a long life of useful service. Ed Brooke.' "

Even after taking their seats there was an up-and-down procession of spectators with programs to be signed. "During the half we walked over to the B.U. stands," Nathan recalls. "The boss put his arm around Evan, who looked young enough to be a student, and as we passed each section, fans rose and cheered Brooke." Later the U. Mass. president asked why Brooke hadn't let him know he was coming so he could sit with him. Brooke knew he would get better visibility on his own, further grounds for the claim made by Bay State pundits that he is "the smartest politician in the state."

Nathan, former president of the Young Republicans of North-ampton and Brooke's coordinator in Hampshire County, had ar-ranged for Brooke workers to spend two days in Northampton and nearby towns, coordinating his efforts with those of Dobelle. Brooke's workers had set up Women for Brooke, Lawyers for Brooke, Busi-nessmen for Brooke and, for a scattered group, Volunteers for Brooke. Sally Saltonstall headed the Youth for Brooke Committee, which visited 70 campuses, after canvassing 113 colleges and universities. They posted signs and addressed groups to get their support. In a homemaking contest at Garland Junior College in Boston, prizes were given for the best design for a campaign dress. Brooke's girls made a dozen dresses and wore them while handing out stickers, campaign buttons and literature at fairs, clambakes, village greens and city squares—wherever crowds gathered. Girls from Smith College, Mt. Holyoke and other colleges left classes to work for Brooke. Nathan arranged for the mayor of Northampton to give a tea so his candidate could charm old ladies. "Even the kids got excited," Nathan said "In Northampton a bunch of kids on tricycles and bi-cycles, with Brooke banners trailing after them, paraded through the neighborhood, and their enthusiasm was contagious."

During two days in Northampton, Students for Brooke, stationing themselves in shopping centers in the area, put bumper stickers on cars after getting permission from drivers, and passed out campaign literature to drum up interest in their candidate. This tour meant being at factory gates before dawn, speaking engagements at college and university campuses all day, with home receptions and afternoon teas in between. In freezing cold outside the Brass Rail Restaurant in Pittsfield, Brooke, wearing a tan trench coat, stayed outside while his workers took turns going into the restaurant to get warm. "Some of the factory workers who waited in line to greet him were still there after the 8:00 A.M. whistle," Dobelle recalls.

On this swing Brooke neared the breaking point once after retiring to a motel after midnight. A skunk, killed in the parking lot outside his window, kept him awake most of the night, and it was a frazzled candidate who left the motel around 5:00 A.M. to put in another 17 hours on the trail. That day, accompanied by six carsful of Smith and Mt. Holyoke girls, Brooke drove all over the area, with stops at factories and shopping centers before meeting with students and touring newspaper offices and radio-TV studios.

Hamilton H. Wood, a nephew of Harcourt Wood, after majoring in government at B.U., had joined Brooke's staff in the spring. During the campaign he drove almost 15,000 miles around the state. "For the first few months we coasted, with no momentum," he recalls. "It was chiefly because we had a money crunch at a time when we needed TV exposure and strong advertising. During this period Brooke was at his best in street encounters. He introduced himself and while shaking hands looked everyone straight in the eye until he got a glimmer of recognition. Some folks walked away in a trance."

"Tony" Wood said the boss knows how to work a parade. "In one trek in North Adams during the foliage festival, he made side trips to lawns and porches, shaking hands and pausing long enough for another aide and me to take Polaroid shots of himself with persons he greeted. By the end of the march we were winded, since we had to sprint to catch up with him. I coated so many Polaroid glossies I ruined a new sports jacket with smudges. We used about 200 dollars' worth of film during the parade." Wood said he was in good enough shape to run the Boston Marathon after the biggest parade of the campaign—the annual Columbus Day march in East Boston, usually witnessed by about 250,000 persons. "The applause Brooke got gave us a shot in the arm. I distinctly remember that Chub Peabody didn't get the same reaction."

Endicott Peabody, just as energetic and tireless, in the final weeks hoped President Johnson's projected visit (which never materialized) to Boston would spur his candidacy. To counteract the possible impact, Brooke, telling workers, "We're going to hit them head on," mingled with workers in Boston's Democratic wards, picking up support that otherwise might have gone against him.

It was a clean campaign except for a few heated exchanges. Brooke told voters the Democrats had not renominated Peabody after his single term as governor, and Peabody, noting that a Brooke victory would cancel the vote of Ted Kennedy, said his opponent was most un-Republican. "He is trying to run on my platform. He should resign from his own party."

Brooke, using an argument which white politicians had previously advanced to exploit anti-Negro sentiment, campaigned on the idea that "we can't have the so-called Great Society until we have the Responsible Society—the society where it's more profitable to work than not to work. You don't help a man by constantly giving him more handouts." Like Charles Percy of Illinois, Brooke felt the GOP should be "a party of proposition rather than opposition."

In his harshest outburst Peabody accused Brooke of being a principal in a slime-throwing tactic and of administering one standard of justice for Democrats, another for Republicans. His charge stemmed from Brooke's threat to convene a special grand jury the day before the election to probe a possible conflict-of-interest charge against Francis X. Bellotti, Elliot Richardson's opponent in the race for attorney general. Five days before the election Richardson had charged that while serving as lieutenant governor Bellotti accepted 12,000 dollars in legal fees from Nationwide Insurance Company in a successful effort to get the company licensed in Massachusetts. The Richardson-Bellotti feud put Brooke in the middle and cost him votes on the eve of the election. At a rally at Blinstrub's Village in South Boston (which accommodated more people than any other nightlife center in New England) on the Sunday before the election, Brooke was close to being frantic because of the simmering situation, fearing it might cost him the election.

This development was countered by unexpected support Brooke had received a few days earlier. On November 2 *The Boston Globe* said the 67-member Committee of Religious Concern About Vietnam, representing congregations throughout Greater Boston, endorsed Brooke "on the basis of religious conscience and moral conviction." Another boost came from 46 college professors, including Ervin N. Griswold, Dean of Harvard Law School, and Max F. Millikan, head of MIT's Center for International Studies. In a letter to every faculty member of every college and university in Massachusetts, the professors said in part: "At few occasions in our history has there been greater need for men of stature in public life—deliberate and independent thinkers who can also act with vigor and effectiveness. We believe that . . . Brooke is such a man. His intelligence, experience and independent judgment are qualities that Massachusetts and our nation need in the U.S. Senate." The professors said Brooke's proposals on Vietnam were "relevant, practical and realistic." Their endorsement was significant because of their influence among supporters of Professor Thomas D. Adams of Harvard University, who had run in the primary. About 50,000 persons had voted for Adams, and one of the imponderables of the campaign was where those votes would go.

Thus the endorsements of ministers and professors were a major breakthrough. The Committee of Religious Concern sent its letter to 2,300 clergymen, pointing out that Brooke's position was more likely to bring about a negotiated settlement of the war. "Mr. Peabody, on the other hand, has given his unequivocal support to the present policies of the Administration."

On election eve Brooke worried about backlash. He knelt in church and prayed. "Don't worry," he told his mother. "It's going to come out all right. When I prayed I said it would be all right with me either way, but that it would be a great help if I could know which way it would be. I know now that I am going to win."

On election night Brooke supporters in the Sheraton Plaza grand ballroom tensely watched Walter Cronkite on his CBS-TV program. Nancy Porter recalls the scene:

"Al Gammal, Roger Woodworth and I, with other members of the staff, staked out chairs on the stage as returns started trickling in around eight o'clock. Television cameras were waiting, and the ballroom was full of reporters and photographers. The hotel had set up a temporary stage on one side of the ballroom, where monitors kept a running total of votes on a blackboard. We worried because of last-minute predictions that Brooke's involvement in the contest for attorney general between Richardson and Bellotti would damage our chances." For a while there seemed to be cause for worry, as a *Globe* reporter noted.

"As the polls closed, one prominent former official of the Peabody administration visited the Brooke encampment in the . . . grand ballroom. He said he had stopped by to 'view the scene of the concession.'" Some Brooke supporters who were watching the TV program were worried even after Cronkite predicted that Brooke was winning.

Woodworth and Gammal did not share the concern. They had assembled an army of volunteers (boys and girls) at 11 Beacon Street, given each a dime and delivered them in car pools all over Boston. When the polls closed, a student at every precinct in the city recorded the tallies on the voting machines and called in results to campaign headquarters, where other volunteers were manning telephones. Woodworth relayed the totals to Gammal, who projected the figures on a screen.

"We had a dozen phones operating at 11 Beacon," Woodworth recalls. "We had the Boston returns long before cops took the tallies to City Hall. By 8:40 P.M. we had Boston complete."

Even earlier Gammal knew Brooke was winning, after getting results from six key places, including the towns of Monroe and Mt. Washington and a ward in Northampton. He told a WBZ newsman at 8:15 that Brooke would win by 300,000 votes. When his prediction was passed on to John Powers, one of the political commentators at WBZ who had been president of the Senate, he said: "Gammal doesn't know what he's talking about." Even a political pro such as Powers thought it was too early to tell.

Ironically it was a Peabody win in Holyoke that gave Woodworth and Gammal further indication that Brooke was winning. Holyoke, with its two-and-a-half-to-one registration in favor of Democrats, had gone Democratic by fewer than 300 votes. News came later that Brooke had taken Peabody's home city of Cambridge by a slim margin, along with the "ancestral Peabody-Saltonstall city of Salem" by a wider margin. As these encouraging returns dribbled in, Brooke partisans sang and danced around the ballroom.

In an upstairs suite Remigia and her mother-in-law sat with a few old friends, while the burly Willie Davis (a black who is now a U.S. magistrate) stood outside the door fending off the press who tried to crash their quarters. Late in the evening Brooke, who had been in another suite on the fifth floor, followed William Hayden through the crowded corridor. Hayden, finally getting the door open, grinned at Mrs. Helen Brooke.

"The Senator is here," he said. Mrs. Brooke and Remigia weren't the only ones in the suite to weep. Brooke and his wife slipped into the bathroom and sat on the edge of the tub for a tearful moment of privacy, while newsmen milled around, clambering over beds and furniture. Ten minutes later, when Remigia's aide, Barbara Masters, brought in Remi and Edwina, their parents were still seeking cover in the lavatory, unable to close the door all the way. Herbert Tucker, who had been sitting with the ladies when the new Senator walked in, kept saying, "We made it, we made it!"

"I was a very proud mother," Mrs. Helen Brooke said later. "You see, my son is a Christian boy . . . always has been from a mere child,

189

and when he told me just before the elections that he had gone to church . . . we knew everything was going to be all right." That election night she was sad, wishing both candidates could have won "I'm sorry he had to run against Chub. I'm very fond of him. He runs a clean campaign."

In a long emotional concession which should have been made an hour earlier, Peabody, always a gentleman, called the victory one of which the entire nation could be proud With his lovely but now tearful and inconsolable wife Toni at his side, he told his followers that Brooke's family and organization could be proud along with "all of the United States of America as well." Viewers were touched by the heartbroken look on the face of his daughter Barbara as Peabody thanked his campaign workers and told the TV public that Brooke had waged a "wonderful campaign."

While Peabody was speaking, Governor Volpe was congratulating Brooke. There had been an embarrassing moment when Willie Davis, failing to recognize Volpe, elbowed him away.

"Brooke then descended into a mob scene that for sheer emotion rivaled anything seen in Masachusetts political life since the late President Kennedy's election eve rally at the Boston Garden in 1960," David Wilson wrote in *The Boston Globe*. As Brooke entered the ballroom, Leo Martin, Gammal and Jack Bottomly made way for him and his family as they headed toward the stage to the swelling cadence of "We want Brooke." Excitement was at concert pitch, and as Brooke started to talk, weighing every word, he could scarcely be heard. Suddenly he paused, startled. The platform wobbled, and the rear section collapsed, sagging three or four feet, as some persons lost their footing. Though no one was hurt, it was a frightening moment.

"The crush of victory on a platform collapsing under her husband's senatorial acceptance speech prodded Remigia's memory," a reporter said. "Twenty years were spanned in a split second." Remigia recalled a tragedy when 685 persons were killed in a human stampede in a tunnel under the streets of Genoa during World War II. The searing memory clouded the moment of triumph. "For a moment I could see the thing that happened in Genoa happen again. I am so happy today I never think of those times in Italy during the war. But once or twice, I think how it was."

Shortly after midnight, in what many consider his finest speech, Brooke addressed 1,500 campaign workers and supporters: "I have just heard a very moving, a very heartfelt and warm speech by my opponent, the Honorable Endicott Peabody. And I want to say to

190

him that a man of his quality and his integrity, and with the campaign that he has waged—he has not lost. This great Commonwealth, founded by the Pilgrims, has given to this nation and to the world Leverett Saltonstall, Henry Cabot Lodge, Christian Herter, John Fitzgerald Kennedy and John Anthony Volpe.

"And they have given to the world the answer that it has been awaiting, that so many people have questioned. I had faith in their answer. I knew what their answer would be: people in Massachusetts judge you by your merit and your worth. The people . . . have answered all of the George Rockwells, have answered all of the people who would divide us and who would keep men from being brothers; and I intend to merit their confidence and their support and their faith in me as a man!"

He predicted that the "freshman class" he was joining would be the greatest in the history of the Senate.

"But I am mindful of my pledge to Democrats and independents, a well as Republicans, who have supported me; and I say to you that I go to Washington to do all that I can do to give equal opportunity to all Americans for decent housing, quality education and equal justice under law; and I go to Washington to unite men who have never been united before and bring across this nation and across this world the brotherhood of man!

"And when I walk down that aisle in January with the senior senator, Edward Kennedy . . . and hold up my hand I assure you that I will take my oath and that oath will include to be a man among men, as you have, Mr. Saltonstall, since you have represented this state.

"Remigia, my wife—my daughters, Remi and Edwina—and I extend to Chub and Toni best wishes for a campaign well run and a campaign of high level."

In 1971 a reporter, in recalling memorable moments of his career, mentioned election night in 1966 at the Sheraton Plaza Hotel when early election returns were coming in and Brooke realized he was going to the U.S. Senate: "Brooke stood there smiling in that fifth-floor suite, and he said it was 'too early to tell' but the answer was there in his eyes. He knew he had won, and he was going to Washington as a United States Senator. It had to be one of his happiest moments." It was.

"To the people of this great Commonwealth of Massachusetts," Brooke said in his acceptance speech, "I extend my profound gratitude for giving me the supreme moment of my life."

No matter how late Brooke stays up on election nights, he has taken his shower before 7:30 A.M. and is at his office before nine. At 9:15 the next morning he held a staff meeting after walking past a large sign outside the door, put there by his staff. "Good morning, Senator Brooke." There was another emotion-packed scene as Brooke, with tears streaming down his face, told his workers how much he appreciated their efforts. "I'll never forget you, no matter where I go, and I hope you'll never forget me." Women in his Chippendale blue suite sobbed as he told them their loyalty had placed great responsibility on him.

"Victory was sweet last night," he said. ". . . I'm going to call 'em as I see 'em."

The November 8 election was the fourth straight in which Brooke rolled up more than a million votes. He won three to two, getting 1,213,473 votes—a plurality of more than 400,000. He did well in poor Irish and Italian neighborhoods, and held his strength or increased it in suburbs, old-line Yankee areas and among Brahmin families "who have always, if somewhat uneasily, supported him," *Newsweek* reported.

If there was any white backlash, it was mostly confined to middle-age groups. According to the authors of *The Republican Establishment,* "It is even a Massachusetts joke that Brooke was elected to the Senate . . . on the strength of the white backlash—his white opponent, Endicott Peabody, being the more outspoken liberal on civil rights. But this hardly means that Brooke is indifferent to the plight of the Negro. He has argued civil-rights cases before the Supreme Court and argued for a strong civil-rights plank in the 1964 Republican platform." The authors further noted that Brooke, "in the racial tinder box," seems to be one of the few black or white persons who has made his own private peace with the race issue. "It is probably this quality, even more than his fine record or the bend-over-backwards effect of a Negro candidate on liberal white voters, that has won three elections for Brooke in a state with a 98 percent white electorate." A black reporter said he has achieved "absolute assimilation." All this, as John H. Fenton wrote in *The New York Times,* "has resulted in the creation of a personal insulation against the flak that is bound to assail him as he enters the Senate chamber."

"The people here [in Massachusetts] have their prejudices," Gammal said. "Governor Peabody couldn't take advantage of the backlash because his record was even more liberal than Brooke's.

The Crisis, a Negro periodical, called the election "a resounding rebuke to both the white and black advocates of voting for candidates on the basis of race. The election returns indicate that Mr. Brooke was chosen neither because of, nor in spite of, his race. This is as he wished. Come January 1967, Mr. Brooke will assumed the mantle once worn with honor and distinction by that . . . dedicated Boston Brahmin, Charles Sumner, who brilliantly and uncompromisingly espoused the Negro cause both on and off the Senate floor."

Brooke mused the morning after the election: "I'm glad it [the campaign] was conducted on such a high level, on both sides. It enabled people to choose between men; Peabody is a good man and I hope I am, too. But it wasn't the case of being the first Negro elected to the Senate since the Civil War; it wasn't a case of being the first this or that. It was a case of Massachusetts making its choice between two men who differed on some things and agreed on others. What this election means to a lot of people in the nation—because Massachusetts isn't any different from most other states—is that if a man will work . . . he can get ahead." That, he said, is "what America is all about."

Before going to his office, Brooke had breakfast at the Sheraton Plaza. It took him 20 minutes to get from the elevator to his table, since he stopped on the way to greet people in the lobby. "How *are* you, how *are* you?" he asked. Before shaking hands with everyone in the downstairs barbershop, he pretended shaving the lathered face of a man in a chair. A Boston reporter trailing him watched him greet Tom Oliver, an Irish cop, who grinned broadly when Brooke crossed the lobby to shake his hand.

"Hey, Tom, how *are* you? Do you remember the time we . . ."

"And whatever they remembered," Bill Duncliffe of *The Record American* said, "both laughed loudly at it."

"He's just a great guy, a great guy," Oliver said.

Just as jubilant were the dining-room waitresses who flocked around him. Duncliffe asked one if she was glad Brooke won.

"Am I ever!"

Later Brooke called the fight "a campaign by ordeal. I've been going around with two cracked ribs and a bad left foot. I hurt the ribs in a fall this summer, and the foot thing is an old injury." He said political campaigns were too long, feeling the solution would be moving the primary or the convention closer to election day. It would cost less if this were done.

"I'm going to propose legislation to do just that. I didn't want to do it during the campaign because it might have been misconstrued. But the election is over now, and I'll do it before I leave the attorney general's office."

Brooke didn't think the efforts of Ted and Robert Kennedy helped Democratic candidates. "I thought the Democratic ticket had too much reliance on the Kennedys and others. I thought we had better candidates, and we campaigned well."

Brooke felt that Democratic candidates, by relying on the Kennedys and other bigwigs, gave the impression they had no judgment of their own. "The people of Massachusetts don't like people coming in here and telling them what to do."

Brooke himself thanked Republican top brass who promised to speak for him in Massachusetts, but said, "No thanks."

Color was an ambivalent factor in the 1966 fight. Frank J. Meranda, chairman of the Boston Congress of Racial Equality (CORE), said his group neither opposed nor endorsed Brooke. "My opinion is one of understanding. He represented all the people of this state and there is no way he can come out with a Negro position." Meranda said CORE would not expect any more from Brooke in the area of civil rights because of his race, "but, on the other hand, neither will we expect less."

A Harvard government professor summed things up: "He's more white than many white persons in this state in appearance, mannerisms and philosophy. I don't know if you could even call him a Negro candidate. He didn't raise any of the issues that normally would be brought out with a Negro running for office. If he had raised any of the issues of race, it could have been a different story. But he managed to avoid arousing any of the anti-Negro feelings that are in this state as they are in any other."

Kenneth I. Guscott denied Brooke was an Uncle Tom. "That talk was just a lot of propaganda put out by the conservatives. Ed Brooke was supporting the civil-rights cause long before it became the popular thing to do. We don't expect him to march in the streets carrying a sign and demonstrating." Guscott thought Brooke's victory was a boon for everyone, not merely blacks. "He opened the eyes of a lot of white people in showing that he is just as capable as anyone else of contributing to the management of this country."

Brooke's election, which raised him to the most powerful role ever held by a black politician, jarred Democrats, since many Northern states had a greater concentration of Negroes than did Massachusetts. Yet in those states Democratic leaders had historically failed to consider blacks for high office.

Senator Jacob Javits called Brooke's election a triumph of enormous proportions for his ideas, and for modern progressive principles. Senator Everett Dirksen of Illinois said after Brooke came to Washington: "We're happy to have you here."

After the election Brooke and his wife were guests of old friends in St. Thomas. When they returned, he told the press he would be back in Massachusetts frequently.

"People will see more of me here at home than they've seen of any other senator."

CHAPTER ELEVEN

Mr. Brooke Goes to Washington

THREE WEEKS after the election Eric Sevareid interviewed Brooke in a television studio against a backdrop of a Beacon Hill law office complete with ship models and old nautical wall prints, with a view through a small-paned window of what seemed to be old Boston homes. The scene was actually a blow-up of a quiet street in London.

Brooke, called the "most interesting" of the newly elected senators, seemed relaxed, having just returned from a vacation in St. Thomas. He said later he had "butterflies in my stomach" during the half-hour interview. As early as February 1966 a GOP senatorial assistant had said in reference to Brooke, Charles Percy of Illinois, and Mark Hatfield of Oregon: "Just imagine what the likes of three men like them in the U.S. Senate could do for the Republican image." Columnist Mary McGrory that same month had written: "By accident or otherwise, there just happened to be a scarcity of Senate Republicans who are able to capture public imagination and excite voter interest in the style of such Democrats as the Kennedy brothers, Indiana's Birch Bayh or Maryland's Joseph Tydings." Normally, the American public thought of GOP senators in terms of old warhorses like Senators Everett Dirksen of Illinois and Bourke Hickenlooper of Iowa.

Thinking of such attractive, moderate candidates as Percy and Hatfield, Brooke told Sevareid the GOP had a "golden opportunity to secure the ground" by putting together an acceptable program for

196

1968. To that end he again suggested an off-year Republican convention, and again there was no response.

Sevareid asked about possible presidential candidates. "I have great admiration and affection for Mr. Romney, Mr. Nixon, and . . . Chuck Percy," Brooke said. "I don't know Mr. Reagan too well. But I think we have many others." He mentioned Javits and Volpe. In a previous interview a reporter had asked Brooke whether he saw any threat in the election of Reagan, an avowed conservative.

"Words like that are meaningless," he had said. "When Reagan sits in the governor's chair . . . he'll find all the household chores—the taxes, the strikes, the welfare of the people, the everyday business of administration—will alter some of his approach. I think he'll be a good Republican rather than an arch conservative."

He warned that the civil-rights movement had "taken a turn in the wrong direction" with the cry of some leaders for "black power." When asked if he was sensitive to charges that he had not done his duty to blacks, Brooke said he believed "passionately and fervently" in civil rights and said he planned to propose and vote for civil-rights legislation.

The fresh new faces in the Senate, Brooke said earlier, did not mean "acceptance of the Republican party itself. It's just an opportunity to move with all haste to solidify our position. We can be innovators; we can be leaders; we can be creative. . . . But I don't think the freshman class is going to take over the seniors. I do think we'll have a voice and that our views will be given consideration."

In the same interview in mid-November he said: "People ask me what I am going to do about racial strife. The answer is simple. I'm going to work for simple tolerance. We are brothers and we should act like brothers. . . . When I was campaigning I must have talked to thousands and seen hundreds of thousands. I looked into their eyes in the small towns and the big cities, at factory gates and rallies. And I saw no backlash—only friendliness." He assessed his new role: "The Senate is a great body." He laughed. "It's been around a long time and I'm just a beginner. I figure I'm going to be very busy getting on-the-job training."

The U.S. Senate, which considers itself the greatest deliberative body in the world, has long had a tradition that newcomers in the "outfield" don't give their maiden speech until they have sat through a congressional session in silence. This rule has been bypassed in recent years with the election of men already nationally known. For example, writes William Saffire, "the maiden speeches of men like

Robert Kennedy of New York and Edward Brooke, . . . delivered shortly after having taken their places in the Senate, were given careful attention all over the nation. In Great Britain, however, the tradition is current; Winston Churchill called Sir Alan Herbert's maiden effort 'a brazen hussy of a speech.' "

Asked about Southern segregationist senators, Brooke said: "I have great faith that they will do what the people of Massachusetts did. I hope they will judge me as a man and a legislator and a representative of this state in Congress." Thomas Pettigrew, a social psychologist at Harvard University, predicted that Brooke's presence would change the Senate, "the most exclusive club in America," which has for long been a white man's preserve. "If nothing else, I really believe there will be an upgrading effect on the private lives of some senators."

Soon after the election Brooke and Ted Kennedy were guests at a Boston Chamber of Commerce luncheon. Kennedy said he welcomed his friend to Washington and would be glad to show him the ropes and lead him around.

Brooke smiled as he took the microphone. "The only time I will follow Ted will be when, as senior Senator from Massachusetts, he leads me down the aisle before I take the oath of office."

Back from his vacation, Brooke instructed his division chiefs to wind up all difficult or controversial matters so he could leave Richardson, his successor, a clean slate. He "nol prossed" some cases because witnesses were no longer available and asked his assistants to list all civil and criminal cases left to be tried. He did everything possible to make the transition smooth.

One case involved the Governor's brother, S. Peter Volpe, in connection with choosing architects on state contracts. The day after Christmas Brooke cleared him of conflict-of-interest charges stemming from a Senate investigating committee. Brooke also ruled that Richardson's position as incorporator of two Boston banks did not violate the Conflict of Interest Law. Referring to Volpe's appointment of architects for the University of Massachusetts Medical School, Brooke said: "Bad faith, fraud, improper influence and the like cannot responsibly be inferred solely on the basis of innuendo, rumor, suspicion and supposition."

The Boston Globe, chiding Brooke, said Volpe had been invited by Administration Commissioner John J. McCarthy to a meeting at which McCarthy tentatively chose architects for the medical school, adding that Volpe "gave his opinion as to the qualifications of various architects for the . . . assignment." Volpe, at McCarthy's request, telephoned three firms to see if they were interested in the work and participated in the decision-making process at the highest level, thereby acquiring the status of a special state employee subject to the law prohibiting conflicts of interest.

"Despite these facts," *The Globe* said, "Brooke concluded that there was no evidence to show that . . . Volpe engaged in conduct violative of the criminal or civil provisions of the conflict law." Brooke disagreed, declining to rule on whether Volpe violated the Code of Ethics, since his authority under the law did not extend to such matters.

The situation did not hurt John Volpe's political fortunes, since he easily won a third term as governor. During the proceedings Brooke did not mention the case to the Governor, nor would he have accepted any telephone calls from the Governor on the subject. He didn't have a problem in this regard, since the Governor kept out of the case. Thus Brooke could honestly tell the press that he had never discussed S. Peter Volpe with his brother.

Another problem was Richardson's charge against Bellotti in the insurance case, an issue that helped him beat the Democrat (Bellotti) in the race for attorney general. Brooke was caught in the middle. If he stayed out of the dispute he would be blamed for not doing his job, and if he took action he would be accused of bias against Bellotti. Thus the controversy hurt Brooke more than it helped Richardson.

"I guess," Brooke said the morning after the election, "it cost me 100,000 or 150,000 votes. . . . I'm pretty sure that, without it [the feud], I'd have run a lot closer in Boston and probably I would have carried the city." Brooke had felt obliged to make a quick decision, since charges by Richardson and countercharges by Bellotti made headlines. Judge Benjamin Gargill warned Brooke of the explosive situation. "Don't let Bellotti have the opportunity of calling his gang together over the weekend and raising hell just before the Tuesday election," he advised.

"I could have played it smart politically and said nothing," Brooke said; "that was what my . . . advisers suggested I do. But there was more at stake than just an election. A man's reputation, his law practice, his wife and children. I just could not stand aside." He meant Bellotti. "You know," he said in the interview the morning after the election, "if either [Richardson or Bellotti] had said, 'Let's declare a moratorium on this thing until after the election,' I think

I would have gone for that." Richardson was making charges and Bellotti was calling on Brooke to clear his name.

On December 19 Bellotti accused Brooke of a "callous administration of a dual system of justice," of conducting a "whitewash" for Republicans and a "witch hunt" for him. This stemmed from Brooke's order calling for an investigation of charges against Bellotti, who said the "patently political" decision was an effort to "destroy me in every way imaginable." He said in recent days Brooke, while whitewashing Volpe and Richardson—both Republicans—"found cause to recommend further investigation against me. . . . Although I have no doubt of my ultimate vindication, I have been irreparably damaged." Referring to Richardson, the new attorney general, he asked: "How would you like your political persecutor to be your prosecutor?"

Feeling he was caught in a vise between two Republican attorneys general, Bellotti said: "There is the question of whether any man henceforth who constitutes a threat to the Republican high command can be secure against the misuse of the power of the high office of attorney general. Mr. Brooke in a last-minute move has washed his hands of the case, and now, incredibly, the man who was my political adversary and accuser takes over the role of my political prosecutor."

Richardson hurled his charge five days before the November election. Bellotti said Brooke at the time was seeking Democratic votes as a candidate for senator, noting that Brooke said at this time that the feud could be resolved by "a simple correction of the records by properly constituted officials of the Nationwide Insurance Company under oath. . . . Now, however, that he is safely elected and fears no judgment of the people for six years, he is more interested in doing the work of his political allies. He now wants to keep the case alive and to extract from it the last dregs of political advantage."

A 51-page report prepared by Edward Swartz, still in the office of the attorney general, was given to Edward T. Martin, whom Governor Volpe appointed acting attorney general after Brooke was elected to the Senate. Brooke resigned as attorney general on January 2 to take his Senate seat, and Martin served as interim attorney general until Richardson was sworn in on January 18. The Bellotti case, one of hundreds of conflict-of-interest opinions which Swartz wrote for Brooke, had dramatic aspects. Five state troopers accompanied Swartz when he went to the Department of Insurance in Boston to get material pertaining to the case, which was dropped by Richardson, who had promised because of the political ramifications involved that he would insulate himself from any involvement in the Swartz probe.

The Brookes registered at Hotel Madison in Washington on January 8. That night the Senator-elect and his wife were guests of honor at the home of Mrs. Christian A. Herter. The dinner had been arranged before the death of Herter, whose close friendship with Brooke had begun in 1952 when the latter worked for him in the gubernatorial election in which Herter defeated Paul Dever by only 14,000 votes. There had since been close, affectionate relations between the two men.

Barbara Masters shared one bedroom at the Madison with Remi and Edwina. After adjusting Brooke's black tie, she helped Remigia get ready. "She wore a powder-blue, floor-length, princess-style coat over a simple blue brocade gown, and never was she more radiant and stunning," Mrs. Masters said. "But what most impressed me was the way the Senator was bubbling over during those exciting days in Washington. As he told us how warmly he was received everywhere, he reminded me of a little boy opening one present after another on Christmas morning.

"After the Herter party, the Brookes came into our bedroom around 11:30. The Senator asked me to guess who was there, unable to hide his excitement. 'You could have run the country from the party,' he said. Dignitaries included Vice-President Hubert Humphrey and Secretary of State Dean Rusk. 'Was anything memorable said?' I asked.

" 'Well,' Brooke said, grinning, 'the Vice-President gave me some practical advice. He told me that if I forgot a woman's name, or didn't know how to pronounce it, to just call her "dear." ' "

Brooke had a crowded social schedule during his first week in Washington. On Sunday, before having luncheon with the Edward Kennedys in their handsome red brick house on a quiet street in suburban Georgetown, Brooke spent most of the morning accepting the congratulations of fellow senators.

Joan Kennedy had the living room banked with roses and chrysanthemums, and Ted got a fire burning in the hearth. After a luncheon of quiche lorraine, green salad, toast, fresh strawberries and cream, the men talked politics in the den.

"To use a famous Kennedy expression," Brooke said, "we talked about doing more for Massachusetts."

Remigia and Joan chatted about their children and their summer homes. Motioning toward a photograph of her mother-in-law, Rose Kennedy, Joan said: "She is seventy-six years old and has more energy than both of us put together." The conversation switched to the opening of Congress next day.

"I remember how thrilling it was when Senator Saltonstall escorted Ted down the aisle and how exciting it is to sit in the family box of the Senate gallery," Joan said. Did she have any advice for Remigia? "I wouldn't want to begin. I'm still learning myself."

Brooke and Kennedy discussed politics for two hours before newsmen and photographers were invited to join them.

"We were delighted to have the Brookes for luncheon," Kennedy said. "Joan and I wanted the opportunity to welcome them to our home and get to know them better." Actually, Brooke and his wife had often met Joan during the campaign, when she substituted on the platform for her husband, who was hospitalized with a bad back following a plane crash. When a photographer urged the senators to pose for "just one more" picture, Brooke quipped: "I'd rather shake hands with Joan, if we're to continue to shake hands."

Kennedy told reporters he would differ with Brooke on some votes. Both men said they would cooperate in the interests of the Commonwealth.

"I just passed on some of the advice Senator Saltonstall was kind enough to give me a few years ago," Kennedy said. "We've enjoyed during the course of recent years a partnership, and I'm hopeful it will continue through the present session and beyond. The textile, shoe, fishing and other industries and the defense installations up there in Massachusetts know no party. What they need is two effective voices in the Senate working together."

Brooke agreed. "I think we have bipartisan representation that will work closely together. It was a very nice touch of Senator Kennedy's staff to invite our staff to coffee in his office last week. It was very well done and much appreciated. We hope to invite you back when we get situated," he added, turning to Kennedy.

Noting that Brooke had already had a briefing from Saltonstall, Kennedy said: "Ed is way ahead of where I was when I came down here."

As the Brookes left, he told the press Joan was a charming hostess and "an excellent cook." Remigia said later she thought Ted prepared the quiche lorraine.

Both senators went to the House Chamber to hear President Johnson's State of the Union message the following evening.

The Brookes left for their hotel to get ready for a busy evening. "I'm going to take a sauna," Brooke told the press as they left the luncheon. "But Remigia won't, because she doesn't want to spoil her hairdo." Monti, Mrs. Brooke's favorite hairdresser in Newton, had come to Washington at his own expense to take care of Remigia and her daughters, who returned to Newton after three days in the city.

That afternoon Brooke worked out in the Senate gymnasium, played tennis with Senator Mark Hatfield, and took a sauna and had a rubdown before getting a haircut in the Senate barbershop. While in Washington he had seen a lot of Al Benjamin, who was producing a film titled *Mr. Brooke Goes to Washington*. Benjamin had arranged to have a Capitol police officer assigned to show the Senator and him around the city. Once, when Brooke asked the officer to take him to an appointment, the cop said: "Sorry, Senator, you'll have to clear it with Mr. Benjamin."

"Cheese and crackers, Benjamin, I don't know how you do it," Brooke told the newsman.

"I arranged Brooke's schedule and ran him ragged," Benjamin recalls. "Late in the afternoon of the day he lunched with the Ted Kennedys, I was taking a sauna when he came in. 'For crying out loud,' he said. 'I told you I'd cooperate, but interviews in saunas are off limits.' "

Station WNAC had warned Benjamin and his crew to keep expenses to a minimum. They were having dinner after the sauna incident when Brooke walked into the Madison dining room.

"You fellows really know how to live," Brooke said, noticing the wine. "I don't see any wine at my table."

Brooke, who was entertaining several friends, had a message for the waiter who served the table wine that was sent by Benjamin.

"Tell Mr. Benjamin I thank him, but say I have had better wine in my time."

That night Brooke hosted a reception at the Madison. On their 1966 Christmas cards the Brookes had invited many friends to the reception following swearing-in ceremonies to be held the following day, little dreaming of the enthusiastic response. Several hundred Massachusetts friends came to the Sunday night reception at the Madison, where Senator Jacob Javits told Brooke, "You're the hottest thing in town." Brooke was dancing with Remigia while Benjamin's cameraman, getting close-ups for the film and balancing equipment on his shoulder, danced backwards, opposite the couple. Brooke said he was a good dancer.

"So are you, Senator, but you have a better partner."

Seven hundred guests, mostly from Boston, danced until 2:00 A.M. Brooke himself was on the floor most of the night.

Up early for breakfast, he attended a Republican caucus at 9:30, then returned to his suite to get ready for induction "under the stern marble gaze of the busts of Webster, Clay and Calhoun in the galleries," *The Boston Globe* reported, noting that the Senate floor "was deceptively calm. . . . The day seemed to sum up a great deal that is right and a great deal that is wrong with the U.S. The sun shone on the great, imperial stone buildings." Most spectators were well dressed, including Negro women in mink, and all were in a celebrating mood. But, as Senator Edward Kennedy noticed when he stepped outside briefly, demonstrators were massed on the steps of the House wing chanting for Adam Clayton Powell.

Ambassador Henry Cabot Lodge had come from Vietnam to welcome Brooke to his old Senate seat. And that's how it was on Brooke's first day in the Senate, *The Globe* reported—"the demonstration in the smog, and most of all, the war this nation has yet to win or lose and in any event to settle." It takes a special kind of courage and sense of humor to deal with such problems. "Our new senator has both," said *The Globe*.

Before and after the brief swearing-in ceremony, Brooke sat in Saltonstall's seat directly behind Senator Everett Dirksen. It had been a trying morning. Remigia and Mrs. Helen Brooke were sitting with his new administrative assistant, Cammann Newberry, in the gallery, with Remi and Edwina behind them. Governor Volpe was also in the family gallery, but Brooke had only ten tickets for the public gallery, "and admirers from Pittsfield to Attleboro" wanted them. The lucky ones sat near Joan Kennedy in the front row of the same gallery.

It was a solemn moment when Brooke was escorted down the aisle by the youngest brother of the late President to be sworn in by Vice-President Humphrey. It was remembered that Ted Kennedy in 1963 had been presented to the Senate by his senior, Leverett Saltonstall, a Brahmin. "It is a sociopolitical progression that may have further presidential overtones," wrote Broder and Hess.

"I would have loved for Dad to have been in the gallery," Brooke said later. "I thought about the frustrations he must have had because he had the ability but not the opportunity to do more. Never would he have foreseen that some day his son would sit in the U.S. Senate. There was one scene I shall never forget. As I left the Capitol building I noticed hundreds of high-school students crowding the steps, some from Mississippi and some from Cardozo High School in Washington. I thought of what my grandmother used to say—'Stay in your place.' This advice was given to protect me from injury, because if you didn't follow this advice, you knew what would happen. But this was a statement I never could accept. Your place is anywhere you want to make it. And so these Negro high-school students . . . could see a senator of their own race and this sight would encourage them to dream, to aspire and to work toward higher goals." Brooke was delighted to see the Dunbar High School senior class at the reception following the swearing-in.

After shaking hands with colleagues, Brooke returned to Saltonstall's seat, which he occupied until assigned to a back seat in the chamber. Just across the aisle was Senator Richard Russell of Georgia, dean of Southern Democrats, who greeted Brooke cordially. By the second day Russell was calling him "Ed."

At the Capitol Hill reception that afternoon in the New Senate Office Building, what seemed an endless line of people of all races shook his hand. The crowd included affluent blacks from Washington, many of them old friends of the Senator.

"I felt shabby after seeing so many well-dressed Negro women, a number of them in mink coats," a reporter's wife said. Whether these Washingtonians had known him as a child or had never seen him before, they wanted to be proud of him, as did the rest of the crowd made up of people from all over the nation. Some called themselves friends of Brooke. "They all came clamoring after the Senator . . . shouting his name, reaching out to touch him, greeting his every little remark with shouted hilarity," Judith Martin wrote in *The Washington Post*. "He had the biggest crowd of squealing, screeching, that's-right-you-tell-them admirers yesterday for the opening of Congress. A thousand of them, black and white, came down from Massachusetts for the occasion. They grabbed seats on planes, trains and buses and came to Washington."

On congressional opening day, the Brooke family were feted at three parties during a full schedule of official functions, "with the Senator coming through to be kissed and back-pounded and hand-pumped by everyone who could fight through and grab him. The biggest mob scene was in the New Senate Office Building, partly because the Powell supporters came over from the House after they finished demonstrating. One jubilant Bostonian spoke for many when she said, 'We're so grateful when we get an honest politician that we don't care what color he is.' "

Brooke refused to discuss Powell. As a former attorney general, he said he would first have to look into the allegations—a job he would not undertake, since he had no jurisdiction in the matter.

Tired but radiant, Brooke breezed in for 20 minutes near the end of the final party at the Washington Hilton on congressional opening day. The guests, invited for 6:30, had been barred from the door until seven because the Senator hadn't come. They gave him a wild ovation when he did.

At day's end, exhausted by the social grind, Brooke returned to the Madison to dine on what he quipped was his "gourmet" dish: hogmaws and greens. "You can say that I am a soul brother. I enjoy soul food. And this may qualify me for the club."

In *Ebony* magazine Simeon Booker said this admission would be "meaningful for Negroes who jubilantly hailed his election and have been mystified by the tremendous array of news articles picturing the New Englander as a 'conservative' or 'moderate.' Said a lifelong friend: 'Old Ed's the smartest Negro in politics. How in the hell could a Negro with a white wife be elected senator by whites if he was a conservative?' "

In his book *Race and Color in the West Indies* David Lowenthal reflects the view of less jubilant blacks: "The election of . . . Brooke, a light-colored Negro . . . to the United States Senate . . . is a 'first' about on a par with the selection of the Barbadian mulatto, Conrad Reeves, as Chief Justice of Barbados in 1884. Both are protégés of the propertied, 'safe,' 'responsible' men to whom whites proudly point as evidence of the absence of color prejudice." According to Jim Bishop, Brooke's election did not elate Martin Luther King, Jr.: "Brooke's skin was pale, his hair straight [sic]. He had married an Italian girl whom he met while in service. . . . Brooke's origins related to the black middle class, which, as far as the average black is concerned, is closer to the White Establishment than to the Black."

Brooke, who reminded Washington of the early Jack Kennedy ("in technicolor," according to one wag), was a "smash" in a city that prizes glamor. His affable manner won friends. Joe McMahon, conductor of the "Toonerville Trolley," a special subway from the Senate Office Building to the basement of the Capitol, said: "I've been working here for 30 years, and it's the first time a senator has spoken to me." It was as if a Hollywood star had hit town. "When Brooke appears on television the ladies cry. . . . The growing mystique does not reach Kennedy proportions, but it is an impressive start for the former infantry captain . . . known as 'Carlo' to the Italian partisans he worked with in the Apennine Mountains in the years when Jack Kennedy was captaining a PT boat in the Pacific." When Hollywood films the story, a reporter wrote, its title will be *Code Name: Carlo.* In the movie, "bombed-out cellars behind the German lines in Italy will replace the shattered deck of PT-109 for the main setting." Brooke will be played by the "brooding presence of Sidney Poitier," and for the opening the director can use the set from *Advise and Consent.* He adds: "With [Ted] Kennedy and Brooke the Bay State goes to the top of the gallery's hit parade."

Observers said the buzz in glamor-starved Washington over the new senator would hurt him. "Yes," Brooke said, "I suppose every time I sneeze it will be noted. Let's hope I sneeze in the right direction."

Brooke got on-the-job training sooner than he anticipated. During his first month he got over 500 letters a day as "the hottest name on the speaking circuit." He received more than 1,800 requests for personal appearances in more than 30 states, including 70 for the Lincoln Day observance alone. He accepted only three of 65 invitations to give commencement addresses in June. He chose radio and television slots and turned down scores of invitations for dinners and receptions. His new duties forced him to reject most of them. "I want to learn. That's why I was there."

At a Mayflower Hotel reception in honor of the birthday of Senate Republican Leader Everett M. Dirksen two days after Congress convened, Brooke gave another example of good timing when he came into the ballroom just as the receiving line dribbled off. Dirksen and he chatted for a few minutes, then the GOP leader took him around introducing him. After posing for photographs, they were interviewed by Martin Agronsky on television.

"It was unusual for Dirksen to roll out the carpet for a freshman senator," a reporter said. In a group photograph* signed "Congratulations and best wishes to Senator Edward Brooke," the freshman stood with Democratic Majority Leader Mike Mansfield, Dirksen, Ted Kennedy and Vice-President Hubert Humphrey. According to Jerome Sadow, Brooke met Humphrey late one afternoon before

---

* Dated January 10, 1967.

Congress reconvened. Brooke was coming out of the Old Senate Office Building when he saw two black Cadillacs and "furtive-looking men hovering about." They were Secret Service men guarding Humphrey, who paused on his way down the steps to shake hands with Brooke.

The Mayflower reception for Dirksen was on Wednesday. Two days later Brooke lunched with Dean Rusk for a briefing on Vietnam at Rusk's invitation. That night he attended a cocktail party given at a hotel by the publisher of the two leading Worcester newspapers for members of the Massachusetts congressional delegation.

Brooke was ninety-eighth out of a possible hundred in the choice of a Senate office, and suites were allocated on the basis of seniority and state population. His first office was a three-room suite in the Old Senate Office Building, part of the quarters occupied by the defeated liberal Democrat, Senator Paul Douglas of Illinois. (Senator Howard Baker of Tennessee, another freshman, took the other half of the suite.) Later Brooke moved to the New Senate Office Building (Room 1251, where he had more space), then back to suite 232 of the OSOB, remaining there until the summer of 1971, when, as a veteran senator, he was assigned suite 421, larger quarters in the OSOB.

His first quarters were so cramped he found Roger Woodworth, a peripatetic "dictator," dictating to Maura O'Shaughnessy in the lavatory, where Roger was having difficulty pacing back and forth. When Brooke opened the door, he asked Maura what she was doing on his Senate seat. When Attorney Edward Swartz called on Brooke, he was ushered into an office closet to share a light lunch with the Senator. As he left, he asked Brooke about his closet "apartment."

"It's the only way I can get any privacy," Brooke said.

If the members of his staff who accompanied him to Washington felt cooped up in the suite of offices at the State House, in the first two suites in the Capitol they felt "cabined, cribbed and confined," to steal from Shakespeare. Brooke had a large, well-appointed office, but his staff of 20 worked behind desks almost shoulder to shoulder in a world of jangling telephones and clattering typewriters and doors opening and closing. There was hardly room for another bookend. Jerry Sadow's desk was almost hidden in an alcove, and there was scarcely room in the tiny rooms for the voluminous files which Albert Gammal drove to Washington in a rented truck. (He also brought along Brooke's old attorney general's chair.) Governor Volpe dropped into the office the morning the files arrived and was surprised to see Gammal sorting out the cases.

There, on opening day, that formidable and persuasive campaigner Sally Saltonstall sat behind an arrangement of snapdragons and gladioli and greeted visitors. During the confusion, a distinguished-looking gentleman dropped by to pay respects to the new senator.

"May I ask who is calling?" Sally said.

"John Gardner."

Not knowing he was Secretary of Health, Education and Welfare, Sally told Brooke a caller wanted to see him. After a handshake, Gardner said he would be glad to be of help if Brooke needed anything from HEW.

"Thank you, sir," Brooke said. "Do you work at HEW?" Gardner never got past the anteroom.*

A week later *Time* ran a cover story on Gardner. "I guess I *was* a freshman senator," Brooke said grinning.

From the outset Brooke's rapport with his colleagues was cordial. Senators from both sides of the aisle called him Ed, and he enjoyed all the privileges of the exclusive club. He sat with other freshmen in the chamber's "outfield" ("Boys' Town"), as senior senators call the back rows. During the first few months Brooke seldom spoke unless he had something important to say. In one of his first public appearances he shared a platform with Senator Ernest F. Hollings, a Democrat from South Carolina. In his speech to the women's press club Hollings said: "Senator Brooke owes his election to the white people of Massachusetts, and I owe mine to the black people of South Carolina."

Brooke, who had integrated the Senate without a sit-in demonstration, was the first high-ranking Republican who could speak clearly to blacks who had voted Democratic since the New Deal. This posed problems.

"Everybody wants Ed to be the instant Negro hero," a friend said. "Single-handedly he made it to the top in politics and he's not going to change his system for a few hurrahs now."

From the outset he rejected the role of lionized Negro, refusing to let blacks "elevate him to a kind of political sainthood or trample on

---

* There was another embarrassing incident, in the Senate cafeteria, when Brooke greeted Andrew White, a Georgia black who was running for the House. "Andy, it's good to see you," Brooke said. "I'm behind you 100 percent." Young, a Democrat, grinned. "Meet my Republican opponent," he said. Brooke also supported his friend Royal Bolling, even though he was a Democrat, because of his confidence in him.

him if he doesn't do and say what they demand," as Roscoe Drummond wrote even before Brooke took the oath of office. Drummond raised an interesting question.

"Will we allow . . . Brooke to be the kind of senator he wants to be? Brooke is not a Negro senator any more than he was a Negro attorney general. . . . He is a senator who happens to be a Negro, and, on the record, by instinct and character, that's exactly the kind of United States senator he aims to be."

Drummond correctly predicted that civil-rights leaders would try to turn the newcomer into a front-line spokesman for their cause and that the press would insist on making him a symbol of new black political power.

"The fact that . . . Brooke was elected because of himself is far more significant than the fact that he is the first senator who is a Negro in some 80 years," Drummond said, adding that it wouldn't be easy for the press to appraise Brooke as an individual. There would be a tendency to suggest he was speaking "Negro" views and promoting "Negro" policies, Drummond said. "Brooke wants to be a good senator for Massachusetts and for the nation. That will be the finest contribution he can make to racial progress. And the finest contribution we can make is to let him be himself."

Nevertheless, while trying to convince everyone that his Negritude was irrelevant, he advanced the cause of blacks. NAACP Washington Bureau Director Clarence Mitchell, a Capitol Hill lobbyist for more than a quarter of a century, said: "Senator Brooke is more informed and knowledgeable on civil rights than any other first-term senator I have met. He is concerned and interested and I am proud of him." On an individual basis, Brooke proved to be a sensitive, authoritative civil-righter whose greatest service would come in Senate debate and in behind-the-scenes negotiations to initiate legislation.

He declined a post on the Senate District of Columbia Committee, a job which virtually would have made him the mayor of Washington, since the city is controlled on Capitol Hill. The committee is a kind of town council for the voteless federal enclave. Brooke was ideal for the post, since his upbringing and education in Washington had given him an insight into the city and its problems—one few senators could hope to acquire. But, as Carl L. Shipley, chairman of the D.C. Republican Committee, said, "Brooke is too sharp a guy to be concerned with municipal ordinances like the length of dog leashes. We need him on more important committees. . . . He would be run to death by 'alderman duties'—complaints and problems from Washingtonians."

Ed Brooke (back row, far right) *at Loon Lake in Lakeville with Cub Pack 12, Troop 9, in 1948.*

Brooke (far left) *on picnic at Loon Lake in 1953.*

Brooke at NAACP membership drive in 1952. Seated: *Mrs. Satyra Bennett, Governor Christian Herter, Lionel Lindsay.* Standing: *Ed Brooke and Kivvie Kaplan.*

Ed Brooke with Sally Saltonstall during 1960 campaign.

*This photo was taken in 1963 when Edward M. Kennedy was U.S. Senator
from Massachusetts and Endicott Peabody* (center) *was Governor of the
Commonwealth. Brooke was attorney general of Massachusetts.*

(Associated Press)

*As attorney general, Ed Brooke ponders question asked him at press con-
ference regarding reports that the Internal Revenue Service had been
investigating his tax returns. He answered, "I'm a taxpayer and subject
to the same tax laws and investigations as everybody."*

(Wide World Photos)

The attorney general at a staff party at his home in Oak Bluffs, Martha's Vineyard, in 1965.

On Sunday, the day before he was sworn in as senator, Brooke and Remigia had lunch with Joan and Ted Kennedy at the Kennedys' suburban home in Georgetown. Here they are shown leaving.

(The Herald Traveler–Record American)

In the foreground is Betty Hager Francis. Julie Tiernan Allen is in the background. The girls were secretaries in Brooke's first office in the Old Senate Building in Washington.

(The Herald Traveler–Record American)

Brooke with Henry Cabot Lodge at a fund-raising dinner in 1967. Lodge was ambassador to the UN at the time. Brooke holds the Senate seat once held by Lodge, whom he greatly admires.

Senator Brooke and General Westmoreland in MACV-I Compound in March of 1967.

Brooke greeting South Vietnamese during his trip to Vietnam in March of 1967.

Mrs. Edward Brooke, the Senator's mother, embraces her daughter-in-law, Remigia, at a $100-a-plate dinner for Leverett Saltonstall at the Commonwealth Armory in April 1967.

Remigia Brooke relaxing at the Colosseum in Rome during her 1968 trip.

Brooke flanked by President Nixon and Kenneth Belieu, a congressional liaison officer and now Assistant Secretary of the Army. They are shown on a porch of the White House in 1969.

(White House Photo)

Ed Brooke and his aide Roger Woodworth battling cold wind after their arrival at Logan Airport from Washington for the Christmas holidays in 1969.

(The Herald Traveler–Record American)

The Senator in his Washington office in the spring of 1970 when the Oba of Lagos visited him.

During the MIRV controversy Senator Brooke confers with Secretary of Defense Melvin Laird and President Nixon.

In declining the post, Brooke said urban matters had never interested him. But before the year was out he found himself concentrating on two controversial, high-impact issues—the Vietnam war and riots in the cities. And, said a columnist, "he ran with them hard enough to relegate [Senator Charles] Percy to the back pages."

After the 1966 senatorial campaign a reporter asked Remigia if she liked politics. In another charming non sequitur she said: "This is my good time to campaign. I tell my husband I like to campaign all year round. He says *what?*" She had some doubts about the prospect of a quieter life as the wife of a senator.

"Do you mean that for the next six years I can't go out again?" Although thrilled when her husband was elected, she knew he would be "more busy" than ever. "I am proud of him, but I miss him. He worked 16 hours a day when he was attorney general. The sacrifice is not too big. It is much more important now [that he is senator]. I wouldn't change anything."

Remi, who was seventeen and, according to her father, "going on twenty-one," and Edwina, fourteen "and going on eighteen," had by this time learned that one penalty they had to pay for their father's success was that they seldom saw him. Remi could have said then what Edwina, as quoted by *Seventeen* magazine, said three years later: "I often feel sorry for myself because I miss him so much. When he's home, I stay home."

Remigia maintained the modern three-bedroom Newton home so the girls could continue their schooling at Newton High, where Remi was a senior and Edwina a freshman. She said her husband would miss his family. "We are used to missing him, but he is accustomed to coming in, anywhere from nine to 11, and stopping off to say good night to the girls. I think he may say to us soon, 'I would like you to move here with me.' So I do not know how long we shall commute."

Her project was to study English. "I worry about the grammar. My husband said my accent is okay, but I should speak correctly." She hoped to brush up on her grammar with a tutor's help. When the family is together, they often speak Italian. "It is comfortable for us to do so." Mention of politics is taboo. "I still do not know everything about politics," Remigia said. "My husband tells me, 'The less you know the better you are.' But I read newspapers. I like people. I listen."

Their Newton home is backed up against a tree-shaded hill. The

211

den has a piano, record player, television and radio. Early in 1966 a reporter interviewed Remigia against the backdrop of Beatles music in one room, *Madame Butterfly* in the den, and *Sound of Music* coming from the kitchen. Sometimes, during a jam session, Brooke plays the piano, accompanied by Edwina (who also plays the piano) on the guitar. Remi is less musical. "The only piece I can play on the piano is 'Heart and Soul,' which my father taught me." Like Edwina, she speaks French and Spanish, as well as Italian, and both can Watusi and do a fancy Twist.

Remi had a part-time job as checkout girl in a Newton supermarket to earn gasoline money for her 1960 car, which, she said, ran like a 1940 model, "and I practically have to push it to school." After she took the job her father cut off her allowance, explaining that it was the price she had to pay for taking time from her studies.

The handsomely furnished living room is full of antiques collected at auctions and reflects the Brookes' love of Italian Provincial decor. Along with a Louis Quinze cabinet and a Louis Quatorze chair, there are Spanish antiques set off by two Kirman blue and gold rugs. Also in the living room are trophies, plaques, silver bowls and collections of classical records and miniature elephants. Brooke converted the cellar into an office and recreation room for the girls.

Remigia, completely dedicated to her husband's career, is devoted in the Old World manner. "When I marry him, I know he would be a lawyer, but if somebody told me it would be like *this,* I think it is impossible," she told a reporter in Washington in the spring of 1967. She told another she was from the Old World, "where women just don't interfere in their husbands' business." Although she still speaks of Italy as "my country," she is a wife whose home is where her husband is. "I came for him. I like it here. But if anyone say anything against my country I get mad. I am glad I married a strong man. But now he says I must be stronger, with the children. He say I mother them too much, that I am—what do you say, Babra—a mother hen. Some people call me old-fashioned." Brooke's actual words were: "My wife is a lot like a mother hen and does too much for the girls. They need some independence. We sometimes disagree on how much help to give them." Remigia agrees. "Now my daughter [Remi] is eighteen I must think more in the American way."

Raising two teenagers and running the Newton house with its heavy traffic was a full-time job, "and I want to do it well. I enjoy going to the opera and parties with my husband and I like meeting people on a campaign. But the home is first and very often the responsibilities here take up all my time." The Brookes have no room for servants. "I wash and wax my own floor and I may be doing it when you come," Remigia told a reporter, "but my door is open and I will share with you my coffee."

The 2,200 supporters who attended Brooke's 100-dollar-a-plate fifty-second birthday dinner in Framingham, Massachusetts, in 1971 were amused when Brooke turned to President Nixon's son-in-law, Edward F. Cox: "Tricia [Nixon Cox] shares something with my dear wife—the only thing she can cook is spaghetti." Actually, Remigia spends hours in her kitchen preparing Italian gourmet dishes. She doesn't measure ingredients. "I don't even own a measuring cup," she says.

"No, no, no, I never give recipes," she told Nancy Kovel, whose column ("Celebrity Cookbook") appeared in *The Boston Sunday Herald*. After ten hours in the kitchen with Mrs. Brooke and Barbara Masters, Miss Kovel jotted down a few recipes. "Flour flew, eggs plopped, artichokes sizzled and the 'machine' waited patiently on the kitchen table while Remigia's fingers measured by pinches and fistfuls . . . and then everything was pushed back into a borrowed set of measuring cups to ascertain the correct amounts."

While running lasagne pasta through the "machine" (an imported Italian device for shaping noodles), Remigia explained that her mother never cooked a day in her life. Nana, their servant, did the cooking. "But here is different and I remember how she does it." She finds cooking a chore. "I would rather wash windows or polish furniture, but my family likes for me to cook, so I do." The Greater Boston Young Republicans Club and other GOP organizations would never guess that she finds cooking a chore. Several times at fund-raising affairs she has cooked lasagne for large gatherings. Occasionally she raised money for groups by selling her baked lasagne for $2.50 a plate.

When Nancy Kovel visited her in March 1967, Remigia was looking forward to a summer vacation with her daughters. "I don't budge without my girls." She skis with them and sometimes takes them to Tacoma, Washington, to visit her sister, and to San "Francheesco." She loves the city: "I love one day to see a little more."

On weekends, when the Senator is home, they entertain often at candlelight dinners for as many as 16 guests. Mara Cochetto, who lived with the family for nine months in 1967, helps with the cooking. Besides baked lasagne and cannelloni, Remigia often serves ravioli—her husband's favorite Italian dish. Edwina, who, like

Remi, calls her mother "Ma," and sometimes teases her father by calling him "Fast Eddie," says one of her favorite dishes is "squid the way my mother prepares it, in a tasty sauce."

Remigia has other "specials." According to Miss Kovel, her Torta Pasqualina is a choice main dish "that puffs up like an Easter bonnet. It's rather like a chilled artichoke-quiche with a pastry pouf which would be spectacular served in small wedges as an hors d'oeuvre at your next cocktail party." The columnist says Remigia "works like lightning when blowing between the layers to make the dough puff."

Remigia, whose figure is not quite so trim as it used to be, still looks young enough to be her daughters' sister. "I eat," she says, "but always stay the same." She watches her weight and is less apt to sample her cooking than does Julia Child. "I am never fat even when young," she says. "In Italy I eat and eat—I think it is the good air over there that keeps me from fat."

In the bustle of a campaign or when otherwise engrossed, she forgets to eat. Early in February 1972 the writer invited Mrs. Brooke and her daughters to a luncheon interview at the Boston Harvard Club. Answering the doorbell at her Newton home at noon, Mrs. Brooke suggested that it would be easier to hold the interview on the premises, especially because Remi's fiancé was coming over "after lunch." After a three-and-a-half-hour interview with the vivacious trio, Mrs. Brooke suddenly realized it was closer to supper time than lunch. It was a pleasant visit that would have been interrupted if not spoiled by moving into the dining room.

During the first months of her marriage, Remigia retained certain Italian customs. "When I came to this country, I served fresh plates with each main course and thought a buffet was not a hospitable way of entertaining guests. Now, as you can see, America has taught me to eat faster and with fewer dishes." Her husband insists on saying grace before meals, she added, and if she forgets, he reminds her. "He is a very religious man and I think if you do not have that, you do not have anything." Although she was brought up a Roman Catholic, she let the girls follow their father's Episcopalian faith until Remi became a Roman Catholic convert.

While in Washington for the January swearing-in and social whirl, Remigia charmed everyone with her bubbly humor, engaging and impish grin, returning to Newton exhilarated and happy. She had seldom expected her husband home early when he was attorney general, but now had to get used to the idea of living at her Newton home with her daughters, always looking forward to rejoining her husband in Washington for a weekend of parties or a round of politics. The press was disappointed when she decided not to settle in Washington, knowing she would "add a dash of pepper to the Capitol stew." Unlike her husband, whom she has never seen lose his temper, she has fiery moods. "I have real temper, but after two minutes it is gone. You like a little action in the house in 19 years." The Brookes know each other's moods. "When I am upset he tells me you are not today to discuss. We will discuss tomorrow when you are calm." She knows when he has had a rough day from the expression in his eyes. "Then I know if I have something to ask him, this is not the time. I offer him brownies with a cup of tea or milk." It helps if she has ravioli for supper. He loves Italian food, especially meat and salad, but shies away from most desserts.

Generally speaking, their Newton home, as one reporter put it, "is filled with the happiness and trauma of life with two teenage daughters." After Brooke settled in Washington, the family missed him more than ever. "When he is home, he is full of life with them [the girls]," Remigia said. "We play together. He is very close with them. I have to talk ten thousand times before I make them listen. He doesn't have to speak two times."

Although he likes classical music, Brooke never complains about the din that sometimes drowns out conversation, when he calls his home a "madhouse." Sometimes his daughters and their friends have two record players going at once. This, Remigia soberly explains, "is not the kind of music we like. My house is like a central station." She was thinking of Grand Central.

Recalling her own childhood, she thinks young Americans "live too fast. When I was sixteen my mother took us to the country. We had a wonderful time. We would go out early, walk for miles, have a picnic, take an accordion. I climbed trees at sixteen. Now girls are like old ladies."

Remigia, who still calls her husband "Carlo," when not referring to him as "Mr. Brooke," has often said her daughters and she have never experienced prejudice because of her husband's color. That he is a Negro they simply accept and ignore.

"He has never felt any limitation," Remigia told a London reporter. "He has cut through everything. When we were first married, we lived among young couples like ourselves, struggling. We still don't have a lot of money. But me and my children, we have no experience of this kind of thing. We read it in the papers, about racial inequality, and it makes us mad. But we have no experience of it."

With her husband settled in Washington, her daily schedule in

Newton remains flexible. He often summons her to splashy Republican political affairs or White House dinners—sometimes on only a few hours' notice—or telephones her to be ready to entertain a few guests at dinner on one of his sudden trips home. Once, when Edwina was trying to decide on which college to attend, she called her father for advice. He flew right home for the evening.

Brooke lived with his mother in Washington for a few weeks before renting an apartment in the "elegant masonry" of Tiber Island, a huge block overlooking the Potomac River, the dome of the Capitol building where his office is, the Jefferson and Lincoln memorials and Kennedy's eternal flame. His mother and sister live in nearby apartments in Tiber Island.

In his apartment Brooke sips a glass of skimmed milk for breakfast before driving to his office. For a time in Washington he was seen in a chauffeured limousine with a DIR Massachusetts identification plate. Richard I. Robie, a Bay State Republican "angel," loaned him the car until Brooke hired a chauffeur, Richard Daniels of Kentucky, who for 12 years had driven for Congressman Joseph Martin. Brooke prefers to drive himself back and forth to work.

At the time it was customary for the Chrysler and Ford corporations to lease luxury cars to congressmen at low cost. Brooke had a 900-dollar lease deal with Chrysler after coming to the Senate in 1967. Although the practice did not violate any Senate rule or the law, Brooke gave up the car when the Senate's Select Committee on Standards and Conduct so advised.

After a light lunch in the Senate dining room, Brooke, when not on the Senate floor, stays in his office, where, with frequent interruptions, he works until seven in the evening or later. Back in his apartment he prepares a light supper, rarely dining out. During his first year in the Senate he didn't attend a single White House dinner or embassy reception. He simply didn't have time. Even on frequent weekend visits to his Newton home, he brought along a full briefcase. "Relax?" said Woodworth. "I've never seen the boss relax. Every moment is filled with something. He's either writing or reading."

Brooke and his family summer at Oak Bluffs on Martha's Vineyard. Long before the upstart Kennedys moved from Cohasset* to

---

* Joseph P. Kennedy quit Cohasset in a huff after the Cohasset Golf Club rejected his application for membership. According to his chauffeur at the time, Harry Pattison, Kennedy was ired because Edward Moore, little more than a glorified errand boy, belonged to the club. Pattison showed this writer the tiny garden cottage on the grounds where Moore lived.

Hyannis Port, black Bostonians founded a closed society at Oak Bluffs. Nearby Vineyard Haven hosted celebrities such as Lillian Hellman and James Cagney, who still operates his yacht out of the harbor. Oak Bluffs became the preserve of talented black poets, writers, actors and politicians, including Ethel Waters, Paul Robeson, Sidney Poitier and Eddie Haywood, a composer. Neither money nor political or literary status qualifies anyone for the "in" group. Some black Brahmins, in fact, still consider Brooke a parvenu.

Nearby Edgartown, the last WASP stronghold, as late as 1966 barred Negroes from hotels. Meanwhile, Oak Bluffs became a symbol "of the point at which Negroes had more than 'Thursday off.' It commemorates the time when an élite group of blacks (not necessarily wealthy) could join whites in the mad pursuit of leisure."

There in the summer Brooke swims, plays tennis and bicycles around the park near his home, cheerily greeting everyone he meets. There he cooks, cleans out the refrigerator, scrubs the floor, trims the hedge and prunes bushes. He also pores over a briefcase full of papers to keep up with his Senate responsibilities.

Adam Clayton Powell was already a celebrity at Oak Bluffs when his chauffeur, James Mahone, helped Brooke move to his home on 11 acres. Still there summers is Powell's first wife, whose prize possession is a pulley bucket given her by Matt Henson, a black who accompanied Peary to the North Pole and who is said to have gotten there first.

The Brookes like to entertain friends and members of the political organization at Oak Bluffs. The day after the Chappaquiddick tragedy, Al Gammal was on his way to Martha's Vineyard in a cabin cruiser with his host, Malcolm Whitney, a Watertown assessor. While trying to tune in to a Boston Red Sox baseball game, Gammal could hear above the static a disjointed account of a tragedy on the Vineyard involving a senator. He caught the words "girl drowned" and flew into a panic, fearing that something awful had happened to Brooke.

"I hate to admit it," Gammal recalls, "but I sure was relieved when I learned the senator referred to was Ted Kennedy and not Ed Brooke."

On the five-acre site of an old French fort on St. Martin in the French West Indies, the Brookes have a magnificent home built into the side of a cliff rising over 40 feet above the ocean, with stunning sea views in three directions. The 12-room house includes two large living rooms, three bedrooms, three and a half baths, a dining-room-study, a wet bar and a "lanai," a room festooned with greenery and plants, including climbing ivy. Stone steps from a 100-foot-long terrace lead down to a sandy beach. A gardener and housekeeper have this beautifully landscaped garden spot ready for immediate occupancy. It is the one place where the Senator can completely relax with his family. During the holiday recess at the end of 1971, their guest was John J. Coyle, Remi's fiancé. In a "five-and-ten-cent" poker game one night, Coyle kept raising Brooke, confident that his natural full house could beat Brooke's four clubs and hidden card. Brooke won with a flush.

"He took me to the cleaner's," Coyle said.

Mrs. Helene Amos no longer owns a home on St. Croix, where the Brookes used to visit. Lester Zwick, a Hearst newspaper executive, recalls the night on St. Croix when he introduced Senator Brooke to a Southern couple. "He is the first colored person I've shaken hands with in my life," the Virginian said. "He is really quite charming." The Governor of the Virgin Islands agreed. On September 14, 1966, he made Brooke "honorary ambassador to the Virgin Islands."

Brooke, who enjoys opera, once, while working, played the full record of *La Bohème* three times in one day. "I couldn't listen to it that many times in one day," Remigia said, "but I think he wanted to learn it word for word." Brooke was president of the Opera Company of Boston soon after he became attorney general and, after becoming senator, served as chairman of the board. Brooke learned to appreciate good music as a young boy, and ever since has been more interested in opera than in orchestral or instrumental music. "I remember that as a child I was very fond of *Carmen* and *Cavalleria Rusticana*. Among my favorite operas now are *La Bohème, Madame Butterfly* and *The Puritans*."

He is devoted to an old friend, Sarah Caldwell, whom he calls "the genius who founded the Boston Opera Company in 1957." He lauded the Boston Opera Company's home-produced operas, with much talent coming from the Boston area.

On October 22, 1966, Brooke announced that the opera company wanted to raise 610,000 dollars for the season. The money was especially needed because the Back Bay Theatre was gone, he said. Five years later, he said the lack of an opera house in Boston was a disgrace to a city known throughout the world as a cultural center. "The Opera Company of Boston is tired of living hand to mouth, year

after year, always facing one crisis or another. Opera is growing . . . and we should support it so that five out of ten American
opera singers don't have to go to Europe to perform in European
companies," he told the thirteenth annual meeting at the Harvard
Club of Boston.

In October of 1967 Brooke and Metropolitan Opera tenor Richard
Tucker were featured performers at the concert of the 108th Worcester Music Festival. Brooke narrated the Detroit Symphony Orchestra's performance of Aaron Copland's *Lincoln Portrait*.

The Brookes, who have been opera buffs for years, according to
their daughters, who prefer rock and roll, really "dig classical music."
They were among guests in 1966 when Mozart's *Don Giovanni*
brought proper Bostonians out in mink stoles, heirloom jewels and
evening gowns as the Boston Opera Company opened its ninth season
at the Back Bay Theatre. Earlier that day they heard the Monte
Carlo National Orchestra at Symphony Hall. If traffic jams around
the Back Bay Theatre and Symphony Hall meant anything, Boston
was indeed a center of culture. Governor Volpe was ten minutes late
in welcoming Prince Rainier and Princess Grace's Monaco musicians
in the name of the Massachusetts Federation of Republican Women
because his S-1 couldn't get close to Symphony Hall. Heinrich
Knappstein, the German ambassador to the U.S., addressed the
federation at the Harvard Club before members went to see Sarah
Caldwell conduct *Don Giovanni*. And, to cap things off, Mayor
John Collins' car was buried two deep while he saluted the Boston
Opera Company dinner guests at the Harvard Club. Bill Jackson
drove the Brookes right up to the front doors of all destinations that
day.

Early in March 1967 Remigia came to Washington just before her
husband left for the Far East. At Howard University she and Mrs.
Helen Brooke watched him in scarlet robes receive an honorary de-
gree at Howard's centennial. Of all the distinguished guests, a re-
porter wrote, "two men above all electrified the audience. One was
Ed Brooke . . . outstandingly handsome and magnetic in presence."
The other was President Johnson, who had come to reaffirm his com-
mitment to civil rights. Johnson in his speech meant to compliment
Brooke when he acknowledged his presence: "Senator Brooke, whom
I'm sorry to say I didn't appoint."

Remigia loved their Washington apartment: "He did this as a

surprise for me, all himself," she told a reporter from *The London Times*. Blues and browns dominate the suite, which has the Spanish-type furniture which Brooke likes.

With Barbara Masters, Remigia walked around the apartment showing it off. "This is the first time I've slept here," she said. "Babra, can you find some spoons? The only thing Carlo forgot to buy was a coffee pot. I can't manage without coffee. In the morning, I never get ready if I don't drink one cup of coffee."

During the Senate campaign Brooke had promised that, if elected, he would go to Vietnam. In 1967 he missed many roll calls because of a trip he made to Southeast Asia, the Middle East, the Mediterranean and Massachusetts.

CHAPTER TWELVE

Ambassador Without Portfolio

D URING his first two months in Washington Brooke saw how the war was taking the time of the President and Congress. The whole executive branch was tied into it, and the nation's prestige was at stake. Sitting in the Senate, he said, "You get this briefing and that briefing." When the bombing in North Vietnam was resumed, Brooke felt he could not make intelligent decisions without getting firsthand knowledge of the situation. "For when I was a boy, my father told me that the quality of a man's judgment was no better than the quality of his information."

After being cleared by the Senate Banking and Currency Committee to make a fact-finding tour of Japan, Taiwan, Hong Kong, South Vietnam, Cambodia, and Thailand, he left on March 1. With him was William I. Cowin, a legislative assistant. Before leaving Dulles Airport, Brooke found he had another companion. Peter Lucas, a *Boston Herald* political reporter, was covering his trip.

In Washington Lucas huddled with Theresa McMasters of the *Herald's* Washington bureau. "I was not to be seen by any *Globe* reporters, to keep coverage exclusive," he said. In a taxicab Theresa told of the difficulty she was having with Jerry Sadow, Brooke's press secretary, who refused to release the Senator's itinerary because she wouldn't tell him whether the *Herald* was sending a reporter on the trip. If the story was to be covered at all, Sadow wanted coverage from two competitive Boston dailies. The morning before Brooke was to leave, Theresa again called Sadow while Lucas listened in on an extension. Sadow parried questions with feigned ignorance, saying the schedule was incomplete, several times asking whether the *Herald* was sending a reporter. Theresa slammed down the phone, saying something unladylike. Then she phoned the airlines and had Brooke's schedule in two minutes. "Just make out a third ticket," she told the reservationist.

Lucas drew 5,000 dollars from the bank, of which about 2,000 dollars went to the airlines. He was excited, knowing that Brooke, after touring Southeast Asia, hoped to talk to Ho Chi Minh in Hanoi. A U.S. senator—a *black* U.S. senator, intent on crossing over into enemy territory! Lucas thought it was "one hell of an idea. Had Ho Chi Minh agreed, a picture of their meeting would have circulated throughout the world, and Brooke would have become an instant global hero."

Lucas heard that President Johnson and the State Department were upset by Brooke's project. "In fact, it was reported to me that the CIA would be watching Brooke and that I was to report any CIA man I saw. What does a CIA man look like? And suppose it was a CIA woman?"

Early Saturday morning Lucas hid in the airport so as not to be seen by Brooke, Cowin or any *Globe* reporter who might be covering the departure. After a Washington television newsman interviewed Brooke, he and Cowin climbed into the bus to be driven to the plane. Suddenly Lucas joined them. "I'm going with you," he said. Brooke frowned.

Washington to Cleveland, Cleveland to Chicago, Chicago to Anchorage, Alaska. Midway between Chicago and Anchorage, Lucas, who had been sitting behind Brooke, changed seats with Cowin. Brooke said he wanted no publicity.

"I'm going to report to the State Department and the Senate."

"Fine. But the paper's not sending me halfway around the world on a vacation." Lucas felt strange talking to Brooke as a senator. For four years at the State House, he and other reporters had called him "general" or simply "Ed." Now it was a different ball game. Brooke wanted to talk to Ho and end the war.

Lucas said he wanted at least two briefings a day, since he had to know what Brooke was doing. "I'm going to Hanoi with you if I can," he said. Brooke looked out the window instead of answering. Finally breaking the silence, he said he wanted to learn about the political and military situation in Vietnam and surrounding areas. Lucas asked about Hanoi and the State Department's reaction to the idea; also, about the personal security of a senator. Brooke said if personal security was the State Department's only reason for discouraging his trip to Hanoi, "I would not refrain from going in."

He admitted the State Department was "unhappy" with his decision to try to go to the North. "I wouldn't do anything to impede any possible negotiations," he said, adding that the State Department even objected to his visit to Cambodia, since the U.S. then had no diplomatic ties with that neutral nation.

The plane set down in Anchorage during sunny but windy weather. Lucas had typed his story on the plane. It was 2:00 P.M. in Anchorage, 8:00 P.M. in Boston. During the half-hour layover Lucas got the city desk and dictated his story. The editor asked whether there were "any *Globe* guys around," adding that the *Herald* editor wanted to promote the story if it was exclusive. It was.

The group flew to Taipei, Taiwan (Formosa—the Republic of China), after a stop at Tokyo. On the way Brooke ordered one Bloody Mary while Lucas drained three glasses of tomato juice. Not until he felt woozy did he realize that the Japanese stewardess had given him the three Bloody Marys and Brooke the tomato juice.

In the spring of 1971 Brooke was prophetic when he said Nixon's overtures toward mainland China might be the most significant legacy of his administration. Three months later he again praised Nixon for opening the way to trade and travel with China and announcing his intention to be the first American President to visit mainland China and the first to visit a country with which we have no diplomatic relations. What he said in the spring and summer of 1971 had been on his mind when he visited Thailand in 1967: "Communication with Red China does not mean we reject the Republic of China. Nor does it mean we are seeking to pit one Communist nation against another [Russia]. It means we are committed to the concept that world peace must be nurtured in the soil of world understanding. Nixon has made a wise and courageous move toward world peace."

Brooke was pleased when the UN seated Red China in the fall of 1971. He regretted that the United Nations had kicked out Taiwan, but realized it was inevitable.

"To travel from Japan to Taiwan is to travel from an already developed, highly sophisticated nation to one that is well on the way to similar economic and social well-being," Brooke said later. "Taiwan is literally moving from a bicycle economy through a motorcycle economy and into an automobile economy."

In each place he visited, he conferred with government officials, and with a variety of private citizens, including youth groups, Communists, soldiers, professors and other intellectuals, politicians and farmers. "I took full advantage of the wisdom and experience offered by the competent men and women whom I found in the Foreign Service of the United States. I spent as much time as possible seeing at first hand examples of those things which had been discussed in briefings, asking questions, and testing fundamental American policies against the harsh light of the realities of a distant and far different continent." One major purpose was to look into the commodity import program of each country he visited.

In Taiwan he consulted with the Vice-President and Prime Minister, C. K. Yen; the Economic Minister, K. T. Li; and the Vice-Minister for Foreign Affairs, H. K. Yang. As elsewhere, he also talked with private citizens, including the governor of the Central Bank of China, Kan Lee, and the president of the China Development Corporation, Felix Chang. Also, he visited the Legislative Yuan as well as a variety of industrial and agricultural projects and academic institutions. "I was most favorably impressed with the quality and dedication of the political and business leadership in Taiwan," he said. He thought Taiwan had the potential of West Berlin, "something we can show and sell to the rest of Asia." Brooke suggested that Taiwan might consider improving its own economy rather than trying to return to the mainland. "It's what they talk and think about, no matter how impractical it may seem." American know-how and show-how was having an impact.

Brooke spent a day in Taiwan inspecting factories and in a moment of leisure bought four sets of ivory chopsticks for his family. "I like to use them myself," he said.

Brooke next went to the Asiatic listening post of Hong Kong, a British crown colony with a population of 3,750,000, of which over 98 percent are Chinese. It is a hazardous descent into the airport, which is cupped between mountains and the harbor, with a quick drop to the runway. Two weeks after Brooke's plane landed a plane went down in the harbor. All passengers were rescued, including Melinda Hall, once on Brooke's staff.

On a warm, humid evening Brooke and Cowin checked into the Mandarin Hotel. Next morning they applied for visas to Cambodia, hoping it would be a stepping stone to Hanoi. A spokesman for the U.S. consul general in Hong Kong said Brooke's prospects of getting to Hanoi were almost nil. "I think he has a ten percent chance. He would have no chance if he were not a Negro." Brooke spent two hours with Allen S. Whiting, a China expert at the American consulate, who briefed him on conditions in Red China. Then Brooke, Cowin and Lucas toured the business district of the city and crossed the harbor to visit refugee settlements on the Kowloon Peninsula with Lynn Olson, chief economist at the U.S. consulate.

Unimpressed by merchandise in a huge department store owned by Red China, the Americans bought nothing. Nor was Brooke interested when "Mr. Sam," a local tailor who counted diplomats and other high officials among his clients, telephoned him at the Mandarin Hotel and tried to sell him a custom-tailored suit.

"Other senators buy them. You will be the first who does not."

"I'll be the first who does not," Brooke said, hanging up.

Hong Kong's business community, finance, port and related facilities are highly developed, and unusual wealth and affluence can be found within its total 397.75-square-mile area. "Unfortunately," says Brooke, "there is also dire poverty in Hong Kong, the likes of which I personally have never witnessed in the worst part of the United States or anywhere else in the world. Sampans mired in the mud and housing four, six, or eight persons, and filth and disease surpassing description are found within 500 yards of beautiful homes owned by successful businessmen. Within a mile of the colony's impressive business center are hillsides containing ramshackle huts housing thousands of Chinese refugees. Although the government of the colony has made progress in refugee relocation by the development of public refugee housing centers, several of which I visited, the major problems posed by the refugee influx must still be resolved."

Until it became illegal in 1962, Hong Kong admitted more than a million refugees from Red China, and by 1967 they were about a fourth of the crown colony's population. Lucas, who was amazed by the poverty nuzzling opulence, said about 90,000 refugees lived in dilapidated sampans in one two-mile stretch. One sampan was a home for a dozen refugees clad in what looked like dirty, ragged underwear shorts. The sampans are moored in muck so filthy its stench is nauseating. There the poorest of the poor sit with vacant stares.

After crossing from sampan to sampan on a slimy bridge of rotting planks, Brooke came away shaking his head. During the 20 minutes he spent in this squalid setting, children badgered him for handouts. He discovered later in Saigon that kids no older than six become your friends to pick your pocket. The Aberdeen section, where starving refugees live not far from the apartments of the affluent Chinese, is not far from Repulse Bay, a garden spot with a sprawling hotel, golf course and tennis courts.

The Brooke party took a five minute ferry ride from Aberdeen to Aplichua, a district of Hong Kong where Chinese artisans in a picturesque setting strip junk machinery and build fishing boats. Another five-minute drive from Aberdeen to the crown colony's shopping center offers a world of bargains. There some of the world's best pearls can be bought for a fraction of the cost in the U.S. Brooke bought some for his family. At a resettlement site on the outskirts of the city, he was impressed by the discipline of Chinese children as they lined up for milk and crackers. Some swarmed all over him, wrapping themselves around his legs in a friendly gesture.

Back at the hotel Lucas tried to get Brooke's reaction to the contrast between the haves and have-nots in Hong Kong and was miffed when the Senator clammed up. Lucas walked off in a huff. That night Brooke, realizing the reporter was angry and not knowing what he was going to write, was guest of honor at a political dinner.

"I sat beside him," Lucas said. "After a glass of Chinese wine he felt more relaxed, loosened up and gave me a story. But it was a running battle most of the time getting him to talk."

Brooke's primary purpose in going to Hong Kong was to talk with as many "China watchers" as possible, to get information about economic, political, social, and military problems on the mainland. China watchers get information from Chinese radiocasts, Chinese newspapers, Chinese refugees from the mainland, and Chinese living in Hong Kong who correspond and visit with relatives and friends on the mainland. "Recently," Brooke said after returning to the U.S., "much information has also come from 'wall posters,' an institution which is somewhat familiar in the Orient and at times surprisingly accurate. In addition, much knowledge is gained from the wisdom of Chinese citizens who reside in Hong Kong and from their frequently informed, sometimes intuitive, sense of what is transpiring within China's closed society."

Landing in Saigon on March 11, the party stayed at the Hotel Embassy, where, as in less plush hotels, lizards scamper across the walls. In the musty elegance of Saigon, according to Lucas, you "have to curve as you walk to avoid stepping on a woman and two young children sleeping on a mat on the sidewalk, or you will have to cross the street to avoid a woman suckling a baby as she squats along the walkway and begs for money. After a strenuous day, you can relax at a sidewalk café with a bottle of San Miguel beer from the Philippines and watch the Edsels whip by."

Brooke helicoptered around the countryside, visiting installations, talking to troops and listening to innumerable briefings. In one of the refugee camps around Saigon he told Staff Sergeant Gilbert Broner of Fitchburg he was glad to meet him. "I carried that city [in the Senate election]." He talked to other New Englanders as he climbed over sandbags piled up by American and Vietnamese troops. Children at an elementary school welcomed him with a Vietnamese army tune.

In Saigon Brooke was guarded by a cordon of troops. One day he visited Bao Trai, 30 miles west of Saigon, to inspect reconstruction programs. The village had been attacked four times during the preceding year, and only hours before Brooke's arrival the Vietcong had staged a brief firefight in the streets. As his jeep drove up, American and Vietnamese infantrymen lined the route.

Brooke talked with South Vietnamese officials, including Prime Minister Nguyen Cao Ky and Foreign Minister Tran Van Do. He conferred with Ambassador Henry Cabot Lodge at a luncheon at the embassy and was briefed by General William C. Westmoreland and the general staff. He attended a session of the Constituent Assembly and was present when South Vietnam's new constitution was finally adopted. He rode a patrol boat up Saigon River to chat with Massachusetts members of the 199th Light Infantry Brigade at Cat Lai, south of Saigon. He told the men about the Boston Strangler and "the war going on between other armed forces" in Greater Boston, meaning gangland slayings.

"Most of the GI's seemed fed up with the war," Lucas wrote. Brooke sat down with them, reminding them that civilians, not the military, run the government. "Write my office in Washington if you have any complaints." Brooke also talked with knowledgeable members of the international press corps in Saigon, charming them, according to Lucas. "What a hell of a guy," a reporter said.

In army fatigues Brooke inspected a captured Vietcong mine. On March 13 he visited Mekong Delta, looking down from a helicopter at a hamlet just liberated from the Vietcong. In the Chieu Hoi prison camp on the outskirts of Saigon he asked a Vietcong deserter through an interpreter why he had defected to the South Vietnamese side: "Because I could not live with the Vietcong any longer. I lost my freedom. They made me work very hard. They gave me no food."

Another VC deserted because he feared American air strikes. The U.S. Army paid VC deserters for bringing in weapons. The camp near

Bien Hoa, not far from Saigon, is a field enclosed by a maze of barbed wire. South Vietnamese police run the camp, one of several rimming the city.

Lucas tells of a typical day for Brooke: "Your arms ache as you awake before dawn to catch a lift to the airport for the chopper ride in the country to cover the daily travels of Brooke. They ache because you have been shot full of holes as a precaution against disease." After being inoculated against plague, typhoid, typhus, tetanus and being revaccinated, Lucas felt awful. "You remember that somewhere along the line you are supposed to get some other shot, but you feel now that the only protection you really need is a bulletproof vest."

On the way to the U.S. Mission Press Center, where a truck picked up reporters, Lucas saw women cooking breakfast on the sidewalk. Along walls on side streets men and boys were urinating. In the helicopter Lucas sat in a seat next to the open door.

"Don't worry," a photographer told him, "it's almost impossible to fall out of these choppers." As they flew over lush terrain they could see winding rivers, rice paddies, rubber plantations, the jungle and bomb craters dotting the countryside. After a long ride they got into a jeep and followed Brooke to a refugee center, hoping no VC would throw a bomb. "I can just hear one VC telephoning his cousin in the next village," an English photographer said. " 'Let Senator Brooke's car go by but get the one carrying the tall English photographer.' "

While talking to Massachusetts GI's, Brooke saw panic in the eyes of a young soldier who asked him to call his mother when he got back to say, "I'm all right." Lucas could see "fear and frustration in his handsome face. His arms look as though they were better made to carry a baseball bat than a rifle."

In a hospital ward the first wounded soldier Brooke spoke to had a look of resignation and defeat. Brooke continued down the ward, "offering a word here, a joke there, a handshake, encouragement, sympathy. He glances through the windows of an operating room and says later, 'I wish I hadn't done that.' It takes three or four minutes to complete the walk down the one ward and by the time Brooke reaches the end the first wounded soldier has died."

Even hard-boiled reporters came away misty-eyed. "The sun is still bright when you leave the hospital," Lucas says. "Your arms do not ache anymore."

In South Vietnam Brooke visited every echelon of command from generals down to infantry in foxholes and explored some of the tunnels uncovered in one massive drive. He found corruption when he walked the port at Saigon. "I flew over it by helicopter, and I talked with seamen on barges and ships, and rode in a Navy patrol boat up the Saigon River." He found "seemingly unresolvable congestion." Perishable commodities remained unloaded in ships and barges docked in port for weeks and sometimes months. "Goods ordered when prices are high may not arrive until such prices have fallen considerably." Thus consignees often prefer to leave the cargo in port rather than claim it and suffer a loss caused by low prices. Brooke said consignees who refuse to claim cargoes when they arrive should be denied import licenses.

Cambodia had approved visas for Brooke and Cowin in Hong Kong on the fifth day of their tour. Lucas was denied a visa only because he was a reporter. Had he known this, he would have posed as a tourist. At Saigon's airport Brooke said he would talk to any available representatives of the National Liberation Front or North Vietnam in Phnom Penh, hoping eventually to learn how Hanoi was weathering the war. He had no peace feelers. "I have no authority to negotiate. I want to correct any false impression that I go [to Cambodia] as an agent of the U.S. I go as a member of a legislative body."

Cambodia had severed diplomatic relations with the U.S. in 1965, two years after Senator Mike Mansfield of Montana had conferred with Prince Sihanouk in Phnom Penh. Since then, South Vietnam had charged that Cambodia provided a sanctuary for the Vietcong fleeing superior allied forces.

After they had spent the night in a hotel in Phnom Penh, a limousine sent by Prince Norodom Sihanouk picked up Brooke and Cowin shortly after 7:00 A.M. and drove them to a ceremony to inaugurate the opening of a bridge at Sangkum. Since Sihanouk had been in France from the beginning of January until early in March, this was his first opportunity to speak publicly with respect to the affairs of Cambodia and its international relations.

"I was politely accorded a place of honor on the platform directly behind the Prince as he addressed a crowd of several thousand," Brooke said. "During his remarks, which were delivered in Cambodian, French, and partially in English, the Prince stated his esteem and good feeling for the American people and expressed the belief that Ho Chi Minh undoubtedly felt the same way. He took pains to express his fondness and admiration for Senator Mansfield,* for whom an avenue had been named in Cambodia. The Prince reiterated his familiar position that Cambodia did not wish to be a party to the ideological struggle between the East and West, but wanted simply to be left in peace to develop in its own way. . . . In the portion of the Prince's address which was delivered in English, he referred to the war in Vietnam as a civil conflict which in the beginning could not have been considered a threat to world peace. Although he expressed his understanding why the United States might intervene in a controversy which really jeopardized the peace of the world, he insisted that U.S. intervention in the Vietnamese war had in fact created the very threat to world peace which the U.S. sought to avoid. He said American intervention had transformed a primarily internal controversy into a struggle of worldwide concern. At the conclusion of his remarks we crossed the new bridge together, but there was no opportunity for me to present my own belief that the real threat to world peace had been posed by North Vietnamese aggression."

Seated on the temporarily erected platform for dedication ceremonies for the new bridge with Brooke and Cowin were the Australian ambassador and envoys from Peking and North Vietnam. Their presence explained some of Sihanouk's barbs at Americans during his two-hour speech.

"Sihanouk spoke several minutes in Cambodian, translated his remarks into French, then spoke in English, repeating this cycle in his talk," Cowin recalls. "When others on the platform applauded when he spoke in French, I clapped my hands. My textbook French, little remembered from high-school days, is not as good as Senator Brooke's, and when I noticed that he did not applaud the Prince during the French intervals, I refrained. It turned out that Sihanouk had been attacking U.S. policy in Southeastern Asia in all three languages. When he spoke in English he bitterly blamed the U.S. for the war in Vietnam."

After the ribbon-cutting ceremony, Brooke and Sihanouk talked for several minutes. The Prince showed Brooke a downed U.S. airplane as proof of U.S. incursions and asked how they could handle the problem of resuming diplomatic relations. In his speech Sihanouk had described his country's foreign policy as reciprocity—Cambodian

---

* Senator Mansfield, a close friend of Prince Sihanouk, had contacted the Prince through Cambodia's permanent representative to the United Nations to assist in arranging Brooke's visit.

attitudes toward other countries would depend primarily, even solely, upon the attitudes of such other countries toward Cambodian sovereignty and independence.

Prince Sihanouk was official host *in absentia* at a luncheon and dinner in Brooke's honor. Cowin got drowsy at the ten-course luncheon, and a 14-course dinner that night made him even drowsier. "I don't know how Brooke got through those official receptions. With about 20 persons present at the dinner, almost everyone toasted everyone else, and it was evident that were expected to drain our small glass of Chinese wine each time. It was an insult not to." Host at the dinner was Son Sann, private counselor of Sihanouk. Among prominent Cambodian officials present were the Secretary of State for Commerce, Seng Bun Korn; the Secretary-General of the Council of the Kingdom, Khieu Vann; the President of the Foreign Affairs Commission of the National Assembly, Keuky Lim; and members of the Foreign Affairs Ministry and the Ministry of Information. Also present was His Excellency Noel St. Clair DesChamps, the Australian ambassador to Cambodia, who was highly knowledgeable and most cooperative. According to Brooke, "Since the break in diplomatic relations between the U.S. and Cambodia, Mr. DesChamps has performed effective consular-type services in Cambodia for the U.S. government."

During the dinner, which lasted several hours, the Cambodian-American rupture was discussed. "Toward the close of the evening," Brooke said, "I asked why Cambodia still retained diplomatic relations with Australia, despite Australia's participation in the war in Vietnam. Son Sann responded that participation in the war was a private matter for the governments of the U.S. and Australia, and not the concern of Cambodia. He pointed out that the difference in the Cambodian view of the two countries was based upon the fact that at all times during the war Australia had respected the sovereignty of Cambodia and the inviolability of her borders, whereas the U.S. had clearly violated Cambodia's borders."

At the end of the dinner, Son Sann, in a brief improvised speech in English, said he was happy to receive Brooke in the name of the Prince, adding that he was pleased that the Senator seemed to understand the Cambodian policy of strict neutrality. Son Sann said he hoped Brooke's mission would "contribute to the development of mutual understanding."

In his Senate speech on his return from the tour, Brooke said there had been many "unfortunate incidents in which troops have crossed the border and planes have flown over Cambodian territory. Perhaps the most unfortunate incident occurred at Thlok Trach, where American bombs were dropped upon a town which, for as long as all observers can remember, had been governed by Cambodia, although French maps located the town in South Vietnam. Such incidents give Cambodia cause to doubt American respect for Cambodia's sovereignty."

When word spread that Brooke wanted to see spokesmen from North Vietnam, there were inconclusive phone calls in the middle of the night. The procedure was like playing a game of chess with an unseen and unidentified opponent.

Brooke, in his hotel lounge, had a long sit-down with Wilfred Burchett, an Australian correspondent for *The London Daily Express* in World War II. He had sailed with the U.S. Navy in the Pacific. Despite his reputed contacts with Hanoi, he could do nothing about arranging a conference between Ho Chi Minh and Brooke in North Vietnam.

Brooke queried Cambodian officials about rumors of Cambodian peasants along the South Vietnamese border being armed. Officials blandly explained that these peasants usually wore black pajama-like outfits—the uniform of the Vietcong—and were often mistaken for the Vietcong fleeing into the safety of Cambodia.

After visiting Cambodia, Brooke had planned to fly to Vientiane, capital of Laos, which, with Vietnam, formerly constituted French Indochina. The next stop was to be Thailand, which had become a launching site for U.S. raids against North Vietnam. Brooke canceled his trip to Laos and went directly to Bangkok, Thailand, where he spent a Friday morning in bed recovering from a stomach upset believed caused by impure water he drank in Cambodia. He recovered in time to confer with officials, who reminded him that Thailand and the U.S. had a common cause: a will to resist a Communist takeover in Southeast Asia. Thailand's ambassador to the U.S., Sukichic Nemmanheminda, assessed the situation: "When Southeast Asia is gone, half of Asia is gone. If half of Asia is gone, all of it will be gone. The time to put out a fire is when the fire is a small one."

When Brooke left Saigon, he thought he had lost Lucas. The reporter knew a plane flew once a day from Saigon to Bangkok, with stops at Phnom Penh and Vientiane. He was frustrated when there was no vacancy on this plane. Noticing an old peasant woman carrying a mesh bagful of carrots and beets in the waiting line at Saigon airport, Lucas called aside the clerk behind the counter and offered him ten dollars if he could squeeze him onto the plane. The clerk dumped the woman and sold her reserved ticket to Lucas.

"I felt like a heel when I realized what had happened," he said, "but I had been stymied too often in Southeast Asia, and I had deadlines to meet. I sat in second class up front behind a curtain. When nobody was allowed off the plane at Phnom Penh, I figured this was Brooke's flight to Bangkok. It was. As I flapped open the curtain, he was putting a package* up on the rack. He was surprised, but pleasant, when he saw me."

In Bangkok, Cowin said Brooke was not cutting short his trip because of contacts made in Phnom Penh. He was returning to Washington merely because he had gathered the information on U.S. overseas aid programs which he needed as a member of the Senate Committee on Banking and Currency.

Brooke landed at Dulles International Airport Saturday night, after flying home from Thailand by way of Anchorage. He brought back new thoughts on Vietnam after his talk with Ambassador Lodge in Saigon and exchanges with combat veterans and VC prisoners of war.

Soon after his return, in a speech at Johns Hopkins University in Baltimore he said he was tired of the terms "hawks" and "doves," so tired he was thinking of complaining to the Audubon Society. "What the President needs is fewer hawks and doves and more owls." He grinned when asked about GI opinion of Senator Robert Kennedy, who had recently toured Vietnam. "They were still talking about his hairdo," he said. (This was before long hair became more fashionable.) When he mentioned Governor Ronald Reagan, several students hissed.

"Thank you for helping me make up my mind," he said. In this well-received talk Brooke showed his wit. "The Japanese have developed a great society—did I say 'great society'? I'll have to watch that."

On another theme he said the Harlem district in which Adam Clayton Powell had been reelected deserved representation, noting that although the issue properly belonged in the House of Representatives, one reason for his censure was that he dramatized and brought to light existing abuses. "I don't rule out race," he added, as one

---

* In the package was a silver cigarette case given to Brooke by Prince Norodom Sihanouk, with whom Brooke has corresponded since his 1967 visit.

reason for the censure. He did not think, however, that race was a supervening consideration. At a press conference before his speech he said the publicity concerning Powell and Senator Thomas J. Dodd a Connecticut Democrat who had been censured, pointed up the need for reform. Brooke said a "full disclosure" law might be the best way to prevent abuse.

On the day before he gave his Vietnam report to the Senate, he met with Vice-President Hubert Humphrey and Secretary of State Rusk.

Wearing a black suit, Brooke seemed relaxed as he entered the Senate chamber shortly after noon. His mother, wearing a black dress with a red bow, sat with tourists in the gallery. Fewer than ten senators were on the floor, and Brooke waited until they had finished lauding Paul H. Douglas, the Democratic senator from Illinois, who had lost his bid for reelection. Brooke took the floor after Senator William Proxmire, a Wisconsin Democrat, said: "The junior senator from Massachusetts has a very important speech."

As a man of peace, Brooke returned from his trip with a demand that the U.S. use tear gas instead of napalm in some actions, since napalm killed civilians. In other comments he did not sound so much like a dove:

Noting that in the main the American people do not and have not differed on their basic commitment, Brooke said in his maiden Senate speech: "And let there be no doubt in the mind of Ho Chi Minh or anyone else that the American people will persevere in their fundamental support of the South Vietnamese. That commitment is a willingness to discuss an equitable political settlement in Vietnam; and a readiness to continue our military and economic assistance to the South Vietnamese so long as is necessary.

"The American people are beginning to accept, reluctantly but definitely, that this struggle could conceivably last another decade. On the other hand, there can be no doubt that the North has suffered severe losses during the past year and a half. The North Vietnamese–Vietcong casualty rate has continued to soar, and defections from their ranks have increased dramatically. . . . It is possible that continued military pressure may end the war sooner than we dare to hope."

Later in his speech Brooke said he had hoped "that a cessation of bombing in the North would bring about negotiations for peace, that if we did cease our bombing, Ho Chi Minh would come to the conference table and honest negotiations for peace could commence. I am discouraged by his recent statement affirming his original position that negotiations are impossible without cessation of bombing in the North coupled with a unilateral withdrawal of American and allied troops from South Vietnam. This reassertion of his original and fixed position shows no intention on the part of Ho Chi Minh to negotiate for peace at this time."

Brooke said that while in Cambodia he had tried through intermediaries to talk to North Vietnamese representatives. "The representative of the Hanoi government sent back a message that he believed that any discussions between us would serve no useful purpose at this time." Brooke went on to say the burden of responsibility had shifted from the U.S. to the Hanoi government. "I firmly believe that this continuation of the war is based on the influence of those in Hanoi who believe the U.S. will falter." Brooke, favoring containment of the war, advised patience until Hanoi realized negotiated peace was the only solution. Brooke did not favor escalation of U.S. military commitment in Vietnam, nor did he advise any military action which might arouse Communist China's fears that her borders were threatened and that her intervention was imperative. His assessment:

"Since I believe that North Vietnam is not prepared to negotiate in a meaningful way at this time, I must reluctantly conclude that the general direction of our present military efforts in Vietnam is necessary. This is far from an easy conclusion for me to reach. I know war. I am familiar with its consequences. I like to think of myself as a man who loves and desires peace for all men. But all too frequently what we desire and what reality thrusts upon us are very different."

Brooke says *The New York Times* read too much into his speech when it reported the next day: "President Johnson won a prize convert today in the congressional debate on the Vietnam war. Senator Brooke, who had advocated a reduction of the American military effort, said he had changed his mind after touring Southeast Asia."

On the CBS television program *Face the Nation* Martin Agronsky, Alex Kendrick and Robert Novak, in a series of skillful questions, forced Brooke to admit that the war in Vietnam had brought the civil-rights movement to a dead halt. *The Nation,* a liberal publication, came to the same conclusion. By endorsing the President's direction of the war, the magazine charged, "Brooke has not merely let the peace movement down, he has left American Negroes in the lurch." During the interview Brooke had said, "If we show strength within the confines of a limited war I believe [Hanoi] will come to the peace table sooner than at any other time."

Minutes after the program ended, President Johnson phoned

Brooke from the White House retreat at Camp David, Maryland. Brooke, who took the call in the monitor room at the CBS studio in Boston, fought back tears as Johnson praised him for giving "a clear statement of the situation" and invited him to confer with him at the White House. Johnson told Brooke he had performed a great service by saying the best path to peace lay in continued military pressure against the Communists, adding that he "had never heard the U.S. position presented more clearly, more succinctly, or more forcefully." Soon thereafter the President sent Brooke a photograph (which hangs on the wall of his Washington office) inscribed: "To Ed Brooke from Lyndon B. Johnson." Ted Kennedy has never received such an autographed photo from Johnson.

On the show Brooke said he would have been pleased to return recommending immediate withdrawal of U.S. troops, negotiating for peace immediately and ceasing bombing of the North. "But when I saw the men dying as I did in the hospitals and I saw the soldiers at the front who believed in the cause for which they were fighting [then I realized that putting U.S. troops] into the ring with one hand tied behind [them] just wasn't right." In defending his revised position he said, "I'm carrying no brief for the President. The President has never brainwashed me." He said he had had serious doubts as to whether the U.S. should be in Vietnam in the first place. "But the fact is, we are there." He also said he found no evidence that Cambodia was giving sanctuary to Communists, but found that American forces had violated the Cambodian border.

The Senate speech moved Brooke closer to the GOP center. Most Republicans then favored a strong military posture in hopes of ending the war quickly. William S. White, a syndicated columnist, said Brooke's stance might aid the GOP, noting that his "private courage and public honor" had earned him the respect of a great majority of both political parties. "But he has become almost a traitor to the little band of peaceniks who had thought they had captured him." White pounced on Martin Luther King, Jr., and other black leaders:

"Never in memory has a single act by a freshman senator had such profound effects as has Brooke's simple act of intellectual gallantry here. For one thing, he has largely broken the long attempt of extremist Negro leaders to force a halt to American military resistance in Vietnam on the false argument that this help to a dark-skinned people in Southeast Asia was somehow harmful to the civil-rights movement at home."

Brooke won praise from an unusual quarter when Senator John G.

Tower, a GOP Texas conservative who was one of Goldwater's first supporters, lauded him on the Senate floor for "one of the most courageous acts on the part of one of my colleagues I have witnessed since being in this body." He inserted in the *Congressional Record* quotations from several Texas newspapers which commended Brooke's stand.

A fortnight after the Senate speech *The Nation* reported: "Anyone reading the headlines of March 24 might conclude that history was a plot. One read, 'Dr. King to Press Anti-war Stand'; another, 'Brooke Shifts View and Supports President.' No doubt the timing was coincidental, but accidents can be politically important. In this instance, what would have been a setback for the President turned into a day of triumph. He had won a prize convert whose timely conversion offset Dr. King's renewed attack on the administration's war policy, which he first launched at the National Institute in Los Angeles on February 25."

Brooke's support was indeed welcome at the White House at a time when black leaders were escalating their war against the war. After his maiden address, Brooke received 8,000 telegrams, letters and postcards—divided about two to one against his stand. Constituents blasted him as a cheap politician and accused him of betraying his trust by selling out to President Lyndon Johnson. It was the worst lashing the Senator had ever received from his public.

There was no doubt that his speech, which elated hawks, further split the already divided black civil-rights movement. The Boston chapter of CORE sent him a letter after his speech which ended by urging President Johnson to end immediately the bombing of North Vietnam and to enter into immediate negotiations aimed at the earliest possible withdrawal of U.S. forces.

"It is hypocritical in the extreme for the administration to seek justice in Vietnam at the expense of racial and social justice at home," the letter said in part. "Boston CORE in its attempts to serve racial justice has become keenly aware of the enormous economic needs of our nation's ghettos and slums. Here is America's greatest problem. Against this background, we see the war in Vietnam using billions of dollars every year and laying waste to the beginnings of progress in this country. The disproportionate number of Negroes who fight and are killed is an ironic commentary on a society in which the only promise of full manhood and economic security for black men leads through combat."

Although Brooke and Martin Luther King were not enemies predestined to meet in a narrow alley, their clash was of particular interest, especially since *Time* in 1963 had named the minister "Man of the Year," explaining that he was chosen "as a man but also on the representative of his people, for whom 1963 was perhaps the most important year in their history. The American Negro made 1963 the year of his outcry for equality, of massive demonstrations, of sit-ins and speeches and street fighting, of soul searching in the suburbs and psalm singing in the jails." In 1964 King won the Nobel Peace Prize in further recognition of his efforts as a black leader of blacks. The press noted that he had "succeeded in keeping his followers to the principle of nonviolence. Without King's confirmed effectiveness . . . demonstrations and marches could easily have become violent and ended with the spilling of blood."

Said King: "I accept the Nobel Prize for Peace at a moment when 22 million Negroes of the United States . . . are engaged in a creative battle to end the long night of racial injustice."

In ensuing years King's luster dimmed. Dr. Ralph Bunche said he was guilty of a tactical mistake in trying to lead both a civil-rights campaign and a crusade against American involvement in Vietnam, and the NAACP shared this view. *Life* magazine went a step further: "In linking the civil-rights movement with total opposition to our position in Vietnam, Dr. Martin Luther King comes close to betraying the cause for which he has worked so long."

A few weeks after his Senate speech Brooke challenged King's stand on Vietnam, saying his efforts to brand the conflict a Negro war were harmful. "His advice to young men not to obey the draft laws is dangerous. It unquestionably has hurt him and it unquestionably will hurt the civil-rights movement. This is a time for sane, calm deliberations. Inciting violence is not going to bring about civil rights for the American Negro. It will not be won with bloodshed."

Brooke said King's plea for a cease-fire was suicidal, but he credited the minister's leadership of civil-rights demonstrations as the forerunner of the 1964 Civil Rights Act. He equally blamed the change of direction in the movement for the defeat of new civil-rights legislation in 1966.

Brooke had further comment on Southeast Asia when he was interviewed by Senator Clifford P. Hansen, a Wyoming Republican conservative, on Hansen's weekly television show: "We've not sent troops into North Vietnam. We've not crossed the seventeenth parallel and our bombing is justifiable because we are doing interdiction bombing and we are bombing strategic military targets. I do believe that if we mine Haiphong harbor, or if we send planes into mainland China and bomb the airbases near North Vietnam, that very possibly could provoke Red China into the war."

A personal letter dated April 23, 1967, from Prince Sihanouk further verified Brooke's remark that American forces violated the Cambodian border. Sihanouk said "our hostility toward the policy of the United States government has no ideological motive, but is inspired by the frequent and brutal violations of our borders by the American forces, who thereby show their contempt for our sovereignty and our territorial integrity. You have shown in your report* that you recognize the existence of these violations, that you deplore them, and that you demand that they be avoided in the future. . . . And may you be heard by your government when you declare that the existence of a truly neutral Cambodia is of great importance for the U.S. and the peace of Southeast Asia."

Before many more months had passed, Sihanouk was ousted by a coup and was living in exile in Peking.

Most comments on Brooke's maiden speech were favorable. At the request of Francis T. Galbraith, U.S. ambassador to Singapore, the U.S. Information Service produced an illustrated booklet with the full text of the speech for overseas distribution. Later Galbraith said the booklet had been distributed to 12,500 government officials and news media representatives in Singapore and Malaysia.

Brooke, who had contracted an intestinal infection in Asia, was sipping skimmed milk and munching on cookies one morning when a *Boston Traveler* reporter interviewed him for a story captioned: "Brooke All Set to Go on More Peace Trips." Noting that the Senator was "becoming a self-styled peace ambassador, traveling the countries of the world wherever he found a ray of hope for peaceful coexistence," the reporter said Brooke was about to leave for Pacem in Terris II, the second international convocation on the requirements for peace to be held May 28–31 in Geneva.

Enroute to the Geneva peace conference of 70 nations, Brooke planned to stop in Frankfurt and Berlin, hoping to visit the East Berlin wall as well as the western sector. "I want to see both sides."

---

* After he returned to the U.S. Brooke sent Sihanouk a report he had made to the U.S. Senate. In a letter he wrote: "I take the liberty of inviting your attention to pages 11 through 13 wherein I sought to summarize my impressions of my all-too-brief stay in Cambodia."

He also said in the interview that he wanted to visit the Arab nations in 1967 and expected to tour eastern European Communist countries and Africa in 1968.

"Peace and understanding in this world are what I said I would work for," he said as he paced the hooked rug (which Helen Cavelle had made for him) in his Senate office. "I don't care if they criticize me," he added, referring to a published report about his missing roll calls. "Whenever I find a ray of hope for peaceful coexistence and understanding, I'm going to reach out for it. I said in my acceptance speech that peace was my great concern."

He didn't travel for fun. "It's hard work. I'm up at 5:30 and seldom get to sleep before one A.M. after long interviews and talks. There is also the fatigue of the travel and the time changes." Asked whether he thought he was neglecting his constituents, he said there had been little Senate activity while he was in Southeast Asia. "I'll be here when there are important votes and committee reports," he said, adding that he spent less time traveling around the country making speeches than most senators. "I have turned my back on no domestic problems."

Brooke has a cartoon mounted on the wall beside his desk showing him in Bermuda shorts and a flowered sports shirt, his valise plastered with travel stickers as he arrives at an airport after a trip to Greece, the Virgin Islands, Africa, Vietnam, Thailand, Cambodia, Japan, Hong Kong and Israel: "I also have high hopes of visiting Washington one of these days," the Szep cartoon reads.

Brooke was in Jerusalem, Israel, on April 24, about a month after his return from Southeast Asia. While touring the campus of Hebrew University, he met a student in the central library. "I'm Kenneth Kupisch from Walton," the twenty-one-year-old student said. "My brother Clay worked for you during the [Senate] election campaign." Brooke introduced the youth to his wife and others in the party, some of whom had known the student's late father, Clarence Kupisch, a Boston attorney.

Brooke went to Israel primarily for the laying of the cornerstone of the aeronautical wing of the Amal Comprehensive Trade School which was named for him. The trip was sponsored by the Boston Histadrut* Committee, which had honored the Senator in the fall of 1966 with its Brotherhood Award for his help in building technical educational institutions in Israel. Brooke was touched when the foun-

---

* "Histadrut" is the name of the Israeli Federation of Labor Committee.

dation stone was laid, as Remigia, the Herbert Tuckers, the Maxwell Shapiros and other friends looked on. The friends represented a group who had donated 100,000 dollars for the Brooke School, which is in the desert city of Beersheba, now one of the biggest immigrant centers in Israel. One side of the school brushes a woodland. It is flanked on the other side by a pasture where Bedouin shepherds graze their sheep. Brooke and his party signed the foundation scroll, which was put into the ground.

"While we are looking for outer-space discoveries," Brooke said while standing by the Sea of Galilee, "we must not forget man and his struggle."

At the end of the speech Herbert Tucker motioned toward the Sea of Galilee.

"Here at last is your chance to walk on water," he said.

At that precise moment the sun streaked through the cumulus clouds.

"Herb, do you see what is happening up there?" Brooke said. "Father is telling me, 'Don't try it now.' "

While in Israel the Americans visited the Room of the Last Supper and the Tomb of David and toured Nazareth, where Christ had lived from the ages of three to thirty-three. "As a youngster," Brooke said later, "I read and studied so much of the Old and New Testaments. And last week it all seemed to have a special meaning and significance for me when I stood in those places in the Holy Land. . . . The Bible did come to life for me while I was in Israel!"

Brooke lauded the ingenuity of the Israelis, who had turned what had been a desert a quarter of a century earlier into an agricultural community. Water was a serious problem in Israel until a power plant was built. "They take the water from the Sea of Galilee," Brooke said, "and mix it with sweet water from various streams that come into the pipe, and it is pumped into the country by massive pipelines so they are able to irrigate the various fields and grow bananas, oranges, figs, dates, and flowers."

Brooke and his party were guests at a seder (ceremonial dinner held on the first night of Passover) at Kibbutz (a collective settlement) Kineret, near the scene of recent border clashes. "The seder was a beautiful and impressive ceremony and quite a revelation to me," Brooke said. "I was given the interpretation by a friend who sat at my side and explained the complete service." While in the Holy Land he met Israeli President Zalman Shazar and Prime Minister Levi Eshkol, as well as mayors of the cities.

"I went to the Middle East as a guest of Histadrut, which named a school after me, and while there had an opportunity to look at the East-West arms race, and I reported my findings when I came back," Brooke said. On the same trip he visited Greece—the first American to go there after the military coup. He conferred with the American ambassador and met his old friend Constantine Costamanos, who with Margaret Byers had done a photo essay on Brooke for *Life* magazine. Costamanos showed him points of interest during his two days in the country.

Soon after his return from Israel and the Mediterranean, Brooke told the press the First Secretary of the Soviet Embassy in Washington had invited him to Moscow. At a Boston press conference prior to addressing the National Association of Mutual Savings Banks, he said the invitation stemmed from his report on Vietnam. The Soviet official said his superiors were impressed with his objectivity in reporting on Red China's position concerning the Vietnam conflict. He turned down the invitation because of his commitment to be one of three panelists at the international conference in Geneva. By this time his trips as a one-man State Department or self-appointed ambassador-at-large conducting his own negotiations had enhanced his stature. But *The Boston Herald,* commenting on his role, warned that he was "playing a dangerous game."

At an airport press conference on his return from Pacem in Terris, Brooke said that unless the U.S., Russia, Great Britain and France acted to head off an Israeli-Arab test of strength, "I feel we are very definitely in for a very disastrous war." He warned against testing the Egyptian blockade of the Strait of Tiran. If Israel ran the blockade and was fired on, there might be war. He thought the UN could help solve the problem. "U Thant has not used up all his credit . . . and once the Arabs recognize that Israel cannot be exterminated, border disputes and international waterways questions will be ripe for solution."

Although little was accomplished for world peace at the Pacem in Terris colloquium, Brooke said it was not a complete waste of time, since there was an exchange of ideas. If it was a failure, it was because Russia, Red China, North Vietnam and the Vietcong did not attend.

A week later Brooke spoke to a group of Massachusetts Jews who had come to Washington for an afternoon rally in a Senate hearing room. Brooke warned that Israel would be annihilated if the U.S. and the Soviet Union interfered in the Middle East war.

"If the Soviet Union sent in troops, the U.S. would also send in troops. If the Soviets sent in arms, we would have a serious retaliatory situation." He blamed the U.S., Russia, Great Britain and France for the situation in the Middle East, noting that the four major powers had used the smaller powers by sending them arms and economic aid in the name of ideology.

Brooke would continue his interest in foreign affairs with an important tour of Africa in 1968. Meanwhile, domestic issues took his attention.

CHAPTER THIRTEEN

The Troubled Cities

B ROOKE had finished raking leaves on the lawn of his Oak Bluffs home and was arranging wildflowers he had picked when the telephone rang. It was President Johnson, who told him in a 30-minute conversation that he was impressed with his "patriotism and objectivity."

Johnson had just formed a Commission on Civil Disorders, a panel whose aim was to investigate the 1967 summer's racial riots in cities and to propose ways to prevent their recurrence. As the only Negro in the Senate, it was inevitable that Brooke would serve on the commission. He asked the President whether the commission would include men from public and private sectors, and whether it would have conservatives as well as liberals. The answer to both questions was yes.

By midsummer of 1967 the Senate was concerned with what Whitney M. Young had described as the "chronic depression [which] hangs like a shroud over the nation's Negro ghettos, stifling hope and eroding the lives of young and old alike." As a member of the President's Commission Brooke visited many of these ghettos and inspected damage in riot areas. What he saw further convinced him that the nation was coming perilously close to a second civil war.

"The causes span a century," he said in *Look* magazine. "The consequences are awesome. What a nation sows, it must inevitably reap. In this year of 1967, America reaps a harvest of violence." He likened violence to a sniper's bullet. "It is a brick through a store owner's window. But violence can take other forms. It is an act of violence to deny or infringe or violate a man's constitutional rights or his individual dignity. It is an act of violence to deny a man a job because of his race or religion."

Brooke blamed the administration for failing to enforce existing civil-rights legislation and for not appropriating funds needed for social progress. He said the failure of state and local governments to deal with legitimate grievances also contributed to riots, arguing that riots are neither Communist-inspired nor the result of an interstate conspiracy. Hunger, bad housing, ill health, lack of work and the absence of law enforcement need no allies to create a climate of violence, he said. He dwelt on this issue again and again, until he saw more light in the tunnel.

On June 4 Senator Edward Kennedy spoke at dedication ceremonies of new buildings at Assumption Preparatory School in Worcester, and Brooke, who left an hour before Kennedy arrived, gave the commencement address. The junior senator, who later that day received an honorary degree from George Washington University, told the graduating class that life was no stagnant pool.

"You must get into the current of life and swim with it." He told them not to fear being a member of a respected minority, since minorities often become majorities. He said there were other crises besides Vietnam and the Middle East.

"The atomic genies have been let out of the bottle and are abroad in the world. The Chinese calendar tells us this is the year of the sheep, but I am sure you will agree that history will record it as the year of mounting tensions."

Brooke mentioned two nights of turmoil in Roxbury and the nearby South End after mothers on welfare staged a sit-in which triggered violence. Brooke said these mothers were the same type of people who had come to him with their problems when he was attorney general. "These are people who live in a continuous state of hopelessness and despair. The course they decided to follow is the wrong course, but many of them can see no other." The Senator said there would be more Roxbury-like riots in the nation unless society solved the causative problems: "social and economic problems, not racial problems." "No one can condone rioting, but certainly we have to give people on welfare enough money to live on, and not restrict them to a standard of poverty." Later in Washington, enlarging on the theme of the economics of the situation, he said Negroes who become black-power militants represent "sort of an acceptance of defeat

because they haven't been able to integrate into the American society."
Again and again Brooke complained that Congress gave more attention to anti-riot legislation than to measures to get at root causes.

"It is past time the U.S. prepared itself for a monumental assault
upon the crisis which has attacked America's urban centers." He said
the nation was reluctant to devote the time, energy and money to
overcome poverty, which he called "far more frightening and disgraceful than any poverty which appears in Africa, Asia, or Latin
America. . . . We are fierce in our defense of a small nation thousands
of miles removed from our shores. We are relentless in our attempts
to put a man on the moon." He insisted that the U.S. must become as
excited about education as it is about the war or putting a man on the
moon. "In the long run, the development of a superior educational
system may well be far more important than success in either of the
other endeavors." Calling riots symptoms, he said "each time we are
called upon to treat a symptom we are forced to admit that the sickness which has caused the symptom still exists unabated." He also
said that in the mind of the destitute "sometimes violence alone can
give him a shred of dignity when all other avenues to human respect
have been destroyed."

America has held out a promise to all citizens, but has denied it
to blacks, Brooke and the late Whitney M. Young, Jr., then executive
director of the National Urban League, told its convention in Port-
land, Oregon. The time was August 1967, when the Urban League,
considered the most conservative of national civil-rights organizations,
was being pressured by delegates and other members to adopt a more
militant position.

"Negro citizens know that responsible militancy is the most effective way they can achieve their equal rights and develop the community strengths which make for power in our society," Young said.
Said Brooke: "Organization and the exercise of power are the antithesis
of the conditions and mood which lead to riots. Democracy is a
system which provides an outlet for grievances and frustrations because it provides the possibility of peaceful change. It must be made
to work equally for the have-nots in America as it has for the haves."

Noting that fewer than one-fourth of the poor in the U.S. are black,
Brooke said they "are the most conspicuous poor, mostly crowded
into urban ghettos. They are largely powerless to effect change in
their own behalf. In addition, the Congress is affected and inhibited
by the myths and prejudices of constituents and by the fact that racial
prejudice is a working force in this country. There is also a kind of

'creeping Horatio Algerism.' This promulgates the notion that 'anyone can make it and that government need not play a role.'"

Brooke asked what blacks could do when national leaders refuse to lead. "The people must give direction. I am not an advocate of Black Power in the sense that that term has come to mean violence. But power as the ability to change conditions is the essence of the democratic process. The poor, especially the Negro poor, must become full participants in that process. The slum communities must create political institutions to bargain with and confront the existing political structure."

Brooke said the Urban League should take the lead in providing this leadership. "The civil-rights movement must evolve into a grass-roots political organization or it will be irrelevant to the needs of the people it represents."

Brooke accused the news media of giving too much attention to Stokely Carmichael and H. Rap Brown and not enough to responsible Negro leaders. "The emphasis should be placed on the great, great majority of people in the Negro community who merely want improved conditions, who want government to respond responsibly to their needs and who at the same time recognize the need to help themselves." He said the U.S. needed more taxpayers "and not just tax consumers."

On the same day (September 11, 1967) *The Boston Globe* reported Brooke's speech, it ran a story about a riot in East St. Louis, Illinois: "Within hours after black-power advocate Rap Brown came, several hundred Negroes massed downtown, tossed fire bombs and stabbed a policeman. . . . There were also three or four sniping incidents." It was this kind of violence that Brooke lashed out against time and again· "We will not tolerate killing, looting, burning, sniping. . . . Those on the lunatic fringe who make statements to incite riots do a disservice to their nation and to the cause they profess to serve. . . . And those who shout, 'Kill Whitey,' or 'Burn Whitey,' do it only to get on television or get their picture in the paper. They are not concerned with civil rights or with poverty."

In mid-July 1967 *The Boston Globe* assessed Brooke's role as a civil-rights spokesman: "Brooke, after more than a decade in and out of public life, is just this week choosing to emerge as a civil-rights leader. His thoughtful and eloquent speech to the NAACP here . . . coupled with his fight for principle on the Senate floor in Washington [the next day] cast the former attorney general of all the people in a new light."

Repeating that he was not a proponent of black power and that he didn't think bloodshed and the destruction of property would lead blacks or any other minority to equality, Brooke told the NAACP meeting that the civil-rights movement was a "second American revolution" to realize America's "promise of liberty and justice for all—white and Negro together, not apart." At this fifty-eighth annual NAACP convention Senator Edward Kennedy presented Brooke with the Spingarn Medal, an award "for the highest achievement of an American Negro."*

Brooke told the assembly that the only civil-rights legislation enacted during the first half of 1967 was a bill to make promoting a riot a federal crime. It was an attempt, he charged, in the name of civil rights, to create a reaction in the U.S. to the civil-rights movement "which appears to be a punitive reaction." He said violence should not be used as an excuse for halting progress toward equality and justice for blacks. He noted that the 1966 Congress defeated proposed civil-rights legislation; the first session of the Ninetieth Congress took no action on the Civil Rights Act of 1967; the executive branch failed to act with force and speed to implement laws already on the books. One comment drew loud applause:

"Many who are denied those basic rights are serving this nation in Vietnam. Before a member of the Congress casts a nay vote for the Civil Rights Act of 1967, he should write to his Negro constituents in Vietnam explaining why the federal government cannot assure them the right to live where they choose or why racial unrest in their community makes it politically inopportune to vote for civil-rights legislation at this time."

Brooke was honored again in 1967 when the Negro Omega Psi Phi fraternity gave him its Outstanding Citizen Award at the Sheraton Plaza.

Brooke lost his first civil-rights battle on the Senate floor on July 12, when, by a 36–47 vote, the Senate rejected his amendment, which would have killed initial funds to build the 300-million-dollar atomic-energy project in Weston, Illinois. "Here is a golden opportunity not to talk about providing equal rights for all Americans, but to act," Brooke said, embarrassing his friend Senator Charles Percy of Illinois, who had advanced the dubious argument that his state should not be punished for failing to pass open-housing legislation when the federal government had also failed to do so. Brooke lost his

---

* Named for the late J. E. Spingarn, former president of the NAACP.

pitch: "We should see that federal money from this day forward doesn't go into projects where there is discrimination." The floor fight came hours after Brooke had given his first major civil-rights speech at the NAACP convention in Boston.

In the summer of 1967 the two Massachusetts senators, along with Senator Philip Hart (Democrat of Michigan) and Senator Clifford Case (Republican of New Jersey), held a long meeting with civil-rights leaders in the privacy of a Capitol caucus room. Present were Roy Wilkins and Clarence Mitchell of the NAACP, Whitney Young of the Urban League, and Attorney General Ramsey Clark, who once said: "A great many people in this country are worried about law and order. And a great many people are worried about justice. But one thing is certain: you cannot have either until you have both."*

Young said blacks were criticized universally because of riots. "For every kid who threw a brick in Newark there are 200 Negro kids in Vietnam. And for every Cassius Clay there are 2,000 white boys up in Canada avoiding the draft."

By the time of this meeting there was less talk about Brooke being an Uncle Tom. He had said earlier that almost everyone was called an Uncle Tom "who is not a militant leader, who does not condone violence. The word is overused and misused." He said he had gone alone into some of the worst neighborhoods in Spanish Harlem to talk to people on the street about their problems. "I sat with a group of 49 . . . some with weapons, and they said, 'How will you get out of here? The police won't help you. The National Guard won't help you. And you're powerless.' I told them I had come voluntarily and would go out on my own."

Brooke strolled through Harlem, East Harlem and the East New York section of Brooklyn, exchanging views with local civic leaders and ordinary citizens. That night he walked with Mayor John Lindsay to cover some of the toughest sections of the Bronx after a meeting at Gracie Mansion.

Stephen C. Luce, president of the Martha's Vineyard National Bank, was master of ceremonies for "Ed Brooke Day" held in Oak Bluffs on July 29. Brooke flew to the island after a two-and-a-half-hour conference in Washington with President Johnson and ten other members of the Advisory Committee on Civil Disorders. He spoke in The Tabernacle, an open-sided building with a cross on its dome on

---

* Clark said this on the *David Frost Show*.

the former Methodist camp meeting ground. On his way to The Tabernacle he passed thousands of people lining the dockside at Oak Bluffs Harbor, where sloops and cabin cruisers swung at their moorings. Governor Volpe introduced him.

"As a member of a winning team, as a hardworking teammate, Ed Brooke this year went to the big time and the bright lights of the U.S. Senate. There is only one answer, and the road that Ed Brooke took points to that answer. The answer is teamwork on the part of all Americans, regardless of race, religion, heritage or political party."

In The Tabernacle Brooke told 3,000 persons there was no more important domestic issue than insurrection. He counted six riots in 1961, five in 1962, 40 in 1966, and there had already been 30 racial riots in 1967, when the situation was worsening. "We have a war going on in this country and we have got to respond." He asked what children had to look forward to: "Eighty riots in 1968 or a hundred . . . in 1969? There is nothing wrong in this country that we can't correct. We don't have to wait until the next generation. We can begin to do it now."

Before his speech a reporter asked how future riots could be averted. "If we convince the urban centers that their government is concerned, that relief is on the way, that it is also a concern of state and local governments, and that this commission will not produce just another report to gather dust on the shelf. This is a war that must be won just as the war in Vietnam." He said anti-riot legislation was not the answer.

"Senator, if you were President right now, what would you do?" a reporter asked.

"Number one, I'd listen to the commission I had appointed. Number two, I would press forward with such programs as the Model Cities program.* To turn our backs on these problems is a great mistake. The entire poverty budget appropriation is a negligible

---

* Actually, the Model Cities was an example of President Johnson's Great Society at its worst. The idea was to choose certain neighborhoods in selected cities for funded projects that would serve as a model for other communities. But when the Nixon administration took over on January 20, it found chaos in the Department of Housing and Urban Development. There was no clear blueprint of how the money was to be spent or what to do about projects elsewhere. The Johnson administration did not decide which cities would get pilot projects, nor did it set up guidelines for choosing the cities. The result was a widespread clamor by mayors asking to have their cities included in the Model Cities program. To satisfy even half of them would have cost far more than the $750 million budgeted for Model Cities by Johnson during the ensuing fiscal year.

amount of money. If I were President I would insist on more. We need to wage a war on poverty, and if I were President I would go before the Congress and say it in just those terms." He said it was unfair to accuse civil-rights leaders of being instigators of all riots. "I don't think . . . Carmichael in Cuba is dictating what happens in Detroit. I don't think he has that influence."

After his speech a tall black smiled and held out his hand. "I'm Willy Jackson. I came all the way from Louisiana to be with you on Ed Brooke Day."

Brooke gave the essence of the presidential commission when he told his summer neighbors not to be vindictive about the rioting. "But ask yourselves, 'Why did they happen?' That's the mandate of the President's commission."

In mid-1963, less than six months before his assassination, President Kennedy had finally taken a firm stand on civil rights by placing before Congress legislation that would bar discrimination in places of public accommodation. Kennedy's death and the emotional mood it caused gave President Johnson a chance to enact more legislation in the field of civil rights than any President had accomplished during the nineteenth century.

"We have talked long enough . . . about equal rights," Johnson said. "We have talked for a hundred years or more. It is time now to write the next chapter—and to write it in the books of law." Senator Everett Dirksen, agreeing, quoted Victor Hugo: "Nothing in the world is stronger than an idea whose time has come."

The time for other ideas was slower in coming. Later Brooke scored President Nixon's veto of attempts made by HUD to push low-income suburban housing for blacks. "If it doesn't violate the letter of the law, it violates the spirit of the law," he said. "I think the President has a responsibility to lead in this direction. Secretary Romney [head of HUD] has pursued this, but it has been vetoed by the White House."

It was in the field of housing—especially for the elderly—that Brooke was to score one of his legislative triumphs.*

In September 1967 Brooke called for a massive new effort to remedy the failure of the antipoverty program in opening up job opportunities for the poor. "It is my firm conviction that education, rehousing, slum improvements . . . will prove of value in ending the

---

* For Brooke's major congressional achievements see Appendix.

cycle of poverty only if they increase the number of the poor who through these and other programs can find productive and rewarding employment.

He said men and women were prepared for jobs in fields with no openings. "They are given the equivalent of a fifth-grade education when a minimum of a tenth-grade education is required for gainful employment anywhere in the state." Brooke outlined a program that could be implemented through legal initiative without using federal funds. It included:

1. Businessmen employing and training previously unemployed or underemployed persons.

2. Tax incentives to industries that lower employment standards and start training programs.

3. A program in public schools by the U.S. Employment Service to provide information on career opportunities.

4. The extension of minimum-wage laws to include uncovered jobs such as hospital aides, unskilled restaurant helpers and unskilled retail workers.

Brooke also urged urban centers to help rural immigrants find jobs and adequate housing and to provide counseling and health services. He advocated raising Social Security benefits beyond the requests of President Johnson.

Meanwhile, in his former backyard, Brooke announced a federal grant of 197,000 dollars for the training of Roxbury residents in the management and ownership of small businesses. (He wanted a pilot program to serve as an example to a federal program.) The funds were made available to the Joint Community Center for Inner-City Change, a project sponsored by Boston College and the Urban League. The center added enough money to bring the total to 266,500 dollars.

This single project trained 60 potential managers and owners and was expanded to set up seminars to help Roxbury residents solve problems blocking the growth of the area, still largely a slum.

In the spring of 1969 Brooke inspected the new Avco printing plant in Roxbury, which was built by black contractors and operated by blacks an an example of cooperation between big business and the ghetto. The training program and Liberty Mutual key-punch facility (in Grove Hall, Roxbury) impressed him. "Isn't this better than the Job Corps?" he asked a worker.

Brooke began his tour at the Afro-American Institute, where he met Elma Lewis, the dynamic organizer of the project taking shape in the former Temple Mishkan Tefila. Brooke and Miss Lewis stood before the vast shell of the old synagogue and looked up at the inscription chiseled into the building: "Not by might, not by power, but by my spirit, saith the Lord."

"We're going to keep that," Miss Lewis said. She told Brooke it would cost two million dollars to restore the shabby shell, which would be the heart of a black cultural center; more money would be raised to restore an adjacent building that housed her school for the arts. The Elma Lewis School of Fine Arts has since won national recognition.

"When Brooke left my art school," Miss Lewis said, "the girls dropped everything and followed him out the door, surrounding his car in the parking lot. Nobody stayed inside the building, even to handle the telephone." This writer asked why she didn't take care of this detail.

"I was out there with the girls," she said.

In his next stop Brooke revisited old haunts, stopping at the Humboldt Avenue headquarters of Metco, which sends hundreds of black Roxbury students into suburban school systems. Later Brooke helped Metco officials in their campaign to have state funds restored to the program. At the Unity Bank and Trust Company on Warren Street he told the staff: "I've got stock in this bank. I had to come to see how things are going." The bank, starting from scratch, had developed assets of 10.5 million dollars in its first year of operation and was expanding into space next door. With Brooke when the Senator dropped by an automobile agency in Roxbury taken over by black owners was George Lodge, who recalled the crisp eloquence of a brief talk Brooke gave.

During his first five years in the Senate, Brooke won the respect of black leaders, although he disappointed one admirer, Clarence Mitchell (a black who had witnessed lynchings of blacks), when he refused to co-sponsor an antifilibuster resolution that would substitute a 51–49 vote for a two-thirds majority. This was the first substantive issue Brooke faced, and he resented any pressure to catalogue him. This was his first significant warning against second-guessing him. He said he would listen to the debate on the issue before making up his mind, a procedure he has always followed in the Senate.

As national spokesman for NAACP, Mitchell had asked Brooke to promote a petition against the filibuster rule, which liberals had been trying to change for years. When Brooke balked at signing until he studied the bill, Mitchell asked: "What the hell kind of Negro is he?"

But when the time came to vote, Brooke took the most liberal position on the question. Mitchell still insisted, however, that Brooke, had he signed the petition earlier, would have reminded the public that the filibuster rule had often been used by Southern segregationists to keep civil-rights bills from becoming law. Hence a change in rules was in effect a vote for civil rights.

Brooke co-sponsored a resolution to allow female pages in the Senate, joining with 17 other senators, including Javits, Percy and Fred Harris of Oklahoma, and the measure passed. He refused, however, to co-sponsor the Women's Rights Amendment. In a cartoon the bitingly satirical Szep showed Brooke in a beaked hat standing in front of a snarling personage representing a congressman waiting to club a woman representing women's rights. "Here come one of them damn integrationists," the caption read. The amendment was debated and dropped. Brooke is a strong believer in equal rights for women. "Of course," Roger Woodworth quipped, "as a moderate he takes a dim view of suffragettes like the late Mrs. O. H. P. Belmont, who comforted an equal-righter by saying, 'Call on God, my dear. She will help you.' "

Since joining the Senate, Brooke, rather than posing as a civil-rights leader, has concentrated on luring blacks into the GOP fold. In his first speech in California he had reminded a Lincoln Day audience that "the heritage of the GOP was based on the concept of human freedom and human dignity," then went on to score Governor Reagan for failing to win the support of 95 percent of California's black voters. Brooke said the GOP had to capture the votes of America's youth and urban dwellers, as well as blacks, to win the presidency in 1968. "If we turn our backs on these two groups they will turn their backs on us." He said the GOP must "profit by the past, not live in the past. I don't want to see people chained to the White House gates for generations to come. . . . I don't want to see racial strife, poverty, and war." He said Republicans should take the lead in solving urban, social and economic problems. The first item would be to create a society in which it would be "more profitable to work than not to work."

During his first year in the Senate, Brooke learned everything he could about the job and spent much time with a staff considered one of the most efficient and devoted on Capitol Hill. It was a demanding year in terms of time and study, with rules and procedures of the Senate to learn, as well as "the legislative process," which, Brooke said, "is quite different from anything I've done before." He said his assignments to the Banking and Currency Committee and the Aeronautical Space Science Committee required an in-depth study of banking principles and practices and space techniques, adding that he tried to "couple academic study with travel to gain firsthand knowledge of conditions at home and abroad."

Big investment bankers in Boston wanted to meet Brooke when he was named to the Banking and Currency Committee, and they asked Donald Whitehead, whose father was a partner in the Wall Street firm of Nye and Whitehead, to arrange an unpublicized luncheon meeting in Boston. The bankers thought the freshman senator would be overwhelmed at the prospect of having the counsel of leaders in the monetary field, feeling he would not have enough time to delve into the intricacies of high finance and would be glad to have their ideas on pending legislation affecting mutual funds. Donald Whitehead warned the investment bankers not to press Brooke, who dislikes being wined and dined, and suggested that they deal with him at his office in Boston or Washington. By the time this came about, Brooke was well versed in the field of banking and currency.

Brooke drew criticism from a Boston reporter for failing to do enough homework on a few issues affecting his constituency during his first year in Washington, including getting federal aid for a medical school to be built in Worcester and a proposal to build a new kind of Navy ship that could bring multimillion-dollar contracts to the shipbuilding plant in Quincy. "He did well on the probe of the Cape Kennedy fire that killed three astronauts," the reporter said, not meaning to be gratuitous.

Another Boston reporter criticized Brooke for a 1966 ruling made while he was attorney general in connection with the filming of *Titicut Follies,* which showed demented persons at the Massachusetts Correctional Institution at Bridgewater in naked and otherwise embarrassing situations in what medical experts called an outrageous invasion of privacy. Brooke had ruled that there "does not appear to be any provision, whether statutory, constitutional or common law, to the effect that a consenting inmate at the institution may not be photographed (assuming that such inmate is mentally competent to give his consent)." This matter followed Brooke to the Senate. According to the reporter, Brooke failed to explain how patients confined to an institution for the criminally insane could possibly be competent to sign legally binding documents such as releases.

In his voting record Brooke favored antipoverty legislation, several amendments to the existing act to strengthen the Social Security program and the Model Cities bill; also, legislation setting quotas on textile, fish and shoe imports—industries important to Massachusetts economy. Brooke urged legislation to permit wiretapping and other electronic eavesdropping by law enforcement officials under close supervision by the courts, although President Johnson had asked Congress to outlaw all use of wiretaps or electronic surveillance except in cases directly related to national security.

"It seems apparent that ultimately the most valuable weapon against organized crime will be a statute which permits certain kinds of wiretapping," Brooke said in a speech to the National Council on Crime and Delinquency in New York.

He also recommended immunity status for informers, wider use of grand jury investigations and the establishment of a special organized-crime unit by state and local police as other steps to fight crime. On the other hand, he filed an amendment to abolish the Subversive Activities Control Commission, "because it hadn't been doing its job." He said the attorney general's office, the FBI and the Justice Department have legal means of giving constitutional protection, "and this is the best way of rooting out communism."

During his first year in the Senate, Brooke logged more travel time than any other senator and received more awards than many senators get in their entire career. He had unusual experiences. He got a tumultuous welcome from blacks and white officials when he went to South Carolina in November. A high-school band played "El Capitan" when he landed at Columbia airport, where Mayor Lester Bates, a Democrat, gave him a key to the city and said the state was "honored with your presence." The Mayor said Columbia had "the finest racial relations in the U.S." A reporter asked Brooke if he was friendly with South Carolina's Republican Senator Strom Thurmond, a vocal segregationist.

"We are friends. We don't always vote alike, but I like him and I think he likes me; we play tennis together."

Later on that visit Brooke went to the predominantly white University of South Carolina and received honorary membership in the college's Republican party organization. He also addressed Negro students at Allen University and Benedict College at an outdoor assembly, speaking of racial disturbances he had witnessed in Detroit, Newark, Harlem and other Northern cities. Referring to the "war" between haves and have-nots, he said, "I am encouraged. I believe your generation will win this war."

Over the years Brooke, who is a Fellow of the American Bar Association and the American Academy of Arts and Sciences and the holder of 23 honorary degrees, has been frequently honored. An early honor was the Distinguished Service Award, American Veterans of World War II, Am Vets. In 1963 he received the annual Americanism Award "for exemplifying the principles of Americanism" on Flag Day, June 14, on the Battle Green at Lexington. The following year the national Pigskin Club honored him at the annual awards dinner at the Statler Hilton in Washington. Brooke, Humphrey and Javits were feted for "outstanding achievement in human relations."

In 1966 he received the Herbert H. Lehman Ethics Medal from the Jewish Theological Seminary of America "for embodying high ethical ideals in public service." In his acceptance speech at the New York Hilton Hotel Brooke said he wanted to be like Lehman, "the conscience of the Senate," adding that he had the greatest respect and admiration for him, "especially when he said, 'I serve my conscience.' " Rabbi Louis Finkelstein, chancellor of the seminary, praised Brooke as having a career marked by an unceasing concern for humanity and highest ideals and principles "and the probity and morality which have been the hallmarks of your personal and political life."

Late in 1966 Brooke "exposed" an "illegal" honorary award given him by Roxbury's Freedom House, a community and civic center founded in 1949 by Otto and Muriel Snowden. Brooke had been called to Caesar's Monticello, a nightclub in Framingham, to receive the fourth annual Freedom House Recognition Award.* When Mrs. Snowden handed him the flowered scroll he noticed that it had not been signed.

"I want the record to show," he told the 500 persons at the benefit party, "that Freedom House has given me an unofficial, illegal honorary award." He paused during the laughter. "I'm very sorry, Muriel, that I had to expose you, but in keeping with my promise to the people of Massachusetts, I have to call them as I see them and this is the way I see them."

Mrs. Snowden said Freedom House "wanted to give the award to Ed Brooke so that when he looks at it he'll remember the years of work he's done with us."

At the annual Charles Evans Hughes Award (National Conference

---

* Earlier awards went to Jacqueline Kennedy, the New England Telephone and Telegraph, and the Roxbury–North Dorchester Parents Association, which sponsors Operation Exodus.

of Christians and Jews) dinner at the Waldorf-Astoria in New York in 1967, the citations went to former President Harry S Truman, former Senator Paul H. Douglas, and Brooke, all cited for "courageous leadership in governmental service."* Margaret Truman Daniel accepted her father's award. In his acceptance speech Brooke urged passage of the Johnson administration's bill to provide 2.6 billion dollars in antipoverty funds. "I don't want to see this country exist with people demonstrating in the streets and stores burning indefinitely." Brooke had earlier received an award from the Massachusetts Committee of Catholics, Protestants and Jews at the annual Goodwill Dinner at the Statler Hilton in Boston.

Brooke found life in Washington more pleasant than ever, although his social activities were so limited that Maxine Cheshire, gossip columnist of the *beau monde,* who frequently mentioned Senators Edward and Robert Kennedy, didn't mention his name once over a span of five years.

Despite an increase in salary of 5,000 dollars (senators receive 41,500 dollars a year) over what he had received as attorney general, he found living costs high. He had to maintain two residences, and the federal government, unlike the Commonwealth of Massachusetts, did not provide him with a limousine and chauffeur. However demanding, it was, Brooke said, a challenging and rewarding year. "I like to think I've made some contributions."

Richard Stewart, Washington correspondent for *The Boston Globe* until he became Senator Edmund Muskie's press secretary in the 1972 campaign, wrote of the 10,000 congressional aides who are "the anonymous backbone of the U.S. Congress, "They . . . make sure your veteran's pension check gets taken care of or a Chinese citizen's immigration papers are handled properly. They write the speeches, answer the mail, come up with ideas and protect their big-name bosses from public harassment. They work in the backrooms huddled over typewriters and stacks of mail."

"In the long run," wrote Richard Harris, "few of the countless forces that pull and push at senators are stronger than the influence of their staffs. While influence is not the same as power, at times strong aides can make the two seem identical." There is a special rapport between Brooke and his staff, whether in his Springfield, Bos-

---

* One of the recipients in 1966 was former President Dwight Eisenhower.

ton or Washington office. There is an atmosphere of camaraderie and affection. "You have a function and a role," Nancy Porter said, "and your performance is noticed. You are encouraged to excel."

Included in the staff Brooke took to Washington were Cammann Newberry, Roger Woodworth, Sally Saltonstall, Nancy Porter, Marilyn Dexheimer, Barbara Masters, Hamilton Wood, Clarence Elam, and Betty Hager, the only black members of the Washington staff until Rochelle Fashaw, Delano Lewis, Eather Higginbotham and Eleanor Harrison were added.* Newberry, who for six years had been administrative assistant for Senator Henry Cabot Lodge, Jr., recalls that Lodge's total staff numbered eight, as compared with Brooke's 30. When in Massachusetts, Lodge's office was in the basement of his elegant home at Beverly Farms. Newberry, who supervised Lodge's staff, wrote speeches and handled legislative work but never remembers being rushed or having to work nights, even though it was a time of the Korean War, the Marshall Plan and McCarthyism. He thinks the media—especially television—have stepped up the pace for modern senators.**

Soon after he was settled in Washington, Nancy Porter took the staff on a tour of the city in a chartered bus equipped with a bar. Sitting up front with Brooke behind the driver were his mother and Clarence Elam. As the bus got underway, Brooke rested his hand on Elam's shoulder.

"Well, Clarence, how does it feel to be sitting up front of a bus for a change?"

Later, on a muggy night, Elam chartered an excursion boat and took the staff on a band-concert tour down the Potomac. Miss O'Shaughnessy, an attractive blonde, had had her hair done that afternoon, but by the middle of the evening her gorgeous hair was frizzy.

"Looks as if you and I have the same problem," Brooke said, grinning.

"We were new to Washington," Sally Saltonstall recalls, "and everyone was hosting parties for us." Later most of the Washington group, joined by Georgia Ireland and others from the Boston staff, took a Metroliner to New York City to be entertained by Nancy

---

* Elam, Fashaw and Lewis are no longer on the staff, which in 1972 numbered 32, counting five in Boston and two in Springfield.
** Brooke, who has great respect for Henry Cabot Lodge, Jr., didn't know of Newberry's relationship with the Senator when he (Brooke) named Newberry his administrative assistant. "You mean you were *Lodge's* administrative assistant?" he asked.

Porter and Joseph McMahon, who were no longer with Brooke. At least once a summer Brooke and most of his aides attended a baseball game in Griffith Stadium when the Boston Red Sox came to town to play the now-departed Washington Senators—"first in war, first in peace, and last in the American League." On the program were beer, peanuts, and no political talk. There are also the senatorial softball games.

Miss Saltonstall captains the Brooke Bombers, or Brooke Bas-TARDS, as Woodworth calls the team. When Senator Walter Mondale's team beat the Brookes 14 to 4 one summer, Brooke suggested that his team be renamed the Saltonstall Bloopers. Other teams are the Javits Jets, the Russell Longshots,* Maggie's (Magnuson's) Mules, and the Fulbright Dissenters. When Brooke plays for his Bombers, he takes his pick of an infield position. Each team has to play three girls. There are no team standings, and sometimes it takes a filibuster to decide who is safe at first base or home plate. Woodworth, a can of beer in his hand, stands behind the pitcher and umpires, but has no official status. In 1971 the Bombers won ten, lost four and tied Senator Ted Kennedy's team 3–3. The only game Brooke came to see (against Colorado Senator Peter H. Dominick's team) was rained out. "And they were pushovers," said James Mc-Cauley, coach of the Bombers. "The boss was delighted when we edged Senator James Pearson's team, since they are close friends. In a memo to Pearson he said he was launching a VISTA program to teach the fundamentals of softball, primarily for the benefit of the Kansas Senator's team."

Interns who work without pay for Brooke during the summer include college athletes. There is fierce tennis rivalry in the "Brooke Invitational," played annually in Washington or on Brooke's private court at Oak Bluffs. Brooke usually wins the singles and pairs with Sally Saltonstall to take the doubles.

"There won't be a Brooke Invitational in 1971," an aide said. "One intern is David Burwell, captain of the Dartmouth tennis team." (Burwell is now at the University of Virginia Law School.) Brooke laughed when told of the remark. As it turned out, the press of Senate business left no time for the event.

Brooke's interns come to Washington in June at the height of the legislative season, when many major bills move from committee to

---

* At the Dallas-Miami superbowl game in New Orleans in January 1972 Brooke was a guest of Senator Russell Long.

the Senate floor. "Our mail, heavier than usual," Brooke said, "reflects Massachusetts' concern about issues of the moment."

Congressional interns help the regular staffs answer thousands of letters, telegrams and postcards which come across congressional desks. They expedite the receipt of a tardy Social Security check, arrange to bring a GI home from Vietnam for his grandmother's funeral, cut red tape for a constitutent at one or another federal agency and do legislative research. Usually three or four interns are chosen from a field of 300 or more and become a vital part of Brooke's organization.

While Brooke's offices in Springfield and Boston are swamped with incoming mail, the real deluge pours into the Washington office, especially during a crisis. After the Cambodian incursion Brooke's Washington staff handled about 70,000 letters, 55,000 of which opposed Nixon's decision to move into the neutral country. Letters are filled with complaints, requests for help and advice. A man has lost his job because he is black, a woman is not getting enough money under Medicaid, a dealer who sold a man a car is not honoring the warranty. A Coast Guard helicopter flying out of Otis Air Force Base in Massachusetts is damaging a farmer's crops. An aide writes to say the chopper will fly in another direction when the wind permits.

A Boston tourist is jailed in Vienna for stealing a flamingo from a zoo; an aide contacts the U.S. embassy and arranges for his release. A Ph.D. in biochemistry has been put in the infantry by a computer; the Brooke office has him transferred to a medical unit. (Linda Bunce, who handled this assignment, also arranged for a soldier to fly home from Okinawa to see his father, who was dying of cancer.)

Three residents of nursing homes in Massachusetts who write Brooke daily are "Old Sarge" Barney, "Mother" King, who was invited to the wedding of Remi Brooke, and Laura Miller, who sent Brooke five Valentines on one day to be sure he got the message. Another friend outdid her by mailing him 25 Christmas cards. Brooke answers as many of the "Dear Ed" letters as possible and sends flowers occasionally to favorites such as Mother King and Laura Miller. A conservative critic in Greenfield who scolds Brooke at least two or three times a week was once chided by Woodworth for an extremist view.

There are crank notes, letters from paranoids and odd telephone calls. A Cape Cod resident wrote the Senator about a niece and uncle who were living as man and wife. "She has a retarded son. . . . The state pays all of her son's bills, as well as hers. The niece has an aunt in California with money, so why should the state support her?"

"The foremost analytic theorist on logic" said he had "detected the most heinous crime since Creation affecting the decisions of Presidents and Congress and the life of the entire world with the result of solving the most perplexing problem of his day. Criminal or Einstein?"

During a 15-minute interval a taxpayer who had bought a new house called to say a toilet was backing up. An aide advised her to see her insurance agent after getting a plumber. An old woman who said she was writing her will wanted the name of an Indian tribe to whom she could leave money. Any tribe would do.

Because of its accessibility, the Boston office is the most frequent target of oddball droppers-in. A furtive-looking man wearing dark glasses, after assuring Maura O'Shaughnessy that he no longer wished to be crucified although he was Jesus Christ, said his real reason for coming to Brooke was to complain about night riders in New Hampshire who had arrested him because he hired blacks to work in his bamboo-shoot factory. Maura suggested that the matter came within the purview of the attorney general, whereupon he flew into a rage, shouting that Brooke hated blacks. That same afternoon a policeman escorted him from Senator Edward Kennedy's Boston office in the same building.

A dowdy woman claiming to be a disbarred nurse said people followed her everywhere, even when she went to confession. When she went to New York to help her cousin elect Ralph Nader President, she was shadowed. Also, a dentist filled her tooth with an electronic eavesdropping device wrapped in microfilm. She didn't want to trouble Brooke, she said; she merely wanted him to investigate the FBI. She brightened and left when Maura advised her to ask a different dentist to insert a silver filling in place of the device and microfilm.

Most of the business is more serious. Eddie Harrison, a black convicted murderer who was jailed in 1960 for the shotgun slaying of a Washington gambler and who stayed in prison until 1969, spent part of his time on death row after being sentenced for life. His conduct was so exemplary he was released without bond while preparing a final appeal. On the day Chief Justice Burger was sworn into office (June 27, 1969), one of his last opinions was being released by the Court of Appeals. It rejected Harrison's plea on the grounds that there was no alternative under the law. Burger, noting that Harrison had benefited from rehabilitation, suggested that the case be considered for executive clemency.

Harrison gave Ann Cunningham, an aide in Brooke's Washington office, insight into the need for prison reform, rather than jailing people and throwing away the key. After reading the Harrison story in *The Washington Post,* she called him and told Brooke of his plight. Brooke wrote Attorney General Mitchell in support of a commutation petition filed in Harrison's behalf. Ann, with assistance from Marilyn Dexheimer, Cynthia Hill and Alexander Hewes, Jr., co-workers in Brooke's office, got further help from Senators Charles Mathias and Marlow Cook, and in her spare time on Saturdays she went to the White House to seek help for Harrison from her friends on the White House staff.

In March 1970 President Nixon announced that Harrison's sentence had been commuted. He would not have to return to prison. "Ann really pushed the whole effort on Capitol Hill," Harrison said. "Dedication. That's the word. She was more concerned about this thing than I was. Senator Brooke is fortunate to have her."

Early in 1971 Brooke sponsored a performance by the Inner Voices, a group of inmates in Lorton Reformatory near Washington, D.C., in the Senate Office Building auditorium. Rhozier Brown, a lifer at Lorton, founded and directs the group after conceiving the idea of the Inner Voices during eight months of solitary confinement. The 37 prisoners in the company, who act out scenes of prison life, now bring their songs and heart-wrenching stories to audiences in the District, Maryland and Virginia. Their stories deal with life in the ghetto, hunger for dignity and equality, and the destruction of human life by drug addiction. Brooke says most of the actor-inmates were considered incorrigible until they joined the Inner Voices.

Ann Cunningham took the cast (wearing blue jeans at a black-tie party) to the first balcony of a theater to see *Hair.* In the first act the "police" were on stage and the audience was "under arrest." The convicts, who came with two guards in a bus, were frightened, so real was the illusion.

Brooke operates a taut but friendly ship. Girls on his Washington staff think he is old-fashioned in some ways. Linda Bunce, known as the "organizer" or "union leader," said it took time to overcome his bias against mini skirts, and he has never eased his ban on pant suits. Linda, after polling aides in the other 99 Senate offices, set wheels in motion that resulted in longer vacations and higher salaries for the staff. She is the only staffer who ever left the boss speechless.

Brooke was standing beside her desk at 9:03 A.M. with a "good evening" look in his eyes when she walked in, one arm behind her back. Before he could say a word, she handed him a bouquet of flowers plucked that morning from her garden. For once the boss was startled, embarrassed and tongue-tied.

The Washington office functions smoothly even in the absence of the Senator, but there is more levity when Brooke is away. Nancy Dickerson of NBC called one afternoon and asked to talk to Betsy Warren. Roger Woodworth picked up the phone and, thinking he was talking to a friend of Betsy (Brooke's personal secretary), said: "Yes, Betsy is here. But I'm afraid she is terribly inebriated right now. You see, she has just returned from a martini lunch." Another time he told a startled caller that one of the girls was no longer with Brooke, explaining that drugs had been found on her person. Then, realizing it was a serious call, he handed the receiver to the "addict." He is also apt to tell callers that one of the girls is out of the office. "Call back in a few minutes. She is in the ladies' room."

Brooke staffers take dignitaries in stride. In *The Brooke Report* the Senator recalled early in 1971 that President Nixon is so busy during normal business hours with appointments, conferences and paper work, he often spends his evening hours on the phone. "It therefore wasn't too much of a surprise to my personal secretary when her telephone rang about 8:30 P.M. A polite voice said, 'This is the White House calling. The President is anxious to speak to Senator Brooke. Do you know where he can be reached?' "*

Betsy asked if she could take a message. "Just a minute, please," the operator said. A moment later she heard a familiar voice: "Hello, Miss Warren, this is the President." She was about to ask the caller to cut the comedy when it occurred to her that it *did* sound like Nixon. She scrambled for something on which to jot down the message he gave her. "My Rose [Miss Rose Mary Woods] takes all my messages," Nixon said jovially.

Betsy recalls how friendly and informal Nixon was. "We must have chatted for six or seven minutes. Not realizing I had a special line at home, he asked me why I was working so late."

Betsy Warren was on another line one day when her mother called her from the Warren home in Brookline, Massachusetts. Brooke picked up the phone: "Hello, Mother," he said. "Betsy will be right with you."

Subdued merriment keys the annual Christmas party held in the Washington office. The girls set up the tree and mistletoe and distrib-

---

* Washington operators first try the Brooke office, then his home or apartment—then Miss Warren, to see if she knows where he is.

ute "joke" gifts. One year Brooke received two dead tennis balls (from Sally Saltonstall), a pair of false sideburns and a prison hat with his Senate number on it.

"How do I look?" he asked, trying on the sideburns and hat. The girls passed around sherry and champagne. During one Christmas party* Ann Cunningham was doing her part in an impromptu pageant when the telephone rang and someone asked to speak to her.

"Sorry, but she can't come to the phone," Woodworth cheerily told the caller. "Ann is dressed in swaddling clothes and is lying in a manger."

Another time Sally Saltonstall answered the phone when a fourteen-year-old volunteer on vacation from prep school called from the Boston office to say there was an important message for the Senator. "Where can he be reached?"

"He's on the floor," Miss Saltonstall said.

Marc Goldberg, who didn't realize she meant the Senate floor, was embarrassed. He thought the Senator was drunk.

One of the hardest workers on Brooke's staff is Roger Woodworth, a lawyer who was chief of the Employment Security Division when Brooke was attorney general. Woodworth is a keen student of local, state and national politics and government, and serves "the boss" in many capacities—primarily as a political adviser and troubleshooter. He is married to his job, often working around the clock, with perhaps a brief nap on a leather sofa or in an office closet. During campaigns he sometimes lived on milk and cookies as he typed well past midnight. He has been known to wash his socks and underwear and hang them up in the men's room in the Old and New Senate Office Buildings in Washington, just as he did earlier in Boston. Melinda Smith, one of Brooke's Washington secretaries, asked Woodworth whether he wanted his milk delivered and garbage removed, while warning that he was in danger of being evicted from the Old Senate Office Building for slum housing. "I file his laundry under L," she said.

There is always a Woodworth story circulating, but the prize incident happened in 1970 in Boston, when he had zipper trouble. He went into a small room next to Brooke's office in the Kennedy Building and, after removing his trousers, asked Maura O'Shaughnessy to see if she could fix the zipper. He became nervous when

---

* Brooke sponsors an annual Christmas party at Anthony's Pier Four in Boston for friends and workers.

Brooke buzzed for him, and asked her to hurry. Maura was still tugging away when there was a second, rasping buzz. "It sounded sarcastic," Woodworth said. Maura told him he'd better go in.

Brooke shook his head when he saw Woodworth standing in front of his desk. Roger, grinning nervously, had a jacket over his underwear.

"Get dressed and come back," Brooke said.

When Woodworth returned, his garters could be seen under his raincoat.

"You should have seen the look on the faces of the constituents waiting to see the boss when Roger came out," Maura said.

Brooke seldom expresses any real annoyance. Early in 1970 he made an exception when, after visiting Nixon at the White House, his black Chrysler wouldn't start and he had to be driven back to his office by a White House aide. The girls in his several adjoining offices in Washington are proud of the boss, while recognizing his foibles. "When he slips into his tuxedo he comes in on some excuse so the girls can see him," Melinda Smith said, adding that he is an inveterate tease. Although Brooke has only one administrative assistant (Timothy Naegele), the phrase is used loosely to describe any aide. "When *The Philadelphia Inquirer* called me an administrative assistant," Melinda said, "I told the boss I deserved a raise. 'You're overpaid as it is,' he said. None of us mind when he calls us a bunch of hopeless old maids, but sometimes I wonder just how much he is kidding. Whenever any of us gives a party, he drops in for a while, knowing how much we appreciate it."

One staff assignment is to draft material which Brooke recasts for radio and TV shows on which he appears. He and Senator Claiborne Pell used to put on a bipartisan television show as a public service, and Miss Smith called Pell's aides for an exchange of ideas and a list of possible topics. Brooke picked it up from there. On this informal show he might tout Ted Kennedy as a likely Democratic nominee in 1972: "I can see him standing by a plane in Hyannis, waiting for a call." The staff drafts material for other shows and for weekly radiocasts used on scores of stations.

Brooke finds time to greet visitors, old and young. One day he spent half an hour answering questions from Amherst (Massachusetts) High School. "As usual, some of the most penetrating questions ever asked me came from these students." He addresses Washington high-school assemblies and meets his public on Constituent Day. An aide had a boy in a Montessori school in Washington. When the boy's teacher brought his classmates (aged four and five) to his office, Brooke let them sit behind his desk. "You're a senator now," he told the children.

Another day he visited an integrated school in the city and talked to a nine-year-old black, asking how he got along with his white classmates and whether they invited him to their homes. "Do you solve all disputes by fighting?" he asked.

Brooke told Senator Walter Mondale it was quite a switch from the days when, as attorney general, he was used to hardened criminals. He found it relaxing to talk to children. Mondale, also a former attorney general, smiled and nodded.

In April 1971 Girl Scouts, Boy Scouts and members of the Catholic Youth Organization (CYO)—all from Massachusetts—filled the Caucus Room of the Old Senate Office Building, after a luncheon arranged by Sally Saltonstall in the Senate cafeteria. Sally also provided House and Senate gallery tickets for the group, which included two vanloads of ninth-grade Cadette Girl Scouts. Mrs. Dennis Kullgren, one of the leaders of the Cadettes, described the scene:

"After our flying tour of the Senate and House, we scurried back to the Old Senate Office Building and up the wide staircase to the Caucus Room. . . . First one, then another group joined us, until by the 3:00 P.M. appointment time we were wall-to-wall Girl and Boy Scouts and other youth groups from all over Massachusetts. In hopes of a quick word with the Senator beforehand, I went down to the lobby, where he was engulfed by the Boston CYO. When a group picture ended their interview, I walked back up with him and his staff. There was none of the terse 'turn off the frozen smile, let's get on with it' attitude I've often encountered when politicians get together with kids too old to kiss and too young to vote. He was really enjoying these young people, obviously feeling this was an important part of being their Senator. Wearing a blue blazer and white slacks, he had their undivided attention while he addressed the entire group, and all waited while he met with each group individually to have his picture taken with them on the front steps of the building. Despite the fact that he was late for an appointment with an adult group, he took time to tell the girls to have pride in their organizations and in their uniforms, which they had gone to great lengths to conceal by whisking off hats and buttoning up coats, despite regulations and the repeated protests of their leaders. This appointment with Senator Brooke, which many of the girls had been reluctant to 'waste time on,' was *the* highlight of a week's trip, which included a visit to Williamsburg, and was completely on a par with running all the way down the Washington Monument!"

Senators Brooke and Edward Kennedy greeted two Massachusetts officials one day to discuss state and national problems. Romney and Elliot Richardson were also on hand. After the joint conference, Kennedy bused the visitors to his Georgetown home for cocktails, along with senatorial staff members. One of Brooke's secretaries, Caryle Connelly, spoke to the host before leaving.

"I used to work for you, Senator Kennedy. Now I'm with Brooke," she said.

"Well, there's always next year," Kennedy said.

When the girls give a surprise birthday party for the boss, as Betsy Warren did one year at her apartment in Georgetown, they usually invite the Senator's mother, along with friends, husbands and wives of staff members. Brooke dutifully sits down and opens his presents. At one such party he saw that his mother had given him a shirt.

"Oh, Mother," he said, pretending to be embarrassed.

"Well, I didn't think you would open it here," Mrs. Brooke said.

Brooke was so tired of reading about strife and discord by the summer of 1967 that he asked Marilyn Dexheimer, a legislative assistant, to find him something cheerful in the newspapers. Marilyn couldn't find anything worth showing him, so she wrote a memo to the boss, titled "Good Morning":

> Ah, woe is me, great statesman,
> There's no good news today.
> The Reds have not retreated,
> The Greeks have lost their way.
> The Germans are unhappy,
> The French still think we're fools;
> And in the land of China,
> Now no one knows who rules.

After three more stanzas recounting other troubles of the world came this quatrain:

> The world is in a turmoil,
> Or so it would appear.
> But let's enjoy it while we can—
> Next comes election year!

Brooke enshrined the doggerel in the pages of *The Congressional Record*. Doggerel intruded again, in October, when Brooke told the

Senate the Boston Red Sox had won the American League pennant. Before he could get the floor to read the roll call of Red Sox heroes, he sat patiently while the Senate paid tribute to its presiding officer, Carl Hayden (Democrat of Arizona) on his ninetieth birthday. Brooke then revealed that during a crucial part of the baseball season he had sent some verse to Dick Williams, the Red Sox manager. It read in part:

> Of all the teams in baseball,
> The Red Sox are the best.
> You've vanquished all contenders
> From the East Coast to the West.
>
> Your fans are all excited
> With this year's performance.
> We couldn't be more delighted
> With your encouraging transformance.
>
> You've won the praise of all of us,
> Win, lose or draw the race.
> And it is my humble prediction,
> You'll end up in first place.

The Senator didn't insert this verse in *The Congressional Record*.

CHAPTER FOURTEEN

A Swing Through Africa

S ENATOR BROOKE was the third prominent American to visit Africa in 1968. Early in January, U.S. Supreme Court Justice Thurgood Marshall had accompanied Vice-President Hubert Humphrey on a 13-day trip through the continent. Traveling with Brooke were two aides—Clarence Elam and Marilyn Dexheimer—and two journalists. One was Anne Chamberlin, who had been assigned by *Cosmopolitan* magazine to profile Brooke. Unable to corner him in his Washington lair for an interview for her close-up story, she concluded that it would be easier to "track him through the bush." Later, after trying to keep up with him, she said: "There may be a lot of things I still don't know about Senator Brooke, but I'm beginning to get the picture about his work habits. I don't know whether that Scottish explorer named Livingstone could have kept up the pace."

The other journalist was Howard S. Knowles, political editor of *The Worcester Telegram and Evening Gazette*. Knowles was standing beside the Senator at the Pan Am gate at Kennedy Airport when a photographer assigned to get a picture of him with Brooke came up. "Where's Knowles?" he asked the Senator.

Brooke smiled. "Who's going on this trip?" he said.

Before leaving the airport for a projected 26-day fact-finding tour of 12 African nations south of the Sahara Desert as a member of the Senate Banking and Currency Committee, Brooke held a press conference. "He was the only one in the room who didn't look like a tossed salad," Mrs. Chamberlin said. As usual, Brooke was dressed to the nines, in a tailored gray suit, conservative tie and a shirt "that could have starred in a Clorox ad."

Brooke wanted to study social and political developments and American aid programs in Africa and to determine its possible future in world affairs, he told newsmen. "I hope to find out as much as I can about the opposition parties, where they exist, to talk to knowledgeable press people, when I can, to check out information at firsthand." He felt Africa was looming in importance because of the swift and revolutionary changes taking place. Recent cutbacks in foreign aid to emerging African nations were unfortunate, Brooke said, adding that his trip had nothing to do with any impression Stokely Carmichael had made abroad. "I wasn't asked to go as a goodwill ambassador."

Marilyn Dexheimer during the 1966 Senate campaign was a research assistant who dug up information on such matters as the New England economy and wrote position papers on foreign policy. For months, in preparation for the African trip, the twenty-eight-year-old Miss Dexheimer, who had left her pursuit of a doctorate in American government and international relations at Boston University to campaign for Brooke in 1966, had been interviewing African scholars and reading volumes of assorted information, which she condensed in a loose-leaf notebook. Meanwhile, she was a legislative assistant in Brooke's Washington office.

Dr. Adelaide Hill briefed Brooke while he familiarized himself with the warehouse of data in Miss Dexheimer's "black book." Later she startled African officials along the route by asking involved questions studded with words such as "infrastructure," then filling copy books with detailed notes on the answers.

During the seven-hour nonstop flight to Dakar, Senegal, a country with a one-crop economy sometimes called "a nation sitting on a pile of peanuts," the stewards served malaria pills with the champagne, along with a note warning of mosquitoes in Africa. At the Dakar airport Ambassador Dean Brown, present ambassador to Jordan, and his embassy staff met the party at 4:30 A.M. local time and drove them to the ambassador's villa, which had sliding doors opening onto a pool.

"For another of my wild, misguided moments," wrote Mrs. Chamberlin, "I thought we might have a chance to swim in it. The Senator is a keen swimmer and may be the only member of the U.S. Senate who was once a lifeguard." Like the rest of the party, she quickly learned that business came before pleasure.

271

After having coffee and Danish pastries (there was no time for sleep) Brooke talked at length with President Leopold Senghor, a poet who, like the Senator, has an honorary degree from Howard University. The party saw no tigers or lions in Dakar streets as embassy cars took them past turbaned women in floating boubous who "sailed like galleons along the sidewalks." At bus stops men in long robes riffled through comic books, "with transistor radios glued to their ears," all in a setting of honking automobiles and traffic jams. The sights and sounds were unsettling to anyone with a preconceived notion of Africa.

The guide, the first vice-president of the Senegalese National Assembly, answered Brooke's questions: "Does the future of Africa lie in federation?" "Do you foresee a racially integrated Africa?" "How much cotton do you import?"

At a Dakar press conference Brooke said the many black Americans identified with Africa, "which is good and healthy. But I think we must live in an integrated America, just as you must live in an integrated Africa." Some questions were unanswerable. At the International Relations Club of the YMCA in Monrovia, Liberia, someone asked a question ten minutes long and very involved. Brooke, giving him a coolly appraising look, said, "I'm with you."

The first day in Dakar, after lunching on paella, salad, papaya and vin rosé at the home of an embassy official, the party toured the Senegalese countryside in Land Rovers enroute to a Peace Corps project. Brooke paid his respects to the governor of the province at his villa in Thiès. Served in a large reception room were Scotch, champagne, soft drinks and pineapple juice. Brooke waved off the Cordon Rouge. "One drink of that champagne and you'd have another house guest," he said. He sipped a glass of orange pop. When nobody else wanted champagne, the Governor refused to open a bottle for his wife. In lieu of small talk, Brooke questioned the Governor on the economy and demography of his region.

Next stop for the three Land Rovers was the dusty village of Pout, where the natives had a street festival (*tam-tam*) for Brooke. Three Senegalese drummers thumped out a native rhythm as Brooke met the village leaders. After chairs were set up in a courtyard, turbaned women, clutching up their spangled, billowing boubous, twisted and stamped to the drum beat as a troupe of dancers and blue-jean-clad Peace Corps volunteers clapped in cadence. Brooke climaxed the performance by suddenly improvising—with a native charmer—a fandango to the beat of drums. For several minutes they danced, to the delight of the gathering. A villager said the Senator wasn't a bad dancer for a *toubab,* a word that means "white man" in the local Wolof dialect.

"One day in Africa," wrote Anne Chamberlin, "and Senator Brooke had shot through the color barrier and come out the other side." Mrs. Chamberlin recalls that while she was with Brooke, "the Africans seemed more anxious to ask him as an American senator about economic aid and Vietnam than as a Negro about black power." In Ghana (formerly the Gold Coast) Brooke told a group the Negro had unique problems that needed correction. "I am doing all I can to correct them. I would do the same if I were not of African descent." During the trip he said he didn't know where his ancestors came from —whether from Liberia, Nigeria or elsewhere, "but my ties are in Africa." Then he quickly added: "I am here not as a Negro but as a man."

After driving along a dusty, winding road, the caravan stopped at the hill village of Khinine, where two young Peace Corps workers were helping to build latrines. Not realizing it was a signal of distress, the natives flew the American flag upside down in honor of the visitors. In Wolof dialect a Peace Corps volunteer told the elders the Senator "was happy to be with them, loves them, and hopes to be with them again." That night in Brooke's honor the party dined at a buffet featuring a shark mold shaped like an airplane.

Knowles remembers a swimming party one hot midnight when a young embassy official fished a frog from the pool. "Senator Brooke, unaware, was doing a slow breaststroke as the youth took aim, intent on landing the frog in front of the senatorial nose. 'Now don't do that,' the ambassador said. He shrugged as the youth let fly." It was a clear miss.

Next morning the group flew from Senegal to Guinea in a 1945 model DC-3. A steward pointed out the life preservers and canned food on board in case the plane was forced down, and warned against having more than one person behind the bulkhead at the same time, because it made the tail heavy, causing the plane to lose air speed. He didn't say what would happen in that case.

"He's not as pretty as a Pan Am stewardess," Brooke said. "But he sure scares you more."

Ambassador Robinson McIlvaine met Brooke at the Conakry Airport in Guinea and an embassy car took the Senator and his two aides to one of President Touré's villas. An hour later the party boarded Ambassador McIlvaine's inboard cruiser for a picnic on Tamara Island. The Senator also inspected the Harvey Aluminum

Company's bauxite operation on a neighboring island, and the party returned in the evening to attend a reception at the palace honoring Toure's almost unanimous reelection to another seven-year term. After speaking fluently in French at the National Palace Touré drove Brooke in his Citroën to a guesthouse with a thatched roof and tiled bathrooms, where Brooke enjoyed a long talk with the President through an interpreter. Brooke asked Touré about prospects for American private investment and an African federation. Touré gently chided the U.S. for its slackening interest in foreign aid to Guinea, but said American and Guinean relations were cordial. He said Guinea would work with any nation that respected its dignity and independence. "We will not devalue our money even if it means we do not import one needle," he told Brooke, who knew that Guinea was the only French colony to reject President de Gaulle's offer to enter the French community. The discussion lasted long enough to make Brooke two hours late for McIlwaine's dinner party.

Next morning the group visited a Mack truck assembly plant and a technical training school, leaving after lunch to fly to Monrovia, capital of Liberia, where Ambassador Benjamin H. Brown, Jr., welcomed the Americans at the airport. The president of the Liberian Senate toasted "Senator Edward W. Brooke of Massachusetts. May he accelerate."

At the formal lunch at Hotel Ducor Intercontinental, overlooking the South Atlantic, guests drank champagne toasts to Liberian President William V. Tubman and President Lyndon Johnson. Brooke had a private talk with Tubman on his second day in Monrovia. The parents of Tubman, who graduated from Ohio University, were slaves who migrated to Liberia from Georgia. During Tubman's 27 years in office Liberia became the first black African nation to join the UN Security Council. Along with Emperor Haile Selassie of Ethiopia and President Jomo Kenyatta of Kenya, Tubman was one of the African elder statesmen who led the movement which resulted in the Organization of African Unity in 1963. He died in London in 1971 at the age of seventy-five.

Liberia reminded Brooke of home. Its flag has stripes and one star, and its currency is the U.S. dollar. Policemen wear American-style uniforms, as do members of the National Guard, and Liberian people speak English with the Southern accent of the first freeman settlers who migrated from America in 1822.

After a conference at the embassy, Brooke was badgered at a Monrovia press session by a Tass correspondent who asked about the "typical American boy" who had admitted torturing people in Vietnam, he said.

"I am also a typical American boy," Brooke told the Russian, who referred to an interview with a GI printed in a Paris newspaper in which the soldier had said Americans tortured North Vietnamese prisoners. Brooke, noting that he had talked to people in all walks of life in South Vietnam, "including some Communists," said he at no time heard of atrocities. "I can assure you, sir, I have seen no evidence of any such thing."*

In Harbel, Liberia, Brooke toured the largest rubber plantation in the world—220 square miles of rubber trees owned by the Firestone Rubber Company. Before his inspection, Peace Corps workers complained of the low wages Liberians, who lived in dismal shacks, were getting. Firestone managers told Brooke natural rubber was getting tough competition from U.S. synthetics, one reason for low wages.

A tapper showed Brooke how to slice a wafer of bark from a tree to start the latex oozing, while the Senator shook hands with some of the plantation children. Brooke shook his head when the tapper said his maximum salary was $1.40 a day.

Abidjan, capital of the Ivory Coast, is called "the Paris of West Africa" and "the pearl of the lagoons." Its Hotel Ivoire is the most elegant on the continent. An official of the African Development Bank told Brooke no West Coast African nation could go it alone, even one as affluent as the Ivory Coast. "We cannot have poor nations looking in at one rich nation." This, he said, could foment a revolution.

The Senator was impressed by the West African showplace with its superhighway leading into the city. The official said the U.S., instead of spending money to bring Africans on tours of the United States, should spend half that amount to bring congressmen and other legislators to Africa so they could see the problems. After the conference, wrote Anne Chamberlin, "another fat bundle of documents headed for his [Brooke's] Washington office."

On a drive to the interior the group passed women carrying buckets on their heads, herds of goats and mounds of coconut shells. It stopped at a village for a conference with the subprefect, who briefed Brooke on politics, budgets, schools and hospitals. During the African trip the Senator suffered from a recurring intestinal upset, but at this time was feeling well enough to enjoy lunch in a pleasant

---

* This, of course, was before disclosure of the My Lai massacre.

restaurant in Aboisso which included banana foufou, poyo and a liberal serving of ganguey, a palm wine. Everyone drank toasts in pink champagne to Ivory Coast and U.S. good relations.

The next stop was in Ghana, which, according to Mrs. Chamberlin, "lay gasping under the *harmattan,* a dry, dust-laden wind from the Sahara, so the Senator headed straight for the hottest place in the country, an aluminum smelting plant, to learn about U.S. investment in Ghana. Hard hat on head, I took notes and sweated." The Valco Aluminum Smelter is the largest outside North America.

At a press conference in Accra, Ghana, a reporter, noting that the American public had often criticized congressional junkets, asked Brooke whether he was learning anything from his trip, and whether his report to the Senate would be "carefully prepared." Brooke said there had been no criticism of any trips to Africa. "I think there could be criticism of the lack of trips. Much has been written in America about Africa, but I'm afraid little has been read by the average citizen. Many Americans still have the impression that there are tigers and lions in the streets."

This drew a comment from another newsman that some American institutions fostered that idea, citing "cannibals" in Disneyland. Later, at a conference held at the home of Ambassador Franklin Williams, Brooke learned that "Tarzan and the Apes," a comic strip widely distributed in Ghana and Kenya, affronted the Africans.

Brooke and U.S. Ambassador to Ghana Williams may be remembered as "the most swinging Americans ever to represent the U.S. in Ghana," Knowles wrote, noting that the African reunion of these two high-school friends included joining the "chorus line" of a professional Ghanaian dance group which entertained at the embassy with a performance of authentic Ghanaian tribal dances. Forty prominent Ghanaians and American embassy officials attended the party in Brooke's honor. The dance group of 14 men and women performed on the dimly lit terrace of the embassy with a series of fantastically intricate and authentic maneuvers to the cadence of drums. Suddenly Williams, grabbing Brooke's arm, brought him onto the floor, urging the percussion group to "make those drums roll." The pair improvised an American Twist in the center of whirling Ghanaian dancers.

In Accra, Brooke talked to General J. A. Ankrah, who came out of forced retirement at the time of the 1966 coup against former President Kwame Nkrumah to lead the country. Touré gave Nkrumah sanctuary in Conakry after his corrupt one-party rule in Ghana toppled.

Williams took Brooke on a shopping tour for Ghanaian artifacts and arranged a tennis match. Brooke and his partner won the mixed doubles in three straight sets. The ambassador, once director of the Peace Corps in Africa and proud of his athletic prowess, was displeased.

Nigeria was in the midst of a civil war at the time of the Senator's visit. The Ibos in the vast country's eastern region had tried to break away and form an independent nation; the rest of the country believed that strength lay only in federation. As the fighting wore on, reports began to circulate that the Nigerian federal government was engaged in a campaign of genocide against the Ibo people. The Senator was particularly anxious to learn more about this accusation. He found that 38,000 Ibos lived in peace in Lagos alone, that many of the government officials with whom he met were Ibos, that careful plans had been made for the return of personal property and the reconstruction of the Eastern region once the war was over. Subsequent events confirmed both the seriousness of the Nigerian government's intentions in this regard, and their capacity to carry through.

Brooke still corresponds with Major General Yakubu Gowon, head of the federal military government in Nigeria, and with the Oba (the traditional chief) of Lagos, with whom he played Ping-Pong at the palace. Nigeria is Africa's richest and most powerful nation, with a population of about 60 million. Gowon, who took much of his military training in Britain when Nigeria was a part of England's colonial holdings in West Africa, took over the military government of Nigeria in 1966, when he was not yet thirty. A moderate with no wish to prolong military rule, he told Brooke early in 1968: "I will not stay a day longer than necessary. There is no doubt whatever that the war will soon come to an end."

During their conference, Gowon told Brooke he had been reading Carl Sandburg's life of Abraham Lincoln. "I can see real similarities," Gowon said in Lagos. "I ask myself why we haven't learned from history." Brooke said he hoped Nigeria would not adopt America's Reconstruction Era as a model. Gowon said that if needed, he would run for president of Nigeria, if there was a return to constitutional government. "I cannot run away."

About a year after his meeting with Gowon, Brooke wrote the general of his concern over new claims of Nigerian attacks on innocent civilians, hospitals, and relief planes in the war zone. "Recurrent press dispatches assert that aircraft under the command of the Nigerian federal government have bombed and strafed market places, aircraft carrying supplies of food and medicine, and other non-military targets. They are said to have inflicted hundreds of casualties, including many fatalities among women, children, and other non-combatants. I respectfully urge you to do everything in your power to determine the extent to which incidents of this character have occurred and to provide guarantees against terror attacks in the future."

In September 1969 Brooke wrote his friend again: "I was most heartened to learn of the Executive Council's decision to permit the operation from Dahomey of daytime Red Cross relief flights into the rebel-held territory. The human suffering from starvation has been great; the cost to present and future generations cannot be measured. It was your government which made the concessions necessary to bring relief to the innocent victims of war." On January 13, 1970, the "Biafrans" surrendered and their leaders fled the country. Brooke wrote again telling Gowon how happy he was to hear about the end of the war.

While in Nigeria, Brooke met many Nigerian officials, including the Oba of Lagos. The Oba, a dignified elder statesman whose several wives share his palace, personifies the merger of the ancient and the modern in much of Africa: he sleeps in a bed built over the graves of his ancestors, but keeps his Scotch whisky and glasses in a modern aluminum sphere. It was the Oba who, on a visit to the United States three years later, met at length with the Senator and his staff in the Washington office and presented the Senator with an elaborately embroidered hand-made robe.

Acting Chief of State and Minister of Interior Etienne Tshisikedi welcomed Brooke to Kinshasa, Congo, and recalled that the previous summer President Johnson had given his country three transport planes that were used to ferry Congolese troops to a border region near Katanga province to quell a revolt of white mercenaries. Acting Foreign Affairs Minister Victor Nendaka praised Brooke, saying his election to the U.S. Senate was "very important to us." He gave Brooke an elaborately carved elephant tusk, a kind of totem pole depicting events in Congolese history.

"As a man with historic ties to Africa," Brooke said, "I can understand your pride in my election . . . and you can understand my pride in seeing young black men in roles of leadership in a free country. . . . I hope we can continue as partners."

There was no mention of the deposed Moise Tshombe, who had led the Katanga secessionist movement shortly after the Congo won its independence from Belgium in 1960. Tshombe was a captive in Algeria, after his plane had been hijacked in midair by persons eager to return him to Kinshasa for trial.

Herchelle Challenor, who had gone to Dahomey to study for a Ph.D. and married an American physician there, had been recommended to Brooke by Dr. Adelaide Hill, and she joined the party in Dakar. She was his interpreter during the tour of the Congo. She collected data for Miss Dexheimer's bulging black book until she left the party at Lumbumbashi in the Congo.

From the Congo the party drove across the border to the mining town of Mufalira in Zambia. Here they met with expatriate managers of one of the world's largest copper mines and descended 2,000 feet into the depths of the mine. While taking an elevator to the top of a shaft, the Senator could not help but notice that the prevailing winds blew the copper dust and smoke over the homes and gardens of the black workers. Wages were quite low, and the living and working conditions for the workers were quite poor in contrast to the beautifully landscaped and appointed homes and guesthouses of the managers.

After luncheon with local African officials, the party flew on to Lusaka, the capital of Zambia, where they met with Vice-President Simon Kapwepwe (since jailed for his political opposition), with all of the Cabinet members and with officials of the national bank.

The after-dinner entertainment at the ambassador's residence was interrupted by an unscheduled event: The ambassador's cook chased a cabinet minister's driver through the shrubbery with a butcher knife.

One day the party took an all-day excursion by Piper Aztec to Botswana, a prairie nation of half a million people south of Zambia. President Seretse Khama was their host in Serowe, where most of the inhabitants live as they have for generations—in clusters of tiny mud huts.

The pilot was determined to show the party all the sights. The tourists, from the diving plane, had a breathtaking view of Victoria Falls in the southwest corner of Zambia, as the pilot stood the Piper on its wingtips in a tight figure eight only a few hundred feet above the swirling gorge. "For an encore," Knowles wrote, "he drove the plane through the heavy mist which rises into the air high above the lip of the falls. The craft shot skyward in the updraft and thumped down heavily as it cleared the spray." Did the Senator want a second swing over Victoria Falls? the pilot asked. He did not.

He was less nervous when the plane made strafing runs above grazing animals which turned out to be herds of cows. They returned to Lusaka, where they held a late night meeting with representatives of several Southern Africa liberation movements. The next morning they boarded a flight to Dar es Salaam, where Brooke swam in the Indian Ocean. He canceled a scheduled talk at University College in Dar es Salaam, capital of Tanzania, a state composed of Tanganyika on the eastern coast of Central Africa below Kenya and above Mozambique, and the tiny island kingdom of Zanzibar, just off the coast. Brooke had a long, off-the-record talk with President Julius Nyerere, an articulate, cultured and outgoing, if sensitive, ruler whose policy of African socialism steers a course between East and West but who is a bitter enemy of the U.S. position in Vietnam. Early in 1968 Nyerere let the National Liberation Front (Vietcong) open a diplomatic mission in Dar es Salaam.

Shortly after Brooke's visit, Calvin Cobb, a disbarred black American lawyer, came to Dar Es Salaam to address the students. He said the white establishment was using some civil-rights leaders to stall any chance of changing the status quo in the U.S. and called Brooke an Uncle Tom. Tanzania denied a U.S. request for extradition of Cobb, who had been convicted of embezzlement in New York City.

Knowles, who has covered Brooke for years, said the only time he ever saw the Senator upstaged was by Nyerere. It happened in a magnificent setting in a government building overlooking the Indian Ocean, with doors opening onto a patio.

"Brooke was sitting beside Nyerere at a huge conference table. Nyerere, fingertips together and head lowered, listened as Brooke explained the purpose of his trip. The more the Senator talked, the less attention Nyerere seemed to be paying. Finally, Brooke's voice trailed off, as if he didn't know what to make of the situation. Nyerere startled him by suddenly asking: 'What do you think of our Godforsaken country?' "

A half-hour flight to the clove-producing island of Zanzibar provided the Senator and his party with an opportunity to meet with Sheik Abeid Karume, the longshoreman turned political leader who had wrested control of the government from the island's Arab minority in 1964. He is now Tanzania's first vice-president. Karume's wall was adorned with photographs of Lenin, Mao and Nasser, and Brooke promised to send him a photo of "the next Republican President of the United States" to add to his collection. After the 1968 elections, a color photo of President Nixon was sent to Zanzibar.

Dar es Salaam also gave the Senator an opportunity to hold further extensive meetings with the leaders and members of the various Southern African liberation movements. In these discussions, a picture emerged of consistent economic, social and political repression of blacks. Most of the liberation leaders, like the famous Eduardo Mondlane, who was assassinated less than a year after dining alone with Brooke in Dar, were educated by Protestant missionaries from the United States or Western Europe.

From his talks with the liberation leaders and with political leaders in the black African states, Brooke returned with a strong conviction that the United States must disassociate itself from any policy of implied complicity with the racist regimes of Southern Africa.

Finally exhausted by the grind, Brooke made a rare slip while addressing a dozen student leaders at Makerere University College in Kampala, Uganda. At a coffee hour Brooke said one aim of the U.S. in South Vietnam was to guarantee the right of the South Vietnamese to choose their own form of government in peace and security. One student, knowing that the history of many emerging nations in Africa had been punctuated by coups and countercoups usually resulting in the suppression or postponement of constitutional regimes, asked Brooke why the U.S. had not broken relations with African nations whose governments had been taken over in coups.

"Why is this different from the question of self-determination in Communist-threatened nations?"

The students gasped when Brooke said "military coups are an accepted form for changing governments. They are a legitimate means." He told newsmen later he hadn't meant to endorse military coups, but had in mind that nations, including the U.S., have given diplomatic recognition to governments installed through military takeovers.

After his startling comment, a student asked if he knew how to promote democracy in Africa, noting that the "new democracy has apparently failed."

"I don't think Africa is going Communist. I think Africa is headed toward democracy," Brooke said.

The Kampala press corps quizzed Brooke on a connection between his trip and Vice-President Humphrey's, noting that it was a presidential election year. Wasn't the basic idea merely competition for the American vote?

Brooke said he wasn't running against Humphrey or anyone else, and that his trip had been planned a year earlier. "And nothing he [Humphrey] or I say will have any great bearing on the United States election."

Another reporter asked about the CIA's role in overthrowing African governments. Noting there was no evidence of this, Brooke said the CIA didn't have that power "and it should not have that power." A hostile reporter said Brooke was the first black senator since the Civil War. "Is this because there is a feeling that Negroes are incapable of holding office?"

Knowles recalls a frenzied ride to the airport in Uganda after one of the group missed an early morning call, raising the question of getting to the plane on time.

"The embassy official in the front seat [of the car] kept growling to his African driver to step on it. Roadsides were crowded with natives walking or bicycling to work. As you bowl along at sixty, horn going, your embassy man keeps making waving motions through the windshield, muttering, 'get out of the way, you bastards.' "

In Nairobi, Kenya, where Brooke finally saw herds of zebras and giraffes in a game preserve, as well as a cheetah and her five cubs gnawing on the carcass of an antelope, he was asked by university students how he could reconcile the rejection of violence in the U.S. civil-rights struggle while advocating it in Vietnam. He said they were different situations: in the U.S. change *can* be achieved peacefully. He expressed sympathy for the "freedom fighters" of Southern Africa seeking to overthrow white regimes, including the one in Rhodesia. Students who had heard that Brooke was the only black in the U.S. Senate were anxious to meet him but puzzled when they did, for, as a correspondent wrote, "when an American Negro meets an audience of Africans for the first time, he is too urbane, too Western, and, in fact, too light-skinned even if he talks of his 'African brothers' and describes himself as an 'Afro-American.' "

This happened when Brooke met 200 students at the university. The student chairman, misreading his notes on Brooke's wartime service, introduced him as "the leader of the American Army during World War II. "The laughter was mingled with warmth and understanding. It semed to touch a chord of identification: He was a privileged American Negro just as they were privileged Africans."

The students were more interested in Brooke as a "leader of the American Army" and as a representative of the U.S. government than as a Negro. Some assailed U.S. policy in South Africa and Portugal, as well as in Vietnam. Brooke said that as a member of the opposition party he was critical of American policy in Vietnam, although he understood why the U.S. was trying to check communism there. He said he would detail his views about Southern Africa in his report on his trip.

Why was he—a Negro—a Republican? Why do Afro-Americans make up such an out-of-balance share of troop casualties in Vietnam? Brooke calmly answered the questions. Then a student said he had been elected to an all-white fraternity while attending college in America. This was for window dressing. Was this also true of the Senator?

"Nobody in Massachusetts decided they just wanted to put a Negro in the Senate," Brooke said. "If they had, I wouldn't have been their man. It isn't a question of race. It's a question of power politics, frankly."

Was there a sharp cleavage between rich, professional Negroes and poor Negroes in the U.S.? During the long question period, Brooke's patience at times wore thin because of repeated insinuations that prosperous American blacks had no interest in the civil-rights struggle. It was silly, he said, to criticize American Negroes for being successful. "For you to believe that American Negro middle-class society has turned its back on the other Negroes just isn't true." Brooke said the students, like himself, were God's chosen people. "Otherwise you'd be out in the bush, not sitting in the chairs. You people don't go back and live in that bush. You'll never live in that bush." He said blacks like himself who were lucky enough to get an education were no different from young Africans lucky enough to be attending the university, with its handsome, modern facilities. The students laughed when he said cutbacks in foreign aid were made because the U.S. had its own problems, and they were again amused when he said 20 percent of Americans live on or below the poverty level.

Brooke canceled his trip to Ethiopia to return to Washington for an imminent Senate civil-rights legislation vote.

During his arduous trip Brooke saw little of the bush. He was guest of honor at 75 luncheons, cocktail parties and formal dinners arranged by U.S. embassies and African officials and attended by several hundred African officials, journalists and prominent citizens. In each country he was briefed by embassy and AID (Agency for International Development) officials and talked with Peace Corps volunteers. He thought his tour improved Afro-American relations.

By the end of the trip he had shipped home bales of statistics. He concluded that Africa, because of its location, natural resources and vastness, loomed as a crucial area. "The people are not too concerned with ideology yet. They're too concerned with food and shelter. Illiteracy is too high. But this is certain to change, not in five or ten years, perhaps, but eventually it must come." He called Africa "a continent still hanging in the balance. It may be pulled into the Communist sphere. But this is something only the future will decide. If the West deals wisely with Africa, it need not happen. No one can visit this continent, however, even for a brief time and not feel that the effort might be made."

Brooke remembered promises on his return to Washington. On April 28 he asked the Johnson administration to cut its trade with South Africa unless that nation ended its policy of oppressing blacks. In a 10,000-word speech on the Senate floor he proposed a policy that would isolate all white regimes of Southern Africa which subjugate black majorities: South Africa, Rhodesia, Angola and Mozambique. He also proposed an end to military treaties with Portugal, which controls Angola and Mozambique.

"I believe the time has come to wrench ourselves from this pattern of implied complicity with the Southern African regimes. I do not fancy that maximum American pressure will bring early and easy political change. . . . I realize that firmer action on our part may increase tensions with our European allies. But I believe we must remove from the United States any hint of sympathy for the minority dictatorships of Southern Africa." He said that in the eyes of most Africans "the record of what we have not done speaks more clearly than the verbal condemnations and token sanctions against the white regimes. We have done nothing to discourage American private investment in South Africa, which . . . serves as a vital pillar of support for that unpopular government."

Brooke said the U.S. regards Southern Rhodesia as "a British colony in rebellion, yet because of the limited nature of our investment and trade, our economic sanctions have had no impact at all, and we have done little to persuade the British to increase pressure on the rebel government of Premier Ian Smith." Brooke also charged that our allies sell arms and military equipment to the South African government and that we have done little to discourage the practice. "Portugal receives considerable military assistance from the U.S., and the African freedom fighters insist that it is American weapons which are killing their people in Angola and Mozambique." He said the U.S. should support the British proposal in the UN Security Council for mandatory economic sanctions against Rhodesia.

He also noted in his speech that the U.S. could prejudice its case "severely if we allow our preoccupation with the Cold War to dominate our policies, or if we . . . chastise nations for accepting Communist aid. So long as these nations are diligent in protecting their independence, we should share their satisfaction that both East and West are prepared to aid their development."

The Washington Post published two letters rebuking Brooke's position: "Senator Brooke's recent call for an end to our trade with South Africa at the same time that he supports expanded trade with Communist countries is a source of concern to all who had admired his work to date. South Africa's apartheid policy is not to be condoned, but to suggest that we continue to trade for Russian products built by forced labor is to join the far-left demagogues who find the Russian brand of slavery acceptable." The second writer said Brooke would do "more service to his own country and people if he concentrated on helping to solve problems here, rather than telling South Africa how to manage its affairs, Portugal how it must commit itself in Angola and Mozambique, and Britain how it must increase pressure in Rhodesia. The old saying, 'Better clean up your own backyard before you start on your neighbor's,' seems applicable here."

Brooke, taking a more pragmatic view, continued his interest in Africa. Early in October 1968 he disagreed with Senator Edward Kennedy's proposal that the UN be the prime organization for helping victims of the Nigeria-Biafra war. In a statement before Senator Eugene J. McCarthy's Foreign Relations Subcommittee on African Affairs, Brooke said UN support should be offered through the Organization of African Unity. A UN debate would likely be long and inconclusive, and would involve the broader East-West controversy in the United Nations.

McCarthy's subcommittee was investigating steps the U.S. could take to help civilian victims of the war that began when the eastern region of Nigeria seceded and proclaimed itself the independent nation of Biafra. Nigerian federal troops under Major General Gowon reoccupied most of the breakaway territory, which, as Brooke noted in his correspondence with Gowon, suffered from widespread starvation and disease. Brooke said Biafran leaders "must bear a large share of the blame" for the starvation. Genocide is not and never has been a policy of the Nigerian government, which, he said, "places unity and domestic peace far ahead of tribal differences."

Brooke told the subcommittee Nigeria had acted to "quell the rebellion in a responsible manner," and there had been no confirmed evidence of massacres. He said Colonel C. O. Ojukwu had promised to fight to the end for the Biafrans, but "it is not heroism to take millions of innocent people to their deaths as well." Brooke linked

Ojukwu, the leader of the Biafran revolt, with Hitler: "Once before in modern history a national leader chose to rule or die and to take his people with him.

While Brooke was in Africa he was the target of widespread criticism by both the press and his Senate colleagues.

"Is Washington burning?" a reporter asked. "Many say yes, but apparently . . . Brooke, junior senator from Massachusetts, takes a cooler view. He is not here. With problems worsening, the Senate this week [January 1968] embarked on a legislative quest to improve the economic and social development of the U.S. in the form of a rather modest civil-rights bill."

The reporter noted that Brooke and Senator Walter Mondale, a Minnesota Democrat, served notice that they planned to expand current civil-rights legislation into a fight for a national open-housing law. "This news was greeted with some bemusement by such Republicans as Jacob Javits, Hugh Scott, Thomas Kuchel and Clifford Case, who have been fighting that battle for years with some skill but no success." The consensus in the Senate was that an ambitious bill could not pass in 1968 and that a modest bill should be proposed. The modest bill before the Senate in January would offer federal protection to persons exercising their civil rights, such as students and marchers who previously had "been beaten and maimed while FBI agents took notes in case the matter ever developed into a federal case."

Brooke and Mondale, said the reporter, planned a "kamikaze" approach—all or nothing at all. This proposal "was not greeted as bitterly as was the absence of both men when the liberals caucused to discuss strategy to counter a Southern filibuster." Some liberals were openly criticizing Brooke's untimely absence. "No senator claiming to be a leader in civil rights could afford to be away from his desk during the coming debate," the reporter continued. "While Brooke tours Africa, Mondale is in Europe." He added that a bloc in the Senate had "taken to joking about Brooke's performance in the past year." According to one story, during the civil-rights debate one senator motioned toward Brooke and said: "What do you call him?"

"I call him senator," the second solon said.

"The first one laughed sarcastically," according to the reporter.

But Brooke had the last laugh.

CHAPTER FIFTEEN

An Emerging Spokesman

O N FEBRUARY 19, 1968, Brooke spoke on the cloture vote scheduled for the following day on the civil-rights legislation then before the Senate. If cloture could be invoked, amendments to the bill including the Brooke-Mondale open-housing amendment could be called up and voted upon. "We are on the eve of the most important vote which we shall probably take in this session," the Senator said.

When the vote was taken the following morning, cloture failed by seven votes. It was evident that the proponents of the legislation were unlikely to obtain cloture, and a vote on the unmodified Brooke-Mondale amendment, in that session of the Congress. In a series of strategy meetings with the leadership, it was determined that a less comprehensive but nevertheless stringent open-housing amendment should be proposed by Senate Minority Leader Everett Dirksen, who could bring enough votes with him to shut off debate and invoke cloture. Instrumental in these negotiations was the junior Senator from Massachusetts, without whose efforts the open-housing bill would not have been enacted.

Two days later a colleague of *The Boston Globe* reporter who had rapped Brooke's "untimely absence" said Brooke's motion, if successful, would force the Senate to end its filibuster and vote on the civil-rights package in 1968.

"Its chances were enhanced by the behind-the-scenes efforts of a handful of men, including Brooke, who was criticized for being away on a trip to Africa when the civil-rights debate—now in its twenty-fourth day—began in the Senate. Brooke cut his trip short when it appeared a vote was imminent, but the criticism was not dulled. He teamed with Javits and Percy."

Noting that Javits was "abrasive when passionately involved in an issue," the newsman added that Brooke had charm and "deals with people in a disarmingly diplomatic way. He also is the only Republican senator on the President's Advisory Committee on Civil Disorders, which has been investigating last summer's urban riots."

An aide to a Democratic senator who was a leading proponent of the civil-rights bill commented on Brooke's efforts: "This guy has done a hell of a job. I criticized him, too. But once he swung into action he was a real pro. I'm very impressed. He's a clear thinker. Some of these guys agonize in a telephone booth. He doesn't. He's a doer."

An aide to a Republican senator also had a comment: "He's done great yeoman service. He did his homework and played it cool—they listened to him."

The move to table or kill the fair-housing amendment to the civil-rights bill that was co-authored by Brooke and Mondale lost 34 to 58. "I have no doubt that we will succeed," Mondale said after the vote. "One of the fundamental reasons for my belief is that the Senator from Massachusetts is providing great leadership and tireless devotion to this issue."

On March 5 *The Boston Herald* reported: "During the cliff-hanging moments yesterday when the Senate roll was being called to end the civil-rights-bill filibuster, Senator Brooke made the final deal which pulled across the one necessary but elusive vote." It was the third time in less than a week that the Senate had voted on cloture, and the only time civil-rights proponents had received the two-thirds count required to end the verbal marathon. "Brooke," *The Herald* said, "who dramatically snared the one required extra vote with no time to spare was the hero of the day, although many senators had worked tirelessly for days to pass cloture." The vote Brooke snared came from Senator Jack R. Miller (Republican of Iowa), who, as an opponent of cloture, demanded a commitment from Brooke. To get Miller's vote, Brooke promised to vote for the Iowa's senator's amendment to the open-housing section of the bill. Miller's amendment would allow the owner of a single-family house to be exempt from the antidiscrimination bars in the bill if no military veteran was involved. In brief, the owner could sell to anybody of his choice and refuse to sell to anyone he didn't want except a veteran. He would have to sell to a veteran regardless of race, religion or for any other reason.

Brooke had been angling for the vote of Senator Karl Mundt (Republican of South Dakota) as the roll was being called and learned that Miller has passed without voting on the first call. Mundt suddenly disappeared, although he ended by voting against cloture. Brooke collared Miller, urging him to vote for cloture. At this point Miller agreed, provided Brooke backed his amendment.

"What about the others?" Brooke asked.

Miller said he would forget Dirksen, Mondale, Javits and Philip Hart, since it would "mean something" to him to have Brooke's vote. Brooke said he would have to check with Dirksen and the others. Dirksen then released Brooke from his earlier obligation, and he made the deal with Miller. However, Brooke did not promise the Iowa Republican that he would not speak against the amendment prior to the vote. In an impassioned speech, Brooke's real position was made crystal clear. The rest of the Senate concurred with his stand and the Miller amendment lost by a vote of 13 to 73.

The Senate, *The Boston Herald* noted, "can generate more high suspense than an Alfred Hitchcock film."

The Congress finally passed the civil-rights bill with its open-housing section. The Congress, Brooke said, had made a noble beginning, adding that it was "a landmark in our national history. The fair-housing provisions of this act will go far toward making the U.S. a more open and equitable society. By establishing the first housing principle in federal law, this legislation will make an immeasurable contribution to the nation's capacity to cope with the domestic crisis now wrenching our social structure. The ghetto will not disappear overnight, but this legislation is a positive declaration that the American people will no longer tolerate the rigid practices which make urban captives a disadvantaged minority."

Without ceasing to identify with the goals of the black community, Brooke worked within the system to achieve those goals in a steady effort to effect meaningful change, "to make it equal, to make it right."

Late in February 1968 Brooke said he hoped Martin Luther King's proposed April Poor People's March* on Washington would

---

* At the National Governors' Conference in Cincinnati in July, just before the Miami Beach GOP National Convention, Spiro Agnew called national political reporters to his hotel suite and lashed the Poor People's March, then camping on federal land in Washington. He said Nixon could best deal with such menaces.

be peaceful. "I have known Martin for many years. I know he's absolutely sincere in his devotion to the nonviolence ideas of Gandhi. I am also convinced that his first march on Washington was responsible for the passage of the first civil-rights legislation."

At the Geneva conference the year before, Brooke and King had discussed ways of ending the Vietnam war. King admitted then that he had lost allies for the civil-rights movement by taking such a strong stand on Vietnam. Articulate in calling for a halt to the bombing of the North, he asked for a negotiated settlement based on the participation of the National Liberation Front—the political arm of the Vietcong—in any coalition government. When King was assassinated before he could organize the April march, Brooke said: "He told me, 'I was a minister before I was a civil-rights leader and have a duty to follow my conscience first.' " Brooke praised King's steadfast adherence to peaceful change through democratic process. "King knew that a revolution just wasn't going to occur here and saw the way the races could live together. Society—both black and white—wasn't listening. It was they who created the militants and the riots and they must be blamed for King's death."

Without King to lead them, Brooke feared militants would get control of the April 22 Poor People's March on Washington. "The slightest spark could set it off," he said, recalling that two weeks earlier in a Senate speech he had questioned whether even the late Martin Luther King could have controlled the Washington demonstration, considering the "inflammable climate and tension in the country. It is so different today from the way it was when King led his magnificent marches in the South in 1963–64. I pray that the march on Washington will take on aspects of a memorial to King. This is the time for the people who adhere to his philosophy of nonviolence to stand up."

Brooke said the martyrdom of King tore "from us our most brilliant and most beloved civil-rights leader. The crime is unspeakable, the grief unbearable. In our anguish and bitterness over this awful event we must not lose sight of the meaning of this great man's life." Brooke added that the "savage act of his assassin must not be allowed to overshadow this higher vision which Martin Luther King shared with us all. The sorrow which all Americans of goodwill feel at this terrible loss must bind us together, not rend us apart."

In the emotional wake of King's death, the late Richard Cardinal Cushing of Boston suggested that the Negro be canonized, and Brooke, on April 8, urged Congress to make King's birthday, January 15, a day of commemoration of the birthday of King. "At this time, more than any other," Brooke said in a Senate speech, "this nation needs to raise up from itself and its posterity, the image of reconciliation encompassed in the person of Reverend Martin Luther King, Jr." The holiday, he said ". . . would symbolize in fitting manner our reverence for the man and our devotion to his principles." Congress took no action on the proposal. Congress, however, was worried by extremist talk of avenging King's murder. There was talk of assassinating a white conservative like George Wallace, and Nixon and Reagan were also mentioned in this context in secret sessions. Wallace and Reagan hired bodyguards, and Nixon was warned to be more careful.

An ugly mood was sweeping over the nation. On May 7, Brooke deplored the rude reception given former Alabama Governor (later reelected) George Wallace a few days earlier at Dartmouth College, calling it a "disgraceful spectacle." Brooke said he disagreed with Wallace on the issues, but he had a right to speak. "If he can't speak at one of our highest institutions of learning, it's a sorry situation," Brooke said in a televised interview.

A month later, less than six hours after Senator Robert F. Kennedy was shot, grim members of Congress kept a promise to visit Resurrection City (the area in the District where the marchers congregated) to listen to the poor recite their wants. Brooke, chairman of a special *ad hoc* committee serving as a liaison between the poor and Congress, and Representative Edward P. Boland of Springfield, Massachusetts, a member of the committee, were in this delegation. Brooke met privately with Ralph Abernathy, promising to ask President Johnson to press Congress for passage of supplemental appropriations bills to start an immediate relief program. The special committee was named when the 2,000 "poor marchers" came to Washington in April.

Brooke and other members of the Commission on Civil Disorders were concerned because President Johnson had not made any dramatic statements to focus national attention on the commission's findings. Johnson's first comment on the report came when he told a group of bankers that the report was "recommended reading" and was being evaluated throughout the government. Brooke urged Johnson to do everything possible to put political and social institutions into action as recommended in the report. "Failure to do so can only postpone the day of reckoning with the sinister trends in the American heartland."

At first, Robert C. Weaver, head of the Department of Housing and Urban Development, thought the government would be unable to implement the crash housing program that the commission recommended be done in five years. Weaver said the program, which involved building 26.2 million new housing units and rehabilitating two million others, would take ten years. On the following day he indicated that the commission's proposals might be met.

Brooke, noting that the nation was tense, spoke of the volatile atmosphere and ominous mood as the country awaited another summer. "I firmly believe that the work of the commission has illuminated the path. Now the President must inspire our people to pursue it. The nation has never faced a sterner task; the President has never faced a stiffer test."

Brooke co-authored the report of the Commission on Civil Disorders, which blamed white racism for the movement in the United States toward two separate and unequal black and white societies. At the Charles Evans Hughes Award dinner Dr. Sterling V. Brown, president of the National Conference of Christians and Jews, said race relations in the U.S. had deteriorated because of the "pernicious doctrine" of white supremacy, which had "wrecked" the patience and hopes of American blacks. He said the hostile attitudes of Negroes had become explosive; their impatience, because of rising and unfulfilled expectations, had mushroomed. "We can no longer tolerate social and religious discrimination. The time has come to speed the work of human relations." It was a theme that Brooke expounded on college campuses in 1968 and in speeches in following years. He also focused on militant black students who advocated a separatist movement because integration was proceeding far too slowly. "I think the great majority of the black people in America want to opt in, not out. I think the great majority of black Americans want integration rather than separation. The great majority is not following this small minority. I've always been an outspoken foe of separatism. I'm more convinced than ever that it is wrong, and that it will not lead the black man to a just place in American society."

In recent years some black leaders have recommended establishing a separate state within the United States by having Negroes emigrate in great numbers to an established state and assuming all political power. Julius Lester, author of *Look Out, Whitey! Black Power's Goin' Get Your Momma!*, argues that separation is the only assurance blacks have of being regarded as human in their own nation. Lester says all effort should be turned to finding a way to establish a black nation within the territorial confines of the U.S., adding that if this movement gained momentum, whites would join in support simply as a good way to rid society of blacks. He cited precedents such as the creation of Pakistan and Israel for persecuted minorities. He said Vietnam, Korea and Germany were all partitioned within the past quarter of a century and cited growing separatist movements in Canada, Belgium and Spain.

"For 300 years we tried the impossible—integration—now let's be rational."

Roy Wilkins praised black militants for the pride they have infused into black communities, but feels that "integration into American life today remains the best way out of our situation." Brooke agrees, feeling that blacks have reached a point where they can determine their own destiny in America. He argues that separatism would mean a cutting off from important advantages that the total society can provide.

"Where integration is possible, separatism is nothing more than abject surrender to injustice." Brooke is more optimistic than many black leaders about the movement toward true equality. He agrees with the late Whitney Young, who said: "The black man's best hope lies not in a narrow separatism or in the cultural suicide of assimilationism, but in an Open Society, a society founded on mutual respect and cooperation and pluralistic groups, self-consciousness and pride."

Early in 1968 Remi Cynthia Brooke, then eighteen, moved into her father's apartment in Washington, bringing her rock and roll records with her. Previously the apartment had "heard no sounds sprightlier than opera."

"She says she's come to keep house for me," the Senator said. "But so far, she's fried one egg, and I've had to pick up her clothes." Remi, who had graduated from Newton High School, was a sophomore at Northeastern University in Boston and was looking for a job as an airline hostess. She wanted to save enough money to attend a modeling school and said she hoped to return to college in December 1968.

"September," her father said.

Remi became a ground hostess with Eastern Airlines at Logan International Airport in Boston under Northeastern's cooperative education plan and returned to school in December.

In the fall of 1967, through college friends in New Jersey, Remi had met Donald R. Hasler of Milford, New Jersey, a freshman engineering student at Monmouth College, New Jersey. The couple had met at a party at Hasler's house and had dated ever since. When they talked of getting married, the Brookes feared at first that they were too young, but were convinced by the Haslers that their son was mature enough to marry. Donald's father, Eugene Hasler, is a machinist for Lever

Brothers in Edgewater, New Jersey, and Mrs. Hasler, a Democratic committeewoman, works for Stock Forms Company in Englewood. Asked about the interracial marriage, she said, "It makes no difference: they are in love."

It is not generally known that a justice of the peace married the couple in Troy, New Hampshire, on March 8, 1968. The Brookes, wanting their daughter to have a formal ceremony, persuaded the couple to be "married" again in an afternoon wedding on June 22 at Oak Bluffs, with a Roman Catholic priest officiating. (Remi by this time had become a Roman Catholic convert.) The ceremony was held before a bay window in the guesthouse ballroom behind the main summer home, and a reception followed on the lawn. More than 400 guests attended, including Senator Charles Percy, Governor John Volpe, Lieutenant Governor Elliot Richardson, Attorney General F. Lee Bailey, and island celebrities such as Katharine Cornell, who helped Graham Champey drain a bottle of champagne.

Blue and white—Brooke's campaign colors when he ran for the Senate—dominated the wedding. The bride's white silk gown had blue velvet ribbon threaded through the Venise lace at the neck, and her seven attendants wore white organza over powder blue and carried blue and white flowers. Edwina Brooke was maid of honor, and the bridesmaids included Peggy D. Amos, niece of the Senator, and Carla Ferrari-Scacco, Mrs. Brooke's niece. Bruno Ferrari-Scacco, the bride's cousin, was ring bearer. As a wedding present F. Lee Bailey flew the couple to Niagara Falls in his private jet plane.

Hasler, who had completed his freshman year at Monmouth College, transferred to Northeastern University and after his marriage worked on construction at Logan Airport. The couple rented a four-room apartment in a high-rise complex near Northeastern in Boston, after their wedding trip to Niagara Falls.

On February 4, 1969, Remi won an uncontested divorce on the grounds of cruel and abusive treatment. There were no children of the marriage, no request for support, and Remi assumed her maiden name. She returned to her studies at Northeastern. Although Brooke told Woodworth and his staff not to withhold the information, newspapers did not mention the divorce until December 1969.

Brooke often lapses into an introspective mood on long drives with old friends. A week before Remi's marriage at Oak Bluffs he gave a commencement address at a high school in Shelburne Falls, Massachusetts. He flew from Washington to Hartford, where Hardy Nathan met him, and they flew to Northampton. After having dinner with the Nathans, they drove to Shelburne Falls.

"It must be nice to see so much of your family," Brooke said. "Sometimes I wonder whether it's worth being a senator. You have to give up so much."

There are compensations, according to Hardy Nathan. "On the way I was stopped for speeding, and when I told the state trooper the Senator was late for a speaking engagement, the trooper waved us on."

The next day at Oak Bluffs Brooke and his partner won the men's doubles in the Brooke Invitational, and he played Ronald Rappaport, a Stanford intern, in the finals of the singles. After each had won a set, it was getting dark. Rappaport, who was tired, suggested they settle for a tie. In less formal matches Brooke plays tennis with old friends such as Herbert Tucker and Graham Champey, a telephone company executive who helps Brooke with communications during campaigns. After beating both one afternoon, he wrote Champey to thank him for an extra supply of telephone directories: "If I were you and Tucker, I wouldn't be so overly confident about your avowed agility and finesse on the court. Herb has already admitted he's slowing down, and, as for you, you're a bit confused. Your last name ends in 'ey,' not 'ion.' "

Remi and Edwina agree that the life of a senator's daughter has its drawbacks. They have learned to avoid publicity, conscious always of having to maintain a "perfect" image, as *Seventeen* magazine pointed out: "Edwina [then seventeen] . . . is even careful not to double-park her car. Once when she did, one of her father's constituents saw her and scolded, 'I didn't know *you* were privileged.' " A customer at a discount store where Edwina worked when she was seventeen tried to "embarrass her by loudly calling her 'senator' every time he saw her." Edwina said, "People that I've never before seen rush over to me and say, 'I remember when you were this big!' " She indicates a height of about two feet. "What can I do but pretend I remember them?"

While Remi stayed in her father's apartment early in 1968, Remigia and Edwina had a vacation in St. Thomas, Virgin Islands, and Mrs. Helen Brooke spent a month in Hawaii after being feted at a bon voyage party given by Washington friends. Mayor Walter E. Washington of Washington, D.C., said even his busy schedule couldn't keep him from a party honoring Mrs. Brooke. As a going-away present, he gave her a hundred-dollar bill presented by 33 of her friends who attended the party, given by Mr. and Mrs. Waddell Thomas. Another gift was a grass skirt. Mrs. Brooke thanked the Mayor for the money and did a quick hula with the skirt.

"When Edward was growing up," she recalled, "the junior high-school kids in the neighborhood used to meet at one another's house —both boys and girls—along with their mothers. In this way mothers got to know one another—not as chaperones—and also became acquainted with the children, who called me 'Aunt Helen,' and still do. They send me gifts on my birthday and on Mother's Day. Most of the guests at the Thomas party were these old friends of mine."

Mrs. Brooke meets once a week in the Old Senate Office Building with wives of senators to roll bandages and make baby clothes for the Red Cross. "Mrs. Spiro Agnew heads our group," she said. Among the wives who attend are Mrs. Stuart Symington and Mrs. William Fulbright. The Senator, whose office until recently was just down the corridor, doesn't see much of his mother during the week, but he phones her almost every day. She spends summers at his home in Oak Bluffs, where she prepares seafood dishes and bakes pies.

The Brookes are a happy family.

CHAPTER SIXTEEN

Brooke and the 1968 Campaign

W HILE she was campaigning for her husband in 1966, a reporter asked Remigia Brooke how she would react if he was chosen vice-presidential candidate in 1968. "I will see about that . . . when the time comes," she said.

The time seemed far off until Brooke won national fame. True, in 1888 Negro Senator Blanche Kelso Bruce of Mississippi received 11 votes for the Republican vice-presidential nomination, and Frederick Douglass, the illegitimate son of a white man and a Negro slave, got a vote for President at the same convention. But the idea of a black on the national ticket was considered so far out in 1892 that Eugene Field, the poet-columnist for *The Chicago News*, who wrote so often with tongue in cheek in his column "Sharps and Flats," said H. H. Kohlsaat, publisher of *Inter-Ocean,* a rival paper, would nominate a Negro for Vice-President at the GOP National Convention. The publisher, moreover, would pay the expenses of anyone wishing to join him in the venture. The upshot was that Kohlsaat had to tell a delegation of black volunteers who came to his office that Field's item was a joke.

By 1968 it was no joke to talk about such an able, attractive and plausible candidate as Brooke, who in 1963 said it was just a matter of time before a Negro could be elected President of the United States. "Not too many years ago, one would never have thought a Negro could be elected attorney general of Masschusetts." Two years later he said in a *Newsweek* interview: "I like to think that any man in this country—including a Negro—could be elected President . . . if he has the qualifications. I see no goal as unattainable. . . . I know of men in my father's generation and even earlier who had the qualifications to be President, if they had had the opportunities." Brooke spoke in the same vein when President Johnson put him on the commission to probe race riots: "The sky is the limit. I . . . believe that any man, regardless of race or religion, can aspire to be President." The late Senator Robert F. Kennedy agreed. In 1962 he said a Negro who was sufficiently neutral and bore enough non-Negro traits and attitudes could win an election in which most of the electorate was non-Negro. He thought this could happen by the year 2000. Kennedy was thinking not of a black politician, but of a black in politics, which is precisely what Brooke is. His observation drew a shaft from author-philospher James Baldwin:

"I resent that. What right does the son of a first-generation Irish immigrant* [sic] have to tell me when I can be President. I've been here for 400 years."

John H. Johnson, founder of *Ebony* magazine, foresaw the possibility of a Negro Vice-President by 1985. Later Simeon Booker, an *Ebony* writer, said Brooke upset the timetable when he was elected Senator in 1966.

Early in 1962, Brooke expressed concern because blacks are often represented by white office holders, but blacks "rarely, if ever, today, represent a cross-section of whites and Negroes." When Brooke was re-elected attorney general, Al Herman, deputy chairman of the GOP National Committee, called him a priceless asset for the party nationally: "Attorney General Brooke can be a symbol that the Republican party is not a party of racism. His importance is increased because he is the only Negro elected official in the country who represents a predominantly white constituency." Herman had in mind a political axiom that voters tend to give national recognition to members of minority groups in inverse proportion to their "ethnocentricity." In any case, political seers by 1964 agreed that Brooke's reelection put him in the forefront of national politics. "Republican leaders regard him as their biggest bonus baby of the 1966 season," David Farrell wrote two years later, just before Brooke was elected to the Senate. "If elected he will be one of the Republican 400 hitters by 1968. . . . In Brooke and Volpe," Farrell went on extravagantly, "the Republican

---

* Actually, Robert Kennedy was a third-generation Irish American. His father, Joseph P. Kennedy, was the son of Patrick J. Kennedy, whose father, Patrick, sailed to America in 1849.

party has the potential to wrest the presidency from the Democratic party in 1968."

In 1966 Walter Lippmann, asked whether the U.S. was ready for a Negro for the presidency, said, "Yes. I say yes because I don't think that at this time Brooke's color would be any more of a problem than Humphrey's liberalism." He said color would have made a difference 15 years earlier. "But not today. Not with such a qualified and attractive candidate as Brooke apparently is." He advised the GOP to use Brooke as a symbol to erase the Goldwater image. Lippmann, however, rejected the notion of Brooke's being on the national ticket in 1968: "In '72, well maybe, but I can't really see that far. But he's young. He has time."

Like Herman and other political leaders, Lippmann agreed that Brooke had not come far enough to run on a national ticket. Former vice-presidential candidate William E. Miller of New York saw Brooke as a definite prospective candidate for Vice-President in 1972: "He has the potential to become the first Negro senator since Reconstruction. And regardless of color, when a man is a governor or senator he automatically becomes a prospective national candidate. However, Brooke is still serving his apprenticeship in the national party. He'll have to get out and work with the grass-roots Republicans across the country and work for the party."

Brooke reestablished the GOP's appeal to Negro voters—some 70 percent of whom were registered Democrats when he was elected attorney general. Liberal Republican governors early in 1966 felt Brooke could not only wipe out the Goldwater ultraconservative stigma, but could also snatch the entire Negro vote from the Democratic party where it had fled en masse to escape Goldwater.

After going to the Senate, Brooke was first considered a potential candidate for Vice-President. The GOP saw in him a black who could attract white liberal votes, along with normally Democratic Negro votes. But Brooke vetoed the suggestion, saying he wanted first to master his new job. "Yet he is plainly on a path that goes beyond whatever personal summit he may reach," *The Reader's Digest* noted. "The achievements of . . . Brooke will be as much a standard of a whole society's progress as they will be the measure of an individual who happens to be a Negro."

Republican leaders knew Brooke had a power base no other senator could claim. "Not only is he in a position to show his race the way out of apartheid politics; he could also considerably influence the selection of the GOP presidential candidate in 1968—and beyond."

By the spring of 1967, red, white and blue stickers appeared reading

"The New Look—Romney and Brooke '68." The stickers amused the Senator, who at the time didn't think he could wind up on the national ticket in 1968. In an interview in the spring of 1967 he called Romney "the leading candidate" and praised him. In answer to a question, he said he would support Nixon were he nominated, recalling that he (Brooke) had actively campaigned for him in 1960.

Although Brooke said in 1967 that he hoped there would be few favorite son candidates so the 1968 convention could promptly pick a presidential nominee, he put Volpe on the presidential list. What the GOP needed, he said at a 100-dollar-a-plate "Stars of Victory" dinner at the Commonwealth Armory in Boston, was a "hard, tough moderate committed to peace . . . who won't be pushed around" in the arena of world politics. Among candidates who filled the bill were Romney, Nixon, Percy, Volpe, Governor Raymond P. Shafer of Pennsylvania and Governor Daniel J. Evans of Washington, in that order.

Brooke's mention of Volpe came after the Governor tried to scotch the rumor of a rift with Brooke over control of the Massachusetts delegation to the 1968 GOP convention. "There is absolutely no foundation to reports of rivalry between Senator Brooke and myself about delegates," Volpe said. "We haven't even talked about it."

Volpe was considering a favorite-son candidacy in the preferential primary in May 1968. That would have given him strong control over the delegates and increased his chances of winning the vice-presidential nomination. Brooke, privately committed to Rockefeller, hoped to see the Bay State delegate strength go early to him.

On May 17 Roscoe Drummond wrote: "Before the 1960 Democratic convention, President Truman suggested that the nation was not ready to take Senator Kennedy, a Catholic, as President. Before the 1968 Republican convention a similar question is arising. Is this nation ready to take Senator Brooke, a Negro, as Vice-President?"

Drummond speculated that Brooke might team with Romney, Percy or Nixon if it was felt he would draw more Negro votes to the GOP than he would drive away white voters.

"Would his choice . . . look like a crude means to buy Negro support or an act of statesmanship to help unite the country at a moment when unity is at a premium?" Drummond asked. "If Brooke were white, he would be high up on the vice-presidential list. That is a fair measure of his capacity and personal attractiveness and political talent." On the other hand, if the GOP's posture on racial questions enabled it to carry some Southern states, Brooke would not be considered. But if George Wallace ran as a third-party candidate, the reasoning went,

300

the Republicans could kiss off the South and choose a ticket which would have a maximum appeal outside the South. This would bring Brooke into the picture.

At about the same time as Drummond's column appeared, John Chamberlain, another syndicated columnist, wrote in the same newspaper (*The Washington Post*): "By his single speech on Vietnam, in which he reached a reluctant conclusion that we must continue to counter Ho Chi Minh force with even more force of our own, Brooke has made himself a prime candidate for Vice-President on the 1968 Republican ticket." Brooke's switch from moderate dove to moderate hawk brought him in line with the thinking of most influential Republicans.

When the five freshmen GOP senators appeared on *Meet the Press* in January 1967 they were asked whether they favored cessation or continuation of U.S. bombing of North Vietnam. At that time Hatfield and Brooke favored cessation, while Baker and Clifford Hansen wanted the bombing continued. Said Charles Percy: "I would like to see it stopped if we get something back for it."

"That," said a wag, "makes the score 2½ to 2½."

Noting that Brooke called himself an owl after his return from Vietnam, Chamberlain wrote: "An 'owl' who is also a Negro and a 'moderate' Republican from an eastern industrial state would make a wonderful second man on any Republican ticket. Romney, Nixon and Reagan had better look Brooke over."

Brooke, who said riots and Vietnam would be key issues in the 1968 elections, called the Johnson administration vulnerable and said Republicans could win with the right candidates; they could also improve their position in both Houses of Congress. He was no longer ruling himself out as a possible vice-presidential nominee. "I've never ruled myself out of anything." Another time, when a friend asked if he was interested in the nomination for Vice-President, he said, grinning: "What makes you think I'm interested in the second spot?"

Still playing cat and mouse, during this same September (1967) interview, Brooke again endorsed Volpe for the VP nomination, calling him an excellent governor who had been "a big winner—a Republican winner—in a Democratic state."* Earlier Brooke had spoken of Volpe's unique position on the basis of section, religion and ethnic

---

* In the 1966 elections in Massachusetts, Volpe did better than Brooke. Volpe even took the Democratic citadel of Boston by 10,063 votes, while Brooke did well in holding his loss in the city to 23,868. There is a heavy concentration of Italian-Americans in Boston.

background. "Catholics and Italian-Americans are strong in the cities where we Republicans are weakest. So John Volpe could bring much to the national ticket.

By the spring of 1968, however, Brooke's romance with Volpe had waned. He stepped up his campaign to draft Rockefeller when Romney faded in a move that portended a struggle with Volpe for control of the Massachusetts delegation at the Miami Beach convention in August. As early as mid-December 1967 Brooke had predicted that GOP moderates would swing behind Rockefeller if Romney ran out of steam. He said only Rockefeller could keep former Vice-President Nixon from getting the nomination if Romney flubbed the primaries.

"The moderates feel Nixon can't win. They are less troubled by his philosophy than by his image and his ability to win elections. A lot of people, both Republicans and Democrats, think Nixon is the one Republican who can unite the Democratic Party." At this point, Nixon had not won an election on his own in 18 years.

Brooke had talked to Rockefeller at a New York dinner honoring Senator Javits and believed the Governor was ready and willing to step into the breach if and when Romney faltered.

That was in December 1967. At a press conference in Boston in April 1968 Brooke said Rockefeller "has always been available for the presidential nomination," adding that his temporary withdrawal from the primaries on March 21, 1968, widely interpreted as a swan song, was simply "sound political strategy."

"I expect to do everything I can to encourage Rockefeller's nomination. I will be talking to delegates, and I will even talk to Governor Volpe."

Volpe, in Japan at the time, preferred Nixon, who had reportedly told him that he [Volpe] was definitely in the running for the vice-presidential nomination. Brooke made his intent clear: "I intend to live up to my commitment . . . Volpe as our favorite son on the first ballot, but I hope we can carry the Massachusetts delegation for Rockefeller on the second."

The 34 Bay State delegates were expected to include a majority of "Rockefeller liberals," but many who leaned toward the Governor were understood to have a prior commitment, through state politics, to follow Volpe's lead. Brooke guessed there would be about 10 or 12 votes for Rockefeller no matter what Volpe did.

Brooke criticized Nixon on both domestic and foreign policy, calling his response to the President's riot commission report unfortunate. During the campaign in March, Nixon said more blame should be put on rioters. "I was frightened and disappointed by his reaction," Brooke said. "He seemed not to understand the social and economic conditions that had given rise to rioting."

Brooke, who was scored for his own zigzagging on Vietnam, said he was confused by Nixon's stance. "When Mr. Nixon first spoke out on Vietnam, he was talking about mining Haiphong, sending more troops and doing more of everything that President Johnson was doing. More recently he's said that we must get peace and be sure we don't have to send boys back to Asia. But I don't believe Rockefeller asked for the mining of Haiphong or an increase in our troop level."

Brooke saw evidence of a national change of heart in race relations. "In the Congress I don't sense the punitive reaction to the riots that I felt when I first went to Washington. No one would have predicted the passage of the open-housing law this year. Just recently, we have restored funds for summer jobs and the Head Start program. This is a time for Negro militants and the white majority of the country to realize we can make great progress now." He slammed Mayor Daley's orders to "shoot to kill" arsonists and "shoot to wound" looters. "I believe in law enforcement, but I believe you must use only the amount of force necessary to do the job. I don't want to see this country turned into a police state where we're shooting lots of kids with little provocation." His feelings on this issue colored his attitude toward Nixon and Rockefeller.

Rockefeller's reentry into the presidential sweepstakes on April 30 resulted in a stunning, unexpected write-in victory over Volpe, who ran as a favorite son pledged to Nixon. Emmet John Hughes, one of Governor Rockefeller's close advisers, said he didn't even know there was a primary in Massachusetts that day. Relations between Brooke and Volpe (who blamed the press for giving so much coverage to Rockefeller's candidacy) became suddenly strained, as *The Washington Post* noted: "Governor Volpe was in a white-hot fury immediately after his humiliating defeat by a Rockefeller write-in, but his wrath was not directed at Rockefeller. The target was his intrastate Republican rival, Brooke. Talking to a friend, Volpe blamed Brooke for undermining him and for advising Rockefeller to announce his candidacy on the day of the Massachusetts primary. Moreover, Volpe privately promised to wage a campaign for control of the state's 34 national convention delegates, who will be pledged to Rockefeller for only one ballot." Later bitterness developed within the convention delegates as Volpe tried to win second-ballot support for Nixon.

Volpe had himself to blame. Lulled by polls that wrongly showed

Rockefeller unpopular with Massachusetts Republicans, Volpe did little organizing for the primary. "And despite his intentions, at least two-thirds of the delegates are likely to be controlled by Brooke and Rockefeller on the floor at Miami Beach," the press reported.

Late in June, as he leaned back in his chair in his Senate office, Brooke told a reporter: "Look, if the organization people in the Republican party feel that both Nixon and Rockefeller can win, they are going with Nixon. He has that many accounts receivable and it has to pay off." Brooke recalled Nixon's offer to come to Massachusetts to help with the Senate campaign, "and if I didn't want him, he would stay out. I assume he did that with a lot of candidates. And I think he has a lot going for him."

Brooke then spoke about the kind of politician who wins conventions and the kind who wins elections. "Nixon is a convention politician. He's really good at it. And Rockefeller is an election politician. It seems to me that Rockefeller recently is moving. But I admit it's all uphill."

Brooke denied any philosophical rifts in the GOP in 1968, as there had been in 1964 because of Goldwater and his shock troops and their resentment of the challenge that Rockefeller had made to Goldwater. "These same people this year want to win."

Brooke thought Nixon had already fallen into a trap because his Southern supporter, Howard Callaway, a Georgia Republican national committeeman, had said George Wallace should join forces with Republicans. Actually, Nixon had merely said he didn't want Wallace's support. Brooke thought Rockefeller's chances were better. "I wasn't sure about Rockefeller at first. But now I am. He wants it and is willing to make the fight for it."

Brooke and Governor John Chafee of Rhode Island were Rockefeller's chief supporters in New England. Governor Shafer was another backer. Brooke was surprised to find Hatfield, a leading dove, supporting Nixon, but was less surprised that Volpe was for Nixon. Volpe had seriously considered voting for Goldwater at the 1964 convention, and in the end had seconded the nomination of the candidate's running mate, William Miller.

"Brooke has gone down the line for Rockefeller," the political editor of *The Boston Globe* wrote, "and Brooke's support is not to be taken lightly. In the Senate he is highly regarded and his support on measures is sought."

A political reporter on *The Boston Herald* sized things up: "No question about it, the old master-politician has done it again. After a few months of partial eclipse Brooke, whose political savvy is rivaled perhaps only by his luck, is back in full sunshine, standing next to Rockefeller. And left in the dark is Brooke's major rival for leadership in the Massachusetts party, Governor Volpe." The shift came on primary day when the Bay State GOP voters denied Volpe a blank check with which to bargain for himself in Miami. Rockefeller's write-in win over the favorite-son governor was "a stunning surprise." The reporter noted a significant clue on the TV screen that day, however. "There was Brooke in Albany, New York, seated close to the podium, when Rockefeller said yes, he was running for President. It was a good place for a Massachusetts Republican leader to be. Suddenly, the Volpe who stormed to such an overwhelming reelection victory two years ago appears as a man now going nowhere. In Miami he will have one vote, not 34. And when whatever presidential nominee looks for a running mate, Volpe will be the governor who lost his own state."

Citing Brooke's "casual emergence among the angels," the reporter compared the differing political styles of the two men: "Volpe works hard—from hod carrier to millionaire contractor to appointive administrator to governor. He schemes hard—somehow deciding Nixon was his best hope for the vice-presidency, even though Nixon is now a New Yorker. Brooke operates on foresight and the bold strike." He boldly ran for attorney general in 1962 and went into orbit, later maneuvering first and fast to outflank Volpe for his Senate seat. "Now he pops up beside Rockefeller nationally and as patent heir apparent to the party leadership in Massachusetts."

On the eve of the Miami Beach convention, Drew Pearson and Jack Anderson were referring to Brooke, "a Republican moderate who has proved his popularity with both black and white voters in the North," when they wrote: "It hasn't been mentioned outside of the smoke-filled back rooms, but Nixon's top aides are talking seriously of offering the GOP vice-presidential nomination to a black." The columnists said Nixon strategists who favored Brooke wanted to abandon the South to Wallace and focus on winning the North, feeling that Brooke could get enough black votes from Democrats to win such populous states as New York, Pennsylvania, Michigan, Illinois and California. "The white backlash would be counteracted, they [the Nixon strategists] contended, by white suburbanites who would vote for a black for Vice-President as a dramatic gesture of racial unity. This might convince blacks that they were no longer second-class citizens and it would lessen racial strife." The columnists called Nixon a political realist who realized he had to appear conservative to win the GOP nomination, but would have to appeal to moderates to win the election. Thus he needed a moderate running mate.

Came the showdown at the GOP National Convention. *The Boston Herald* said Brooke's "neatly phrased and positively delivered speech before he assumed the duties of temporary chairman undoubtedly impressed delegates (and observers) that his national reputation is well deserved. Brooke "called ringingly for rejection of white and black separatism, whether in the ghettoes or in the suburbs, and urged the Republican party to pursue as its goal 'an integrated society of magnificent pluralism.' "

Speaking at the first night session on August 5, Brooke said: "Democrats have time and again raised the expectations of the disadvantaged only to dash them on the hard rocks of reality." As did the keynoter, Governor Daniel Evans, Brooke blasted Democrats for being "feeble in inspiration and overbearing in application, intrusive in operation and incompetent in administration." He cited millions of Americans "who remain frozen in the deadening life of urban ghettoes and rural backwaters."

The Volpe-Brooke split was there for all to see on August 7, when Brooke seconded the nomination of Rockefeller, while Volpe seconded Nixon. Brooke hailed the New York governor as "the man who can unite not only the Republican party, but all Americans—black and white." He cited Rockefeller's record of action and compassion in the field of civil rights, adding that he was "big enough to assume the tremendous duties of the presidency . . . humane enough to forge the new unity with which our nation and our President can face the future with confidence. With his leadership the Republican party can transform social discord into social harmony, social lethargy into social energy, and social paralysis into social progress." Crediting Rockefeller with having "the broadest appeal to Americans in either political party," Brooke said the candidate would "shatter the solid labor vote on which our Democratic opponents are counting for victory."

In seconding Nixon, Volpe said he "accepts adversity not as a foe, but as a teacher to enrich his growth and development as a leader." He stressed Nixon's personal qualities, noting that at a time of "crisis" and "testing," the delegates should nominate "a leader who has met and passed the test, who has the strength and character to restore the confidence of the people in their government."

After Nixon won the nomination, Volpe, who had long been associated with the moderate wing of the GOP and who had no worrisome enemies within the Republican party, knew "up to the last half-hour that I was in contention [for the vice-presidential nomination] . . . I'm somewhat disappointed." When the pendulum swung to Spiro Agnew, he again said he was "rather shocked." Indeed, when Agnew got the news, he was about to check out of his hotel. The pendulum swung, apparently, because Agnew was less offensive to Senator Strom Thurmond than was Volpe.

Nixon admitted his decision was "very, very close," and one of his aides snidely observed: "It just shows what happens when you keep Dick up all night and then ask him to make an important decision."

In analyzing the situation, the Ripon Society sized up Agnew as an obscure governor who not only had no glaring liabilities, but who also created a tough law-and-order image for himself because of one well-publicized crackdown on militant dissidents when he chewed out "moderate Negroes for supporting militants." Strategists saw Agnew as a "Joe America" who followed the Baltimore Colts and drank beer, and as a candidate who would be popular in suburbia, considered the heartland of the U.S. in the 1960s. Nixon reasoned that glamor candidates like Reagan, Percy and Lindsay might lose as many votes as they would win. According to the Ripon Society, "perhaps more importantly, he [Nixon] had no wish to hitch his campaign to a more glittering star after having engineered one of the greatest political comebacks in decades. It was far better, in Nixon's opinion, that his running mate be a lightning rod to draw criticism away from him." (If the Ripon Society's analysis was correct, Nixon could not have made a better choice.) Nixon's rationale, according to the Ripon pundits, was, "I think if I want to win this, I'm going to have to win it on my own."

Rockefeller was so ired at the choice of Agnew—considering it a personal insult—he thought of packing his bags and leaving his hotel that afternoon. Agnew, after all, had been chairman of his campaign in the spring. It is possible that Agnew himself was miffed when Rockefeller failed to call him before temporarily withdrawing from the presidential race on March 21. A Rockefeller aide called it the "most important un-made phone call in history."

Brooke embraced Volpe as the runner-up, telling the press: "I was disappointed our Governor was not chosen," adding that he thought someone like Volpe, Percy, Hatfield, or Baker, "men in my opinion with long experience in state and urban affairs, would have been chosen."

Meanwhile, other progressives, including Governors Shafer and Chafee who, like Brooke, had not been consulted in the decision-making, engineered a bolt that might have succeeded if John Lindsay had agreed to spearhead it. Brooke was in on the "conspiracy," which finally managed only to delay convention proceedings for an hour. Said Lindsay later:

"There was no mystery about what happened there [in Miami]. Sure, I was under terrific pressure to go for the vice-presidency, from liberal governors, senators and congressmen up for election. They were very worried about their chances on a Nixon ticket and thought I could help if I was part of it. But I kept telling them I didn't want the job."

Shortly before the convention, when Lindsay was being discussed as a possible Nixon running mate, the Mayor was surprised that anyone would even consider his candidacy, *The New York* magazine reported. "A few weeks later, in a campaign trailer at Miami, Lindsay found himself being badgered by Governor John Chafee and Brooke into leading a floor fight of liberal Republicans against the imminent designation of Agnew." At that moment Herbert Brownell, who had just toured Nixon's suites discussing strategy with Nixon's brain-trusters, pushed everyone out of Lindsay's trailer, including Chafee and Brooke. "It would have been politically suicidal," Brownell explained, "if Lindsay had tried to take the vice-presidency by delegate vote, since the delegates were all committed to vote for whomever Nixon wanted." Also, Brownell knew that without Agnew, Nixon might lose Southern support and the nomination itself. Thus Nixon's advisors had offered Lindsay a deal provided he did not make a "kamikaze attack" on Agnew and, instead, seconded Agnew's nomination. "Lindsay's support would help give a liberal urban imprimatur to their rural strategy, and in return he could expect help in his reelection campaign [in 1969]." Lindsay could also expect more assistance from Washington than he was getting.

"When the trailer opened," according to *The New York* magazine, "Brownell was at Lindsay's side. Chafee and Brooke, waiting outside, said they had already amassed 45 delegate votes for Lindsay; he could not turn his back on his liberal GOP supporters now. Lindsay shrugged. Chafee and Brooke waited a few moments for an answer, but none came." Instead, Lindsay, without speaking further, walked onto the convention stage and seconded the nomination of Agnew. "Lindsay received sustained applause from 1,333 Republican delegates, and even the 26 black delegates cheered."

In June 1969 Brooke, breaking his policy of not taking sides in primary contests, supported Lindsay for reelection instead of the

GOP nominee, John J. Marchi. Lindsay won as the Liberal party's nominee. In endorsing him, Brooke said, He's been a good mayor. He's a registered Republican and he's been a Republican mayor."

After the convention, Brooke gave his full support to the Nixon-Agnew ticket: "By the character and substance of the campaign they mount, Richard Nixon and Spiro Agnew will demonstrate to America that they deserve the honored responsibilities of the highest office in the land." Nonetheless, Brooke, disappointed because of Rockefeller's failure, was especially displeased over the choice of Agnew. On August 8, during a joint press conference with Volpe, Brooke said Nixon and GOP leaders "certainly could have done better" than Agnew.

Albert A. Gammal, Jr., one of Brooke's brain-trusters and a former Massachusetts representative, thought Brooke should have been picked to run with Nixon: "If they consulted with a hundred party leaders, I don't know how they could have missed him." The next move, Gammal said, was Nixon's. He should contact Brooke to discuss how he could help the ticket. Nixon did not consult Brooke on his running-mate choice.

A racial incident marred the convention. One night Brooke ate a sandwich alone rather than attend a dinner party given at the exclusive Bath Club for Senator Dirksen, because the club barred blacks. Brooke, who had been invited, said he knew Dirksen was unaware of the club's bias, which also kept out Jews.

"I never knowingly, nor will I ever knowingly, go any place that discriminates against Jews, Negroes or any other race." He was sure that Dirksen would not have arranged the dinner had he known of the policy, adding that he hoped the day would come when "there will be no such places left in the U.S."

Opening his campaign from New York on September 3, Nixon moved triumphantly to Chicago, San Francisco, Houston and back East during the first week. In Chicago an estimated 400,000 persons jammed the Loop as officeworkers rained down confetti. With Nixon were two recent strong supporters of Rockefeller—Brooke and Thruston Morton of Kentucky—to demonstrate party loyalty. There was another enthusiastic turnout as Nixon's motorcade drove through Chinatown in San Francisco.

Early in the campaign Brooke was irked when Nixon repeatedly introduced him as the only black in the Senate. At the airport in Oklahoma City Nixon told the crowd that Brooke was a prime example of "what can be done if given the chance," adding that Brooke had been elected attorney general "not because he is black, but because he is a great lawyer," and he was "an outstanding senator not because of the color of his skin but because he is a great senator." He said Brooke typified the "American dream—the kind of America we're going to build—an America where a man can rise as high as his talents will take him."

In an aside Brooke told newsmen his colleagues were not called "the Jewish senator" or "the Italian senator," "but I understand the practicalities of life and I have learned to live with them." He said Nixon's repeated references to his color "did not offend any sensitivity."

In Houston Nixon again referred to color, telling the press he was "rather amused" when they had suggested that Brooke wouldn't dare go to Texas. "He was there and I thought it was quite exciting that he received the wonderful reception that he did in Houston. It gave the lie to the idea that Texans were so prejudiced that they would not accept a fine Negro senator."

In Houston Brooke told the UPI he was concerned because Nixon was running his campaign on a "safer than safe" basis, reminiscent of the overconfidence which may have cost Thomas Dewey the 1948 election, when he lost to Truman. Morton, Nixon's other co-star during the campaign, discounted the possibility that Nixon was falling "into the trap of 1948" and was sure that the candidate would not let the "heady wine" of big crowds and heavy applause dampen his drive for the presidency.

Brooke and Morton warned Nixon against generating a negative image which the Democrats might counter, aware of the hazards of linking him with his past.

In Oklahoma City early in September Nixon's "well-oiled unity campaign . . . showed its first signs of friction" when Brooke expressed differences with the candidate's approach to the crime issue. Nixon embarrassed Brooke when, after inviting the Senator to appear with him, he began stressing crime in cities where, in the minds of voters, crime meant a race problem. On September 7 Brooke told newsmen he was dropping off the tour, not because the Nixon caravan was moving South, but because he wanted to return to Washington to take part in the Senate debate on the gun-control bill. He said he would rejoin the Nixon "road show" later. He never did.

On the wall behind Brooke's desk in his Senate office a Szep cartoon shows Nixon, looking more sinister than usual, with an arm around Brooke in the stern seat of a rowboat entering the Tunnel of Love.

Brooke is casting a wary look over his shoulder, noticing in the water the fins of two sharks following them. The sharks are labeled "law" and "order." Szep was lampooning the concern Nixon strategists had over establishing enough rapport with blacks so that the candidate, after being elected, could govern effectively. Confident that he could win the election without cutting into the George Wallace vote, Nixon was worried that the repeated mention of the law-and-order issue during the campaign would incite revolt in the ghettos while he was President.

With this in mind, Nixon had met secretly with Glenn Olds, who had left the State University of New York to join the candidate's staff. Olds, who is now president of Kent State University, had a private meeting with two black leaders, Attorney James Pierce of New York and Samuel Jackson, who had served on President Johnson's Equal Opportunity Commission.

"More important than backstage contacts," *The Washington Post* reported, "is the front-page appearance of Brooke in the Nixon campaign. Its origin stems from their conversation in Manhattan [in mid-August] when Nixon invited Brooke to lunch as part of his wooing of disappointed supporters of Rockefeller." At this luncheon Nixon told Brooke he was not turning his back on Negroes and that he would campaign in the ghetto, thereby giving the impression that he would not cultivate the backlash. Then came the invitation for Brooke to join the coast-to-coast road show. Although Illinois and California were the most conservative big industrial states, Brooke was conspicuous both in Chicago and San Francisco. In a statewide telecast from Chicago Nixon introduced Brooke as "one of my top advisers," Evans and Novak reported in *The Washington Post,* "although they had scarcely known each other three weeks ago." Having Brooke at his side, according to the columnists, was "a subtle signal that Nixon is *not* competing with George Wallace for the extremist law-and-order vote and wants to develop Negro contacts."

Brooke, welcoming Nixon's responsible position on law and order, was satisfied with the civil-rights record of Nixon and even of Agnew. Brooke noted that in Agnew's home state (Maryland) there was "much difference of opinion as to whether Agnew is a strong civil-righter or not. I find that there are many things that he has done in Maryland which would indicate that he is progressive." But Brooke said he wished Agnew would use the phrase "order with justice" rather than "law and order" in describing crime in the streets, realizing that many Americans equated the term "law and order" with a hard-line police-state attitude toward urban problems. The phrase had racist overtones. Nixon mentioned this during his Chicago telecast, in a state where backlash was intense. He said law and order was "a code word for, basically, racism," and that "law and order must be combined with justice."

In a taped interview for a CBS half-hour radio program, *Capital Cloakroom,* Brooke, referring to Nixon's wish to have him by his side while campaigning in ghettos, admitted he was "being used to some extent" in these joint billings. "I'm there because we want to attract votes. There haven't been many black people in the audience so far—I hope there will be. But I'd like to believe that I can attract others to the Republican party." Brooke told gatherings that Nixon wanted to bring in new ideas and programs, including black capitalism. He "wants to take Negroes off the relief rolls and make them productive members of society. He's talked about more Negroes on payrolls than on relief rolls."

When Nixon first proposed his plan of federal aid for black enterprise, it jolted Attorney General Mitchell, the architect of the "Southern Strategy" approach, and other advisers who were against any acts or measures favorable to blacks. Against their advice, Nixon attended the funeral of Martin Luther King in Atlanta on April 25, but kept mum on the subject of black enterprise for the rest of the campaign. Jerris Leonard, a conservative GOP state legislator from Wisconsin whom Nixon later named assistant attorney general for civil rights, let the cat out of the bag when he pounced on the wooing of the South: "The South . . . the South, I'm so goddamn tired of hearing about the South," he said during the campaign. "When is somebody going to start worrying about the North? That's where the votes are, to begin with. Instead, we're fighting over the law in order to give something to a bunch of racists."

During the contest Brooke was becoming increasingly disenchanted with Nixon, who was advocating the freedom-of-choice route to desegregation. The flaw in this policy was that, with minor exceptions, fearful Negro families left their children in black segregated schools. "Put bluntly," wrote Evans and Novak, "freedom-of-choice plans of the kind envisaged by [Senator Strom] Thurmond [of South Carolina] were seldom more than a subterfuge for maintaining the status quo." A flagrant example of the way Nixon was scaling his message to sectional audiences came during a closed-circuit Charlotte, North Carolina, telecast when the candidate said he thought the 1964 school desegregation decision of the Supreme Court was proper. He said he could not condone a freedom-of-choice program that was an escape hatch to permit segregation to continue. Then a news director said: "We have had in this area several communities threatened with the withholding of federal funds because the freedom-of-choice plan has been held not valid and not sufficient. Do you have a position on this?" Nixon's answer foreshadowed his stance on civil rights during the first year of his presidency:

"Well, the freedom-of-choice plan is one as you know [that] has been extremely controversial, not only in HEW, not only in the states in the South in which it has been applied, but within the two great parties. . . . My view, generally speaking, is that there has been too much of a tendency for both our courts and for our federal agencies to use the whole program of the—of what we could call school segregation for purposes which have very little to do with education and which as a matter of fact, I do not—I do not believe serve a very useful purpose in so far as the long-range desire that we all have to bring up the educational level of all people within the South and other parts of the country.

"Uh, with regard to freedom of choice, I would have to look at each one of the states involved to see whether it was a true freedom of choice. If it were, I would tend to favor that. I tend to look with, I could say, great concern, uh, whenever I see federal agencies or whenever I see courts attempting to become in effect local school boards. I think the decision in the local areas should be made primarily by people who are more familiar with those problems. Now, if you come to a school district or to a state where freedom of choice is simply used as a device to perpetuate segregation, that's something else again."

This sop for a Dixie Cerberus was a typical Nixon slant when he was out of television range of Northern viewers. Nixon was saying in effect that extreme caution should be exercised in using federal funds as a bludgeon, even though this threat had been the only viable plan the government had to get compliance with the 1954 decision in many Southern school districts.

"I just wondered what he had in mind," Brooke said of the interview. The media also wondered, but when newsmen sought clarification they were stymied. "It was a perfect example of how the pesky national press was being outmaneuvered and bypassed while the candidate pitched his message to a sectional audience," two veteran reporters wrote.

Brooke did not always see eye to eye with Nixon from a legal point of view. He differed with the candidate on whether the Supreme Court

313

made law enforcement more difficult by its recent rulings, including the Miranda decision, which broadened the rights of defendants held on criminal charges. "I do not believe the court went too far in the Miranda case," Brooke said. For his part, Nixon said; "Senator Brooke is a very fine lawyer and I am a lawyer and we may differ with regard to the Supreme Court decisions, but he agrees with me that we need a new approach."

Brooke became more certain as the campaign wore on that Nixon needed a new approach to the problem of civil rights. Discounting angry demands of GOP leaders in states with a heavy black population, Nixon, still listening to his mentor, Mitchell, visited only one black ghetto (in Philadelphia) during the entire campaign, even though—during the final two weeks—Brooke encouraged him to go into black ghettos, where Nixon had nothing to fear. He would "get more of the black vote than most people expect," Brooke said. In refusing to canvass black ghettos, Nixon was establishing a pattern that would continue over the following years, despite Brooke's prediction that Nixon "would pleasantly surprise many people by what he does in the area of programs and policies benefiting the black communities."

Although, before the election, Brooke had been mentioned as a possible U.S. Attorney General, he never discussed this with Nixon. "He's never brought the subject up," Brooke said. "I've never given it any serious consideration. I would much rather be in the Senate." He refused, however, to say flatly that he would not accept the position: "Leave me some running room."

Would he reject other Cabinet offers? "You know I never say what I would do before it happens," he hedged.

In late September there was speculation that Brooke was a good bet to wind up in the Cabinet at the expense of Volpe, but some soothsayers considered it unlikely that Nixon would choose a former Rockefeller backer for such a sensitive post as Attorney General, since such an appointment might irk the moderate and conservative wings of the GOP. Late in October Brooke, reaffirming his wish to stay in the Senate, predicted that Nixon would offer Volpe a Cabinet post.

"Governor Volpe does have unique talents that certainly qualify him for a high position in government." Brooke banished any lingering doubts about his own plans when, on October 26, he said on Boston's Channel 5 *The Week Ends Here* program: "I think I can do more for the country and for Massachusetts in the Senate. Under no circumstances would I accept a Cabinet position if I were offered one."

After Nixon defeated Humphrey in the close election, Brooke, at his own expense, toured Europe and the Scandinavian countries on another private fact-finding mission. On his return, he said in mid-December he was disappointed that Nixon had not named a black to his Cabinet. Knowing Nixon had offered a Cabinet post to several blacks who declined, Brooke said the President could have looked further, since there were other qualified blacks who were not asked.

A few months later in an address to the Young Republicans at Hotel Lenox in Boston, Brooke gave Nixon "an A for effort" in his first hundred days in office, noting that some progress was evident in Vietnam. But although Nixon had put 64 percent more nonwhites in top jobs than Johnson had, the President still could not shake off the "White Only" label of his administration—primarily because no Negro was in the Cabinet.

"He's been turned down quite a lot," Brooke conceded. "There are some blacks who do not want to work in the Nixon administration."

Nixon appointed Volpe Secretary of Transportation, opening the way for the lieutenant governor, the able and congenial Francis Sargent, to succeed him as governor of Massachusetts.

On January 18, 1969, Secretary of State William Rogers phoned Brooke and asked him to head the U.S. Economic Commission for Africa, scheduled to meet in Addis Ababa, Ethiopia. Following the conversation, Rogers sent Brooke a letter which said in part: "Our spokesman at this important meeting will be listened to with great attention throughout Africa. Because of the coincidence of a new administration in Washington, this meeting will have particular significance for U.S.-Africa relations and will be a unique occasion for the U.S. to reaffirm its strong support for African aspirations."

In his January 27 reply Brooke pointed out that with a new administration in the White House there were two possible roles which the American delegation might serve: fact-finding, or, alternatively, to announce a new direction in American foreign policy toward Africa. "If the primary purpose of the mission is to be fact-finding," the Senator suggested that, "In all candor, I believe this function might best be performed by members of the Department of State."

Brooke knew that the administration was not ready to announce any new directions or policies for Africa and, in light of his own well-known views on African policy, felt that his presence as the head of such a delegation "could leave an erroneous impression as to our future policies and programs."

315

In answer to reports that he rejected the assignment because of a growing coolness between him and Nixon, he said: "Any suggestion that my absence from the U.S. delegation reflects some tension or coolness between myself and either the President or the Secretary [of State] is wholly without foundation. It has no more basis than the recurrent and erroneous reports during and since the campaign that my association with Mr. Nixon has been strained and difficult." Brooke said his relations with the President were "cordial and constructive," adding that the President had made "an excellent beginning on both the domestic and international fronts. For my part I will do everything I can to help him deal effectively with the critical challenges before the nation."

Nevertheless, the incident illumined the uneasy alliance between the two men at a time when Nixon was trying to gain the respect of the black community which had scarcely supported him in the election. The press kept things on the front burner:

"The unsettled state of the political alliance between the President and Senator Brooke went back to the early days of the 1968 campaign and continued through the postelection period of Cabinet selection," *The New York Times* reported on February 11. After mentioning that on early flights of the campaign plane Brooke was a guest who posed with Nixon as they deplaned at various urban airports, *The Times* added: "But after a few weeks Brooke dropped out of the traveling entourage and did not reappear." Brooke, according to the paper, said he spent the rest of the fall speaking over the country for Nixon and other Republican candidates; also for GOP candidates in Massachusetts. There was no decline in his political activity, but simply a shift in emphasis.

According to intimates, however, "he was angry and bitter over the role he had been assigned—one that emphasized his being seen with the candidate but did not give him any real opportunity to contribute his political expertise or knowledge on issues." The rift broke into the open early in September after Nixon had publicly placed urban problems at the bottom of a national priority list, the article continued. Soon after that Brooke gave up his seat on the campaign plane.

"Not so," says Roger Woodworth. "Brooke never planned to stay on the campaign plane with the Nixon entourage. He had too many other commitments for that."

An incident in the 1968 campaign in Massachusetts shows the interest Brooke has in the GOP. He sent Carroll P. Sheehan, a Re-

316

publican who lost his bid for the House of Representatives, a letter analyzing his tactics and telling him not to get discouraged. "And I had never even met the Senator," Sheehan said.

The Times article asked whether Brooke had been manipulated for political effect in the Cabinet selection interval. "The Senator has said, both publicly and privately, that he considers the offer of jobs made him by Nixon to have been genuine and legitimate, not merely a proposal made with the sure knowledge that it would be rejected and thus that it was aimed solely at enlisting Negro support for the incoming administration." Nixon offered Brooke the post of Secretary of Housing and Urban Development, but also gave him a choice of being Secretary of Health, Education and Welfare or ambassador to the United Nations. *The Times* cynically observed that "Nixon was not averse to publicizing the fact that he had attempted to enlist Brooke at a high level in his administration."

The first talk about Cabinet posts was at the St. Regis Hotel in New York when the President-elect was putting together his staff and Cabinet in 1968. The second came in November 1970, during a 90-minute conference at the White House during which a broad range of issues was discussed. At the second meeting, when the only post open was ambassador to the UN, Nixon wanted to find out whether Brooke would accept a Cabinet position, if one was suitable and available. Brooke, saying he was deeply honored, felt that as the only black senator he had a responsibility to both Massachusetts blacks and blacks across the nation who constantly sought his help. Wishing also to retain the freedom of action that his role as U.S. senator gave him, he cherished his independence. Nixon asked him not to discuss the matter publicly. More offers came later.

CHAPTER SEVENTEEN

Haynsworth, Carswell and Rehnquist

A LTHOUGH President Nixon wishes Brooke would support him more often, he knew, before taking office, that part of Brooke's political success lay in his independence, both as a black and as a Republican. The Senator rarely lets race or partisanship control or even color his decisions.

During the 1968 presidential campaign Nixon told Brooke he knew there would be times when the Senator would oppose the administration's position because of philosophical differences. Thus the President was more disappointed than surprised when Brooke broke with him on the Haynsworth, Carswell and Rehnquist Supreme Court nominations, in the deployment of the antiballistic missile system, in the SST and the Lockheed affairs.

Early in 1967 five GOP freshmen senators appeared on the TV program *Meet the Press*. They were the front wall of post-Goldwater Republicans: Howard Baker of Tennessee, Clifford Hansen of Wyoming, Mark Hatfield of Oregon, Charles Percy of Illinois and Brooke. Of the five, Percy and Baker loomed as future leaders in the changing GOP power structure.

Percy, a moderate from a conservative heartland state, was a contender for the 1968 presidential nomination. Baker, the son-in-law of Senate Minority Leader Everett Dirksen, was a moderate Republican from a key border state, one of a "rare breed."

By 1970, however, Brooke, having outdistanced the other four solons, was a pivotal figure in the Republican hierarchy.

The two top candidates for the post of Republican Whip left open by the primary defeat of Senator Thomas H. Kuchel of California were Roman Hruska, a Nebraska arch conservative who thought he had the job in his pocket, and Pennsylvania's Senator Hugh Scott. Dirksen, a close friend of Hruska, made it clear that he wanted his senatorial assistant to share his conservative views. Several of his associates, in a move to get Senate freshmen to vote for Hruska, suggested that a favorable vote might give them better office quarters and committee assignments.

Brooke, after a telephone call to Scott in December 1968, joined Senator Richard Schweiker of Pennsylvania as his campaign manager and in the brief weeks remaining, playing a key behind-the-scenes role, turned the leadership fight around. Scott had called him from Philadelphia to say he was discouraged by the way the contest for the number-two leadership spot was shaping up at a time when Hruska had taken an early and apparently decisive lead. Brooke invited Scott to meet with Percy, Senator J. Caleb Boggs of Delaware and Senator Charles E. Goodell of New York to map a winning strategy.

The Scott forces felt they could count on 18 votes of the 22 needed to win. The strategy would be to get the support of three GOP freshmen: Marlow Cooke of Kentucky, Robert Packwood of Oregon and William Saxbe of Ohio. Brooke and Scott checked progress daily. At the caucus the secret vote apparently went exactly as the liberals had planned. The 18 sure votes went for Scott right down the line, and the liberals picked up one vote from the swing group—probably John J. Williams of Delaware, known as the "conscience of the Senate," or Wallace F. Bennett of Utah, and the three freshmen mentioned all voted for Scott, who also got a bonus vote from Senator Theodore Stevens, who had been named to the Senate on December 27 to succeed the late Senator E. L. Bartlett of Alaska. Hruska's staff was waiting to pour the champagne when the vote was announced. After Scott won, 23 to 20, Hruska asked Brooke for a copy of his remarks before the Republican conference, so effective had they been in winning the election for Scott.

A few months later, when Dirksen's death left a vacancy in the minority leadership, the conservative anti-Scott forces rallied around Howard Baker. Brooke, again Scott's manager, was so sure of victory he was surprised when Baker, instead of conceding, forced a vote rather than move the unanimous election of Scott. Had Baker played ball, he would undoubtedly have been named Republican Whip by acclamation.

The moderates, concerned over Baker's Southern and conservative support, now mobilized their forces to deny Baker the Whip post. This time Brooke had to maneuver in an intricate four-candidate race. After persuading two to drop out, Brooke let the remaining moderates—Robert Griffin of Michigan and James Pearson of Kansas—test their strength in the moderate caucus. Brooke held the votes together for Griffin. The result was a moderate victory "that probably changed the direction of the Senate GOP for a decade to come."

Meanwhile, Brooke kept in touch with Bay State affairs. In mid-January he headed a list of dignitaries in St. Paul's Cathedral in Boston when Bishop John M. Burgess was installed as head of the Episcopal Diocese of Massachusetts, the first black to have full responsibility for administering an Episcopal diocese. Brooke was also in Boston on New Year's Eve to arrange a meeting in Governor Volpe's suite at 21 Tremont Street in an effort to convince Elliot Richardson to stay on as attorney general.

Secretary of State William Rogers had phoned Brooke earlier: "I want you to know that we want Elliot Richardson as our Undersecretary of State." Brooke told Rogers he knew Richardson would "do a splendid job." He already knew of the situation, for Richardson had called to tell him he didn't know what to do about the offer.

"You have to decide that yourself," Brooke told him. "Do what you think best. But you were elected to a four-year term, and if you come to Washington, your job will fall into Democratic hands."

Attending the Boston meeting were the "Big Four"—Brooke, Volpe, Sargent and Richardson—along with Roger Woodworth, Albert Gammal, Jr., and Joseph Tauro, Jr. When it became clear that Richardson would go to Washington, the group tried to persuade him to resign before midnight, a tactic that would permit Volpe to appoint a Republican successor as attorney general. Richardson refused to do this, arguing that it would look too patently political. Besides, he said, Representative Robert Quinn, the Democratic Speaker of the House, who would probably succeed him, would do a creditable job. Gammal and Woodworth disagreed to no avail, and when Richardson went to Washington Quinn succeeded him.

Brooke was disappointed, knowing the Massachusetts GOP would be hurt, especially since Volpe, after serving only two years of the first four-year term for governor, was leaving to become Secretary of Transportation. Brooke feared the Democrats would make this an issue in 1970. "At one time, Richardson agreed with me," he said. Brooke did not oppose the nomination, which was approved by the Senate.

Robert Finch was HEW Secretary in 1971 when he called Dr. John Knowles, head of the Massachusetts General Hospital, to interview him for the post of Assistant Secretary for Health. Finch was so impressed by the dynamic physician that he offered him the job ten minutes after they met. Through a slip-up, however, Knowles' name was not sent to the White House for Nixon's nomination.

Then the American Medical Association, still smarting after the passage of Medicare in 1965, entered the picture. By this time the AMA, which Senator Edward Kennedy has often denounced, had a powerful lobby: the American Medical Political Action Committee (AMPAC). This committee omitted Knowles' name from a list of acceptable names for the post, remembering what the liberal physician had told Congress: "I do believe in comprehensive prepaid health insurance for all Americans on a public and private basis." To the AMA this smacked of socialized medicine.

Senator Dirksen and powerful allies of the AMA tried to dissuade Finch from naming Knowles to the post, even though both Massachusetts senators endorsed him. The appointment was put on the back burner for five months "of Kafkaesque indecision and intrigue that was to sear permanently everyone it touched." Dirksen finally stepped aside, saying: "When Napoleon sent Marshal Ney to Russia, he told him he would have plenty of time to discuss with him how he conquered that country and no time to discuss how he lost the battle. And I have not time to discuss Dr. Knowles." Nevertheless, bowing to pressure, two days later Finch told the press: "I have reluctantly and regretfully decided . . . that the protracted and distorted discussion . . . has resulted in a situation in which he would not be able to function effectively in this critical position." Finch then named Dr. Roger Egeberg, Dean of the University of California Medical School, who is as liberal as Knowles and *also* a Democrat. It was too late for the AMA to oppose the appointment.

Brooke was dejected when Nixon withdrew Knowles' name: "Those who have denied the American people the services of this . . . able man—who have made it impossible for the Senate even to consider his qualifications—have performed a singular disservice."

Knowles was honored at a dinner in January 1972 when he left his post as director of Massachusetts General Hospital to head the Rockefeller Foundation, Finch, then a special adviser at the White House, recalling the six months of turmoil in which he boosted Knowles for the HEW post, quipped: "The real reason he didn't get the job—he didn't conform to a statement I put out, urging a maximum of two children per family." Finch alluded to the fact that Knowles, who will work at the foundation to control population, has six children.

"After the Inauguration," Matthew V. Storin wrote in *The Boston Globe,* "Brooke was wearing the Republican colors with ease until the 'Southern strategy' began to emerge by way of extending school desegregation deadlines and later in the form of Haynsworth's nomination among GOP dissidents." Brooke teamed in this fight with Senator Birch Bayh of Indiana, and later the two joined in blocking the nomination of Carswell. "In this period," Storin said, "Brooke often had difficulty getting to see Nixon."

On August 18, 1969, Nixon nominated Clement F. Haynsworth to the seat Justice Abe Fortas had vacated three months before under threat of impeachment for having accepted and kept for 11 months a 20,000-dollar check from a foundation run by Louis Wolfson, a financier later imprisoned for illegal stock manipulations. Haynsworth, fifty-seven, of Greenville, South Carolina, after graduating from Harvard Law School, became Chief Justice of the Fourth Circuit Court of Appeals.

The vacancy Fortas left had been called "the Jewish seat" since Louis Brandeis was named to it in 1916. He was the predecessor of four other brilliant Jewish lawyers: Benjamin Cardozo, Felix Frankfurter, Arthur Goldberg and Fortas. "But Nixon, hearing other political trumpets, was to break the Jewish succession which had lasted for 53 years," wrote Evans and Novak. The President wanted a white Southern conservative federal judge under sixty. Nixon felt he was keeping a campaign promise to put proven strict constructionists on the Supreme Court. The first to fill the bill was Warren Burger, Chief Judge of the U.S. Court of Appeals for the District of Columbia, who replaced Earl Warren. Burger was easily confirmed, with only three Democratic senators dissenting.

The AFL-CIO lined up organized labor against Haynsworth's appointment. President George Meany, who headed the 13-million-member AFL-CIO, said the judge not only was antilabor, but was also not sufficiently interested in the "legitimate aspirations of Negroes." After hearings running from September 16 to October 9, the Judiciary Committee approved the nomination ten to seven. Attorney General Mitchell, as surprised as Nixon by the foot-dragging, quipped that "if we'd put up one of the 12 Apostles it would have been the same."

Hugh Scott and Robert Griffin had been urging the President to withdraw Haynsworth's name when, early in October, Brooke wrote a letter to Nixon which was credited with being a major influence in increasing Senate opposition to the appointment of the Southerner to the Supreme Court. Brooke, noting that he had refrained from commenting on the nomination, added: "The time is now at hand when I shall have to do so and I wanted to tell you of my deep distress in the matter and of my decision.

"My review of Judge Haynsworth's record convinces me that his treatment of civil-rights issues is not in keeping with the historic movement toward equal justice for every American citizen. Combined with some of the judge's business activities, which have created the appearance of conflict with his judicial duties, this consideration raises grave questions about the wisdom of his confirmation."

Brooke went on to ask whether Haynsworth was the man to restore the nation's confidence in the utter integrity of the Supreme Court and "the man to maintain the faith of that vast majority of fair-minded Americans, not to mention the disillusioned minority, who look to the court as the indispensable instrument of equal justice under the law." Brooke said the widespread discontent with his nomination showed he was not, adding that if the nomination were put to the Senate it would "be extremely embarrassing to those of us who face a great conflict between our principles and our sense of obligation to you." He asked Nixon to reconsider his decision not to withdraw the nomination. If there was a consensus in the Senate, he said, "I think it is the view that Judge Haynsworth is not the distinguished jurist whom the country expected to be nominated." A month later Brooke again urged Nixon to withdraw his name, citing Haynsworth's "insensitivity to his apparent conflict of interest and his record in labor and civil rights" as reasons enough to disqualify him.

Brooke's eloquence helped block the confirmation. On November 21 the Senate rejected Haynsworth by a vote of 55 to 44, with 17 Republicans voting against. Among them were Brooke; Senator

Williams of Delaware, a flinty conservative who was chairman of the Committee on Committees; Hugh Scott, Minority Leader; Assistant Majority Leader Griffin; and Margaret Chase Smith, chairman of the Senate Republican caucus. Nixon blew his top. Aides who had not heard him raise his voice in anger during ten months in the White House were astonished at the emotion that Haynsworth's rejection aroused in him. "In the privacy of the White House Nixon inveighed against the liberal press, against organized labor and most of all against the GOP senators." Nixon felt the Republican senators had betrayed him.

He looked for another candidate with the proper qualifications. "You know," a White House aide said, "the President really believes in that Southern strategy more than he believes in anything else."

Whether Haynsworth should have been nominated is debatable, but there is no question that Federal Judge G. Harrold Carswell should never have come into the picture, as Richard Harris makes clear in his book, *Decision*. "Aside from a stratum of racism that ran through his background and his behavior," *The Boston Globe* noted in a review of *Decision,* "his judicial record was so inadequate as to raise the question of his fitness for the position he held on the Fifth Circuit Court of Appeals, let alone his worthiness for so exalted a role as U.S. Supreme Court Justice." Senator Hollings of South Carolina, who had led the fight for Haynsworth's confirmation, said Carswell was "not qualified to carry Judge Haynsworth's law books," yet he voted for Carswell's confirmation.

In view of Carswell's record, it is hard to understand why pressure from the legal profession, which ultimately defeated him, was so slow to mobilize. In 1948, before a meeting of the American Legion when he was campaigning for a seat in the Georgia Legislature, Carswell said: "I am a Southerner by ancestry, birth, training, inclination, belief and practice. I believe that segregation of the races is proper and the only practical and correct way of life in our states. I have always so believed, and I shall always so act." When this speech was uncovered two days after his nomination, Carswell said on television: "Specifically and categorically, I denounce and reject the words themselves and the ideas they represent. They're obnoxious and abhorrent to my personal philosophy."

Harris tells how opposition to Carswell developed, and how pro-Carswell forces, including the White House, "bumbled and bungled and not least among them, Senator Roman Hruska of Nebraska, who said that Carswell was a mediocre judge but that the mediocre people in the nation should have representation in the most sacrosanct body in the U.S. government." George Frazier called Roman Hruska "the most ignoble Roman of them all."

At least one of Carswell's backers lacked conviction. Senator George Aiken of Vermont, who had voted against a major presidential nomination only once in his 30 years in the Senate, told a colleague he would vote for anyone the President named unless the man had murdered someone—lately.

Brooke keeps an open mind in these matters. In this case, knowing that timing was crucial, he waited until all the evidence was in and until the Judiciary Committee held hearings on the candidate. This meant, in effect, that he held back until the anti-Carswell forces were losing momentum and were blindly looking around for new support. Brooke's failure to speak out earlier was the last straw for some black militants, who again criticized him. Not once during the first 14 months of the Nixon administration had he attacked its policy on racial issues.

He finally exploded in mid-March 1970 when, on a CBS radio show, *Capitol Cloakroom,* he accused the administration of making "a cold, calculated political decision" to hand blacks the hot end of the poker. It was "a suburban as well as a Southern strategy," Brooke charged, predicting that Nixon and his advisers would "continue along the road they took during the campaign." Recalling a Nixon campaign slogan, he said: "President Nixon said he wanted to bring us together, but everything he has done so far appears to be designed to push us further apart." Nixon forgot so many promises made to blacks that he became the target of jokes. Mark Russell, a comedian at the Shoreham Hotel in Washington, quipped early in 1971: "The Nixons had a black caucus and they really are making progress. At Tricia's wedding, the flower girl carried African violets."

Commenting on the (*Capitol Cloakroom*) show, *Time* magazine noted: "Somewhat naïvely, he [Brooke] says that, though he was aware of Nixon's Southern-oriented statements during the campaign, he did not endorse them. He made no public protest because he thought Nixon's pro-Southern attitude would change radically after the election." Brooke said, according to *Time,* "I had gathered this from personal, private conversations with Nixon."

"Then in succession," *Time* reported, "came administration policy on school desegregation guidelines, voting rights, the nominations to the Supreme Court of Clement Haynsworth and G. Harrold Carswell, and the departure from the Department of Health, Education and

Welfare of Leon Panetta,* who had been a determined fighter for desegregation of schools in the South. 'And let's use the right word,' said Brooke. 'He was fired!'" On the program Brooke said Nixon was aware of racial tensions and problems in the U.S. "I can't believe that he is oblivious of the ills of the urban centers, where so many blacks are living. . . . I know that he does have advisers around him who do advise him more along political lines than as to what is best for the country, and I think unfortunately, he has listened to them." He said some of Agnew's recent remarks, which disturbed him, could be interpreted as "support for the cold political decision" to downgrade programs to aid blacks in order to win reelection.

When he remained silent on the Carswell issue, the black caucus, angry and frustrated because Brooke was not fighting the nomination, after several unsuccessful attempts to get into his Senate office to "jawbone him into submission," sent him a scorching telegram. The message, which might have driven a wedge between Brooke and the caucus, was given to Western Union a few hours before Brooke's emotional and effective speech that turned the tide against Carswell's nomination.

"When the news of the speech reached the caucus," a Washington reporter said, "a staff member dashed down to the telegraph office and retrieved the telegram before it was sent." The reporter added: "This illustrates the differences in style."

In an hour-long formal speech on February 25 without any notes Brooke outlined several reasons for opposing Carswell. In a moving address he said that, after a "searching" review of the private and public life of Carswell, he concluded that he had tended to pursue from the bench the white supremacy views he had spoken 22 years earlier, when he was twenty-eight, and which he had repudiated only after Nixon nominated him.

"I cannot in good conscience support confirmation of a man who

---

* Although he did not mention it on the program, Brooke was irked when Leon E. Panetta, civil-rights chief of HEW, resigned. He said the resignation could "only be viewed objectively as a victory for segregationists. I am disturbed. . . . He was committed to integration. It was a regrettable move on the part of the administration. . . . If we are going to have a civil rights office in HEW, we want a man of Panetta's dedication." Brooke, who had discussed the matter with Finch, said the White House was dissatisfied because Panetta was dedicated to integration. The dismissal had to have Nixon's approval, he added. "They couldn't have done it without him." The White House announced the resignation before Panetta submitted it. Brooke had hired Panetta to join his Washington staff after Panetta's boss, Senator Kuchel, lost in 1968, but Panetta left to take the HEW post.

has created such fundamental doubts about his dedication to human rights." Brooke, in reviewing Carswell's career, found that his record included "a number of actions which either confirm or invite suspicion that his anti-constitutional inclinations continue to hold sway. This man shows no indication of having changed [from his 1948 views]. I certainly would like to support my President . . . [but] the country cannot afford Judge Carswell on the Supreme Court at this time." Referring to Nixon's inaugural pledge to "bring us together," Brooke said the choice of Carswell "does not serve this vital goal." The strife dividing the country "is not only racial. It is the young versus the old, it is section against section, and religion seems to be getting deeper in conflict after the beautiful time under Pope John XXIII." This, he continued, "is a most inappropriate time in history that this man should be appointed to the Supreme Court, a man who at one time in his life spoke out for white supremacy. I have fought black separatists every step along the way. I do not believe they are right. I do not believe there is any master race, black or white."

Senator Edward Kennedy was one of several senators who applauded Brooke's eloquence, saying he had shown "great courage. We all recognize the significant impact your voice had during the discussion of Judge Haynsworth and your statement here today is of no less significance." Lauded by Senator Charles Mathias (Republican of Maryland) for being "both eloquent and dispassionate at the same time," Brooke said: "I tried to be objective. I am not an angry man."

Birch Bayh was in the Senate chamber when Brooke took the floor and said: "I will vote against confirmation of Judge Carswell." The senators knew this was significant, because Brooke, though reticent for a politician, was "an adroit leader when he decided that the time and the issue were right for him to make a move." The few senators present, including Charles E. Goodell of New York, who had been the first Republican to announce his opposition to Carswell, and Edward Kennedy, the Majority Whip, along with Hatfield, Percy, Mathias and Griffin, the Minority Whip, knew that Brooke had rounded up many of the 17 Republican votes cast against Haynsworth.

Brooke had waited five weeks before announcing his opposition, because he wanted to be sure that Carswell was sufficiently disqualified to justify a concerted effort to defeat him. He also weighed the possibility of rounding up enough senators to show the blacks and young people across the country that their pleas did not go unheard.

327

Otherwise he did not feel justified in opposing Nixon twice in a row on a Supreme Court nomination without losing whatever power he had at the White House. Before he acted he wanted to read and study all the evidence and review the full record.

In her thoughtful commentary, Mary McGrory in *The Washington Evening Star,* referring to the first of two Senate stands Brooke took against Carswell, called it "the most powerful speech against the Carswell nomination," noting that it was also "the least attended [because] few Republicans want to hear the Senate's only black member eloquently laying out the case against Carswell and removing, one by one, the props they are leaning on to justify a vote for a Southern judge whose partisans have admitted he is mediocre."

Bayh told his staff after hearing the speech: "If we really mean what we're saying about the Voting Rights Act and all those other civil-rights matters, how can we let Carswell go through without making a fight?" The Bayh-Brooke camp considered the White House their strongest ally. Senator Robert Dole of Kansas, who fought for Carswell, later called the White House aides "those idiots downtown." Nixon himself seemed unaware of the dimensions of the growing opposition to his choice. After Senators Schweiker, Mathias, Packwood, Percy and Fulbright had joined Goodell and Brooke in opposing Carswell, Brooke, in the White House on another matter, told Nixon: "I want you to know that I am working day and night to defeat your nomination to the Supreme Court." Nixon, apparently thinking Brooke was "merely playing to the liberal and black grandstands back home, smiled indulgently and went on with the previous conversation."

Brooke was one of the liberal and moderate Republican senators who founded the informal Wednesday Club, which met fairly regularly once a week in one or another of their offices for lunch and an exchange of ideas. The club, which had been formed in February 1969, gave the senators a united voice that could be heard at the White House, "which ignored most of them individually." Members of the Wednesday Club played a significant, if subtle and behind-the-scenes, role in defeating Carswell.

Five weeks after Nixon submitted Carswell's name, only three Republicans—Goodell, Javits and Brooke—had come out against him. *The New York Post* rebuked Javits for his indecision. The day after his conference with Nixon at the White House Brooke won more converts after his second speech on the Senate floor: "I've seen no evidence that this is not the same G. Harrold Carswell who comes before us in March 1970 but also was the twenty-eight-year-old man who supported white supremacy while campaigning for the Georgia Legislature." Speaking calmly yet emotionally to an almost empty Senate floor, but to an intent visitors' gallery, he said in an aside: "Some might say that because I'm a black man I might be excited about this issue. But I was an American before I was a Republican, and I believe I'm an American before I'm a black man. I love this country—I don't want to see this country torn asunder." Brooke paced the Senate floor as he added that, if he could find an indication that Carswell had changed his views on white supremacy, "I might be able to change my mind, but I cannot." Brooke further noted that Carswell's involvement in founding a private white-only club in Florida "was one of the most damaging pieces of evidence" to come before the Senate Judiciary Committee.

After this brief, impromptu speech against the fifty-year-old Florida judge, Senator Mike Gravel (Democrat of Alaska) rose to praise him, saying the speech was not made by "Senator Brooke but [by] Ed Brooke, the man."

At this time Carswell's supporters still outnumbered his opponents in the Senate, but Capitol Hill observers felt that, if the vote could be delayed, public sentiment might force some backers to change sides. Brooke's second speech upset Nixon so much, Brooke was called moments later to the White House to discuss current issues with party leaders.*

In the waning days of the debate Hugh Scott told Majority Leader Mike Mansfield that the anti-Carswell forces definitely had the votes to defeat the nomination on the upcoming vote. Agreeing, Mansfield conferred with Bayh, suggesting that, after the recommittal motion failed, he move to take an up-or-down vote on the nomination two hours later—not two days later. Bayh nodded.

He took the floor after the vote and asked for a unanimous-consent agreement to take the final vote at three that afternoon. "Hruska was so flabbergasted by the proposal, a clear sign that Scott hadn't mentioned it to him," Harris wrote, "that he jumped up and shouted, 'The Nebraska from Senator objects!' That was enough to kill the motion."

---

* On March 31, 1970, *The Boston Herald* reported a rumor that Nixon might nominate Brooke to the Supreme Court if Carswell was not confirmed. The White House wanted to silence Brooke's criticism of the administration. Nixon knew that Governor Sargent would replace Brooke with another Republican senator—probably Congressman Silvio O. Conte of Pittsfield.

Nothing daunted after this session, Hruska told the press the administration would win two days later by three or four votes. Brooke paused at his table a few minutes later in the Senate dining room: "Roman, you can count, and so can I. If you had had the votes, you would have agreed to Birch's motion on the spot."

In *Esquire* magazine George Frazier spoke of "that memorable moment when he [Brooke] saved Maragaret Chase Smith's vote from going to . . . Carswell." Brooke had warned his forces not to approach Senator Smith, because she resents any intrusion when facing an important decision. According to Harris, she had refused to tell Nixon how she would vote, "and the next morning, a few hours before the vote was called, she told Brooke that she wouldn't decide until her name came up."

Late in the morning, while the final debate was going on, a Republican colleague told Brooke that he had just learned from the White House that Mrs. Smith had pledged her vote to Nixon. Brooke, worried, found her in the Senate dining room and asked whether the White House was correct in claiming her vote. Noting her embarrassment, he said he was not trying to influence her, but merely to tell her what was being said. Mrs. Smith, flushed with anger, immediately phoned Bryce Harlow, Nixon's senior congressional adviser at the White House, and asked about the leak. Had he told any other senators she was in favor of Carswell? When Harlow tried to sidestep the question, Mrs. Smith castigated him, slammed down the receiver and hurried to the Senate floor, but not until she told Harlow he had "impugned her honor" and that she would *not* vote for Carswell.

Roger Woodworth remembers seeing her turn to talk to Schweiker. After he and Senator Mathias confirmed what Brooke had heard, Mrs. Smith sat down at her desk, "tight-lipped, waiting for the roll call to begin." When the clerk called her name, she quietly said, "No." At that stage she was the twelfth Republican opposed. At the end of the first roll call the count was 46 to 44. Six senators had not voted. The final tally was 51 to 45 against the nomination.

At the White House President Nixon, with Mitchell at his side, said: "I have reluctantly concluded, with the Senate presently constituted, I cannot successfully nominate to the Supreme Court any federal appellate judge from the South who believes as I do in the strict construction of the Constitution." He charged that the vote had been the result of "vicious assaults," "malicious character assassination," and an "act of regional discrimination." He ended by saying he would be compelled to find his next nominee in the North.

Brooke, who had assembled the Republican coalition that defeated the Carswell nomination, found Nixon's statement "incredible, mistaken and unfortunate." He disputed Nixon's contention that "it is not possible to get a Supreme Court nominee from the South confirmed," and suggested that the President delivered his remarks in anger. His assertion that he cannot get "confirmation of any man who believes in the strict construction of the Constitution as I do if they happen to come from the South," Brooke added, "is untrue."

Contending that the Senate reached its judgment strictly on the merits of the nominee, Brooke said among those who opposed the nomination were many distinguished Southerners. He correctly predicted, as events proved, that the Senate would gladly confirm "a Southerner and a strict constructionist who is qualified. I regret the President's statement deeply. I hope that, after his anger has cooled, he will reconsider his remarks. It would be an act of great injustice to overlook competent nominees from the South on the utterly false assumption that the Senate will not confirm them."

Brooke got no personal satisfaction from Carswell's rejection. There was a sad look and a glint of tears in his eyes when he told a reporter in his Washington office on April 8: "I don't know the man." Although he had for more than a month done everything possible to beat Carswell, he felt sorry. "I don't understand why they didn't withdraw his name. This is a difficult thing to put a man through."

It was the second time that day that Brooke had showed emotion. When he walked out of the Senate chamber on his way to the old Supreme Court chamber for a television interview, a crowd of children and adults in the corridor broke into cheers. "The emotion of the moment washed over him and tears flushed his eyes," a reporter wrote.

Carswell described the 80-day struggle for confirmation as "an agonizing experience for me, my family and friends." An hour after the vote he drove with his wife to the Florida Bar Association's office in Washington, where reporters waited. He shook hands with Governor Claude R. Kirk, Jr., of Florida, before speaking briefly. Two minutes later he drove back to his home on Lake Jackson, seven miles north of Washington. One of hundreds of visitors said, "It's just like a death-visiting."

Carswell said he was not bitter and would remain a judge on the Fifth Circuit. A fortnight later he said he was "taking his case to the people" by resigning from the bench and running for the U.S. Senate.

Senator Spessard L. Holland (Democrat of Florida), whose retirement paved the way for this announcement, said the judge "certainly is going into his race well known from recent events." In Washington some senators were amazed to think a man would want to join America's most exclusive club after a majority of its members had blackballed him.

"The boss thinks you're pulling his leg," Roger Woodworth told a reporter who called about Carswell's announcement. Convinced it was true, Brooke refused to comment. Carswell lost his bid.

On April 14 Nixon named Judge Harry Blackmun of the Eighth Circuit Court of Appeals to the seat. Blackmun, a friend of Burger, was, like him, a strict constructionist and a Minnesota Republican. He was easily confirmed by the Senate.

Later Nixon had two more vacancies to fill when veterans Hugo L. Black and John Marshall Harlan resigned. With but one dissenting vote, the Senate confirmed the nomination of Lewis F. Powell, Jr., thus showing how false Nixon's charge was that the Senate would not approve a Southerner or a conservative. As Brooke had said, when a well-qualified nominee of professional stature and a belief in the basic guarantees of the Constitution is voted on, no regional bias or philosophical disagreement bars his way.

Brooke was the first Republican senator to say he would vote against Nixon's nomination of William H. Rehnquist to the U.S. Supreme Court. Brooke said he found Rehnquist's published statements on human rights "unsupportable." He was especially concerned by a letter Rehnquist had written to *The Arizona Republic* newspaper in 1967 opposing a school desegregation plan.

"The time he made that statement was a very relevant time in civil rights. Rehnquist was going backward while the country was going forward on civil rights," Brooke said, adding that the nominee had said he was "not committed to either a segregated or an integrated society; I find this point of view unsupportable."*

The day before Brooke said this, 20 Harvard Law School professors came out in opposition to Rehnquist, to join a growing list of opponents, and at about the same time *The New York Times* (on December 12) backed Brooke, noting that the nominee had repeatedly opposed judicial or legislative efforts to eliminate racial

---

* President Nixon said on September 26, 1969: "It seems to me that there are two extreme groups. There are those who want instant integration and those who want segregation forever. I believe that we need to have a middle course between these two extremes."

discrimination. *The Times* found the grounds for rejecting Rehnquist different from those on which the Senate had turned down Haynsworth and Carswell.

"His record does not show either insensitivity to potential conflicts of interest or deficient professional qualifications. Rather, his are the defects of basic insensitivity to racial equality and seriously deficient understanding of the Bill of Rights."

On the Senate floor on December 7 Brooke spoke for more than an hour in the first full day of arguments on the nomination, saying Rehnquist had shown a "persistent unwillingness to permit the law to be used for the purpose of promoting 'equal justice under law' for all Americans."* Citing the forty-seven-year-old nominee's record as a Supreme Court clerk in Phoenix, Arizona, and as an assistant U.S. Attorney General, Brooke called him an "activist" in opposing civil rights who would "take the nation back rather than continue its forward progress" in this area. Brooke did not oppose Rehnquist because he is conservative, a Southerner or a strict constructionist. He simply felt the nominee is lacking in commitment to an integrated society. Brooke understands perfectly what Saul Alinsky** meant when he said in connection with liberals' concern over Nixon's appointees: "A lot of men change when they're appointed to the court. [Earl] Warren was a terrible racist with the Japanese in California during the war, and look what he became. Frankfurter started out great and turned completely around in his last years. Blackmun was supposed to be an absolute conservative, but Whizzer White makes Blackmun look great, and White was appointed by Kennedy. Let's wait and see about Nixon's people."

This comment drew a wry smile from Brooke, who, noting Rehnquist's relative youth and active posture, said his views on civil rights would influence court action "not only in the last third of the twentieth century, but into the twenty-first century and affect our children and our children's children."

Rehnquist in testimony before the Senate Judiciary Committee commented on his opposition to the Phoenix City Council regulation guaranteeing equal access to public accommodations. He said the ordinance worked well in Phoenix: "It was readily accepted and I think

---

* Two presidential candidates for the Democratic nomination—Senators George McGovern of South Dakota and Edmund Muskie of Maine—also opposed the nomination.

** Known as the champion of the underdog against the establishment, Alinsky heads the Chicago-based Industrial Areas Foundation.

I have come to realize since . . . more than I did at the time, the strong concern that minorities have for the recognition of these rights. I would not feel the same way today about it as I did then."

Brooke said: "How could an intelligent . . . man not know in the 1960s that minority groups felt so strongly about their rights? Now he understands, but he doesn't say he was wrong in 1964, he just says the Phoenix ordinance worked well and he was surprised it worked well. . . . Even now he does not feel strongly enough about basic human rights to categorically, without equivocation, reject his former actions."

On December 12 the Senate confirmed Rehnquist 68 to 26. Nobody was surprised. Senator Birch Bayh spoke for the dissidents when he told a nationally televised audience he hoped Rehnquist would mend his ways in the field of civil rights.

CHAPTER EIGHTEEN

More Grief for Nixon

ANOTHER episode in the Nixon-Brooke relationship was the Senator's role in paving the way for a meeting between the President and the 13 congressional members of the black caucus.

Nixon was still smarting over the Carswell affair when nine black members of the House on May 17 charged that his "retreat" on civil rights has created an "alienation as deep as it is dangerous" between him and black America. After waiting 90 days for a requested meeting with the President, the nine Democrats lashed out in a statement by Representative William Clay of Missouri, expressing "outright disgust" with the President for his policies and his refusal to meet with them. They said his position on school desegregation, his nomination of two Southern racists for the Supreme Court, his veto of school funds, his refusal to give high priority to aid the poor "testify to his apathy not only toward black people but toward all poor Americans." Clay said Nixon had his priorities confused when he "declared his disdain for military defeat," but made no effort "to win battles on the home front." In his attack he cited six blacks shot to death in Augusta, Georgia, and two black students killed by police at Jackson State College.

"If there is honor to be won, it is here in this country, where American blood is staining American soil. If there is a potential for this nation to fall, it exists here in the U.S. more surely than in our correction of mistaken involvement in the affairs of Indo-China."

The black caucus had written to Nixon asking for an appointment in

February to discuss problems and "open some line of communication" between the administration and black America. But the White House recalled a visit by the Reverend Ralph Abernathy of SCLC, who, after what appeared to be a friendly meeting, "promptly denounced the administration from the White House steps." On April 20 the caucus finally got a reply from a White House aide:

"We hoped to be able to work this out, but the President's schedule has been such that we have just not been able to work it in. At this point, we do not foresee an opportunity in the immediate future, but will be back in touch with you if an appropriate time arises."

The caucus was furious at the brush-off. "We got about the same consideration as a letter from a guy in Idaho complaining about his garbage collection," Clay told the press. Nixon's refusal to meet with them, he said, "suggests that he prefers to hand-pick the spokesmen for black America." After more unsuccessful bargaining during the rest of the year, the black caucus, then numbering 12 black members of the House of Representatives, boycotted Nixon's 1971 State of the Union message.

They did not ask Brooke to join them. "It would have put him in an unnecessarily embarrassing position," a boycott leader said, realizing that Brooke was a Republican and a senator, whereas the "Black Dozen" were all House Democrats.

"Under the circumstances," a Negro columnist wrote in *The Washington Post,* "there could have been no basis for hard feelings had Brooke simply gone ahead and attended the President's speech; that is precisely what the callers of the boycott had expected him to do. But Brooke changed the circumstances by announcing, well ahead of the message, that he intended to be there." The columnist charged that Brooke's announcement was an implied "repudiation of the black caucus." Brooke had said that both courtesy and duty compelled him to attend the session, listen to the message and weigh Nixon's legislative proposals.

Brooke's recurrent trouble during his career stems from his often expressed wish to be judged as a public servant, not as a black envoy to the white community or "as a symbol of white acceptance of blacks." According to *The New York Times,* not only has this led some black leaders to attack him for lacking in militancy, but his white Republican colleagues also "have been simultaneously provoked by his refusal to appear as a demonstration of integration in their party." This observation points up the relationship between Brooke and the black caucus.

It was not merely that they belonged to different political parties.

Every member of the caucus felt he was "the elected and legitimate representative" of the 25 million black Americans, and almost all of them represented solid black districts. They realized that Brooke considers himself a senator who is black, not a black senator. Nevertheless, his relations with the black caucus, as with the President, were friendly, despite differences of opinion.

"He's our friend, so why should we complain that he's not perfect?" an aide to a member of the caucus said.

Two days after the caucus boycotted the President's message, Brooke told Charles Diggs of Detroit, then chairman of the black caucus, that his group should give Nixon a face-saving two months, but that he would see them. Why was the President loath to meet with the caucus?

According to William Raspberry, a black columnist for *The Washington Post,* it was the "fear of a public put-down that made Nixon deny the blacks an audience for 14 months. And it was pure politics that led him to confer with them after he consulted with Brooke, who advised him to do so." Raspberry thus analyzed White House reasoning:

"A meeting runs the risk of a public blast, with potentially harmful results. Refusal to meet gives the Black Dozen [now 13—all Democrats, with the addition of the District's Walter Fauntroy] a very powerful political weapon." Nixon also reasoned that by meeting with the caucus more than a year and a half after the presidential election, he would have time to "defuse any bombs they planted." Raspberry noted that from a political point of view the caucus was almost better off with a Nixon brush-off than with an audience. Some members felt that Brooke had done them no favor in arranging it.

"For so long as the President's position was an adamant no," Raspberry wrote, "the black congressional Democrats had an issue. But once he agreed to a meeting, they could not have been stuck with the spectacle of 13 congressmen trying to represent the aspirations of 25 million blacks in one hectic hour."

At the White House hearing on March 25 (1971), Nixon told Diggs his door would remain open to the caucus. He cited the administration's record, which had accepted only a few minor black proposals, while rejecting costly demands. It was an opening wedge in improving communications between the caucus and the White House. Raspberry said Nixon, who needed a better spokesman than the departed Daniel Patrick Moynihan "to tell him what black people are thinking, now has a vehicle for accomplishing just that."

A year earlier (March 11, 1970) Brooke had charged the Nixon administration with pursuing a "contrived, calculated, designed" neglect of the black community. "I have seen very little for black people to applaud." Now, asked whether the administration's approach to Negro problems was one of "benign neglect," as stated by Nixon's former adviser, Professor Moynihan, Brooke said: "You might say it's a period of benign neglect. I just think it's contrived, it's calculated; and as I said, it's designed."

Actually, by "benign neglect" Moynihan meant that "the issue of race could benefit from a period of 'benign neglect.' The subject has been too much talked about. The forum has been too much taken over by hysterics, paranoids, and boodlers on all sides. We may need a period when Negro progress continues and racial rhetoric fades." In short, by "benign neglect" Moynihan had in mind a cooling-off of the "rhetoric of denunciation" which had split the nation into angry racial camps, and a new emphasis on "the great commonalities, such as poverty," which could unite different groups and get them co-operating for common concern. Brooke had often said the same thing more simply. In January 1966 he told the New England Daily Newspaper Association that civil-rights demonstrations have more than racial overtones. "In the rioting at Los Angeles the bitterness of the Negroes could have been directed against the Negro businessmen because the battle was the have-nots against the haves. . . . These demonstrations are not based on race or religion alone but on economics. Now is the time to get rid of the battles on the streets and get them into the courts and at the conference tables."

The second meeting between the caucus and Nixon was in June (1971) in the Ways and Means Committee hearing room. *Newsweek* reported: "A panel of black legislators ranged like tribunes on the curving . . . dais in a Capitol hearing room, sitting in judgment on the President. . . . The 13-member black caucus . . . had embarrassed Nixon into granting them an audience last March." The caucus, which handed the President a bill of 60 demands, had received an equally bulky reply, and had come to this meeting to say the response was "deeply disappointing." Diggs said later: "It is undeniable that the old folk saying still applies: 'If you're black, get back.' "

In February Raspberry had chided Brooke for acting as if race were not an issue in the hope that it would make it go away. Noting that Brooke considers himself an American, a Republican and a black in that order, he said he hoped the time would come "when all black Americans can share his sense of priorities. But that time has not yet come, and it may be folly to act as though it has."

The columnist was thinking of Brooke's endorsement of John Nevius, the only white candidate for nonvoting delegate from Washington, D.C.

"Nevius is a capable, wholly honorable man," he wrote. "But few people doubt that what led Brooke to endorse him is the fact that he is a Republican. Since Brooke and the other candidates for the post are black—and also capable and honorable—and since the District of Columbia is overwhelmingly black," Raspberry continued, it wouldn't seem unreasonable for the Senator to support a black candidate. "And if he found it awkward to do so because the others are not Republican, then he could very easily have said nothing at all."

Nevius, an old friend of Brooke, was his chief fund raiser in the District in 1966. He was also considered one of the best qualified candidates for the office. In view of his long period of public service, Brooke felt he could get more done than the other candidates, including the able Walter Fauntroy. When Rochelle Fashaw and Delano Lewis took Raspberry's position, Brooke's fundamental argument was that it was wrong for blacks to favor blacks or for whites to favor whites merely on the issue of color. "According to your logic," he told the two black members of his staff, "I should not represent Massachusetts because it is 98 percent white. Nevius has just as much right to represent a predominantly black community as a white as I have to represent a predominantly white community as a black."

In any case, it was another example of Brooke the lone wolf—the independent thinker. Most black colleagues in the House understand, if they do not fully appreciate, his philosophy and know of his consistently vigorous stand on civil-rights issues. They have worked together on important measures, and several members of the caucus went to the Senate chamber proudly to listen to his speeches during the Carswell debate.

House blacks, who think and act black, are often abrasive and obstructionist, considering this method the best way to hit paydirt. Although in their differing views they are anything but monolithic, they consider themselves the national champions of blacks. They are less effective than Brooke because their power to push through legislation is limited in direct proportion to their isolation.

Brooke has the same aspirations as the black caucus, but his means differ. He bristled when a newsman said he was the only black in Congress who was not working with the caucus: "Of course we are working in a common cause. My record speaks for itself. I defy anyone to say I have not been working for the rights of all Americans.

I don't think there is anyone who has done more for blacks and the poor than I."

Brooke has worked for and voted for most if not all minority causes that were issues during his first two years in the Senate. Along with his leadership in the Senate rejection of Haynsworth and Carswell, it was Brooke who publicly criticized Nixon's foot-dragging in enforcing school integration, a stance that irked Southerners and Republicans alike. Yet it played a big role in speeding up the administration's enforcement of its integration policies.

It was Brooke also who in the summer of 1970 went to Jackson, Mississippi, to pacify blacks after two Negro students were shot by police during a protest at Jackson State College.

Following the tragedy, Brooke wrote President Nixon expressing his "fears of the gravity of the situation" in Mississippi and elsewhere, and asked Nixon to meet with the presidents of black colleges around the country. In a courtesy letter to Senator John Stennis (Democrat of Mississippi) Brooke wrote: "Surely, Americans agree that indiscriminate use of force, whether by demonstrators or by law-enforcement officers, cannot be tolerated. I trust you will share my conviction that we must do everything possible to see that last week's action is not the prelude to further violence in Jackson or elsewhere." He told Stennis he was going to Jackson to "try to bring reason" to the campus, where, while Attorney General Mitchell was meeting with local officials, 500 blacks—some wearing black armbands—marched on the governor's mansion in downtown Jackson to protest the murders. School officials said many black youngsters either failed to show up or walked out of classrooms at about half a dozen high and junior high schools. It was an explosive situation.

If there was anything incongruous about a Northern black Republican mediating in a Southern Democratic state run by whites, Senator Stennis, chairman of the Armed Services Committee, didn't think so. He knew Brooke, without trying to make political hay from it, would try to ease tension and would fairly assess the situation and return with a balanced judgment. The blaze needed no inflammatory remarks.

Brooke was at National Airport in Washington at 8:00 A.M. on a Monday when he heard of the death of an old friend, Louis Berenson of Brookline. He flew to Boston to attend the funeral. In his absence Charles Evers, the black mayor of Fayette, Mississippi, voicing his fear of further strife, called Brooke's Washington office to invite him to Jackson. Unable to contact Brooke at Logan Airport in Boston, his aides reached him at the funeral parlor and told him of the phone call.

"I don't want to see an explosion in Mississippi," Brooke told reporters when he got the news. "I don't want to see any more bloodshed and violence and senseless killings. He [Evers] asked me to come . . . and I'm going."

Brooke's aides, unable to get a commercial flight, called the Pentagon and got an Air Force plane for the trip after Stennis approved it.

Brooke, back at National Airport less than two hours after getting the call at the funeral parlor, was met by Roger Woodworth, who accompanied him on a Jet Star flight out of Andrews Air Force Base in Maryland. Mayor Evers met them at Thompson Airport in Jackson at 2:45 P.M. State Adjutant General Walter Johnson, representing the governor, told a squad of white and black police: "I want this man to receive all the courtesies due a U.S. senator." Then, with sirens shrieking and lights flashing, Brooke was escorted ten miles to Jackson.

Since breakfast Brooke had eaten nothing but a soggy club sandwich which Woodworth gave him during the flight. For the next six hours, always with Mayor Evers, he was on the go every minute.

"The students at Jackson State need and deserve strong evidence of national concern over the tragedy which has occurred there," Brooke said, adding that he was concerned over another possible confrontation between police and students because evidence of the shootings had been removed. He said he was shocked by what he had seen and heard.

The police argued that the violence had been caused by snipers and demonstrators who threw rocks. Students and black leaders countercharged that the police had opened fire without provocation. A twenty-one-year-old student at Jackson State and a seventeen-year-old high schooler had been killed, and 15 other students had been injured. Before Brooke arrived, a crowd of black students had prevented state investigators from removing sections of the dormitory as evidence. Later, a group calling itself the Concerned Citizens of Jackson State College filed suit in the U.S. District Court for a temporary restraining order to bar state officials from removing evidence.

"We don't want to let them tear down these scars," said one of 200 students massed in front of the dormitory. They retired to a nearby athletic field when informed that the holes in the walls were being taken to a laboratory for investigation.

"There was no order to fire, no sniping," Brooke said. "They just opened up on a bunch of kids." Distressed after viewing the battle-scarred dormitory, he urged students to work within the system, "I've always been an advocate of Martin Luther King. There isn't any other way to win."

Brooke learned that the shooting by police and highway patrolmen, which lasted for 25 seconds, was reportedly in response to snipers, as about 200 blacks stood in front of the five-story women's dormitory. When Evers and he came on the scene there was a basket of flowers on the front steps. Inside on the first-floor landing the dried blood still had not been cleaned away. Every window except two small hinged windows on the fifth floor had been shattered by the hundreds of rounds fired in the brief interval. Metal plates between windows had been pierced with holes, some an inch and a half in diameter. Inspecting one hole, Brooke said: "There's one that looks as if it would stop a tank."

"A lot of you wonder why the world isn't shocked when black kids get shot," he told students who had been on the scene when the killings occurred. "I want a thorough investigation. I want prosecution. . . . I know what you've been through and I'm here because I want to focus attention on what's happening in this country and Jackson." He said the nation was lucky "we haven't had a worse situation. We have to make the nation know that a black life is as valuable as a white life and when I get to tell it before the television cameras, I'm going to say it just that way. It doesn't take much sense to tell what happened here. If they [the police] thought there was a sniper in there, they should have gone into the building and checked."

The alternative to working within the system, which Evers also advocated, was mass revolution, Brooke told the students. "Governments have been changed that way, but I don't believe in it. You could get guns but you don't have missiles and you don't have money. . . . I think political power is the way."

A student told Brooke an officer had said before the shooting: "You send those niggers out and we'll take care of them." Later, the student continued, another officer had said: "There's a nigger lying over there in those bushes. Some of you niggers go over there and drag him out."

After this meeting, Brooke walked to the modest home of James Earl Green, the high-school student who was killed, and talked to his mother privately for 20 minutes. Later that evening he talked to nine

342

wounded youths at the University of Mississippi Medical Center. He consoled the family of the other murdered student at a funeral home on that hot, steaming day. He visited the local NAACP headquarters, met with the press corps and called Governor John Bell Williams, asking him to let the punctured panels remain in the dormitory. The students didn't want the building repaired until after Commencement Day.

Brooke was back in Washington on May 20. "It's a miracle they didn't have a real massacre," he told newsmen. "The girls' dormitory is riddled with hundreds of bullets. It now resembles a fortress subjected to a barrage. But this building is not a fortress. It is a residential hall in which large numbers of innocent Americans were placed in jeopardy by a reckless and intolerable assault. Under no circumstances is a wild and indiscriminate fusillade justified." He said that if the FBI report called for a murder charge, the highway patrolmen would be prosecuted. They never were.

Brooke's trip ired a few members of the black caucus, who had planned to fly to Jackson State to show their concern. When Brooke jetted in a day earlier and returned acting "as if everything was being taken care of," most of the House caucus members canceled their flight.

"Brooke's skin is nearly black," one said, "but his mind isn't black at all."

His appearance in Jackson was credited with preventing further bloodshed. He was a peacemaker again in the summer of 1970 when he went to New Bedford, Massachusetts, following racial strife, at the request of *The New Bedford Standard-Times* and the mayor of the city. The newsmen and mayor told him the situation was bad and was likely to get worse, adding, "You have to come."

When he arrived he found the first problem was lack of communications. Local officials were discussing the causes of the violence without inviting blacks to take part in the talks. Brooke rounded up several blacks and persuaded them to negotiate with city officials. After a long meeting with Mayor George Rogers, Congressman Hastings Keith, the City Council and 11 blacks and Puerto Ricans, agreements were reached following five nights of turmoil during which a black youth was killed and 24 persons were injured.

During his first meeting with black leaders at the New Bedford Redevelopment Authority, a dozen policemen in plain clothes raided a nearby social club looking for weapons, infuriating 250 persons who could not understand how the police could raid a building in front of which the seventeen-year-old black had been shot. The mob pushed police cruisers down the street, whereupon the police who found no weapons, abandoned the raid a few minutes before Brooke walked up. Visibly upset, he asked: "Someone tell my why they raided while we were negotiating, trying to bring about peace."

"You're supposed to know that!" a youth shouted.

"They embarrassed you, Senator!" another yelled.

Addressing about a thousand persons at Carney Academy, Brooke said it should not be necessary "for blacks to arm themselves to get protection. If we have any more raidings, we are going to get into the most sickening situation imaginable and it will set this city back a long, long time."

Once prosperous in whaling days and later a great textile center, New Bedford had come upon hard times and by 1970 was one of the leading cities of the U.S. in terms of federal aid received. Brooke promised the assembly he would seek an investigation by Congress or the U.S. Attorney's office as to "why the funds have not gotten better results."

A woman screamed as Brooke was talking at another meeting in a school auditorium, and immediately most of the 150 persons present rose and joined in the shouting. By the time they had settled down it was learned that the woman was drunk.

"That points up how edgy we all are," Brooke said. "Everybody started screaming because they thought there was a riot in this room. . . . You are sitting on a tinderbox. That's what the real danger is. If there ever was a time for clear, sound thinking, it is now."

On the way to the auditorium Brooke had walked through the tension-packed district (the West End), where 200 black youths pushed and jostled him. While he was in the city he received death threats and was insulted several times. The city was in such a state of tension that while Brooke conferred with Keith, Rogers, blacks and Puerto Ricans at City Hall, the building had to be guarded by riot-equipped policemen carrying rifles and shotguns. Brooke went on New Bedford's Channel 6 for 25 minutes in an appeal for sound judgment "during these tension-ridden days. I can't stand to hear anyone call a policeman a 'pig' or a black person a 'nigger.' I can't understand these or any other racial epithets because they hurt and frustrate people, and that leads to violence."

Just as a scream caused a violent eruption in an auditorium, the violence in New Bedford had started with a trivial incident. The police arrested the black youth because his car had a defective tail-light. The city's problems did not start that night, however, Brooke said. "They started long before."

"Amen!" several persons in the high-school auditorium shouted.

One black woman could scarcely be heard. "They started 400 years ago," she said.

When Brooke spoke of the federal money that had poured into New Bedford, blacks shouted, "Where is it? Where did it go?"

Brooke said the federal government should look into the judicial system, as well as this matter. "If the law applies one way for whites, it has to apply the same way for blacks. . . . If a white boy is held 15 minutes [by the police] and then let go, and a black boy is kept four hours under the same circumstances, then something is wrong." At this point the audience in the auditorium burst into the loudest applause Brooke had heard during his visit.

Since the shooting and rioting something has been done about the simmering racial problem in the old coastal city, where unemployment, poverty and slum conditions keep the population of 105,100 on edge (this includes 2,000 Puerto Ricans and 10,000 blacks). The city council, meeting some of the demands of slum dwellers, installed lights in several playgrounds, provided small parks and included the West End in the Model Cities program.

On July 15 *The Boston Globe* editorialized: "The concessions to poverty-stricken blacks and Puerto Ricans which . . . Brooke has obtained from the city government in New Bedford are not the complete answer to the racism and frustration that took one life and injured more than a score . . . on five consecutive nights of disturbances. One man cannot in a day settle problems which had been aggravated by neglect for years."

Brooke had New Bedford in mind a month later when he filed legislation to treat high unemployment in communities as disaster areas eligible for special federal aid. It would use procedures offered by federal officials after floods, hurricanes and other natural disasters.

"Relief would be available immediately for communities which have been hardest hit by layoffs," Brooke said. Co-sponsoring the amendment were Senators Howard Baker of Tennessee and Joseph M. Montoya (Democrat of New Mexico).

Irked by the investigation of the misspent federal funds in New Bedford, Brooke early in 1971 asked the U.S. comptroller general for a new in-depth investigation. In a report to the comptroller three months earlier the federal regional council of New England ruled out malfeasance and deliberate misdirection of federal funds in New Bedford, but it questioned the effectiveness of federal programs in the city.

Brooke criticized the report because it depended on agency officials who investigated themselves. "It seems to me that neither the federal, state or local officials nor agencies which have been involved with these programs are really qualified to sit in objective judgment of the issues I raised."

The New Bedford matter, which has yet to come to a satisfactory solution, was a time-consuming interruption of a busy man's schedule, but Brooke was at least pleased with the resulting benefits for the poor and underprivileged residents.

CHAPTER NINETEEN

War and Weaponry

O N A COLD October day in 1970 the combined League of Women Voters of ten South Shore towns in Massachusetts sponsored a rally on the Scituate common. The league invited all candidates for local, state and federal offices to speak, allotting each three minutes. In the advance publicity, hoping to attract a big crowd, league members announced that Senator Brooke would make his first appearance in the Twelfth Congressional District to speak in behalf of Congressman Hastings Keith, who was running for reelection against an unknown but promising young Democrat, Gerry Studds, of Cohasset, a seacoast town adjacent to Scituate.

Snow flurries filled the air, and the unseasonably bitter cold held the crowd down to about 90 persons, more than half of whom were wearing Studds buttons. Most conspicuous of all, however, was an enormous stationary sign posted on the common about 50 feet from the speakers' platform. Its huge lettering read: "WELCOME SENATOR BROOKE: CITIZENS FOR STUDDS."

Keith spoke first. A league official rang a little bell when his three minutes were up, and he dutifully concluded. Then Brooke took the podium. After three minutes the bell rang. Brooke kept talking. A minute later there was another bing-bing, and still the Senator continued. Two or three minutes and two or three increasingly insistent bing-bings later, he finished endorsing Keith and left the microphone. It was Studds' turn.

He began quietly, chastising the lady with the bell for thinking that she—or any power on earth—could keep a U.S. senator from talking. Then, motioning toward the sign welcoming Brooke, Studds said. I think I can speak for most, if not all, our supporters in assuring you, Senator Brooke, of the genuineness of our welcome. You have our respect, and we are delighted to see you here. One question bothers us, however. Are you sure you are here on behalf of the right candidate? We ask this because on every major issue of this congressional campaign, you stand with us—and not with Mr. Keith.

"I suggest to you in all sincerity, Senator, that the wide respect in which you are held stems from the fact that you have had courage, again and again, to stand up and speak out against the leadership of your own party when your conscience so dictates.

"You and I support the McGovern-Hatfield amendment to extricate this nation from the tragedy of Vietnam. Mr. Keith and Mr. Nixon oppose it.

"You and I oppose further spending on the ABM [antiballistic missile] and the MIRV [multiple independently targetable reentry vehicle]. Mr. Keith and Mr. Nixon support it.

"You and I oppose the environmental and financial disaster which is the SST [supersonic transport]. Mr. Keith and Mr. Nixon support it.

"You and I have called again and again for a reordering of this nation's priorities—for a renewed focus here at home on housing, education and health—and to that end you voted to override Mr. Nixon's veto of the HEW [Health, Education and Welfare] appropriations. Mr. Keith voted to sustain it.

"And so, Senator, I reaffirm our respect for you and our welcome to you—but you will have to forgive me if I ask once more: Are you sure you've got the right candidate?"

Brooke, who can take a joke on himself, smiled wanly for the few reporters with him, thankful for the sparse attendance. Keith beat Studds by a scant vote after defeating State Senator William D. Weeks, son of former Secretary of Commerce Sinclair Weeks, in the Republican primary. In that same campaign, while working for Keith in New Bedford, Brooke had a more satisfying experience, as Weeks recalls:

"One day in the summer of 1970, I was campaigning in New Bedford during the congressional race, calling on Republican voters house to house with three of my campaign workers from that city. One worker, after ringing a doorbell, had a lapse when an elderly woman opened the door.

" 'Good afternoon, ma'am,' he said. 'Do you have a minute? I have Senator Brooke here to meet you.'

"Her face lit up in anticipation. Then, from across the street, another campaign worker shouted: 'Dan, it's not Senator Brooke. Tell her it's Senator *Weeks*.'

"The smile on the woman's face faded into a look of disappointment. She stood in the doorway for a few seconds, hesitant.

" 'I think I'll wait for Senator Brooke,' she said tartly. Then she slammed the door shut."

Weeks, who tells this story on himself, added: "I think this incident illustrates the strong attachment Brooke has for the average citizen, and, incidentally, the lack of concern this particular lady had for senators of lesser rank like me."

After his experience with Studds, Brooke may have recalled Christmas Eve in 1964, when, as attorney general, he had received a present from Louis Martin, then deputy national chairman of the Democratic party, hailing him as a "distinguished Democrat." Martin asked Brooke to send him a photograph and brief biography to be published in *Who's Who in the Democratic Party*.

"We are proud of the record you have made," Martin wrote, "and the national chairman joins me in good wishes."

Despite all evidence to the contrary, Brooke has never totally broken with the Nixon administration. He has generally, however, aligned himself with the so-called liberal-moderate-progressives within the GOP ranks.

In past years his wavering policies on Vietnam had come under fire, but by 1970 his ideas had coalesced. In May he predicted that no pro-Western government would ever be accepted in Asia, adding that the "best [U.S.] hope is for neutral governments in that part of the world." He said this in a televised interview with Representative Margaret Heckler (Republican of Wellesley, Massachusetts) and Senator Claiborne Pell (Democrat of Rhode Island). All criticized Nixon for denying Congress information on activities in Southeast Asia.

Congressman Heckler said she was shocked during a recent visit to Laos to see the extent of American involvement. "While President Nixon proclaims American troops are not involved, we are involved in extensive campaigns on the North Vietnamese supply routes through Laos. I fail to see the difference between a bomber pilot and a man on the ground with a rifle."

Brooke said those who condone U.S. activities in Cambodia "have endorsed the so-called domino theory in which the fall of one Southeast Asian nation to the Communists will lead to Communist domination of the entire area."

A few days later 20 members of PAX (Massachusetts Political Action for Peace) made personal pleas to Senators Brooke and Edward Kennedy to support a pending amendment that would cut off all funds to support U.S. military involvement in Southeast Asia. While Kennedy said he would support the measure, Brooke was undecided. He told the press he would not support the fund-cutting amendment, but was considering filing a resolution of his own that would call for removal of all troops from Cambodia and no more U.S. involvement in Southeast Asia without congressional approval. At this time he doubted that the amendment filed by Senator George McGovern and four other senators would win approval. "I want something more effective," he said. When pressed by the group to back this amendment, Brooke said: "I haven't made a judgment yet. You want to substitute your judgment for mine. I want to do what's right for the country."

He was stung when a Harvard student said: "You are notorious for being noncommittal." The student referred to a statement Brooke had made on the Cambodian invasion. Brooke then read a statement which expressed his opposition to the Cambodian venture.

"My life doesn't depend on whether I'm sitting here [in the Senate]," he said. "I just want to do what's right."

At this time Brooke was concerned about the powers Nixon had assumed in his role as commander in chief. "There are almost no checks and balances left. The Founding Fathers who wrote the powers of the President never would have foreseen what is happening in 1970."

A week later, becoming more specific, Brooke said the Senate proposal to bar future U.S. involvement in Cambodia by cutting off federal funds was drastic, but "one the Senate must take." He said the strikes against Cambodian sanctuaries were wrong. "I believe they are unwise and have served to undermine confidence in the President's commitment to continue deescalating the war. . . . I doubt that such operations will improve prospects for negotiation. I think the risks far outweigh any potential gains." Later, in Honolulu, when he addressed the state convention of the Hawaii Republican party, he said it was unreasonable to call Vietnam "Nixon's war," since he was withdrawing troops. As for Cambodia, "There is no doubt

350

that . . . Nixon believed and believes today that he made the right decision and that this will speed up the end to the war in Vietnam."

Late in May, 200 Harvard Medical School staff, students and faculty converged on Capitol Hill to lobby against the Indochina war. Critical of Brooke because of his silent stand on the end-the-war movement being debated in the Senate, about 50 members of this group confronted his aides and criticized Brooke's lack of commitment and equivocation over the McGovern-Hatfield amendment to end the war. Learning that Brooke was away on vacation, the group, who tried to meet him for a week, was further ired.

For two hours Alton Frye, Brooke's administrative assistant, Hardy Nathan and Roger Woodworth tried to convince the delegation that Brooke's silence on the amendment was "calculated."

"If he was really committed, he wouldn't be acting the way he is," fumed Dr. Channing Washburn, a psychiatrist. "He's got a lot of respect in this country. Why doesn't he use it to speak out loudly on the major issues?"

"If he were in the posture of shouting the loudest on all the major issues, he could not defeat a Carswell," Woodworth said, adding that while Brooke supported a cutoff for funding the Indochina war, he was far more concerned with finding a date which a majority of the Senate would support than with taking a posture himself. As with Haynsworth and Carswell, timing was important. He wanted to bring along other votes with his own.

In June the Senate defeated the antiwar amendment, as leading GOP senators backed Nixon. Senator Smith said the setting of a withdrawal date was a matter for the President to fix, not Congress, and Senator William Saxbe said some of the proposed measures were "attempting a vote of no confidence in the President." Senator John C. Stennis, Senate Armed Services Committee chairman, agreed that setting a deadline by congressional fiat would "impair the effectiveness of the President around the world."

Late in August Brooke threw his support to the losing Hatfield-McGovern amendment to end the war in Vietnam, while commending Nixon for "an historic beginning" of disengagement from the war, noting that costs and casualties had been reduced and that thousands of troops had been withdrawn. "However, the time has come to reinforce the President's commendable new directions by lending congressional sanction to a responsible program for turning the burdens of this conflict back to the Vietnamese people."

During the summer of 1970 Brooke was besieged by Massachusetts pressure groups who cut into his time. John R. Wheatley, former district attorney of Plymouth County, recalls a visit that summer with a group of church people concerned over Vietnam. He was the only Republican in the delegation.

"We were told we couldn't see Senator Kennedy because he was too busy, but the group felt they didn't want to bother with him anyway. We met three congressmen, and at the last minute were told that Brooke would see us. He gave us a half-hour. Nobody in our party except me had ever met him, and when we came out, all were talking favorably that they had been impressed. Brooke told us how painful it was for him to oppose the President, giving his reasons for it. The climax came in the afternoon when we were leaving for home, and the vote on the Cooper-Church amendment was in the paper. Both Brooke and Kennedy had voted for it."*

Brooke split with the administration on the antiballistics program and the multiple independently targeted reentry vehicle (MIRV) deployment. The split can be better understood against the backdrop of the Strategic Arms Limitations Talks (SALT).

In May 1970, in an open letter to *Pravda,* Brooke proposed that the Soviet Union agree to "a modest degree" of on-site inspection that would greatly facilitate progress at the SALT sessions. The response was silence by *Pravda* and a private reply that Moscow had agreed with Washington to avoid discussing SALT in the press.

"In the spirit of honest exchange on this complicated problem," Brooke had written, he hoped mutual agreement on on-site inspection in the U.S. and USSR could forestall the use of MIRV systems. Brooke said it might be possible "to determine whether a missile has one warhead or several by employing suitable instruments which do not require that the missile be opened or disassembled."

One urgent imperative in 1969 for Nixon was to win congressional approval of the new-style Safeguard antimissile missile or antiballistic missile (ABM) to defend against a possible Soviet strike. This defense system had to pass the Democratic Congress as part of Nixon's larger plan to negotiate with the Soviet on nuclear arms control from a position of strength. On March 14 Nixon said the ABM program

---

* The Cooper-Church amendment to bar future use of American troops in Cambodia created a logjam that forced a lame-duck session of Congress. Otherwise, Nixon felt the Cambodian operation was successful enough to be a political asset.

(Safeguard) was vital for U.S. security, since it was intended to protect the nation against a preemptive Soviet strike aimed at paralyzing land-based Minuteman intercontinental ballistic missiles and B-52 bomber bases. Nixon knew he was in for the toughest legislative fight of the year.

Moving to bolster his position, he went after Senator Margaret Chase Smith's vote. "Maggie," the Maine senator, was unpredictable and could be irascible. Even though Nixon knew that Senator George Aiken of Vermont was an opponent of ABM, in an incredibly bumbling move the President asked Aiken to talk Senator Smith into voting for the amendment. Aiken's effort cemented Mrs. Smith's resolve to introduce her own measure to cripple the bill, just as Bryce Harlow, Nixon's congressional adviser, knew it would.

The Senate rejected Smith's amendment to block spending any funds at all on Safeguard. Then it rejected 51 to 47 the Cooper-Hart amendment, which barred expansion of two new ABM sites in Missouri. (There were already ABM deployment sites in Montana and North Dakota.) Moments before the votes were taken on the Cooper-Hart amendment Senator Henry Jackson (Democrat of Washington) walked down the aisles holding a slip of paper labeled "Top Secret" before several colleagues. It was a letter from Gerard C. Smith, chief U.S. negotiator at the SALT conference, defending the ABM as a valuable bargaining tool. Senator Thomas McIntyre, the New Hampshire Democrat who surprised his colleagues by voting against the Cooper-Hart measure, said he did so because of a telephone conversation he had had with Smith which convinced him that the Cooper-Hart amendment limited Safeguard too much to provide the bargaining chip needed to induce the Soviet to limit arms. On the basis of this conversation he felt that an amendment made by Brooke, following the defeat of the Cooper-Hart proposal, would give U.S. negotiators the bargaining chip they needed, since beefing up defense at the two sites would provide more protection against a Soviet take-out strike.

"If the Cooper-Hart amendment fails," Brooke said, "I think we will have a good chance."

Safeguard opponents backed him. His amendment would give the administration its requested 1.3 billion dollars, but would limit the money to the two existing sites.

Brooke hoped to keep the 47 votes for the Cooper-Hart amendment and add three more for a majority.

But Stennis, the Safeguard floor manager, said the anti-ABM bloc had peaked, and Senator Jackson agreed that Brooke's amendment would fail. Most senators knew it was the only chance to block ABM expansion.

"The build-up of Soviet SS-9s and SS-11s has shocked a lot of our colleagues," Jackson said.

The full Senate voted down Brooke's limiting amendment 53 to 44.

Brooke, as he had predicted, had added three votes, including McIntyre's, but Nixon forces, led by Stennis and Defense Secretary Melvin Laird, persuaded four pro-Cooper-Hart adherents to switch to their side, including Margaret Chase Smith and Charles Percy.

"It was a surprise about Ellender and Randolph," Brooke said after the vote. "That was the ball game right there." Both were Southern Democrats.

Perhaps the decisive moment came in the closing minutes of debate when Stennis read a letter from Laird condemning Brooke's amendment: "The Department of Defense cannot support and is opposed to the Brooke amendment. It is the view of the department that adoption of the amendment would both increase the cost and reduce the effectiveness of the Safeguard defense of the Minuteman [offensive missile]."

Brooke admitted it was hard to assess the impact of Laird's letter on uncommitted senators. "But it had some effect and in a close race that could make the difference." Brooke said he would continue to fight to curb further ABM deployment. "I am very hopeful we can stop this insane arms race with the Soviet Union."

He was more vocal and active in the MIRV controversy.

In October 1969 Brooke called for a missile-test ban, saying the future security of mankind was at stake.

"MIRV threatens to erode one of the basic barriers to nuclear war, namely, the utter certainty that neither the Soviets nor the Americans could carry out a nuclear attack without suffering devastating retaliation. But when a single missile becomes capable of destroying several other missiles, nuclear war may become more likely."

Two months later Nixon wrote Brooke a letter saying the administration had decided not to fund development of MIRV systems that would have the accuracy or power to destroy an enemy's missiles. This information was intended to pacify Soviet delegates at the SALT talks underway in Vienna. Soviet delegates had charged that the U.S. was trying to gain strategic superiority over Russia through developing and deploying multiple-warhead missiles, and thereby ruin any chance for agreements on nuclear arms. Russia's major fear was that U.S. multiple-warhead weapons could knock out Soviet missile sites and thus allow the U.S. to attack without fear of nuclear retaliation.

Administration spokesmen said the MIRVs scheduled to be deployed in June 1970 were relatively small and would be effective only against Soviet cities. The Nixon letter made it clear that the U.S. was not developing MIRVs that could take out missile silos.

"There is no current U.S. program," Nixon wrote Brooke, "to develop a so-called hard-target MIRV capability."

Brooke argued that deployment of MIRV warheads designed to overwhelm an ABM defense would create "insurmountable problems for inspection of an arms-control agreement," adding that if MIRV were not controlled prior to deployment, it would probably never be controlled. "Once testing of these provocative systems is completed, it will be unlikely that either side will believe the other is not deploying them." An agreement to suspend tests of MIRV could "buy time" for agreement on mutual limitation of ABM deployment. In March 1970 Brooke proposed a two-year freeze on nuclear strategic weaponry of the U.S. and the Soviet. An arms moratorium at the start of resumption of SALT talks the following month in Vienna, which the U.S. should propose as the first order of business, would, Brooke said, "buy time for a durable strategic equilibrium." He warned that SALT presented an opportunity that might not come again "to promote the security of mankind." He said his suggestion of a freeze was not grounded on a naïve concept of Soviet goodwill, "but on a hardheaded calculation of our two countries' mutual interest . . . where both sides have a credible deterrent." A few days later he told the Foreign Relations Subcommittee on Arms Control that MIRV was "utterly unnecessary. Given the existing balance of forces, no responsible official would argue that MIRV is required." Brooke was testifying in support of his resolution calling for a mutual moratorium of MIRV testing between the U.S. and Russia pending the outcome of the SALT talks. Air Force Secretary Robert Seamans had testified the week before that the MIRV system would be deployed in June 1970. The Pentagon later called this testimony "a slip-up" which was not intended to be made public.

Dr. Marshall D. Shulman, director of the Russian Institute at Columbia University, backed Brooke, saying the U.S. and Russia were roughly on a par with each other in terms of their arsenals and that deployment of MIRV would upset this delicate balance.

In a Senate speech in April Brooke praised Nixon for his restraint.

"This single contribution to mutual security should be reassuring to the Soviet Union. The Soviet leaders can be confident that their forces are not in imminent danger from the relatively crude American MIRV systems which are being developed. They should also find assurance in the knowledge that any specific development program to produce a true hard-target capability in the U.S. MIRV systems would take years and would be highly visible through the elaborate test programs required, not to mention the congressional and public reviews which such a proposal would arouse."

He added that it would help SALT negotiations "if the Soviets were equally prepared to provide credible assurances that the SS-9 and other Soviet weaponry were not being refined for possible use against U.S. missile sites."

Late in July Brooke offered legislation that would make the MIRV weapon more flexible in the event that an agreement on eliminating MIRV weaponry were reached at the SALT sessions. His proposals would also limit the accuracy of MIRV weapons to make it clear they were not designed to wipe out Soviet capacity to retaliate and give the appearance that the U.S. was trying to gain a first-strike capability against Russia. Brooke spoke as a member of the Armed Services Committee.

MIRV weapons had already been installed in some Minuteman III intercontinental missiles and later were installed in 1971 in nuclear submarines in the form of the Poseidon missile.

Brooke's first amendment asked the Pentagon to develop a single warhead for both the Poseidon and Minuteman III missiles so that, if an agreement were reached at the SALT talks, it would not result in a "de facto reduction in U.S. strategic forces."

Elimination of MIRV weapons would mean the refitting of the submarines and taking them off station in the oceans of the world, and would make some Minuteman III missiles ineffective while they were being converted to meet the terms of a SALT agreement.

Brooke's second proposal delineated the limits of accuracy of the MIRV weapon. It would limit them to fields and accuracies no greater than one-third the level considered necessary for a single warhead to neutralize a Soviet missile in a hardened missile silo. Brooke's proposal would also prohibit operational development.

Brooke broke even in getting the Senate to agree with his views on the MIRV program. By a voice vote the Senate adopted his proposal authorizing the Defense Department to proceed with the development of a single nuclear warhead system in the event the SALT talks with Russia banned multiple weaponry. Initially Brooke's amendment to the pending 19.2-million-dollar military-procurement bill would have ordered the Defense Department to follow this course. But the word "directed" was substituted by "authorized" and made it more acceptable to more senators. Then, with the votes stacked against him, and after Senator Stennis promised to hold hearings on his second amendment, he withdrew it. This measure was designed to implement the administration's policy to refrain from a "hard-target" MIRV capability.

"We just didn't have the votes for it," Brooke said, "and I felt if it was defeated, it might be interpreted as a commitment by the Senate to a first-strike offensive capability to the SALT talks."

Laird explained his "procedural objection" to Brooke's "hard-target" amendment as setting a precedent of congressional preemption in fixing the "general characteristics of U.S. military systems." Brooke countered that "Congressman Laird would never have agreed with Secretary [of Defense] Laird," noting that during his many years in the House Laird had "repeatedly and vigorously fought for an affirmative congressional" role in determining national strategic policy and defining weapons systems. Brooke reeled off several Laird-initiated steps in that direction.

Brooke also rapped Agnew for saying the danger of halting MIRV testing might inadvertently aid Russia by reviving interest. Agnew had accused Senator Edmund Muskie of Maine of confused thinking for supporting the unilateral test ban and angered senators who resented "the manner and source of criticism."

In December 1970 Brooke, dead set against the supersonic transport (SST), a new high-speed concept in commercial aviation to be built by Boeing Company under heavy federal subsidy, said that if the Senate voted funds for the project, he would consider voting against the appropriation. It was Secretary of Transportation Volpe who had sold Nixon on the idea of this plane: "Mr. President, how would you like to go to Dulles Airport and see Americans traveling to Europe on an SST with the words 'fabriqué en France'* stamped on it?" Volpe had a point. In December 1971 when Nixon conferred for two days in the Azores with President Pompidou of France, the latter flew in from Paris on a Concorde, the French-British version of the SST, and though the distance from Washington to the Azores is only slightly longer than from Paris, it took the President more

---

* French for "made in France."

than twice the time to get there in his 707 jet, *Air Force One*. And, as *The Boston Herald* pointed out, an American-built SST would not only create jobs, produce revenue and help keep U.S. leadership in the aerospace technology, but "would also bring in billions of dollars' worth of export income in the years ahead, helping to ease our chronic balance-of-payments problem."

In this case Brooke expressed several concerns: he did not believe the government should commit itself to funding private enterprise, and he was deeply impressed by the arguments of environmentalists against the plane. "Considering the massive funding and the development entailed and the danger it brings to the environment, it is simply not worth it," he said, adding that the development of the SST would not decrease unemployment in Massachusetts.

For Nixon the vote on SST came at the wrong time—late in March, during the unpopular Laos operation. When a Democratic supporter of the SST chided Volpe about the number of Republicans who opposed the project, he said: "They weren't voting against SST. They were voting against John Ehrlichman and his German Mafia in the White House." The President's two advisers are often arrogant in interpersonal relations. Haldeman, Nixon's confidant and constant attendant, has been called "a hostile, aggressive, suspicious, crew-cutted oenologist," and except for the word "oenologist" (one who makes or studies wine), Ehrlichman fits the description.

In May 1971 *The Boston Herald Traveler* ran an editorial titled "Salt Yields Sweet Fruit." It said that for more than 18 months the U.S. and the Soviet Union had discussed the limitation of strategic nuclear arms. On May 20 Moscow and Washington simultaneously announced that they had agreed to talk about the offensive and defensive missiles. "This," the paper said, "in the slow and circumspect process of diplomacy, is regarded as a milestone." Nixon hoped the agreement would be "remembered as the beginning of a new era in which all nations may devote more of their energies not to war, but to the works of peace." Until this agreement, Russia had insisted that the first round of SALT achievements, if any, be restricted to limiting defensive weapons, including the ABM. Soviet delegates finally accepted the argument that offensive and defensive weapons are interrelated. "Thus the talks could continue with the aim of limiting both Russian and U.S. antiballistic systems, along with some offensive weapons."

Just how sweet was the fruit? On December 27 Senator Edmund S. Muskie was quoted as saying that the SALT talks were a "story of unfulfilled promise." Muskie also recalled that Nixon, after vetoing a bill for child care on grounds that the one-billion-dollar cost was irresponsible, then persuaded Congress to spend that much for the ABM and MIRV programs in a single year.

It was a memorable day in April 1970 when both Massachusetts senators, who have often clashed with Nixon, wound up on the Senate floor to praise the President for making decisions and taking actions which they approved.

Brooke praised the President for deciding against perfecting MIRVs to such an extent they could zero in on Soviet missile silos, and on the same day Kennedy, a proponent of draft reform and ending draft deferments, told the Senate he thought Nixon's decision to end occupational and farm deferments was "splendid . . . and courageous."

Brooke and Kennedy were on opposite sides of the fence on the draft issue. In August 1970 a measure at issue was an amendment to the military authorization bill that would have paved the way for a volunteer army, which Brooke favors, by substantially increasing salaries of servicemen. Although Nixon favored a volunteer army, the White House opposed the "end the draft" amendment because of the dwindling but still large forces in Southeast Asia and elsewhere, and because the cost could run up to four billion dollars a year. The military-pay-raise rider lost by a vote of 52 to 35, but even if it had been adopted, military conscription would have continued until the Selective Service Act expired in 1971.

"The ephemeral alliances revealed by the Senate's roll-call vote [on the amendment] . . . were almost preposterous," a newspaper reported. " . . . The Republican and Democratic floor leaders voted for the amendment. The Republican and Democratic Whips voted against it. Senator [Edward] Kennedy voted with Senator Tower and against McGovern and Brooke."

After the 1971 expiration date, the draft, with modifications, was extended for two years, with Kennedy voting with the administration throughout the debate, while Brooke joined the liberal Democrats' efforts to end the draft. Brooke argued that the draft is inherently unfair to the poor and minority groups. He voted for amendments that would prohibit assignment of draftees to combat areas; provide enlistment and reenlistment bonuses and a measure to end the draft by July 1, 1971, while increasing pay for military personnel.

Kennedy, since 1966, while working for draft reform, was against an all-volunteer army, arguing that "an all-volunteer army would lead

359

to an all-black army, and this is totally unacceptable."* Such an army he felt, would be a ghetto army manned mostly by minorities and the poor. He preferred a reformed draft with no deferments as the only fair way to equalize risks. Another person who took a dim view of an all-volunteer army was Representative F. Edward Hebert, chairman of the House Armed Services Committee, who said: "I think the only way to get an all-volunteer army is to draft it."

Kennedy's major achievement was the passage of amendments that put a 150,000-man annual ceiling on the draft call and required congressional approval of any presidential attempt to raise this ceiling. When he visited a veterans' encampment in Washington, he was booed when he began explaining his support for a draft and his opposition to a volunteer army. Then he drew applause when he said the administration was willing to offer bonuses for combat enlistees, adding that the volunteer army would set the stage for the poor and black to fight rich men's wars. His confidence that a voluntary-army concept will ultimately prevail took a step forward in mid-November, 1971, when new military pay rates brought U.S. Army pay in line with that of business and industry. Under the new scales, newly enlisted soldiers will receive $268.50 a month, or double what they got under the former bill. Thus the U.S. Army became a more attractive career choice, considering the free medical and dental care and retirement benefits. At the same time the Army offered a chance for volunteers to choose a variety of technical schools and to enlist to serve in Europe, the Far East, Panama, Alaska or Hawaii.

Brooke sees a volunteer army in the future. As Cervantes said, "Patience, and shuffle the cards."

Brooke has pointed out that the draft could be reduced if civilians filled more jobs at military bases. This came to his attention in 1969, when Daniel J. Kearney, a national vice-president of the American Federation of Government Employes, asked him to do something about "the number of military people who are flying a mahogany desk." Brooke discovered, for example, that most of the officers at Hanscom Air Force Base in Massachusetts, although inexperienced in procurement, were assigned strictly to keep military personnel in civilian jobs. "Why spend money to train them when the job is temporary?" Brooke asked.

The change may come. Meanwhile, "Patience, and shuffle the cards."

---

* Kennedy said this in a speech at Northwestern University early in 1967.

CHAPTER TWENTY

Nixon, Agnew and Brooke

PRESIDENT NIXON has often rapped the northeastern part of the U.S. as well as intellectuals, and Vice-President Agnew, whose rhetoric has made him the most controversial and acerbic wordsmith in the nation since the late Harold Ickes called Wendell Willkie the "barefoot boy from Wall Street" and allegedly damaged Tom Dewey's candidacy by remarking that he looked "like the little man on top of the wedding cake,"* prefaced his invective by speaking of "a spirit of national masochism encouraged by an effete corps of impudent snobs who characterize themselves as intellectuals." Agnew wrote this himself, without help from Pat Buchanan or other speech writers. This blast against Vietnam war protesters came between the two massive antiwar demonstrations in Washington in October and November 1969. The only decent sections of the U.S., according to Nixon, were the South and the West. His pet hate is Massachusetts, as Mary McGrory noted in 1971: "The White House long since decided that Massachusetts is another country, not worth fighting for." Nixon dumped the Bay State without dumping its junior senator, even though he has frequently been a burr under his saddle.

Brooke, considering himself a "creative moderate" who is a "liberal in civil rights and a conservative in fiscal matters," has scored Nixon on the domestic front for not pushing his "black enterprise, piece of the action" proposals, part of his 1968 campaign pledge

---

* Ickes borrowed this insult from Alice Roosevelt Longworth.

361

when he promised a scheme of government subsidies and loans for black businessmen. Brooke also criticized Nixon for failing to establish a meaningful rapport with the black community. "He has not even made a significant attempt."

The relationship between Nixon and Brooke highlights the meaninglessness of political semantics. By mid-1971 the President was calling Brooke a "reasonable moderate." At the White House, even in the conservative Haldeman Ehrlichman wing, Brooke is highly respected as a reasonable moderate. Known as the "Germans," John Ehrlichman and H. R. Haldeman are close advisers of the President who cavalierly and sometimes arrogantly treat even their superiors with scorn. Top officials such as Dr. Arthur Burns have to fight their way past Haldeman's Oval Office guard, sometimes called the Berlin Wall. Thus praise from the "Germans" is praise from Caesar.

Broder and Hess in *The Republican Establishment* give an accurate assessment of Brooke as a conservative, not a reactionary. He is "a man who moves with deliberate caution, weighing all the evidence and alternatives carefully, and putting great emphasis on working through duly constituted authorities. This is not a sudden adjustment to political expediency but a deeply ingrained attitude that goes back to childhood."

Nixon's esteem for Brooke is remarkable in light of the President's reputation for being vindictive and hard, "bordering on meanness." Stories have leaked out of the inner sanctum of the White House about his passionate outbursts against his two big hates: liberal Republicans who don't support him and the communications media. He has been heard to say, "Screw the press!" Why is he so tolerant toward Brooke? Despite several abrasions, Nixon, according to Senator Javits, "has always been intrigued by Brooke."

The record shows that Nixon's most humiliating failure was the Carswell setback. When Senator Charles Mathias told him personally that he opposed Carswell, Nixon said he understood, but his assurance that there would be no hard feelings was a sham. When Brooke said the same thing, Nixon said, "That's all right, Ed. We can still make a lot of good medicine together."

According to a recent biography of the President, Nixon puts Mathias and Brooke in separate categories of liberal Republicans. "He felt that Brooke, John Sherman Cooper, Senator George Aiken of Vermont and Senator Jacob Javits of New York were genuine in their liberalism and opposed him . . . only out of conviction and never out of malice." Nixon ranked Mathias, on the other hand, with

Senators Charles Percy, Charles Goodell, Mark Hatfield, "and, most of the time, Hugh Scott of Pennsylvania, as Republicans who took liberal positions and attacked him personally only for personal political gain." Outwardly polite and pleasant with these men, whom he calls "phony liberals," Nixon reviles them bluntly in his White House inner sanctum. An aide said he was amazed "at the intensity of his feeling against the liberal Republicans." Only newsmen who criticized him were more harshly denounced.

According to a Washington reporter, "Brooke's ability to count heads and to lobby undecided senators impressed the White House." In any case, in recent years Nixon has often invited Brooke to the White House for talks. He told Brooke about the procedural breakthrough in the SALT talks with Russia a week before he told congressional leaders. On May 14, 1970, Nixon called Brooke in to discuss foreign affairs with Henry A. Kissinger, the President's national security adviser. "Such private meetings, exclusive of senators in formal leadership positions, are unusual in this White House," according to *The Boston Globe*.

Nixon is aware of Brooke's interest in foreign affairs as a result of his frequent fact-finding missions abroad. Early in 1971, when there were rumors that Brooke might shun reelection to take a Cabinet post or to be Nixon's running mate, there was speculation that if William Rogers went to the Supreme Court, Brooke might become Secretary of State, a post he likes. When Elliot Richardson left his job as attorney general to become Undersecretary of State, Brooke told him it was the kind of post he would welcome.

Early in 1971 there was another report that Brooke had agreed to help get part of Nixon's program through the Senate in exchange for a guarantee that Boston would keep its shipyard. According to one source, Brooke promised to recruit support for Nixon's revenue-sharing plan and the welfare-reform package when they were introduced.

When in November 1970 Brooke learned that a shutdown of the Boston Naval Shipyard (in Charlestown) was being considered as part of a Navy cutback in shore installations, he conferred with Nixon at the White House, part of an unpublicized campaign he waged at the Pentagon and the White House. Republican senators knew Brooke was having remarkable success in getting to see the President. One administrative spokesman thought "Brooke and the President would move closer together" over the following two years.

Brooke, before their personal meeting, had written Nixon that simple geography argued for the maintenance of the Boston shipyard, noting Boston's proximity to the home port of the Narragansett destroyer force at Newport, Rhode Island, and to the Mediterranean fleet. The maintenance and repair work, he said, "should logically and logistically fall to Boston." He cited the "valuable backstop" of the electronic industry in Massachusetts in view of the high technology aspect of Navy ships. During months of parleying, Brooke also talked to Navy Secretary John Chafee and Assistant Defense Secretary David Packard. Brooke is credited with preventing a shutdown of the shipyard.

In disagreeing with Nixon, Brooke has taken pains not to wound his ego or to antagonize him to the extent of being considered another Charles Goodell, for whom he campaigned in 1970 when he came to New York City to seek support from the city's large black and Puerto Rican electorate. In urging his election, Brooke called Goodell, who had been named senator to fill the vacancy caused by the death of Robert Kennedy, "a modern, progressive, creative Republican."

In September 1969 Goodell had proposed a December 31, 1970, cutoff date for withdrawal of all U.S. troops from Vietnam, and he and Senator George McGovern were the only two senators to address the November (1969) antiwar rally sponsored by far-left organizations. Goodell was also one of the first Republicans to attack Spiro Agnew publicly in 1969. The Vice-President dubbed him a "radical liberal" (later shortened to "radilib") and later vulgarly called him "a political Christine Jorgensen," an analogy between his sudden conversion from conservatism to liberalism, and the sexual transformation of a male nurse into the female Christine Jorgensen as a result of an operation. In private, Nixon blasted Goodell more bitterly than he did any other liberal Republican and marked him for political extinction. Agnew's attack on Goodell helped elect the Conservative party candidate James Buckley, whom the administration favored.

Early in 1971, when Brooke supporters were worried about the conservative GOP threat in Massachusetts to Brooke's otherwise safe second-term run in 1972, they breathed easier when Nixon told Brooke "that the unmaking of a radical liberal" would not be repeated in the Bay State. Nixon further blunted the conservative move when he denied financial aid to the coming campaign.

There has been an uneasy truce between Brooke and Agnew. Brooke had denounced Agnew for his "intemperate statements," which, he said, "embarrassed the party and the administration," and chided the Vice-President for his off-year election crusade against radical liberals within both the Democratic party and the GOP. In

1971 Brooke toned down his criticism. "I've known . . . Agnew for a long time. We were both active in the draft-Rockefeller movement in 1968." In the Nixon-Agnew-Brooke troika, it is at times difficult to identify the relationships.

Nevertheless, Brooke warned Nixon's advisers that they would court disaster in 1972 if Agnew repeated his 1970 campaign tactics. In a private talk at an unpublicized White House session with Attorney General Mitchell, other top Nixon strategists, and GOP senators facing election in 1972, Brooke said the GOP lost the congressional elections in 1970 when Agnew was manning the torpedos. Republicans lost the midterm congressional elections because Nixon himself "talked and acted as though he were running for sheriff, not as the great leader of an underdog party." Also, because there was no coordinated campaign by the GOP in 1970. Nixon and White House spokesmen had feebly tried to convince the voting public that their tactics reaped dividends, which was contrary to fact.

Although invitations to this cocktail-dinner meeting were in Nixon's name, he was absent—detained, an adviser said, by a "national security matter." It would be interesting speculation to picture Nixon sitting in this closed session, reacting to Brooke's charge that Agnew's attack on television networks was "negative politics," since Nixon had said that Agnew by his "Media Speech," as it came to be known, had "rendered a public service." The President had approved the speech, which Agnew gave on November 13, 1970, in Des Moines, Iowa, at the Midwest Republican Conference.

The Vice-President blasted network commentators who had "expressed, in one way or another, their hostility" to Nixon's November 3 Vietnam address in their brief commentaries immediately following it. Naming only NBC's David Brinkley, Agnew attacked network anchor men for having "made their minds up in advance" about Nixon's hard-line speech, adding that network newsmen by "a raised eyebrow, an inflection of the voice, a caustic remark dropped in the middle of a broadcast can raise doubts in a million minds about the veracity of a public official or the wisdom of a government policy." Thus did the giant networks and their commentators join the élite and "effete corps of impudent snobs." Lashing out against television networks to Brooke was lost political mileage.

The interrelationship among Nixon, Agnew and Brooke and the Massachusetts GOP power structure was highlighted on March 18, 1971, when Brooke, aware of the political risks involved, escorted Agnew to Boston, where Governor Francis Sargent met them at

365

Logan Airport. By this time Agnew's stock had sunk to its lowest, the decline setting in after his Christine Jorgensen slur. Inside the White House, braintrusters felt Agnew had to be dumped if Nixon was to be reelected. The Vice-President didn't pick up any points in his clumsy world-girdling trip climaxed by his blast at American black leaders delivered in the heart of black Africa. He also "collided head-on with Nixon's most spectacular foreign-policy initiative: a move to break a generation of total estrangement between the U.S. and the People's Republic of China."

The Middlesex Club is staid and starchily conservative. In advance billing, Agnew told the press his talk to members would be "perhaps the most important speech I will make as Vice-President." Without consulting Nixon, Mitchell or any White House strategist except Patrick Buchanan, a former editorial writer for *The St. Louis Globe Democrat* before becoming a Nixon speech writer in 1965, Agnew made another full-scale attack on the national media, and on CBS in particular. Sargent later said he was sorry he welcomed the Vice-President at the airport, and Brooke, "who must run again in 1972," Mary McGrory reported, "flew up with Agnew and he is sorry, too." She said the Vice-President "brought consternation to the Bay State" and "provoked the largest post-Laos demonstration yet recorded and inspired a teach-in which turned into a 'dump Nixon' rally."

The President, according to Evans and Novak, had "carved a role for Agnew as the avenging angel of the silent majority to deal out awful retribution to establishment power centered in the East which was, to Nixon and Agnew, aloof and remote, absorbed in its own self-interest and prepared to foist its will on provincial America." Agnew earned his pay as Nixon's most trusted errand boy. "He was the messenger sent to the door to tell the press that the Laos invasion is not ending in a rout for the South Vietnamese," *The Boston Globe* reported. The Laotian operation, still in progress when Agnew addressed the Middlesex Club, had been planned to cut off the Ho Chi Minh Trail to buy more time for safe withdrawal of American troops by cutting off supplies needed for an attack on South Vietnam. Laos turned into a political debacle for Nixon when South Vietnamese troops, fleeing under heavy enemy fire, in their panic mobbed American rescue helicopters, clinging onto helicopter skids for a ride home. At the Middlesex Club Agnew said Laos bought time for Nixon and mentioned "an orderly, planned strategic withdrawal."

As Agnew talked, Brooke squirmed, for as a persistent critic of

Nixon's war policy he not only opposed the Laotian and Cambodian invasions, but also urged a total withdrawal of U.S. forces from Southeast Asia by the end of 1971. In the spring of that year he repeated his support of the McGovern-Hatfield amendment, but later tempered his criticism in support of the phased-withdrawal plan after Nixon personally pledged to him that all ground combat forces would be out of Vietnam by mid-1972. Nixon had told Brooke earlier that he and other GOP liberals wouldn't be hurt by the war in the 1972 elections.

The writer asked Brooke why he so often voted the same as Ted Kennedy: "My surname begins with B, his with K; he knows how I vote, but I don't know how he is going to vote," he said, grinning. He wasn't embarrassed in voting with Kennedy on the McGovern-Hatfield amendment, since Massachusetts is the most dovish state in the Union, nor was he overtly embarrassed about his friendship with Agnew, who, a month before flying to Boston, had made it clear that he would not back a conservative challenge to Brooke, whom, in Boston, he called "a friend," gratuitously adding that the Senator was no radical liberal. Six months later he piled on praise: "I think there could be a black Vice-President. I think that Senator Edward Brooke of Massachusetts, for example, could be elected Vice-President."* It was obvious at the Middlesex Club, however, that Agnew, who charmed the stuffed shirts, was a strange political bedfellow. While he was indicting CBS for producing *The Selling of the Pentagon,* an anti-administrative documentary, down the corridor the liberal Republican Ripon Society was holding a teach-in applauding "the escalated threats of Representative Paul McCloskey [Republican of California] to run against the President in the primaries." Later, at the Republican Governors' Conference, Agnew said: " 'Pete' McCloskey is in such a money bind that he's been forced to auction off his personal art collection. Yesterday he sold his favorite painting— *Benedict Arnold Crossing the Delaware.*"

"There are so many other problems," Brooke said after Agnew's speech. The light did not shine on the Senator that night, nor did it shine on the other members of the GOP Big Four: Sargent, Volpe, and Richardson, all liberals. It was easy to believe that Agnew's 22-hour

---

* Shirley Chisholm, the black New York congresswoman who is running for President, was discussing her candidacy with Representative Edward Koch, a Democrat, who asked if she would consider him as a running mate if she got the nomination. "No, Ed," she said. "I don't think the country is ready for a Jewish Vice-President."

visit to Boston was his last as well as his first as Vice-President. While Brooke and Sargent were glad when he left, it was not in the sense that Mary McCrory noted in her assessment of the Boston fiasco: "It is unlikely that the groans of Brooke and Sargent will penetrate the White House walls, inside which the 'dump Agnew' talk is firmly put down." Mary was misreading the tea leaves.

Neither Brooke nor Sargent was interested in pushing a falling fence. Neither disputes a place for Agnew on the 1972 ticket, and will have nothing to do with a "dump Agnew" movement, even to the displeasure of the Ripon Society, which endorsed Brooke. Indeed, after the Middlesex caper, Brooke was shocked to hear the Vice-President say he might not be on the ticket in 1972, "because it never occurred to me that Vice-President Agnew would not be Nixon's running mate." Brooke said this on WEEI's *Bay State Forum*. "Now, whether this was just one of those statements, I don't know. . . . Every presidential team, after the first term, has the same speculation." On Agnew's criticism of the media Brooke was at his diplomatic best: "The media has a responsibility . . . to ferret out wrong in government and in the private sector as well. They've done it . . . and I certainly hope there will be no change in this policy or in this procedure."

Massachusetts was one of several states where Agnew was *persona non grata* during the 1970 campaign, when his only New England appearance was a fund-raising banquet in Hartford, Connecticut. Governor Sargent asked him to stay out of his 1970 gubernatorial campaign. Although Sargent said nothing after Agnew's Boston speech, in November he said: "I won't be part of any dump-Agnew movement. I haven't even heard of any talk of a dump-Agnew movement."

If Brooke came away from the Middlesex Club banquet shaking his head, he couldn't be blamed. The same GOP audience that loudly applauded Agnew gave him "the coolest of receptions one could expect from a GOP crowd."

This showed how far out of touch Republican regulars were with Bay State voters, for Brooke's popularity had not waned appreciably, if at all, since the summer of 1970, when a Massachusetts poll showed him to be the most popular politician in the state. He topped the list with a whopping 84 percent of the public favorable toward him and only seven percent unfavorable. Governor Sargent, with a 77 percent favorability rating, was runner-up, followed by Mayor Kevin White of Boston (75 percent) and Senator Edward Kennedy (22 percent).

Only Kennedy had a large negative vote. His popularity waned after July 18, 1969, when Miss Mary Jo Kopechne drowned at Chappaquiddick Island, Massachusetts, after a car driven by Kennedy went off a bridge. The tragedy was probably a factor in his defeat for reelection as Majority Whip in 1971.

Brooke's popularity was not limited to Bay State constituents. In the world's most exclusive club the only Negro member is one of the most popular senators not only because he can be counted on to be affable, equable, logical and willing to admit politics is the art of the possible, but also because his speeches are usually meaty and interesting. He can put on a good show.

As an action man, he has complained of the dilatory tactics used in the Senate chamber. For one thing, he objects to tedious eulogies of retiring colleagues. "It seems to me that anything we could say here could be said in two or three minutes about our colleagues. As it is now, it is almost like a funeral procession as they sit here and hear themselves eulogized for an hour, and then have the time extended for an additional hour." He brought smiles when he added: "I think if we stopped calling each other 'distinguished,' we might save ten working days in the session. All of us are distinguished or we would not be here, or should not be here; and I do not say that too immodestly, I hope, Mr. President."

When he sat down, Senator Mike Mansfield, the Majority Leader, arose: "Mr. President," he said, "I appreciate the remarks of the distinguished Senator from Massachusetts."

Brooke has the same warm rapport with political foes as had John F. Kennedy and Henry Cabot Lodge, Jr., when they vied for the U.S. Senate in 1952. Late one night in South Boston, Kennedy looked out his car window at Lodge, in a car in the next lane. He greeted the Republican, who waved back, shouting above the traffic din: "Jack! Isn't this a hell of a way to make a living."*

At a farewell reception for Speaker of the House John McCormack and Congressman Philip Philbin of Massachusetts, Brooke saw U.S. Representative James A. Burke of Milton for the first time since published reports that he might run against Brooke for the Senate in 1972. Clasping Burke around the shoulders, Brooke grinned. "How *are* you, Senator?"

---

* Kevin White said the same thing to Evan Dobelle in a men's room in a Pittsfield hotel during the 1960 campaign.

Burke returned the smile, knowing it might be a long time before anyone else called him "senator."

Reporters like Brooke's quick wit. When he was nominated for the Senate in 1966, a newsman asked whether he had heard from George Wallace.

"Yes," he said. "George Wallace of Fitchburg." (He is a long-time Brooke supporter.)

Although much wooed in the "rent a senator business," Brooke has cut down on the circuit under the pressure of his schedule. In 1968 he received 21,000 dollars for giving public speeches, an honorarium that was a record until 1970, when Senator Muskie, who is occasionally in Washington, reported fees of 80,183 dollars.* Brooke's take dropped in 1969 to as little as 5,600 dollars and has not risen since. According to Roger Woodworth, Brooke was glad of this: "It indicated that the Senator had more time to attend to Senate business."

In his record year Brooke's speaking fees ranged from 1,000 dollars from the National Association of Life Insurance Underwriters to 200 dollars for a speech at North Adams State College.

As *The Boston Globe* noted, one of Vice-President Agnew's assignments has been based on his "search and destroy mission against media liberals and student protesters, the two biggest forces in bringing the war home to your living room or local picket line." And Agnew really believed in his blistering attacks on the media and youthful protesters. In a commencement address to Ohio State University graduates in 1969 Agnew said: "A society which comes to fear its children is effete. A sniveling, hand-wringing power structure deserves the violent rebellion it encourages. If my generation doesn't stop cringing, yours will inherit a lawless society where emotion and muscle displace reason." Campus unrest has been a problem for the administration and Congress since Nixon's inaugural. When Columbia University was crippled by student violence in the spring of 1968, Nixon called it "a national disgrace," adding that the sanctioning of the rioting by permissive professors was "far more reprehensible than the disgraceful action of the students they encouraged." At the advice of Daniel Patrick Moynihan, executive secretary of the Urban Affairs Council, Nixon toned down his criticism of professors for a while,

---

* Senator Birch Bayh of Indiana earned 44,331 dollars for speeches in 1970. Mark Hatfield, whose usual theme is the cost and immorality of the Vietnam war, earned 41,955 dollars. The national champion is Governor Ronald Reagan, who receives 25,000 dollars or 20 percent of the gross for each speech.

but after President Calvin Plimpton of Amherst College wrote him that campus violence would continue "until you and other political leaders of our country attack more effectively, massively, persistently the major social and foreign problems of our country," the President stepped up his attack, arguing that no group "should be more zealous defenders of the integrity of academic standards and the rule of reason in academic life than the faculties of our great colleges and universities. But if the teacher simply follows the loudest voices, parrots the latest slogan, yields to unreasonable demands, he will have won not the respect but the contempt of his students." Brooke often sounded off on the same theme, but he did not buy Agnew's simplistic contention that all youthful protesters were "avowed anarchists and Communists who detest everything about this country and want to destroy it" by exploiting the freedom of protest.

In 1968 and ensuing years Brooke has made more speeches on college campuses than any other senator, frequently denouncing protesters who "disrupt and paralyze" institutions by using the weapon of protest without discretion. He said "the right to protest is the right to persuade, not the right to paralyze; that the authoritarianism of protest is not better than the authoritarianism of repression; and that the disruption of great universities is a disservice to a free society."

He declared that the practice of carrying an argument to the point where those petitioned "can only respond by appearing to cave in to force or pressure . . . is a sure recipe for failure. Some of the more outrageous student uprisings . . . seem to . . . have gone well beyond the bounds of sensible political action." He was referring to the Columbia University student protest that closed down the campus. He warned that the outbreaks at Columbia and at the University of California at Berkeley seemed intimately related to Watts and Detroit as symbols of "the creeping chaos which threatens society." On the other hand, he praised modern students for making the world "unsafe for hypocrisy" and for creating a pressure to force universities to improve themselves. "Faculty and administration will have to join hands with students in an active collaboration to meet the serious challenges which have arisen to threaten the university."

Brooke's campus talks mirrored his social, economic and political philosophy. In one denunciation of rabble-rousing professors he singled out Professor Howard Zinn of Boston University, after hearing him speak at Newton High School when Edwina Brooke was in the graduating class. Zinn, calling the Vietnam war "stupid and immoral," said patriotism did not mean behaving like sheep. "The real patriots today are the protesters against the war who say that it is against what Americans stand for and that it should stop."

Later that day, in an impromptu speech to the Revere (Massachusetts) High School graduating class, Brooke said Zinn was unfair in criticizing the U.S. as a nation of war. "In this country with all of its ills we still have the best means for bringing about a better world— more than any other country. I'm here today to report with pride that this is still the greatest nation on earth and don't you forget it!"

Campus violence, which subsided for a time, erupted on April 30, 1970, when the Cambodian incursion began. Next morning students all over the nation were marching, picketing, blocking entry to classrooms and fighting police. At the University of Maryland students struggling with police ruined the ROTC building, and at Kent State University a day later students burned down the ROTC building. Two days later Ohio National Guardsmen, trying to clear an area of rock-throwing students, suddenly opened fire, killing four students and wounding 11. Agnew called the tragedy "predictable and avoidable," adding that it pointed up the grave dangers which accompany the "new politics of violence and confrontation." At a demonstration at the University of New Mexico three students were stabbed in a demonstration. One result of the student unrest was the gathering of 100,000 youthful demonstrators in Washington, where Nixon, in a surprise appearance, unsuccessfully tried to mollify them.

Although campus rioting declined late in the 1969–70 school year, higher educational institutions found themselves in danger of being politicized by radicals, with a consequent erosion of educational standards and academic freedom. Brooke was quick to see the danger.

In June 1970 *The Boston Herald* lauded him in an editorial: "Fresh on the heels of Senator Margaret Chase Smith's eloquent 'declaration of conscience' comes an erudite speech by . . . Brooke, who, like the lady from Maine, fears the excesses of the extreme left. Brooke said he was 'greatly disturbed by the tendency of some colleges and universities to jeopardize that heritage [of academic freedom] by adopting, as institutions, specific positions on current political issues."

Brooke was thinking of a movement which would close colleges for a week or so during election campaigns so students could participate, and which would thereby attempt to end relationships between universities and government and to promote relationships between universities and movements popular at a given moment. Brooke argued that colleges and universities should stick to their fundamental mission of

372

stimulating the search for truth "by remaining constantly open to varying opinions, new information and fresh insight. . . . In short, to voice political judgments, colleges and universities must pass from the posture in which the possibility of present error and future truth is the cornerstone, to the posture in which the permanent obligation to root out falsehood is in danger of being subordinated to the prevailing opinion of a shifting majority."

Brooke was not against dissent, but he made a valid distinction between the freedom of individuals on campus to express their views and the effort to impose a collective political judgment on an institution. As far as violence on the campus was concerned, he predicted that students themselves would curb their excesses. "It would be a drastic mistake for the government to intervene. Let the individual colleges handle the problem." He said unrest would run its course "because most students realize it is self-defeating."

Brooke hailed the President's Commission on Campus Unrest, chaired by former Pennsylvania Governor William Scranton and including Erwin D. Canham, editor of *The Christian Science Monitor,* whom Brooke had urged to run against Ted Kennedy in 1970; President James E. Cheek of Howard University; Lieutenant General Benjamin O. Davis, Director of Civil Aviation Security, Transportation Department; and Joseph Rhodes, Jr., a twenty-two-year-old fellow at Harvard who had been student-body president at the California Inistitute of Technology.* Cheek and Davis are blacks.

Governor Ronald Reagan, who had closed the University of California when radicals threatened to take over the academic process, gave Agnew quotes from published statements of Rhodes, who said Reagan "was bent on killing people for his own political gain," and that Nixon and Agnew "are killing people." Agnew told Rhodes he should resign from the Scranton Commission, which had concluded, after the President asked what ailed the campus, that Rhodes was at fault. Agnew assailed the report.

Nixon, who during the long spell of campus turmoil had been a wavering Hamlet who swayed between repression and appeasement, saved his worst performance for a meeting at the White House with presidents of 15 predominantly black colleges five days after the Jackson State College tragedy. During the two-hour conference held

---

* Other members were James F. Ahern, Chief of Police, New Haven, Connecticut; Martha A. Derthick, Associate Professor, Boston College; Bayless Manning, Dean of the Law School, Stanford University; and Revious Ortique, Jr., New Orleans.

to discuss the tragedy and other problems affecting black higher education in the wake of the Cambodian invasion, one delegate said: "If you don't end poverty, racism, and war right now, we'll hold our breaths until we turn blue!" President Herman Branson of Central State University, Ohio, and now of Lincoln University, Pennsylvania, read a statement: "The increasing alienation of black youth," he said, stemmed in no small measure from "the policies and practices of your administration," and especially the rhetoric of Agnew and Mitchell.

John A. Peoples, Jr., president of Jackson State College, who had toured the roiling campus with Brooke and Evers after the shooting, handed Nixon photographs of the killings. Riffling through them, Nixon suddenly stiffened in his chair.

"Look," he said, "what are we going to do to get more respect for the police from our young people?"

Embarrassed as a tense silence hung like a pall over the room, Nixon in his confusion and bewilderment asked Deputy Attorney General Richard Kleindienst to brief the bristling presidents on the new Law Enforcement Assistance Administration in the Justice Department. "The black educators glowered as they listened to what they regarded as a non sequitur of stunning proportions," Evans and Novak wrote in their biography of Nixon.*

Unlike Agnew and Nixon, Brooke commended the idealism of American youth. At commencement in 1970 at Framingham State College, where he received the second honorary degree of Doctor of Humane Letters awarded in the 131-year history of the college, he said in an aside to parents in the audience: "Our generation is going to have to begin to understand this generation." He said the recent student demonstration in Washington proved that youth "are not opting out, but are opting in. They were there because they wanted to improve the system, not to destroy it." At another commencement he said: "To use their own language, when they turn on we ought not to turn them off so easily. The great majority of the people who [protest sincerely want] to end the war. The Communist and criminal elements should be weeded out of these protests, but the majority of the protesters have something to say." This was a frequent theme.

Brooke has been accused of being another Robespierre, the French Revolution leader who said, "There go the people. I must follow them, because I am their leader." Yet he articulated many trouble-

---

* *Nixon in the White House: The Frustration of Power,* Rowland Evans, Jr., and Robert D. Novak (New York, Random House, 1971).

some problems before Nixon and Agnew faced them. At a June commencement in 1969 at North Adams State College he said there were "more similarities than differences between generations in America," adding that "youth and old alike believe in certain principles of justice, equality and opportunity. Coercion is hostile to any system of open politics. Illegitimate force, whether applied by a majority or a minority, is intolerable. There is a balance to be struck between continuity and change." He recommended lowering the voting age to give young people a greater voice in the political systems.

At another commencement that month at Massachusetts Bay Community College, he asked how Americans could walk "freely in space and not on the streets of Hernando, Mississippi," referring to the ambush of James Meredith, who, after a violent confrontation and against the protest of Governor Ross Barnett, had enrolled at the University of Mississippi. In June Meredith and three other blacks were walking south on Route 51 in Mississippi on a 210-mile hike from the Tennessee border to Jackson. While they were passing through Hernando, keeping to the side of the road, "hands in pockets, head down," a shotgun blast came from the brush, and the four men ran. Meredith had 60 birdshot pellets in his head, neck, back and legs. Brooke called the perpetrators "blinded hate-mongers" who threatened the "basis of individual liberty," adding that America's melting pot "was never intended to produce a gruel, a bland people, a country of look-alikes and think-alikes." The "perpetrators" turned out to be a non-Mississippian who told police when asked why he had shot Meredith, "I don't know. I just don't know."

The day before he spoke at North Adams State, Brooke ran into flak when he addressed Wellesley College's commencement assembly. A student challenged him when he said coercive protest was wrong because it was unnecessary.

"There is a narrow line between productive dissent and counterproductive disruption," Brooke said, branding the ideology of the New Left as "a curious hodgepodge of Marxist, neo-Marxist or crypto-Marxist doctrines, fascinating to debate but irrelevant to enact." He said issues tend to get submerged in a contest for power that is justified at first as a means of correcting identified evils, but [they then] persist in their own right." Paradoxically, he added, "the introduction of coercion as an instrument of protest may serve only to legitimize the use of force to deal with the protesters."

"I speak for all . . . four hundred of us," said the president of the Student Government Association. "For too long those who have led us have viewed politics as 'the art of the possible.' The challenge facing them and us is to make what appears to be impossible possible. As the French students wrote on the walls of the Sorbonne, 'Be realistic. Demand the impossible. We cannot settle for less.' Every protest and dissent is unabashedly an effort to forge an identity. A strain of the old-fashioned virtues runs through our generation, a seeking for freedom to create trust, integrity and respect in our relations with one another."

She did not speak for *all* the students. One wore an armband with a small American flag, in contrast to the prevailing blue-dove and black-panther armbands others wore: "It says I support President Nixon's moves in Southeast Asia," said Ellen Carlson of Virginia. "I don't make a big point of my views, because I'm in a minority. It's too much trouble." That Wellesley graduating class was a magnificently pluralistic society.

In other speeches Brooke told graduating classes not to worry about being members of a minority, since ruling classes were once a minority. If Agnew was the spokesman for the silent majority, Brooke had the effect of being the spokesman for the not always silent minority. He told students this was a time to become concerned and involved. "I pray you don't become part of the silent majority, but this doesn't mean yelling or protesting. No one can afford today to sit by the side of the road and watch the race of men go by." He told students not to worry about having long hair or being unconventional. "This nation did not become great because of its sameness. It has become a melting pot because it has combined the best brains of all nations."

The Senator's daughter Remi went through an unconventional phase. "When she was active in the peace movement, wearing blue jeans and carrying a knapsack, my mother was able to communicate with her when Remigia and I couldn't. Mother can bridge any generation gap."

Brooke took his message down to grade-school level, where he could not be accused of seeking votes. In June 1970 he popped into Roxbury's Martin Luther King, Jr., School, where home rooms are named for prominent blacks. He stopped by the sixth-grade room named after him. He told the middle school's graduation class of the importance of education in combating crime, poverty and narcotics. "Be yourself. Above all else, be a man or woman before you're black, yellow, red or anything else."

Few senators have been interviewed more on radio and television, primarily because newscasters know that Brooke is conversant with and able quickly to articulate topical issues. On an interview on radio station WEEI in Boston he was asked about crime in black communities.

"The black man has never really been the top criminal in the country," he said, noting that gangsters move in and sell narcotics "because people are so deprived they have very little else. They are the great users of narcotics because they may be weak from lack of food or good living conditions, or mentally weak from lack of good education. . . . Hopelessness and despair lead to more bars, more liquor stores, more narcotics dealers, more houses of prostitution in disadvantaged communities than anyplace else." He added that the success of the numbers racket and the recruitment of bookies in black ghettos stem from the black man's need for "a sense of fulfillment" amid despair and deprivation. He is looking for one lucky strike.

When the Mafia moves in and takes over the turf, they don't share illicit profits with blacks involved in rackets. Blacks, Brooke said, have "never been, here, as in any other part of the economy, in the high-level, policy-making profit area. . . ."

As a former law enforcement officer, Brooke retains his interest in rooting out crime. He hailed the Organized Crime Control Act approved by Nixon in 1970 because it brings "lawless acts under federal jurisdiction with penalties appropriate to the seriousness of those offenses." In 1970 in the new Congress Brooke traded his position on the Armed Services Committee for a seat on the Senate Appropriations Committee, which reviews and passes on funding programs. Ever since, he has had a voice in deciding how much is spent to fight substandard housing and crime in the streets.

He has teamed with three other senators who have served as attorneys general in their states: William B. Saxbe (Democrat of Ohio), Thomas F. Eagleton (Democrat of Missouri), and Walter Mondale (Democrat of Minnesota). The Brooke crime bill, co-sponsored by these senators, is designed to set up a "model state" and end the "piecemeal" approach to fighting crime. Brooke said the measure is designed to encourage states and their governmental subdivisions to comprehensively reform their entire criminal justice systems, including law enforcement, courts and prosecution and correctional institutions, all aimed at spurring police professionalism. It is more effective than Nixon's Law Enforcement Assistance Administration, which supervised piecemeal programs. Money appropriated for LEAA has been used only to reinforce criminal justice in its traditional modes of operation, according to Brooke. The new legislation forces states to update their criminal-justice systems.

In reviewing Nixon-Brooke relations, Jack E. Molesworth, a persistent gadfly, calls the Senator a Trojan Horse who has been "in the Republican stable for far too long." He asks Brooke to proclaim himself a Democrat, as John Lindsay did in 1971, pointing out that the Senator "has at almost every turn opposed and undercut . . . Nixon in all of his major policies and efforts." But Brooke goes along, he implies, when Nixon acts like a Democrat: "When President Nixon takes a turn left and urges the admission of Red China to the UN (in complete disregard of the UN Charter, which limits membership only to 'peace-loving' nations) . . . it is consistent for Brooke to endorse the . . . move." The critic also thinks Brooke is consistent in approving Nixon's imposition of wage and price controls and in devaluing the dollar internationally, "as the liberal Democrats have been urging for some time."

As early as May 1970 Brooke had urged Nixon to "face up to the need for adequate government revenues" and to "break the back of inflationary psychology." Brooke advocated a return to wage and price guidelines used a decade earlier, but "only if they have teeth." He suggested linking the guidelines to government procurement policy as an incentive for firms and unions to follow them. "Those which refuse to do so would expect difficulty in competing for federal contracts." Brooke anticipated later action by Congress when he said: "I would consider it so urgent to reverse the inflationary tide that I am drawn to an intermediate policy short of direct controls, but beyond a simple promulgation of guidelines. To maximize the opportunity for private initiative and free enterprise over the long haul, we had best be prepared for decisive government action when it is necessary. Such action is needed today."

In August 1971 Brooke and 11 other GOP senators met at the White House with George Schultz, who heads the office of Management and Budget, and Secretary of the Treasury John Connally. The senators had earlier met in the offices of Brooke and Senator Clifford Case. They told Shultz and Connally to rev up the Productivity Board, which makes inflation alerts, and asked for a commission which could take steps to roll back prices. In their discussion of setting wage and price guidelines, they agreed with Harvard Professor John Galbraith that the way to curb inflation is with strict wage and price control. The senators considered the economy the top issue in the 1972 elections and warned that both they and the administration could be in trouble unless Nixon turned things around. Later Congress approved some of the measures the senators suggested.

Putting Out Brush Fires

T HE TWO Bay State senators ended the first week of the Ninety-second Congress in January 1971 with committee positions and legislative proposals defining their goals on the domestic front. Brooke, who ridicules the idea that he overshadows the senior senator, from the outset of his senatorial career has cooperated with him in furthering the interests of Massachusetts and New England. Early in 1971 they also charted a cooperative course on the national level, with Kennedy pledging a concerted drive to seek legislation to improve the physical life of America, while Brooke turned his attention to safety and living conditions. Just as they often voted together, they worked together to promote the best interests of Massachusetts as well as the nation.

Brooke has been deeply involved with housing for the elderly since 1967, when he was named to the housing subcommittee of the Banking and Currency Committee, now the Banking, Housing and Urban Affairs Committee. In the U.S. Capitol on June 16, 1971, he received the Award of Merit from the National Council of Senior Citizens for his outstanding work in their behalf. Congress adopted his two major proposals to aid the elderly. The first "Brooke Amendment" provides that public-housing tenants can be required to pay no more than 25 percent of their income for rent. The adoption of this amendment puts more money for food, medicine, transportation and recreation into the pockets of hundreds of thousands of older Americans. The second "Brooke Amendment" provides funds for improving the quality in public-housing projects: maintenance and repairs for the tenants' comfort, security guards for their protection and recreational facilities for their enjoyment.

"There is no valid reason why personal development must come to an abrupt halt at the magic age of sixty-five or seventy if an individual is both willing and able to do more," Brooke said. "Retirement ought not to mean banishment from private and public affairs. Older Americans have the accumulated skills and wisdom of decades to contribute to their families, their communities and our nation."

There were endless brush fires to put out. Brooke filed ten private bills to aid immigrants of Massachusetts faced with expulsion from the U.S. for overstaying their visas. One publicized case involved Mr. and Mrs. Apolinario Gregorio, a Philippine couple who had lived in Massachusetts before being deported to Manila. They left two young sons with relatives because they thought the children would have a better chance in the U.S. Brooke, after finding that their visas had been extended 12 times since they had come to the U.S. four years earlier, was criticized for refusing to file a private bill in Congress to permit the family to remain. Actually, the Gregorios had been handsomely treated in comparison with other Philippine residents who wanted to migrate to America.

One case involved a naturalized Hungarian who went home to marry his childhood sweetheart. Hungary had given her permission to leave, but there was a delay over her American visa. The young husband stayed in Hungary as long as possible, but finally had to leave his wife, who was pregnant. Two days after Brooke heard about the case he arranged for a visa for the couple, and Dr. and Mrs. Frank Holly were reunited.

"I would like to thank you from the bottom of my heart for your immediate, kind, and most effective help in obtaining an entry visa for my wife," Dr. Holly wrote Brooke. "She was notified in Hungary within 24 hours and is already here with me. Our happiness is complete and your intervention made our dream come true. God bless you."*

Brooke has asked for a reallocation of resources and conversion of major industries because of the drastic reduction in defense and space spending. He says the market must be restructured, adding that it was a good beginning when the Nixon administration released

---

* Bette Richardson, assistant to the chairman of the Heritage Division of the Massachusetts Republican State Committee, asked Brooke to help the Hollys. She works through a group of ethnic chairmen to help immigrants of 19 nationalities.

42 million dollars for retraining unemployed scientists and engineers in a program administered by the Professional Job Center on Route 128 in Boston, home of the depressed electronics industry. Although Brooke feels that this funding was an important step in the right direction, the legislation which he has introduced addresses itself to the more fundamental problem: creating new jobs.

Early in 1971 Brooke said the 1,676,369 dollars under the Manpower Development and Training Act was provided for Massachusetts projects. That same day he announced a grant of 627,500 dollars to the Woods Hole Oceanographic Institution by the National Science Foundation in support of the first U.S. activity in the International Decade of Ocean Exploration. Total awards to Woods Hole and six other institutions in the amount of three million dollars are funding a project to collect data on levels of pollutants and of fission and waste products in the sea, oceanic mixing and the production of organic matter in the oceans.*

The summer of 1971 marked the second year of operation of Brooke's Domestic Action Program in Massachusetts, designed to use the state's military facilities for summer recreational and educational activities. "The Commonwealth," he explains, "is serving as a model for what hopefully will become a nationwide program. Twenty thousand young people benefit from day and overnight camps, where activities include recreation, vocational counseling, discussions on black history, Portuguese and Spanish history, as well as education in home economics, music and drug abuse." A sample project is the camp at Fort Devens called "Project Summertime," which brings inner-city youth from all over the state. There are similar camps at Boston Navy Yard and other military installations. "These young campers," Brooke says, "are able to take advantage of the swimming pools, camping areas, athletic fields and medical services which ordinarily are available only to military personnel."

In August Brooke said he would seek the end of "death row" confinement for 16 convicted murderers in Walpole State Prison, where they are kept in eight-foot-square cells 22 hours a day—a way of life prescribed in 1898, when the original statute was passed and intended to last only the few weeks between sentence and execution. But no one has been executed since 1947 in Massachusetts. Thus some of the condemned have waited for years on death row.

Brooke became interested in the problem the year before when he

---

* This Geochemical Ocean Sections Study is the first major research effort in the IDOE, a multination investigation of oceanic problems that affect man.

spoke at graduation exercises for inmates, who donned caps and gowns to receive high-school diplomas. In a letter to Governor Sargent, Brooke said men on death row were denied basic privileges granted even to lifers. They could not attend plays or movies in the auditorium, work in shops or attend classes.

As a result of Brooke's probe, he received a note from Attorney General Robert Quinn: "I have notified the superintendent of Walpole State Prison that, pending new legislation being enacted, he has 'standing' to seek a court order modifying the conditions set forth in the statute, if he finds such modification necessary as well as consistent with sound prison administration." In essence, this means that the corrections officials may take immediate steps to improve the situation. Brooke was pleased.

"Time and custom, when left unattended," he said, "can erode the principles that underlie human progress. The ultimate resolution of this problem rests with the legislature and we anxiously await their enactment of a modern law on this subject." Brooke continued to lobby vigorously for a change in the law by the legislature and finally saw his position vindicated when United States Magistrate Willie Davis ruled that "death row" was unconstitutional.

Brooke explained how our foreign-aid program can "perpetuate our friends in power and bolster our own economy," noting that nations receiving U.S. aid spend an average of 90 percent of that money in this country; "of the nearly one billion dollars spent by the Agency for International Development last year, 99 percent of the funds were spent right here in the U.S., including more than 12 million dollars of business for the Commonwealth." He said foreign aid was a humanitarian program, adding that it is not a giveaway program "used as a mechanism for controlling other nations." He said this at a meeting of 300 members of the Quincy–South Shore Chamber of Commerce, which ended on a light note. The Republican mayor said: "I hope Senator Brooke will stop by to see me at City Hall. Because of the party we both belong to, Quincy can be a lonely place. I sometimes think I'm the last living Republican in Quincy, but next to City Hall there's a cemetery full of them."

Brooke took home a set of bookends made of granite from Quincy's Swingle Quarry.

Some Massachusetts conservatives call Brooke "the prince of liberals, right after Mr. [Edward] Kennedy," pointing out that Brooke is so liberal his philosophy is virtually indistinguishable from Kennedy's. The American Conservative Union gave Kennedy a zero rating and Brooke a ten percent rating, which means they disagreed on only one and agreed on the other nine of the ten important votes used in the survey. Americans for Democratic Action (ADA) gave Brooke a 90 percent rating and Kennedy 80 percent, which makes Brooke ten percent more liberal than Kennedy. The COPE Labor rating gives Brooke 95 percent and Kennedy 100 percent. These figures prompted Brooke's old adversary Jack Molesworth to conclude: "Brooke has proven even more conclusively by his recent actions that he and Kennedy are two peas in the same pod which is clearly labeled 'Liberal Democrat.' "

The critic misses the point. Brooke has charted a judicious course in the Senate, voting on the liberal side often enough to escape criticism in an anti-Nixon state, while maintaining a good rapport with the White House, which, a columnist reported, "has apparently adopted an attitude of 'We know what you're up against in Massachusetts, Ed.' " The feeling for Brooke even conservatives have often transcends their deep-seated reservations about his liberal tendencies.

The simple fact is that Brooke, courted by both liberals and conservatives of both parties, is the single most admired politician in Massachusetts, not excepting Ted Kennedy. In assessing the 1972 senatorial campaign, a leading Bay State Democrat said: "Ed will get money from the liberal community in the state. He will get money from liberals throughout the country. He will get some help from labor, or at least the promise that labor will not help his opponent. Add to this the fact that there are plenty of Democrats who will not vote against a Negro. He'd be tough to beat." He had one reservation: "But that dinner-pail issue can be tricky. Voters are inclined to identify parties with economic failures. And a voter who is unhappy with the economy can be very tough on the party in power. This appears now to be the only issue that threatens Brooke for '72."

In a whimsical year-end column in *The Boston Herald Traveler* in 1971 Cornelius Dalton, the political editor, said the winner of the (mythical) "Percy Pennypacker Award for the Man of the Year in Massachusetts Politics" was Mayor-Elect Patsy Caggiano of Lynn, who was picked "for his shrewd analysis of why he was elected":

"The people want new faces," explained Patsy, who had run unsuccessfully for mayor six times before.

One Dalton nominee was former Administration Commissioner John J. McCarthy, the man who called Brooke "the prince of liberals, right after Mr. [Edward] Kennedy." His nomination, said Dalton, was for his "contribution to political confusion when he announced the formation of the Conservative party of Massachusetts." At the time McCarthy said the Conservatives weren't against the two-party system, nor were they launching a third party. They were starting a second party, "because you couldn't tell the difference between the Democratic party and the Republican party, which proved that the Conservative party was a second party and not a third party."

In the 1970 Senate race in Massachusetts, Brooke had urged Erwin D. Canham, editor in chief of *The Christian Science Monitor,* to run against Ted Kennedy. "My candidacy is highly improbable," Canham said. "Nonetheless I am grateful for the Senator's remark." The choice of two behind-the-scenes operators—Charles Colson and Murray Chotiner (Nixon's political mentor as far back as the Red-baiting Senate campaign of 1950)—was McCarthy. Not because he was a better candidate than the eventual GOP convention choice, Josiah A. ("Si") Spaulding.* Indeed, as has been noted, when Chotiner proposed McCarthy, he didn't know his first name. The ploy? Neither Republican candidate could beat Ted Kennedy, so why not let McCarthy try? Spaulding, a me-tooer, would be too much of a gentleman to mention items such as Chappaquiddick, whereas McCarthy would claw Kennedy.

This was the prelude to a testimonial held for Brooke on his fifty-second birthday.

Chateau de Ville in Framingham, just outside Boston, is a pale replica of a Las Vegas casino without one-armed bandits. There in June 1971 Governor Reagan was guest speaker in an effort to herd back into the GOP corral the maverick conservatives who had followed McCarthy in 1970. It was an opening move against the possibility that McCarthy and his henchmen might draw right-wing money and votes from the GOP camp.

Recalling that Brooke had once before avoided a confrontation with the conservative Mr. Reagan, critics charged the Senator with fancy political footwork in staying away from the affair. Actually, he was laid up with viral pneumonia. "If anybody thinks the Senator checked into

---

* Also considered to oppose Ted Kennedy—much to the horror of Governor Francis Sargent—was cartoonist Al Capp. Al Gammal, who suggested Capp, was embarrassed to discover the cartoonist was a Democrat.

In campaigning for Si Spaulding, Remigia Brooke told crowds at rallies: "Please vote for 'See.' My husband needs 'See' in Washington."

Bethesda Naval Hospital for six days just to avoid meeting Reagan, they're in pretty bad shape," Roger Woodworth said. While Brooke was in the hospital, the girls on his Washington staff sent him a huge valentine inscribed with affectionate messages. Betsy Warren wrote: "Office in your absence instant insanity. Recover immediately." Melinda Smith told Brooke she had spent the morning talking to his biographer: "Gave him some juicy scoops for the book. Am now accepting any and all blackmail money you care to offer." Sally Saltonstall suggested a vacation: "A complete rest in Bermuda—with a companion." Woodworth, always the "compleat" politician, wrote: "Don't paw nurses. We don't want the Democrats to have anything on us in the 1972 campaign."

Two months before Reagan's visit Brooke agreed at a GOP policy meeting to a moratorium on his own fund-raising program to help the floundering GOP State Committee. The moratorium ended October 26, when 2,300 Brooke partisans paid 100 dollars a plate for a banquet at Chateau de Ville. This, said a columnist, "points up not only what a charmer he is, but what a charmed political life he has led."

It was an evening of good and flowing cheer where levity prevailed, perhaps in anticipation of glowing 1972 prospects. Toastmaster Charles Morin, who opened festivities by saying Brooke had to get his rented tuxedo back by midnight, was the same glib investment counselor who the year before had promoted the candidacy of the far-right John J. McCarthy. Now he was in the Brooke camp. Guests at the head table included former Senator Leverett Saltonstall; former Governor Robert Bradford, another vintage Brahmin in the GOP vineyard; Governor Francis Sargent; President Nixon's daughter Tricia; and Harvard Law School student Edward Cox who, a reporter said, "is related [to Tricia] by marriage." Morin introduced Tricia as "a stranger in our midst who recently starred on national color TV and played a long engagement in Washington." It was clear that the young couple were personal ambassadors of the President at the appreciation dinner, for it was the first time they "had gone public" in Massachusetts. Their presence, according to a columnist, was Nixon's "none-too-subtle way of telling Republicans, Conservatives and independents alike how high the junior senator stands in his book."

Tricia, pert and blonde, read a congratulatory letter from her father which expressed his admiration for Brooke while wishing him many more happy years of service to Massachusetts. Before the dinner, many political seers and columnists had been speculating about the possibility of Brooke as Nixon's 1972 running mate. The political editor of *The Boston Record American* wrote the next day: "The line that Monsignor George Kerr threw away as he turned from the mike after offering the invocation at Ed Brooke's birthday bash was, 'You're on your way, Mr. Vice-President.' "

After Tricia read her father's letter the speculation toned down, and Brooke himself, a few weeks after the affair, told a gathering he had no illusions about being considered as a replacement for Vice-President Agnew on the 1972 GOP ticket.

The spectacular turnout told much about Brooke and added over 200,000 dollars to the campaign till. Unlike an incumbent governor, as a reporter said, "Brooke has no contracts to let, no architects and consultants to hire, no extensive patronage, no unusual number of lobbyists seeking special treatment or special interests." Thus the gathering was more a tribute to Brooke than to the GOP, for it drew Democrats and independents, along with the leaders of separate wings of the Massachusetts GOP headed by Sargent and Richardson. One guest was Judge John Fox, former chief secretary to the late Democratic Governor Paul A. Dever. Present were labor leaders, and one of the big ticket buyers was Daniel O'Connell, a wealthy contractor who normally donates to Democrats. At the head table was Salvatore Camelio, chairman of the Massachusetts Council, AFL-CIO, a powerful voice in organized labor's endorsements in Bay State elections.

Harmony prevailed. Early in January there had been a rumor that Brooke and Sargent were feuding because they couldn't agree on the choice of a new GOP State Committee chairman. In his brief talk at the Chateau de Ville testimonial, Sargent said the only matter on which he and Brooke differed was which one of them really won the war in Italy.* That night Brooke touched all bases. Reggie Smith, the Boston Red Sox star, got away before he could be introduced, but Brooke asked Jim Plunkett of the New England Patriots to take a bow. One Brooke supporter paid 6,000 dollars for six tables for young people aged 18 to 21, and some of them rose when Brooke mentioned them as "the true trustees of posterity." Also asked to stand was Frank Manning, whom Governor Sargent had recently ap-

---

* Sargent, who emerged from World War II a captain, was a ski trooper in Italy with the 10th Mountain Division.

pointed assistant secretary of the Elder Affairs Division of the Commonwealth.*

The theme of a film shown was *The Four Worlds of Ed Brooke,* with photographs and narrative to tell the guests how Brooke's family sees him, how the press sees him, how voters see him and how Brooke sees himself.

The gala could not hide the fact that the Grand Old Party in Massachusetts is skidding. Brooke's often-repeated warning that the nation itself is in danger of becoming a one-party system of government is closer to reality in the Bay State, where fewer than one person in ten is a registered Republican. Party registration late in 1971 was dropping toward the half-million mark. Democrats outnumber Republicans two to one in registration, three to one in the legislature, and eight to none in the Governor's Council. Legislative races in 1972 may find no GOP candidates in half the races. Brooke is further disturbed because young registrants in the state are choosing the Democratic label by a two-to-one margin.

A political reporter gives a dismal assessment: "Brooke is safe; he has his own organization, and Richardson and Sargent have their people, and John Volpe still has *condottieri* in this state. But put them all together, and you still don't have an effective statewide political party."

The national picture also is changing for the GOP, as Robert Finch suggested toward the end of the 1968 presidential campaign. "This is the last election that will be won by the un-black, the un-poor and the un-young." If this is true, Nixon's Southern strategy may be in jeopardy. Nevertheless, the President continues to coddle the South, as he did in Birmingham, Alabama, on May 25, 1971, when he said: "I have nothing but utter contempt for the double hypocritical standard of Northerners who look at the South and point the finger and say, 'Why don't those Southerners do something about their race problems?" Insisting that there was no progress in the North toward school desegregation during the last three years of the Johnson administration, Nixon contrasted that record with "significant progress in the South" during his term.

Brooke has his own version of Southern strategy. Now that blacks are no longer fenced out of politics in the South, he feels the GOP

---

* Manning was formerly head of the Massachusetts Council for Older Americans. In recognizing him, Brooke realized the importance of the senior citizens' votes.

should redouble its efforts to attract them into the fold. Republicans should infiltrate the South, integrate GOP organizations and become identified with Negroes. Young Republicans could begin, he says, by integrating their Southern clubs.

According to Thomas Pettigrew, a Harvard social psychologist, the Negro thrust into Southern politics is "literally a miracle, wrought chiefly by the 1965 Voting Rights Act." Since then, black registration has nearly trebled from 1.3 million to 3.4 million. Alabama has four black sheriffs—one in Lowndes County, where no blacks were even registered at the time of the Selma march in 1965.

Although the Negro vote is nowhere substantial enough to win a state race, it "has at least softened the rhetoric of Southern statehouse politics," according to *Newsweek*. Even crusty Senator Strom Thurmond, the South Carolina Dixiecrat who turned Republican, put a black-voter-registration veteran on his staff in preparation for his 1972 bid for reelection.

The black surge, according to *Newsweek,* has generated "out of the confluence of the old civil-rights movement and the new voting arithmetic, a made-in-Dixie Negro politics of enormous verve and promise. It is pure black but curiously unvengeful."

Mayor Charles Evers of Fayette, Mississippi, who was trounced in his gubernatorial try in 1971, said: "White folks, we ain't gonna treat you bad. We ain't gonna call you honkies. We ain't gonna call you pigs. We just gonna put that vote on you." This is a warning to Democrats, who tend to take blacks for granted, and an even more frightening portent to Republicans, who in past elections have despaired of winning over Negroes.

Politics offers blacks what it once offered earlier immigrant poor— better jobs, prestige and eventual power. "With the swelling of Northern ghettos and reenfranchisement of Southern blacks, votes are there as well, and politics is becoming the cutting edge of what used to be called the Negro revolution." The revolution has gained enough momentum to seat 13 blacks in Congress and to elect an increasing number of mayors such as Gary's Richard Hatcher and Newark's Kenneth Gibson. Brooke's friend Walter Fauntroy, a nonvoting black congressman in Washington, said: "If blacks use their votes intelligently, they can affect the outcome of every election from city council to the presidency."

The total situation leaves Brooke in a position that has generated wide speculation on the national scene.

CHAPTER TWENTY-TWO

After 1972, What?

Early in 1972 Senator Edmund Muskie continued to be haunted by his remark that he would not put a black on his ticket because it would be political suicide for him. Later, when asked whether Brooke could be elected as President Nixon's running mate, he hedged: "I am not a computer, so I don't know what offices Senator Brooke could or could not be elected to."

As Senator Mervin Dymally of California said of his fellow Negroes, blacks dream of the top spot, and to tell them they can't make it, as Muskie did, "means to deny their aspirations to the highest office in this land." Dymally scored Muskie for "dampening the hopes of a struggling people."

Early in January 1972 GOP Representative Paul McCloskey of California, who said he would be "proud to run on a ticket with Brooke as either a presidential or vice-presidential candidate," added: "Race has nothing to do with ability, nor does sex." At this time George Lodge said it would be a ten-strike for Nixon to choose Brooke as his running mate, and others felt that the idea of Nixon choosing Brooke as his vice-presidential candidate would be a stroke of political genius. Others took an opposite view, arguing that a Nixon-Brooke ticket would not draw even limited support among blacks. "The reasons are simple: blacks are thoroughly disgusted with Nixon and his policies. Many blacks resent the fact that Senator Brooke has a white wife, making it impossible for him to identify completely with blacks." In a letter to *Time* the writer added: "We are tired of being second-class citizens, and Senator Brooke, as a black man, would have a second-rate position on the ticket. Nixon is a conservative and Brooke is a liberal; the ticket couldn't run a united campaign."

During the speculation, Lee Auspitz, a leader of the Ripon Society, wrote in the January issue of the Ripon's *Forum* magazine: "To see why a Nixon-Brooke ticket is a realistic political possibility one must remember that the voters with the strongest racial feelings about blacks are Democrats, not Republicans. The Democratic national constituency stands upon four pillars and forms a house divided on civil rights."

According to Auspitz the national constituency is based on white Southerners who traditionally have been suspicious of civil-rights progress, on blue-collar Northerners who, "though remarkably free of racial malice, have become leery of the civil-rights movement because they have borne the major burdens associated with black migrations into Northern cities"; blacks themselves, who are dissatisfied with civil-rights progress, and, finally, "younger business and professional people who often vote Republican in statewide elections, but have begun moving Democratic in national elections because of the GOP's lack of positive leadership on domestic reconciliation."

Auspitz notes that these four voting groups—the backbone of the Democratic party—"split up the middle on the issue of civil rights." For this reason, he adds, national Democratic leaders "must outflank any Republican attempt to give prominence to race and social anxieties that are related to it in the voter's mind." In brief, Auspitz points out that the race issue can only split the New Deal alliance, "whereas economic issues inject new life into this old, but not yet dead, coalition."

As Brooke campaigns in 1972, he has repeatedly made it clear that he is content with his present role as senator. He is still young enough to dream. He turned down a seat on the United States Supreme Court because, at the age of fifty-one or fifty-two, he considered a seat on even such a high tribunal as "being put out to pasture." He has aspirations for higher elective office, and acceptance of a seat on the Supreme Court would curb these ambitions. He also feels the court lacks the action of the Senate ring, with its legislative slant toward national policy.

Fundamentally, Brooke has visions of being the first black to be nominated and elected to the Vice-Presidency. He knows, however, that as one of the hottest political properties in the nation, there is time for all that in 1976 or 1980.

No matter what happens in 1972 at the August 21 National Convention in Miami, Brooke's political star is rising. He has apparently not peaked.

"I hear people say that he could be President," his mother said. "It wouldn't surprise me. He's capable of doing anything." Asked whether she would want him to become President, she shook her head: "No. Not because of the hard work, but because of a selfish reason. I'd be afraid."

Remigia Brooke and her two daughters think the Senator has what it takes to go higher, but they, too, are in no hurry.

"When he says he wants to be reelected, he means it," Remi said during the vice-presidential speculation. "I know my father, and I am sure of this."

Remigia, knowing her husband makes his own decisions, never discusses his political future with him. "Someone said to me, one day your husband will be President. I was laughing, and they said why? 'Not because he couldn't be,' I said. 'He has every qualification to be President. Sure, I know that. I am laughing because he'd have to give me permission to ask all my friends to the White House. . . .'"

Coming closer is the time when this nation will have to face the question of having a black on a national ticket. It is comforting for Brooke to know that when GOP leaders draw up a list of blacks who are of presidential calibre, his name will be high on the list.

Major Senate Accomplishments and Degrees of Edward W. Brooke

ACCOMPLISHMENTS:

Senate resolution calling for mutual suspension of offensive and defensive nuclear weapons (MIRV and ABM).

Export Expansion and Regulation Act of 1970: The "Brooke Amendment" provided that no family in public housing shall be required to pay more than 25 percent of its adjusted income for rent.

Housing amendment allowing subsidies for improved operation and maintenance of public housing.

Experimental funds for refurbishment of abandoned urban property.

Experimental housing allowance for low-income families.

Banking and securities legislation isolating customers' cash and securities from general operating funds, and prohibiting banks from tying loans to the acceptance of other banking services.

American Revolution Bicentennial Commission Act of 1971.

The Senator was also instrumental in blocking the confirmation of Clement Haynsworth and G. Harrold Carswell to be Associate Justices of the Supreme Court.

Among the Senator's major accomplishments for Massachusetts are:

Persuading the Department of Transportation to take over the NASA research center in Cambridge and use it for transportation research.

Persuading President Nixon to appoint a special mediator to settle the disastrous Boston dock strike in 1969.

Obtaining funds for the U.S. Coast Guard to provide a weather ship to warn southern New England of impending storms, and to secure additional planes, ships and personnel to better protect Massachusetts fishermen from foreign interference.

Securing funds for job training and relocation assistance for Massachusetts industry and employees.

Setting up a Domestic Action Program enabling 22,000 under-privileged youngsters to receive camping experience on military bases in Massachusetts.

Securing better treatment for inmates on death row, and setting in motion a far-reaching effort at prison reform.

Housing Act of 1972: provided for mix of low and moderate income families in public-housing projects, and allowed all on welfare to qualify for rent subsidies.

Introducing Aircraft Noise Abatement Bill which was instrumental in persuading Department of Transportation to set standards for aircraft noise reduction and to request funds for such a program.

Introducing S. Con. Res. 4 urging immediate funding for a program to train and place unemployed scientists and engineers in government management positions; program was implemented by the Departments of Labor and HUD, and 100 of the first 400 scientists and engineers came from Massachusetts.

SENATE RESPONSIBILITIES:

Select Committee on Equal Education Opportunity
Special Committee on Aging
Regional Whip for Senate Republicans
Regional chairman of Senate Republican Campaign Committee

The Senator has also served as:
  Chairman, Ad Hoc Congressional Committee on the Poor People's Campaign
  Member, National Advisory Commission on Civil Disorders
  Member, American Revolution Bicentennial Commission
  Member, Franklin Delano Roosevelt Commission

COMMITTEE ASSIGNMENTS:

Banking, Housing and Urban Affairs Committee
Subcommittee on Financial Institutions

Subcommittee on Housing and Urban Affairs
Subcommittee on International Finance
Subcommittee on Securities (ranking minority member)
Subcommittee on Small Business
Committees on Appropriations
Subcommittee on Military Construction (ranking minority member)
Subcommittee on Foreign Operations
Subcommittee on Labor, Health, Education and Welfare
Subcommittee on Departments of State, Justice, Commerce and Judiciary
Subcommittee on Legislative
Select Committee on Equal Educational Opportunity

HONORARY DEGREES:

American International College, Doctor of Laws 1965
Amherst College, Doctor of Laws 1972
Boston University, Doctor of Laws 1968
Boston State College, Doctor of Laws 1971
Bowdoin College, Doctor of Laws 1969
Emerson College, Doctor of Laws 1968
George Washington University, Doctor of Laws 1967
Hampton Institute, Doctor of Laws 1968
Howard University, Doctor of Laws 1967
Johns Hopkins University, Doctor of Laws 1968
Morehouse College, Doctor of Laws 1968
North Adams State College, Doctor of Laws 1969
Skidmore College, Doctor of Laws 1969
The Catholic University of America, Doctor of Laws 1968
Framingham State College, Doctor of Humane Letters 1970
Portia Law School, Doctor of Jurisprudence 1963
Northeastern University, Doctor of Public Administration 1964
Suffolk University, Doctor of Public Administration 1969
Lowell Technological Institute, Doctor of Science 1965
University of New Hampshire (Plymouth State College), Doctor of Laws 1971
Worcester Polytechnic Institute, Doctor of Science 1965
Xavier University, Louisiana, Doctor of Laws 1971

BIBLIOGRAPHY

BOOKS

THE BLACK PANTHERS SPEAK. Philip S. Foner, editor (Philadelphia/ New York: J. B. Lippincott Company, 1970).

BLACK PROFILES. George R. Metcalf (New York: McGraw-Hill, 1970).

THE CHALLENGE OF CHANGE: *Crisis in Our Two-Party System.* Edward W. Brooke (Boston, Toronto: Little, Brown and Company, 1966).

THE DAYS OF MARTIN LUTHER KING, JR. Jim Bishop (New York: G. P. Putnam's Sons, 1971).

FREEDOM WHEN? James Farmer (New York: Random House, 1965).

THE LESSONS OF VICTORY. The Ripon Society (New York, The Dial Press, Inc., 1969).

NIXON IN THE WHITE HOUSE: *The Frustration of Power.* Rowland Evans and Robert Novak (New York: Random House, 1971).

THE REPUBLICAN ESTABLISHMENT. Stephen Hess and David S. Broder (New York, Evanston, and London: Harper & Row, 1967).

THE RESURRECTION OF RICHARD NIXON. Jules Witcover (New York: Putnam's Sons, 1970).

MAGAZINES

"Brooke of Massachusetts: A Negro Governor on Beacon Hill?" by Edward R. F. Sheehan, *Harper's,* June 1964.

"Individual who happens to be a Negro," *Time,* February 17, 1967, reprinted in *Reader's Digest,* May 1967.

Profile of Brooke by George Frazier, *Esquire,* June 26, 1965.

"Edward Brooke: Candidate with Mass(achusetts) Appeal." Authur Myers, *Coronet,* 1967.

Current Biography, 1967.

"Where Do We Go?" Edward Brooke, *Look,* May 1967.

"Negro in the Senate," *Newsweek,* November 21, 1966.

"Where Do I Stand?" Edward Brooke, *The Atlantic*, March 1966.

"A Negro Runs for State Office." *Look*, November 8, 1960.

"Adam Clayton Powell, the Man Behind the Controversy." Simeon Booker, *Ebony*, March 1967.

"Young Politician with a Conscience." *Ebony*, February 1962.

"Massachusetts: Rogues and Reformers in a State on Trial." Edward R. F. Sheehan, *The Saturday Evening Post*, June 5, 1965.

"Bay State's Color-Blind Candidate." Margery Byers, *Life*, April 8, 1966.

"The Black Man Leading a G.O.P March on Washington." John Skow, *The Saturday Evening Post*, September 10, 1966.

"Mr. Brooke Returns to the Nation's Capitol." Ernest E. Goodman, *Howard University Magazine*, January 1967.

" 'I'm a Soul Brother'—Senator Edward Brooke." Simeon Booker, *Ebony*, April 1967.

NEWSPAPER PROFILES

"Portrait of a Political Prodigy." Everett S. Allen, *New Bedford Standard-Times*, February 3, 1967.

James S. Doyle of *The Boston Globe's* Washington bureau, January 8, 1967.

Washington Afro-American, November 19, 1966.

"A Tribute to Mom." Frances Spatz Leighton, *The Cincinnati Pictorial Enquirer*, Sunday, May 14, 1967. Leighton had another piece on the Brooke family in the Sunday edition of *The Indianapolis Star* on May 21, 1967.

Sarah Booth Conroy, *Washington Post*, February 26, 1968.

NOTES

Chapter One / LIGHT IN THE TUNNEL

BLACK PROFILES by George R. Metcalf (New York: McGraw-Hill, 1970). Martin F. Nolan, *Boston Globe,* January 10, 1967; Robert L. Hassett, *Boston Herald,* January 11, 1967; "Brooke and Black Americans," William Raspberry, *Washington Post,* February 13, 1971; Simeon Booker, *Ebony,* April 1967; John Skow, *The Saturday Evening Post,* September 10, 1966; George Forsythe, *Boston Herald,* November 9, 1966; Everett S. Allen, *New Bedford Standard Times,* February 3, 1967; James M. Perry, *The National Observer,* August 9, 1965; Charles E. Claffey, *Boston Globe,* September 18, 1971. Interviews with Elma Lewis and Mrs. Helen Seldon Brooke. Reference to Joe Martin and his remark about huckleberries came from the writer's interview with Senator Brooke. His statement, "If you have to sit somewhere, the Senate is a good place to sit," was made at a testimonial in his honor on his fifty-second birthday, which the writer attended.

Chapter Two / THE VIRGINIA BRANCHES

BLACK PROFILES, George R. Metcalf (New York: McGraw-Hill, 1970); Bryant Rollins, author of a series of biographic sketches of Brooke that ran in *The Boston Globe* from June 27 through July 11, 1965; Robert C. Maynard, *Washington Post,* August 30, 1971; Constance McLaughlin Green, THE SECRET CITY (Princeton, N.J.: Princeton University Press, 1967); F. S. Leighton, *Afro-American,* November 19, 1966; John Skow, *The Saturday Evening Post,* September 10, 1966; *McCall's* magazine, May 1971; *The Washington Post,* December 28, 1969. Much of the biographic data in this chapter came from Dr. Adelaide Hill—especially the references to the Mavrittes. Mrs. Helen Seldon Brooke was a source of other unpublished biographic information. For material in this chapter the writer also interviewed Senator Brooke, Charles L. Fisher, Otto Snowden of Freedom

House, Massachusetts State Representative Royal Bolling, and Alec Pompez.

Chapter Three / THE SHAPING YEARS

Most of the information in this chapter came from interviews with the Senator, Herbert Tucker, Jr., Dr. Adelaide Hill, Clyde Christmas, Clarence Elam, Alfred S. Brothers, and Royal Bolling. Letter from Ruth Kronholm, Onawa, Maine, dated July 11, 1971; BLACK PROFILES, George R. Metcalf (New York: McGraw-Hill, 1970); Gloria Negri, *Boston Globe,* November 1, 1966; the Bryant Rollins series, *Boston Globe,* June 27 through July 11, 1965; James Michael Curley, I'D DO IT AGAIN! (Englewood Cliffs, N.J.: Prentice Hall, Inc., 1957). The author phoned the town clerk in Monson, Maine, for information on the tiny community of Onawa; Remigia Brooke, in an extensive interview, briefed the author on the courtship in Viareggio and progress of the romance, and other pertinent data came from Mrs. Helen Seldon Brooke. There were other fruitful interviews with John Bottomly and Glendora McIlwain. Pat Collins, *Record American,* November 13, 1966; Barbara Kober, *Washington Star,* June 15, 1967; *London Times,* August 1, 1967; Everett S. Allen, *New Bedford Standard Times,* February 3, 1967.

Chapter Four / TWO-TIME LOSER

Boston Globe, January 8, 1967; Everett S. Allen, *New Bedford Standard Times,* February 3, 1967; Gloria Negri, *Boston Globe,* November 1, 1966; Mary Tierney, *Boston Traveler,* November 9, 1966; William Ellis, *The Roxbury Citizen,* September 14, 1950; *Time* magazine, January 25, 1963; "Brooke of Massachusetts—A Negro Governor on Beacon Hill?" by Edward R. F. Sheehan, *The Saturday Evening Post,* June 5, 1965; BLACK PROFILES, George R. Metcalf (New York: McGraw-Hill, 1970); *Boston Chronicle,* September 13, 1952; Richard L. Lyons, *Washington Post,* January 4, 1966. Interviews with the Senator, Alfred S. Brothers, James Mahone, Clarence Elam, Mrs. John David McKinney, Clyde Christmas, Moe Robinson, Mrs. Melnea Cass, Elma Lewis, Mrs. Helen Seldon Brooke, Glendora McIlwain, Harold Putnam, Remigia Brooke, Franklin W. L. Miles, Jr. George V. Medeiros, national service officer of Am Vets, gave the writer data on Brooke's rise in the Am Vet hierarchy. The anecdote about the school for crippled children came from Mrs. James Pye, Duxbury, Massachusetts.

Chapter Five / OFF AND RUNNING

Boston Globe, April 6, 1960; *Look* magazine, November 18, 1960; Tom Lynch, *Chicago American,* December 5, 1966; BLACK PROFILES, George R. Metcalf (New York: McGraw-Hill, 1970); Paul Driscoll, *Worcester Telegram,* July 7, 1960; *Springfield Republican,* June 19, 1960; John Skow, *The Saturday Evening Post,* September 10, 1966; Frances Spatz Leighton, *The Cincinnati Pictorial Enquirer,* May 14, 1967; *Ebony,* February 1962; John Henry Cutler, CARDINAL CUSHING OF BOSTON (Hawthorn Books, Inc., New York 1970); *Boston Herald,* October 29, 1962; "Brooke of Massachusetts—A Negro Governor on Beacon Hill?" by Edward R. F. Sheehan, *Harper's,* June 1964; *London Times,* August 1, 1967; *North Adams* (Mass.) *Transcript,* October 29, 1960; *Springfield* (Mass.) *Sunday Republican,* October 23, 1960; *Springfield Republican,* October 29, 1960; *Boston American,* October 29, 1960; *Winchendon* (Mass.) *Courier,* October 13, 1960; *Haverhill* (Mass.) *Journal,* October 26, 1960; *Boston Herald,* October 13, 1960; *Springfield Union,* October 1, 1960; *Springfield Union,* July 27, 1960, *Fitchburg* (Mass.) *Sentinel,* September 30, 1960; *Newburyport* (Mass.) *News,* October 1, 1960; *Boston Globe,* July 25, 1960; *Lynn Item,* October 28, 1960; *Boston Globe,* October 27, 1960; *Boston Graphic,* October 29, 1960; *New Bedford Standard Times,* August 23, 1960; *Springfield Union,* October 19, 1960; *Holyoke* (Mass.) *Transcript-Telegram,* October 27, 1960; *Gloucester* (Mass.) *Times,* October 27, 1960; *Quincy Patriot-Ledger,* November 9, 1960; *Rockland* (Mass.) *Standard,* August 11, 1960; *Life* magazine, April 8, 1966.

Interviews with Joseph Fitzgerald, Glendora McIlwain, Senator Brooke, former Mayor of Boston John Collins, Secretary of Transportation John Volpe (in Washington, D.C., June 8, 1971), Al Benjamin, Roger Woodworth, Mary Newman, John Bottomly, Harold Putnam, Remigia Brooke, Nancy Porter, Sally Saltonstall, Patricia Becker Caroleo, Carolyn Stewart, Georgia Ireland, Mayor Kevin White of Boston, Albert Gammal, Salvatore J. Micchiche, Donald Whitehead, former Congressman Charles Halleck of Indiana, Gael Mahony, Captain William Jackson, Hardy Nathan, Frank Bucci, and Francis W. Perry.

Chapter Six / THE TURNING POINT

Ebony, February 1962; "Brooke of Massachusetts—A Negro Governor on Beacon Hill?" by Edward R. F. Sheehan, *Harper's,* June

1964; *Time,* November 23, 1962; *Time,* August 30, 1963; *Time,* September 20, 1963; Margery Byers, *Life,* April 8, 1966; BLACK PRO-FILES, George R. Metcalf (New York: McGraw-Hill, 1970), Thomas Gallagher, *Boston Herald,* February 23, 1962; Robert Healy, *Boston Globe,* June 16, 1962; Richard Hart, *Boston Globe,* November 7, 1962; Howard S. Knowles, *Worcester Gazette,* January 9, 1967; *Lowell Sun,* August 11, 1968; Thomas Gallagher, *Boston Herald,* July 3, 1962, *Boston Globe,* July 3, 1962, *Boston Globe,* September 19, 1962; Rod MacDonald, *Boston Traveler,* October 30, 1962; *Ebony,* October 1963; Cornelius Dalton, *Boston Traveler,* October 12, 1962; *Berkshire Eagle,* October 18, 1962; *New Bedford Standard Times,* October 17, 1962; *Boston Herald,* October 29, 1962; *Time,* January 25, 1963; letter from Mrs. Stephen Courtney Gale, 95 Prescott Street, Cambridge, Mass.; "Edward Brooke: Candidate with Mass(achusetts) Appeal," by Arthur Myers, *Coronet,* May 1966; *Boston Globe,* November 7, 1962; *Record American,* November 12, 1962; "Mr. Brooke Returns to the Nation's Capitol," by Ernest E. Goodman, *Howard University Magazine,* January 1967.

Interviews with the Senator, Lionel Lindsay, Hardy Nathan, Harcourt Wood, Mary Newman, Georgia Ireland, Roger Woodworth, Nancy Porter, Howard Knowles, Harold Appleton, Frank Bucci, Gael Mahony, Joseph Fitzgerald, Harold Putnam, Charlotte Yaffe, Mrs. Helen Seldon Brooke, Herbert Tucker, Jr., Moe Robinson, Mrs. Melnea Cass, Alfred Brothers, Clarence Elam, former Mayor John Collins, Peter Lucas, Jerry Sadow, Glendora McIlwain, John Bottomly, Albert Gammal, Wendy Dewire, Thomas Nash, Al Benjamin, Cornelius Owens, Anthony DeFalco, Elmer Nelson, Francis Perry, George C. Lodge, Sally Saltonstall, Remigia Brooke, Remi Brooke, Francis Alden Wood, Mrs. Gael Mahony, former State Senator William Weeks, George Frazier, Dr. Adelaide Hill and Edwina Brooke.

Chapter Seven / A DEN OF THIEVES

Record American, November 12, 1962; Edward R. F. Sheehan, *The Saturday Evening Post,* June 5, 1965; *The Christian Science Monitor,* July 17, 1963; *Boston Globe,* January 8, 1967; *Boston Herald,* December 23, 1969; *Record American,* December 21, 1969; *Newsweek,* October 31, 1966; *Record American,* February 10, 1964; "Brooke of Massachusetts—A Negro Governor on Beacon Hill?" by Edward R. F. Sheehan, *Harper's,* June 1964; THE PSYCHIC WORLD OF PETER HURKOS, Norma Lee Browning (Garden City, New York:

Doubleday, 1970); Richard H. Stewart, *Boston Globe,* January 14, 1968.

Interviews with Walter J. Skinner, former State Senator William Weeks, Judge Herbert Travers, Senator Brooke, George Frazier, Peter Lucas, Salvatore J. Micchiche, Judge Elwood McKenney, Gael Mahony, Roger Woodworth, Judge Benjamin Gargill, Herbert Tucker, Jr., Harcourt Wood, Albert Gammal, John Bottomly, Judge Edward T. Martin, Edward M. Swartz, Francis Perry, William Jackson, Leo Martin, Donald Whitehead, John E. Sullivan, and Rudolph A. Sacco.

Chapter Eight / ON THE FIRING LINE

"Massachusetts: Rogues and Reformers in a State on Trial," by Edward R. F. Sheehan, *The Saturday Evening Post,* June 5, 1965; Timothy Leland, *Boston Globe,* March 1, 1966; *Boston Herald,* August 7, 1966; John Skow, *The Saturday Evening Post,* September 10, 1966; editorial, *Boston Globe,* July 9, 1971; George Forsythe, *Boston Herald,* February 11, 1964; "Edward Brooke; Candidate with Mass-(achusetts) Appeal," by Arthur Myers, *Coronet,* May 1966; John Henry Cutler, CARDINAL CUSHING OF BOSTON (Hawthorn Books, Inc., New York 1970); BLACK PROFILES, George R. Metcalf (New York: McGraw-Hill, 1970); Margery Byers, *Life,* April 8, 1966; *Boston Traveler,* January 3, 1964; Richard J. Hafey, *Worcester Telegram,* March 15, 1964.

Interviews with Mrs. Melnea Cass, Reverend Vernon E. Carter, All Saints Lutheran Church, Boston; Al Benjamin, William Jackson, Jerry Sadow, Roger Woodworth, Remigia Brooke, Remi and Edwina Brooke, Donald Whitehead, Otto Snowden, Albert Gammal, Nancy Porter, Maura O'Shaughnessy, Claire Alfano, Georgia Ireland, Mrs. Helen Cavelle, Melinda Smith, Edward M. Swartz, Marines Nikitis, Herbert Tucker, Jr., Graham Champey, Wendy Dewire.

Chapter Nine / BROOKE AND VOLPE

BLACK PROFILES, George R. Metcalf (New York: McGraw-Hill, 1970); Richard W. Daly, *Boston Herald,* May 9, 1968; David Farrell, *Boston Herald,* March 15, 1964; Edgar M. Mills, *The Christian Science Monitor,* January 7, 1960; "Massachusetts: Rogues and Reformers in a State on Trial," by Edward R. F. Sheehan, *The Saturday Evening Post,* June 5, 1965; Frank Tivnan, *Boston Herald,* April 17, 1965; John Skow, *The Saturday Evening Post,* September 10, 1966; Bryant Rollins, *Boston Globe,* August 9, 1964; Richard J. Hafey,

World Telegram, March 15, 1964; Margery Byers, *Life,* April 8, 1966; "Edward Brooke: "Candidate with Mass(achusetts) Appeal," Arthur Myers, *Coronet,* May 1966, *Boston Globe,* April 20, 1966, *Boston Globe,* May 19, 1965; *The New York Times,* February 21, 1965; *Boston Herald,* June 30, 1965; *Boston Globe,* October 27, 1965; *Boston Herald,* July 10, 1965; *Boston Herald,* July 24, 1965; *Time,* January 10, 1966; Edgar M. Mills, *The Christian Science Monitor,* December 30, 1965, *Boston Herald,* December 30, 1965; *Boston Herald,* January 2, 1966; *Boston Herald,* February 16, 1966; *Boston Traveler,* January 7, 1966; *Washington Post,* February 25, 1966; letter to editor from Elaine Lawrence, *Life,* April 29, 1966; David B. Wilson, *Boston Globe,* January 22, 1966; J. C. Krim, *Record American,* October 27, 1965; *Boston Globe,* December 30, 1965; *Sunday News,* February 6, 1966; *Boston Herald,* November 4, 1964; *Boston Traveler,* November 4, 1964; *Clinton* (Mass.) *Daily Item,* October 21, 1965; *Newburyport Daily News,* October 28, 1964; James S. Doyle, *Boston Globe,* January 8, 1967; *Fitchburg Sentinel,* October 29, 1964; *Boston Herald,* October 27, 1964; *Boston Traveler,* October 27, 1964.

Interviews with Francis Perry, Harcourt Wood, Frederick C. Dumaine, Leo Martin, Remigia Brooke and her daughters at their home, Barbara Masters, Aurora Walke, Cornelius Owens, Roger Woodworth. The writer interviewed Senator Brooke, Secretary of Transportation John Volpe (in Washington, D.C.), Anthony DeFalco, Donald Whitehead and Roger Woodworth to get an accurate picture of the exchanges between Brooke and Volpe after Saltonstall announced his resignation. Brooke told the author of the exchange he had with the late John F. Kennedy.

Chapter Ten / BROOKE AND PEABODY

Thomas C. Gallagher, *Boston Herald,* January 4, 1966; Timothy Leland, *Boston Globe,* June 7, 1966; letter to editor from Donald P. Bell, Fort Dodge, Kansas, *Life,* April 29, 1966; *Boston Globe,* April 29, 1966; John Skow, *The Saturday Evening Post,* September 10, 1966; Thomas C. Gallagher, *Boston Herald,* August 31, 1966; David B. Wilson, *Boston Globe,* January 22, 1966; Mary McGrory, *Washington Star,* January 25, 1966; "Massachusetts: Rogues and Reformers in a State on Trial," Edward R. F. Sheehan, *The Saturday Evening Post,* June 5, 1965; Robert Healy, *Boston Globe,* September 18, 1966; *Newsweek,* October 17, 1966; CURRENT BIOGRAPHY, 1965; Richard Daly, *Boston Herald,* July 20, 1966; BLACK PROFILES, George R. Metcalf (New York: McGraw-Hill, 1970); Carl Rowan, *Boston Globe,* April 28, 1966; *Washington Post,* September 29, 1966; *Washington Post,* October 10, 1966; *Time,* October 17, 1966; *Boston Traveler,* October 4, 1966; David B. Wilson, *Boston Globe,* October 10, 1966; Jim Morse, *Boston Herald,* October 30, 1966; *Washington Daily News,* November 17, 1967; Everett S. Allen, *New Bedford Standard Times,* February 3, 1967; *London Times,* August 1, 1966; Gloria Negri, *Boston Globe,* November 1, 1966; Gloria Negri, *Boston Globe,* October 9, 1966; Jean Cole, *Record American,* November 1, 1966; *Record American,* November 10, 1966; Mary Tierney, *Boston Traveler,* November 9, 1966; *Boston Herald,* January 8, 1965; Vera Glaser, *Fort Wayne* (Indiana) *Journal-Gazette,* January 30, 1967; THE CHALLENGE OF CHANGE, book review in *America* magazine, May 7, 1966; *Afro-American,* November 19, 1966; Margery Byers, *Life,* April 8, 1966; *Time,* November 4, 1966; *Bay State Banner,* November 30, 1966; *Boston Globe,* December 24, 1966; Bill Duncliffe, *Record American,* November 10, 1966; *Boston Globe,* November 2, 1966; David B. Wilson, *Boston Globe,* November 9, 1966; Pat Collins, *Record American,* November 13, 1966; *Boston Sunday Advertiser,* November 13, 1966; *Newsweek,* November 21, 1966; John H. Fenton, *The New York Times,* January 1, 1967; *The Crisis,* November 1966; *Chicago American,* December 7, 1966; David Farrell, *Boston Herald,* January 2, 1966; Peter Lucas, *Boston Herald,* May 6, 1966; letter from J. Alan MacKay describing his fight against Brooke.

Interviews with Sally Saltonstall, George C. Lodge, Albert Gammal, Roger Woodworth, Evan Dobelle, former Mayor John Collins, Anthony DeFalco, Elmer Nelson, Donald Whitehead, David Blair McClosky, Remigia, Remi and Edwina Brooke, Harcourt Wood, Mrs. Helen Seldon Brooke, William Hayden, Barbara Masters, Mrs. Graham Champey, Herbert Tucker, Jr., Jeremiah Murphy, Hardy Nathan, Rudolph Sacco, Hamilton H. Wood, the Senator.

Chapter Eleven / MR. BROOKE GOES TO WASHINGTON

Washington Star, February 3, 1966; *Boston Herald,* November 30, 1966; Allan Keller, *World Journal Tribune,* November 15, 1966; *Boston Herald,* December 28, 1966; Bill Duncliffe, *Record American,* November 10, 1966; *Boston Globe,* December 28, 1966; *Boston Traveler,* December 20, 1966; *Boston Traveler,* December 30, 1966; *Worcester Gazette,* January 9, 1967; Gloria Negri, *Boston Globe,* January 10, 1967; *Boston Globe,* January 11, 1967; *Time,* January 20, 1967;

Judith Martin, *Washington Post,* January 11, 1967; Simeon Booker, *Ebony,* April 1967; David Hern, *Boston Traveler,* January 10, 1967; James S. Doyle, *Boston Globe,* January 8, 1967; Ernest G. Warren, *Boston Traveler,* February 2, 1967; Robert Healy, *Boston Globe,* January 13, 1967; Leslie Carpenter, *Boston Herald,* May 14, 1967; David B. Wilson, *Boston Globe,* January 10, 1967; *Washington Post,* December 7, 1966; *Boston Globe,* November 14, 1966; James S. Doyle, *Boston Globe,* February 4, 1968; Roscoe Drummond, *Washington Post,* May 17, 1967; William Saffire, THE NEW LANGUAGE OF POLITICS (New York: Random House, 1968); Helen Dudman, *Parade* magazine, May 17, 1970; *Washington Daily News,* November 17, 1967; *Women's Wear Daily,* January 24, 1967; Vera Glaser, *Fort Wayne Journal-Gazette,* May 17, 1967; *London Times,* August 1, 1967; Jean Cole, *Record American,* November 1, 1966; Pat Collins, *Herald Traveler,* January 25, 1966; Tom Leach, *Chicago American,* December 6, 1966; Mary Tierney, *Boston Traveler,* November 9, 1966; Everett S. Allen, *New Bedford Standard Times,* February 3, 1967; *Boston Sunday Globe,* October 31, 1971; James S. Doyle, *Boston Globe,* January 10, 1967; Isabelle McCaig, *Boston Traveler,* March 28, 1967; Vera Glaser, *Fort Wayne Journal-Gazette,* January 30, 1967; *Boston Herald,* May 14, 1967; Gloria Negri, *Boston Globe,* November 28, 1967; Amanda Houston, *Boston Globe,* August 24, 1969; Raymond Morin, *Worcester Daily Telegram,* February 15, 1967; Nora E. Taylor, *The Christian Science Monitor,* October 23, 1966; Mary Tierney, *Herald Traveler,* February 8, 1971; *Boston Herald,* June 4, 1967; *Boston Traveler,* February 18, 1966; *Boston Globe,* February 19, 1966.

Interviews with Barbara Masters, Al Benjamin, Senator Brooke, Edward Swartz, Remigia, Remi and Edwina Brooke, Cammann Newberry, Jerry Sadow, Maura O'Shaughnessy, Sally Saltonstall, Mrs. Helen Seldon Brooke, Georgia Ireland, James Mahone, Lester Zwick, Albert Gammal, Caryle Connelly.

Chapter Twelve / AMBASSADOR WITHOUT PORTFOLIO

Boston Herald, March 6 and 7, 1967; Andy Merton, *Herald Traveler,* May 4, 1971; *Boston Herald,* March 8; *The Nation,* April 10, 1967; *Boston Herald,* April 2, 1967; NEGROES OF ACHIEVEMENT IN MODERN AMERICA, by James J. Flynn (New York: Dodd, Mead & Co., 1970); BLACK PROFILES, George R. Metcalf (New York: McGraw-Hill, 1970); *Boston Globe,* May 12, 1967; *Boston Sunday Advertiser,* May 2, 1967; Isabelle McCaig, *Boston Traveler,* May 16, 1967; *Bos-*

ton *Herald,* March 23, 1967; *Washington Post,* March 27, 1967; James Feron, *The New York Times,* April 24, 1967; *Boston Herald,* April 27, 1967; Trude Feldman, *Boston Globe,* May 14, 1967; *Boston Herald,* June 1, 1967; Theresa McMasters, *Boston Herald,* June 8, 1967; Jack Kneece, *Boston Traveler,* April 19, 1967.

Most of the firsthand material for this chapter came from Senator Brooke and his companions on the Vietnam tour: his legislative assistant, William I. Cowin, and *Herald* reporter Peter Lucas. We also interviewed Jerry Sadow, then Brooke's press secretary, who helped make preparations for the trip. The anecdote about "walking on water" came from Herbert Tucker, who accompanied Brooke to Israel.

Chapter Thirteen / THE TROUBLED CITIES

Richard H. Stewart, *Boston Globe,* July 29, 1967; BLACK PROFILES, George R. Metcalf (New York: McGraw-Hill, 1970); *Look,* May 5, 1967; *Boston Herald,* June 5, 1967; *Boston Globe,* August 29, 1967; Richard H. Stewart, *Boston Globe,* October 21, 1967; *The Christian Science Monitor,* August 24, 1967; *Washington Post,* August 24, 1967; *Boston Globe,* September 11, 1967; S. J. Micchiche, *Boston Globe,* July 31, 1967; Richard M. Daly, *Boston Herald,* July 14, 1967; Jo Ann Levine, *The Christian Science Monitor,* July 12, 1967; *Boston Globe,* July 13, 1967; Kenneth O. Botwright, *Boston Globe,* August 17, 1967; *Boston Globe,* July 21, 1967; *Boston Herald,* June 5, 1967; *Boston Globe,* August 29, 1967; Fred Brady, *Boston Sunday Advertiser,* July 30, 1967; BLACK PROFILES, George R. Metcalf (New York: McGraw-Hill, 1970); *Boston Globe,* September 21, 1967; *The Christian Science Monitor,* February 12, 1967, and September 29, 1967; Gloria Negri, *Boston Globe,* November 28, 1967; James Doyle, *Boston Globe,* February 4, 1968; *Boston Record American,* November 3, 1967; Emanuel Perlmutter, *The New York Times,* November 13, 1967; Robert L. Hassett, *Boston Herald,* June 5, 1967; Thomas C. Gallagher, *Boston Herald,* October 27, 1967; *Boston Globe,* November 15, 1967; Richard H. Stewart, *Boston Globe,* March 6, 1970; *Boston Herald,* March 16, 1969; *Boston Herald,* December 19, 1966; Robert L. Levy, *Boston Globe,* May 30, 1969; *Boston Herald,* January 19, 1966; *Boston Globe,* March 12, 1970; profile of Daniel Moynihan, *Harvard Alumni Bulletin,* December 13, 1971; "The 1971 Interns" is taken from *The Brooke Report.* There is a humorous account of the "illegal" honorary award Brooke received in the *Boston Globe,* November 28, 1966.

Interviews with Miss Elma Lewis at her Elma Lewis School of Fine Arts and with George C. Lodge at Harvard Business School, where he is a professor. Some of the material for this chapter came from Donald Whitehead, Roger Woodworth, Cammann Newberry, Marilyn Dexheimer, Nancy Porter, Sally Saltonstall, Barbara Masters, Hamilton Wood, Clarence Elam, Georgia Ireland, Joseph McMahon, Claire Alfano, Maura O'Shaughnessy, Ann Cunningham, Melinda Smith, Linda Bunce, Betsy Warren (Brooke's personal secretary), Caryle Connelly, Ronald Rappaport, Eather Higginbotham, Rosemary Murphy, Timothy Naegele.

Chapter 14 / A SWING THROUGH AFRICA

"Senator Brooke, I Presume?" by Anne Chamberlin, *Cosmopolitan* magazine, June 1969. Chamberlin accompanied Brooke on the first part of his African trip. Also with Brooke, for a longer period, was Howard S. Knowles, political editor of the *Worcester Telegram and Gazette,* who wrote a series of articles on the trip. The author is especially indebted to Miss Marilyn Dexheimer, a research assistant in Brooke's Washington office, who also went on the African trip. Miss Dexheimer carefully edited this chapter and added several pages of pertinent information. Unlike Chamberlin and Knowles, she was with the Senator at all places visited. Knowles' articles ran in January and February in the *Worcester Telegram and Gazette.*

Washington Post, February 1, 1969; *Boston Sunday Globe,* February 4, 1968; James S. Doyle, *Boston Globe,* April 29, 1968; *Washington Post,* April 30, 1968; James S. Doyle, *Boston Globe,* January 20, 1968; letter to editor from C. T. Hellman, *Washington Post,* May 7, 1968; letter to editor from Lois M. Flannery, *Washington Post,* May 7, 1968; Stanley Meisler, *L. A. Times* to *Washington Post,* reprinted in *Boston Sunday Globe,* February 4, 1968; *Boston Globe,* April 29, 1968. Background information came from interviews with Howard S. Knowles.

Chapter Fifteen / AN EMERGING SPOKESMAN

Richard H. Stewart, *Boston Globe,* February 26, 1968; Lester Carpenter, *Boston Herald,* March 5, 1968; *Boston Sunday Advertiser,* April 7, 1968; *Boston Herald,* June 6, 1968; *Washington Post,* May 3, 1968 (Rowland Evans and Robert Novak); Earl Marchand, *Boston*

Herald, May 20, 1968; Milton R. Benjamin, *Boston Herald,* April 29, 1968; Robert L. Levy, *Boston Sunday Globe,* September 13, 1970; Sara Booth Conroy, *Washington Post,* February 26, 1969.

Chapter Sixteen / BROOKE AND THE 1968 CAMPAIGN

Mary Tierney, *Boston Traveler,* November 9, 1966; *Boston Herald,* August 30, 1966; Marianne Means, *Washington Post,* February 24, 1966; *Reader's Digest,* May 1967; Leslie Carpenter, *Boston Herald,* April 28, 1970; Leslie Carpenter, *Boston Herald,* May 14, 1967; S. J. Micchiche, *Boston Globe,* June 2, 1967; Roscoe Drummond, *Washington Post,* May 17, 1967; John S. Saloma, *Boston Globe,* September 11, 1967; Christopher Lydon, *Boston Globe,* April 17, 1968; *Boston Globe,* December 15, 1968; *Washington Post,* May 3, 1968; Robert Healy, *Boston Globe,* June 28, 1968; Drew Pearson and Jack Anderson, *Boston Globe,* August 5, 1968; *Boston Herald,* August 7, 1968; David B. Wilson, *Boston Globe,* August 9, 1968; *Boston Herald,* August 6, 1968; A POLITICAL LIFE: THE EDUCATION OF JOHN V. LINDSAY (New York: Alfred A. Knopf, 1969), by Nat Hentoff; *New York* magazine, January 4, 1971; Matthew V. Storin, *Boston Globe,* June 19, 1969; *Boston Globe,* August 9, 1968; *Boston Globe,* August 6, 1968; *Boston Herald,* September 8, 1968; Rowland Evans and Robert Novak, *Washington Post,* September 9, 1968; *Boston Globe,* September 18, 1968; Milton R. Benjamin, *Boston Herald Traveler,* September 20, 1968; *Boston Globe,* September 18, 1968; *Boston Herald,* October 23, 1968 (J. J. Smith); *Boston Herald,* October 24, 1968; Richard H. Stewart, *Boston Globe,* December 20, 1968; *Boston Sunday Advertiser,* April 27, 1969; Richard H. Stewart, *Boston Globe,* February 13, 1969; *The New York Times,* February 11, 1969; THE REPUBLICAN ESTABLISHMENT: *The Present and Future of the G.O.P.,* by Stephen Hess and David S. Broder (New York, Evanston, and London: Harper & Row, 1967); THE RESURRECTION OF RICHARD NIXON, by Jules Witcover (New York: G. P. Putnam's Sons, 1970).

Chapter Seventeen / HAYNSWORTH, CARSWELL AND REHNQUIST

Boston Sunday Globe, December 12, 1971; *The New York Times,* December 8, 1971; *Boston Herald Traveler,* December 8, 1971; *Boston Globe,* December 4, 1971; William Raspberry, *Washington Post,*

February 13, 1971; Cornelius Dalton, *Boston Herald,* February 27, 1971; John S. Saloma, *Boston Globe,* April 28, 1970; Milton R. Benjamin, *Boston Herald,* January 6, 1969; *Boston Herald,* January 16, 1969; *Boston Globe,* February 2 and February 5, 1969; *Boston Globe,* July 27, 1969; Milton R. Benjamin, *Boston Herald,* September 20, 1968; *Boston Globe,* October 10, 1969; *Boston Herald,* November 7, 1969; *Boston Globe,* February 21, 1970; *Time,* March 23, 1970; *Boston Globe,* March 12, 1970; *Washington Post,* March 12, 1970; S. J. Micchiche, *Boston Globe,* February 27, 1970; "The Carswell Affair," *The New Yorker,* December 5, 1970, and December 12, 1970; *Boston Herald Traveler,* March 20, 1970; *Boston Herald,* April 10, 1970; *Boston Herald,* April 16, 1970; Richard H. Stewart, *Boston Globe,* April 9, 1970; *Boston Herald Traveler,* April 21, 1970. Interview with George Frazier.

Chapter Eighteen / MORE GRIEF FOR NIXON

Washington Post, May 18, 1970; *Newsweek,* June 7, 1971; William Raspberry, *Washington Post,* February 13, 1971; Warren Weaver, *The New York Times,* February 11, 1971; Carnelius Dalton, *Boston Herald Traveler,* February 27, 1971; David E. Lynch, *Quincy Patriot Ledger,* March 10, 1971; *Washington Post,* March 30, 1971; S. J. Micchiche, *Boston Globe,* March 12, 1970; *Boston Globe,* May 19, 1970; Richard H. Stewart, *Boston Globe,* May 20, 1970; *Boston Herald Traveler,* May 20, 1970; Richard H. Stewart, *Boston Globe,* May 21, 1970; *Boston Globe,* July 14, 1970; Jo Ann Levine, *The Christian Science Monitor,* July 15, 1970; Karen Rothmeyer, *Boston Herald Traveler,* August 9, 1970; *Boston Globe,* July 15, 1970; *Boston Globe,* August 4, 1971; *Quincy Patriot Ledger,* February 12, 1971.

Chapter Nineteen / WAR AND WEAPONRY

Boston Herald Traveler, March 4, 1970; Richard H. Stewart, *Boston Globe,* March 7, 1970; Arthur Jones, *Boston Globe,* May 15, 1970; *Boston Globe,* May 26, 1970; *Boston Globe,* June 17, 1971; *Boston Globe,* August 6, 1970; *Boston Globe,* August 13, 1970; Spencer Rich, *Washington Post,* August 14, 1970; *Boston Globe,* August 12, 1970; John Hall, *Boston Globe,* August 13, 1970; Drew Steis, *Boston Herald Traveler,* August 20, 1970; Robert M. Smith, *The New York Times,* April 23, 1970; *Boston Herald Traveler,* April 25, 1969; *Boston Globe,* March 13, 1970; *Boston Globe,* March 17,

1970; Theresa McMasters, *Boston Herald Traveler,* April 24, 1970; Richard H. Stewart, *Boston Globe,* July 29, 1970; *Boston Herald Traveler,* December 13, 1970; *Boston Herald Traveler,* May 22, 1971; *Boston Herald Traveler,* April 27, 1970; David E. Lynch, *Quincy Patriot Ledger,* June 16, 1971.

Chapter Twenty / NIXON, AGNEW AND BROOKE

Quincy Patriot Ledger, March 5, 1971; Mary McGrory, *Boston Globe,* March 10, 1971; Matthew Storin, *Boston Globe,* May 15, 1971; Robert Healy, *Boston Globe,* January 17, 1971; *Newsweek,* June 7, 1971; *Boston Herald Traveler,* August 3, 1971; *Boston Globe,* March 22, 1971; Donald W. Lambro, *Washington Star,* February 21, 1971; David Nyhan, *Boston Globe,* March 21, 1971; *Time,* October 18, 1971; Becker Research Corporation of Cambridge conducted the Massachusetts poll in April and May 1971 for the *Boston Globe;* Mary McGrory, *Boston Globe,* March 23, 1971; Theresa McMasters, *Boston Herald Traveler,* May 10, 1970; David Nyhan, *Boston Globe,* March 14, 1971; David Nyhan, *Boston Globe,* March 22, 1971; *Congressional Record,* Senate, December 30, 1970; John Henry Cutler, CARDINAL CUSHING OF BOSTON (New York: Hawthorn Books, Inc., 1970); *Boston Herald Traveler,* June 2, 1969; *Boston Sunday Advertiser,* June 1, 1969; *Boston Herald Traveler,* June 9, 1970; Mary Tierney, *Boston Herald Traveler,* June 8, 1970; *Boston Herald Traveler,* June 16, 1969; *Boston Globe,* June 10, 1970; *Boston Herald Traveler,* June 10, 1970; *Boston Globe* and *Boston Record American,* June 20, 1970; *Boston Globe,* October 23, 1970; Drew F. Steis, *Scope,* January 31, 1971; *London Times,* August 1, 1967; *Boston Globe,* November 19, 1971; David Farrell, *Boston Herald,* September 19, 1965; *Boston Herald Traveler,* December 15, 1971; *Harvard Alumni Bulletin,* December 13, 1971; *Time,* December 13, 1971; *Boston Globe,* August 5, 1971; Robert Healy, *Boston Globe,* August 7, 1971; David Nyhan, *Boston Globe,* October 26, 1971; Matthew V. Storin, *Boston Globe,* November 5, 1970; S. J. Micchiche, *Boston Globe,* December 22, 1970; *Boston Herald Traveler,* October 25, 1969; *The New York Times,* October 20, 1970; NIXON IN THE WHITE HOUSE: *The Frustration of Power,* by Rowland Evans Jr. and Robert D. Novak (New York: Random House, 1971); *Boston Globe,* November 18, 1971; *Boston Herald Traveler,* June 8, 1970; *Boston Globe,* November 11, 1971; *Boston Herald Traveler,* October 25, 1969; *Boston Globe,* October 19, 1971.

Chapter Twenty-one / PUTTING OUT BRUSH FIRES

Drew F. Steis, *Scope,* January 31, 1971; NIXON IN THE WHITE HOUSE: *The Frustration of Power,* by Rowland Evans Jr. and Robert D. Novak (New York: Random House, 1971); *Boston Globe,* June 27, 1969; *The Brooke Report,* October 19, 1971; Wendell Coltin, *Boston Herald Traveler,* April 23, 1971; *Boston Globe,* April 17, 1969; Theresa McMasters, *Boston Herald Traveler,* May 15, 1971; Peter Lucas, *Boston Herald Traveler,* April 17, 1971, *Boston Herald Traveler,* December 17, 1970; *The Brooke Report,* February 27, 1971; S. J. Micchiche, *Boston Globe,* July 22, 1971; *Boston Herald Traveler,* September 13, 1969; Bill McCaffrey, *Boston Herald Traveler,* August 9, 1971; *Boston Globe,* November 14, 1971; Peter Hayhow, *Quincy Patriot Ledger,* November 16, 1971; *Boston Globe,* June 12, 1971; A. A. Michelson, *The Newburyport Daily News,* October 30, 1971; Carol Liston, *Boston Globe,* January 28, 1971; Harold Banks, *Boston Record American,* October 27, 1971; *Boston Globe,* November 11 and 14, 1971; David Nyhan, *Boston Globe,* November 31, 1971; *Newsweek,* June 7, 1971; BLACK PROFILES, George R. Metcalf (New York: McGraw Hill, 1970); Joseph Rosenbloom, *Boston Globe,* November 14, 1971; *Boston Sunday Globe,* September 13, 1970.

Chapter Twenty-two / AFTER 1972, WHAT?

Boston Herald Traveler, August 3, 1971; Donald Lambro, *Washington Star,* February 21, 1971; Rowland Evans and Robert Novak, *Boston Sunday Globe,* October 17, 1971; Mary McGrory, *Boston Globe,* December 15, 1971; Robert Healy, *Boston Globe,* November 28, 1971; David B. Wilson, *Boston Globe,* January 8, 1972; *Monday,* January 10, 1972; Robert Healy, *Boston Globe,* February 6, 1972; *London Times,* August 11, 1967; *Boston Globe,* January 5, 1972; Robert Healy, *Boston Globe,* December 27, 1971; David Nyhan, *Boston Globe,* October 26, 1971; Cornelius Dalton, *Boston Herald Traveler,* Thomas C. Gallagher, *Boston Herald Traveler,* October 24, 1971; *Monday,* December 6, 1971. Lee Auspitz, a leader of the Ripon Society, has a good article on Nixon and Brooke in the January 1972 issue of Ripon's *Forum* magazine.

INDEX

411